ALSO BY WALTER NUGENT

Habits of Empire

Habits of Empire

A History of
American Expansion

Walter Nugent

Alfred A. Knopf   New York   2008

This Is a Borzoi Book
Published by Alfred A. Knopf

Copyright © 2008 by Walter Nugent
All rights reserved. Published in the United States by Alfred A. Knopf,
a division of Random House, Inc., New York, and in Canada by
Random House of Canada Limited, Toronto.
www.aaknopf.com

Knopf, Borzoi Books, and the colophon are registered trademarks of
Random House, Inc.

Library of Congress Cataloging-in-Publication Data

Nugent, Walter T. K.
Habits of empire : a history of American expansion / by Walter Nugent.—1st ed.
p. cm.
Includes bibliographical references and index.
ISBN 978-1-4000-4292-0
1. United States—Territorial expansion. 2. United States—Foreign relations.
3. Imperialism—History. 4. Aggression (International law)—History. I. Title.
E179.5.N84 2008
970.01—dc22 2007052251

Manufactured in the United States of America
First Edition

To the memory of

Yehoshua Arieli (1916–2002)
Robert F. Byrnes (1917–1997)
Martin Ridge (1923–2003)

Historians and Friends

We should have such an empire for liberty as . . . never surveyed since the creation: & I am persuaded no constitution was ever before so well calculated as ours for extensive empire & self government. . . .

—*Thomas Jefferson to James Madison,*
Monticello, April 27, 1809

Contents

Maps

Foreword

It has been written that the United States is an imperial nation, but Americans are loath to admit it. That is not the half of it. The United States has created three empires during its history. Thomas Jefferson, one of the few historic leaders to talk of empire, claimed that the United States should be an "empire for liberty." Since "liberty" is always equated with good, the word more than compensated for the bad associations of "empire." Most Americans remember Jefferson for writing "all men are created equal" in the Declaration of Independence. Therefore they think of him much more as a defender of liberty, personal and public, than as an imperialist. But imperialist he was.

So were Benjamin Franklin, John and John Quincy Adams, Andrew Jackson, Theodore Roosevelt, and many other presidents and founding fathers. In recent years, the American empire and the popular acceptance of imperialism have been promoted chiefly under Republican guardianship; but Jefferson and Jackson, celebrated as the founders of the Democratic Party, were as good imperialists as they come. Neither party has had a monopoly. Nor has imperialism been an exclusively male activity. Granted, women have not been major names in the standard histories of American builders and defenders of empire; they were never the generals, diplomats, or officeholders, at least not until the Madeleine Albrights and Condoleezza Rices came along. Empire-building involved not only diplomacy and force, however. It involved occupation and settlement of the American continental landmass, and without women that would not have happened. In traditional histories the diplomacy, battles, and politics necessary for empire-building have been written about as if they had no relation to population and settlement. On the other hand, histories of the westward movement, the frontier, and economic expansion have been treated with little reference to how America's territories were acquired. But acquisition and settlement have been the right and left hands of the same imperial organism.

Put most briefly, this book relates a continuous narrative of the territorial acquisitions of the United States and how that history instilled in the American people the habit of empire-building. It describes how Americans acquired each parcel of real estate: by diplomacy, filibustering, armed conquest, cheating and lying, ethnic cleansing, even honest purchase and negotiation. It also explains who the previous occupants were and how Americans displaced them and occupied the land themselves.

Many books have been written on individual acquisitions—the Louisiana Purchase, Oregon, Texas, the erstwhile Philippine colony, and the others. Here, however, is a continuous history, beginning with the peace treaties of 1782–1783, which ended the Revolutionary War and gave international recognition to the United States. It proceeds through each acquisition to the Virgin Islands in 1917 and the Northern Marianas in 1986. And it looks beyond them into the current global or virtual empire, the present "military hegemony." Telling the whole story reveals patterns that individual episodes do not. Central to *Habits of Empire* is the thesis that the acquisitions and occupations of transcontinental territory before the Civil War not only forged the national boundaries as we know them, but also taught well-learned lessons of empire-building. All along, the United States was also a republic. "Republic" and "empire" have not always fit well together. Today there is a good chance that "empire" might eclipse "republic." Old habits can become unthinking practices.

When I began this project, I intended to tie together the diplomatic and military history of the territorial acquisitions with the history of frontier settlement—two fields traditionally treated separately. In the nation's successive Wests, from Revolutionary times to the mid-nineteenth century, these were intimately related. Settlement—"westward expansion," historians used to call it—could not have happened without sovereignty, and sovereignty was empty without settlement. These acquisitions, from Transappalachia in 1782–1783 through Louisiana, Florida, the failed attack on Canada in 1812–1814, Oregon, Texas, and the Southwest, all required not only acquisition (by means fair or foul). They also involved Anglo-Americans displacing whoever was already there and occupying that land. This story, tying together acquisition, displacement, and settlement of the continental United States, is what I intend as the chief contribution of *Habits of Empire*, which is why it occupies most of the book.

But reaching the Pacific was hardly the end of the story. New acquisitions, offshore across the Pacific and around the Caribbean, formed a second kind of empire, a continuation of the first but seldom involving any settlement. The reverse happened; Hawaiians and Filipinos, and later Puerto Ricans, migrated to the continental United States. For the most part, the offshore empire comprised colonies and protectorates. Only Alaska and Hawaii evolved into states, and they took an unusually long time to do so.

Investigating the Alaska Purchase of 1867 made me freshly aware of the expansionism of its architect, William Henry Seward. Seward revived the word "empire" in connection with U.S. expansion as no one had done since Thomas Jefferson. The link between acquisition and settlement before the Civil War, and offshore acquisitions after it, became crystal-clear. The key was the concept and development of American empire.[1] The United States' first empire-building took place from sea to sea and was completed just after 1850. A second phase began almost immediately with Midway and other small Pacific islands and, after the Civil War, with the purchase of Alaska. Offshore empire-building resumed in the 1890s, capturing Hawaii, Samoa, the Philippines, Guam, Puerto Rico, and the Panama Canal Zone. The final true territorial additions came in 1917 with the purchase of what became the U.S. Virgin Islands from Denmark and, after World War II, the Northern Mariana Islands. By then, several Caribbean and Central American republics had been adopted as "protectorates" by the United States, not to be given up until the Depression-ridden 1930s.

With World War II and the ensuing Cold War, however, a third phase of American empire-building, still with us, came into being. An aspect of it is the current "war on terror." The lessons learned in the first phase (continental), and reinforced in the second phase (offshore), have been shapers of the third, the global or virtual empire of today. Thus we have always been an imperial nation, and remain so, but the shape of the American empire has shifted over time. Its present form is different from either our own past ones or historic ones like Rome or Britain. It is still developing.

Books about the current empire appear virtually every day. I say little here about it. My purpose is to describe the long historical context. I conclude, therefore, with the briefest survey of recent times, to demonstrate its continuity with rhetoric, ideals, practices, strategies, and imperial tactics that extend back to the nation's very first days. Although recent history will be fairly familiar to today's readers, the habit-forming imperialism of pre–Civil War days will not be. Hence I treat the early, continental imperialism more extensively in the hope of promoting a better understanding of how Americans got to where we now are.

The three historic American empires have all rested on an ideology of expansion. Military solutions, overlain by rationales and high ideals, have consistently been considered effective and justified. Expansion has also been premised on the conviction that America and Americans are not tainted with evil or self-serving motives. Americans, the ideology says, are exceptions to the moral infirmities that plague the rest of humankind, because our ideals are pure, a "beacon to humankind," and, as Lincoln said, "the last best hope of earth." The three successive empires, each molded by the circumstances and opportunities of its own times, share an imperialistic outward thrust, a commitment to militarism, and beneath everything a profound faith in the axiom of America's moral exceptionalism. As a result, Jefferson's phrase, "empire for liberty," rings just as true and right to Americans today as it did when he proclaimed it.

In a short seven decades Americans exploded from thirteen colonies pinched between the Atlantic and the Appalachians and drove all the way to the Pacific. Theirs was a uniquely rapid extension of a national territory. It depended on good fortune and on aggressive force, on actions both clandestine and public, on grand ideals and at times on base deceit and hypocrisy. With it came the displacement or absorption of people already living there, with more success than most empires ever had.[2] Finally, this empire depended for its success on lust and love, on a birth rate incredibly high. An Indiana congressman named Andrew Kennedy explained in 1846 how the United States would acquire Oregon:

> Our people are spreading out with the aid of the American multiplication table. Go to the West and see a young man with his mate of eighteen; after the lapse of thirty years, visit him again, and instead of two, you will find twenty-two. . . . We are now twenty millions strong; and how long, under this process of multiplication, will it take to cover the continent with our posterity, from the Isthmus of Darien to Behring's straits? . . . Where shall we find room for all our people, unless we have Oregon? What

shall we do with all those little white-headed boys and girls—
God bless them!—that cover the western prairies? [3]

America's first empire was created, indeed procreated, by millions of
young, ardent couples busily carrying out their own individual manifest
destinies, filling up the land with farms and families, while the nation
successfully pursued its grand, apparently inexorable, Manifest Destiny.

It all began in Paris in 1782.

Habits of Empire

Chapter One

Transappalachia, 1782:
First Land, First Good Fortune

This federal Republic was born a pygmy. . . . The day will come when it will grow up, become a giant and be greatly feared in the Americas.
—Conde de Aranda, 1783[1]

American Independence:
Could It Extend beyond the Mountains?

By the end of decisive combat operations in the Revolutionary War, October 1781, American forces with much French assistance had defeated the British in New England, Virginia, and the interior of the Carolinas. Britain continued to occupy New York, Charleston, Savannah, and several forts along the Great Lakes. Despite that, the former colonists had become independent Americans, governing themselves in the areas where they lived. Those areas extended from the Atlantic west to the Appalachian chain of mountains, with a few adventuresome souls beyond. They were, geographically, a nation between ocean and mountains. Only a few had ventured beyond the mountains into Transappalachia, the region running west from the mountains to the Mississippi and Spanish Louisiana, north to the Great Lakes, and south to Florida. Yet the peace treaty with Britain included Transappalachia within the new United States, even though hardly any Americans lived there. Nor did many British or other Europeans. At least two dozen Indian nations did.

The peace treaty covered a number of points besides recognizing America's independence. The main ones were about fishing rights in the North Atlantic, debts owed by Americans to British creditors, and how, if at all, the Loyalists—those colonists who remained loyal to the king—

might be compensated for property losses. The treaty also laid out the boundaries of the United States. Why did the treaty give Transappalachia to the new country when only a few thousand of its people lived there? How did the American negotiators—Benjamin Franklin, John Adams, and John Jay—achieve that territorial coup? Given the lack of an American military or demographic presence, they got much more than they deserved. Why the great territorial success?

The Declaration of Independence that the Continental Congress adopted on July 4, 1776, condemned George III for many things, but it said almost nothing about the boundaries of these self-styled United States of America. It referred to the native inhabitants as "merciless Indian Savages, whose known Rule of Warfare, is an undistinguished Destruction, of all Ages, Sexes and Conditions" (in other words, even old people and children, women as well as men, and slaves). Provinces to the north, now Canada, were invited to join, but declined. Britain scoffed at such "independence," and it took the Americans years of fighting to prove their point, that they were truly independent. In October 1781, six and a half years after the first shots at Lexington and Concord, near Boston, came the decisive battle of Yorktown in Virginia. Almost as many French troops as American fought there, while the French navy cut off British general Charles Cornwallis's evacuation by sea. A year later, on November 30, 1782, the Americans and British signed a "preliminary" peace treaty, which became final in September 1783 when France and Spain made peace with Britain as well. By this Treaty of Paris, the United States became a recognized entity in international law.

It was an exceedingly favorable treaty for the United States. Among other things, it gave the new country a great deal of territory that it had scarcely begun to settle and would not fully occupy for decades. Without Transappalachia the western border of the United States would have been hundreds of miles east of the Mississippi River, leaving it in no position to buy Louisiana in 1803. Without Louisiana the borders would have been nowhere near Texas, the Southwest, or Oregon, and thus could hardly have been extended to these new territories in the 1840s. Without Transappalachia, the new United States would have been squeezed and hemmed in on three sides, as expansionists warned then and later. It would have been confined to the Atlantic seaboard and to transatlantic commerce, rather than to a future of transcontinental settlement. The United States might have acquired these regions later, but

Transappalachia might well have become an independent entity, or might have linked up with Spain, or pursued some other path that would have prevented the United States from seizing the Louisiana opportunity that came its way in 1803. These centrifugal possibilities continued for years after the Revolutionary War, even beyond 1800.

So the 1783 boundaries were an absolutely essential platform for America's further expansion. Yet at the close of the fighting between the Americans and the British in late 1781, the status of forces was such that the British, although defeated at Yorktown, continued to occupy Charleston, Savannah, and New York City, not to mention Canada and the West Indies and the forts along the St. Lawrence and the Great Lakes in what are now New York and Michigan. A few thousand settlers had ventured past the crest of the Appalachians into Kentucky, Tennessee, western Pennsylvania, and future West Virginia. A meager handful of French villages such as Vincennes in the "Illinois country" that had been French up to 1763 had come under American control. Looked at from London, Paris, or Madrid, Transappalachia had been French since the 1600s and became British and Spanish in 1763. In reality, however, it was Indian country. Americans were simply not present, aside from those few settlers and, to be sure, wealthy "owners"—Pennsylvanians and Virginians who hoped to get richer through sales of land to future settlers, land in the upper Ohio River valley.

Why, if so few American forces or settlers were on the ground in Transappalachia in 1782, did the peace treaty bestow it on the new nation? How did the Americans acquire this huge region when they did not live there and did not in any physical way control it? How did Franklin, Adams, and Jay bring home such a good deal? Why did the Earl of Shelburne, George III's first minister and peace negotiator, give it to them? Where did the Americans' allies, the French and the Spanish, stand on the matter?

The short answer is a timely combination of stubbornness on the Americans' part; the historic antagonism of Britain versus France and Spain; how those governments had to protect their own interests, of which North America was only one; some treachery by the American negotiators toward their allies; and large supplies of luck at several times and in several ways.

To explain this combination of favorable circumstances is to tell the story of how the United States' boundaries in the 1783 Treaty of Paris came to be. As agreed to, it placed the eastern boundary at the Atlantic

Ocean; the southern, along the north edge of East and West Florida (Spanish from 1511 to 1763, British from 1763 to 1783, and then Spanish again); the western, the Mississippi River from the edge of Florida northward to the river's source; and the northern, along the Great Lakes, the St. Lawrence River south of the forty-fifth parallel (the northern boundary of New York and Vermont today), and the north-jutting hump of New Hampshire and Maine. The western and eastern ends of the northern boundary were completely confused because of inaccurate geographical knowledge, though they were no real problem until such knowledge caught up with them decades later. The most important—the most surprising—feature of these boundaries is that they included all of the land west of the Appalachian chain of mountains, south of the Great Lakes and north of the Floridas, out to the Mississippi.

Before 1776: The Colonial Charters, the Quebec Act, and Western Lands

Despite not actually being there, many Americans throughout the war years of the 1770s and early 1780s looked upon Transappalachia as their future. It seemed a natural extension of the frontier settlement that had inched westward since the early 1600s into the southern Piedmont, up the Connecticut River in New England, and down Virginia's Shenandoah Valley. Americans often assumed and argued that the West, as they pushed into it, was legally theirs because the charters of their colonies, long since awarded by the English crown, said so. The charters of the Carolinas, Georgia, and most anciently and broadly, Virginia, proclaimed those colonies' rights to almost limitless westward territory. The map of North America that the peace negotiators used, drawn up by John Mitchell in 1755, blatantly showed the charter claims of Virginia, the Carolinas, and Georgia stretching not just to the Mississippi River but far beyond it. Though less extensive, Connecticut and New York had western charter claims too. Prior to 1763, when the previous Treaty of Paris sorted out the results of Britain's defeat of France in North America in the Seven Years' War, colonists had liked to think that the charters meant what they said, and that, indeed, Virginia extended from sea to sea, Atlantic to Pacific, and that other colonies had rights well westward too.

The 1763 Treaty of Paris put more than a slight crimp in these claims, because Britain agreed to Spain's taking over the former French territory west of the Mississippi (Louisiana) while Britain got the parts east of it (Quebec and Transappalachia). Presumably that nullified Britain's earlier charter grants. An additional crimp in 1763, which greatly annoyed the colonists, came when the crown proclaimed that no settlement should take place west of the crest of the Appalachians. This Proclamation Line obviously contradicted, perhaps even repealed, the charter claims, and if enforced would have confined the colonies between the mountains and the Atlantic.

In yet another slap, Britain in 1774 infuriated colonists north and south by extending the southern border of Quebec all the way to the Ohio River. Prior to that the border had been a line from the point where the forty-fifth parallel struck the St. Lawrence River, extending west-northwest almost three hundred miles to Lake Nipissing. The Quebec Act's main purpose was not to discomfit the colonists but to create some system of administration in the Indian lands of the Great Lakes and Ohio Valley. Yet the collective and clear effect of these actions was to slice away the colonies' charter claims. In disputing the royal authority behind the Proclamation Line and the Quebec Act while insisting on the old charter claims, the colonists were not being logical, since it was that same crown that had granted the charters in the first place. Illogic did not reduce the colonists' anger. The Declaration of Independence made that anger manifest, in its references to the Quebec Act and to Indian "troubles" on the frontier. As the Revolutionary War drew to a close, the charter claims were still very much alive. They would figure centrally in Congress' struggle to adopt Articles of Confederation in 1780–1781, and they would stiffen the spines of the American negotiators in Paris in 1782.

Tom Paine's *Common Sense* of early 1776 marshaled every argument possible for complete independence from the crown, and one of them was "the value of the back lands, which some of the provinces are clandestinely deprived of, by the unjust extension of the limits of Canada," that is, the Quebec Act's placing of Canada's southern boundary at the Ohio River. Paine argued that sale of the Ohio country lands would pay the public debt, and "in time" would "wholly support the yearly expense of government."[2] This idea of the West as a realizable endowment for a national government surfaced many times in the coming years, though as it turned out, public land sales never earned remotely enough money to pay off the debt or run the government. Customs duties were always the chief revenue earner before the Civil War. But the logic of land lucre died very slowly.

The Quebec Act's inclusion of the Ohio country produced a lament about future lost income, but much more urgently, it pained the few wealthy and influential Americans who were already speculating there in the expectation of future profits. George Washington was one such person. Benjamin Franklin, John Jay, and most of the provincial governors were others. Dozens of leading citizens were actively involved in one way or another. The Quebec Act threw their plans into great doubt. Now the odds were that the Ohio country would be developed by other investors—based in London—rather than Americans like themselves.

Of the three American negotiators of the 1782 peace treaty, only John Adams had no personal interest in western lands. His strongest concern, other than independence itself, was with New England fishing rights around Newfoundland. But the other two, Franklin and Jay, had personal as well as patriotic feelings about western lands. Congress appointed two other negotiators, Thomas Jefferson and South Carolina's Henry Laurens, and had they been able to participate, the matter of lands (and therefore boundaries) might have played an even greater role, because they were from the South, where charter claims and expansionism were strongest. Investors creating a series of land companies saw a fine financial future in the lands beyond the mountains, both south of the Ohio River and north of it. At the negotiating table in 1782, absolute independence was the top priority for all three Americans. After that crucial demand, Transappalachia and the western boundary were next.

The Quebec Act also riled New Englanders in particular because it promised to recognize and perpetuate Catholic institutions in Quebec. Objections went beyond mere Yankee paranoia that toleration (or worse) of Catholicism might be foisted on them. Franklin and Washington joined other colonists in protesting that the Quebec Act, by establishing "the Roman Catholic religion and French law in the vast country called Canada," created "an extremely grave danger for the Protestant religion, and for the freedoms and civil law of America."[3] The anti-Catholic strain among the patriots further surfaced in an address of the First Continental Congress "To the People of Great-Britain," dated September 5, and approved October 21, 1774. John Jay, who eight years later was one of the three American peace negotiators in Paris, drafted it. In referring to the Quebec Act, he objected to Parliament's establishing "a religion, fraught with sanguinary and impious tenets," "a religion that has deluged your island [Britain] in blood, and dispersed impiety, bigotry, persecution, murder and rebellion throughout the world." Canada, by that act, will be "daily swelling with Catholic emigrants from Europe" and so increase as to "be fit instruments in the hands of power, to reduce the ancient free Protestant Colonies to the same state of slavery with themselves."

Three days later, on October 24, Congress accepted another address, "Lettre addressée aux Habitans de la Province de Quebec." Jay drafted this one too. But this time, appealing to the Quebecois to join the Continental Congress' protests against the crown, he wrote, "We are too well acquainted with the liberality of sentiment distinguishing your nation, to imagine, that difference of religion will prejudice you against a hearty amity with us. You know, that the transcendant [*sic*] nature of freedom elevates those, who unite in her cause, above all such low-minded infirmities."[4] This appeal was translated, printed, but apparently not distributed in Canada. Another, approved on May 29, 1775, was. It is not clear just what the Quebecois thought of this, but somehow they remained unpersuaded. As for Jay, was he a two-faced bigot? Or only an Anglican of "Calvinist severity," as his most recent biographer writes?[5] Or just a nimble-penned amanuensis for the Continental Congress? Whatever the case, the Quebec Act was "intolerable," more in New York and New England because it protected French Catholicism, more in the middle colonies and the South because it failed to protect land speculation in Transappalachia, but for both reasons everywhere.

Transappalachia and Who Lived There

To fully understand how the United States gained Transappalachia, it's necessary to back up about twenty years from the Declaration of Independence and trace what happened in the region with regard to its population. In the chanceries of Europe and in the Continental Congress in Philadelphia, maps showed what "belonged" to Britain, France, Spain, and (soon) the United States of America. According to the treaties that concluded the Seven Years' ("French and Indian") War, France's "possessions" west of the Mississippi reverted to Spain in 1762, and those east of it (Transappalachia) to either Spain or Britain. The region north of the Great Lakes, formerly New France, became British.

These were white men's claims, however. Decisive as they were in their own way, they ignored the fact that few French, Spanish,

British, Canadian, or American people occupied those lands. Indians, of many tribes and configurations, actually lived there. Indian populations prior to 1800 are conjectural, but there were likely 200,000 to 250,000 east of the Mississippi in the late eighteenth century.[6] Cherokees, Creeks, Choctaws, Chickasaws, and others in southern Transappalachia; Shawnees, Delawares, Mingoes, Ottawas, Wyandots, and others in Ohio and on the shores of Lake Erie; Miamis and Potawatomis from southern Indiana north to Michigan; thousands of Ottawas and Chippewas across the upper Great Lakes—these do not even exhaust the names of the significant tribes. When Europeans arrived in the 1600s, Indians were spread more or less randomly from the Atlantic coast westward, guided by topography or their own shifting conflicts and alliances. By 1780 all but a few had been pushed westward beyond the mountains. White people would overtake the Indians in a generation or so in Transappalachia as well. At the time of the peace negotiations in 1782 the numbers of Europeans and Americans beyond the mountains were not even close to the Indian population. Transappalachia was peopled by natives. From their standpoint, the cells of white forts and settlements had not yet metastasized. Experience suggested they soon would.

Indian locations and numbers were always shifting. When the world war between Britain and France took shape in the early 1750s, English-speakers in North America numbered about a million, all living along the Atlantic coast; none had yet crossed the Appalachians. The French "covered" a much larger area from the St. Lawrence Valley to the Gulf of Mexico, but much more thinly. True French settlements were confined to a couple of hundred miles along the banks of the St. Lawrence River from around Quebec City upstream to Montreal, and less than two hundred along the lower Mississippi River from New Orleans up to Baton Rouge and Natchez. There may have been 75,000 French *in toto*—settlers (chiefly in Quebec, a few elsewhere) plus a few thousand fur traders, clerics, soldiers, and officials sprinkled along waterways from Arkansas Post north to Kaskaskia; at Forts Vincennes and Ouiatenon in present Indiana; at Fort St. Joseph and, more importantly, Forts Mackinac and Detroit in present Michigan; and at Forts Niagara and Frontenac on either tip of Lake Ontario. The French had, however, worked out relationships over the preceding century with their Indian hosts. Though uneasy and occasionally lethal, they succeeded better than anything the British or Americans were able to achieve consistently.

Following the British defeats of the French in 1759 and 1760, the

Ottawa chief Pontiac adroitly constructed a confederation of tribes to resist the British, whom they found to be aggressive and ungenerous. For over four years in the mid-1760s, Pontiac's forces bedeviled British posts and forts all across northern Appalachia, from Fort Pitt to the Mississippi and from Lake Erie south to the Ohio River. In 1763 alone, the British suffered more than two thousand soldiers and civilians killed and wounded.[7] But Pontiac failed. After his struggle collapsed, the Indians of the Great Lakes, Ohio Valley, and upland South had no recourse, in attempting to defend and retain their homes, than to make temporizing, short-term, short-range alliances with either the British or the Americans as opportunity arose. For their pragmatic shifts they were condemned by whites as unreliable and treacherous. By the early 1770s, though France's power was gone, some hundreds of French continued living in their villages, now under nominal British or Spanish rule. Virtually no British settlers, and only handfuls of troops, replaced French ones in the Great Lakes forts. At the lower end of the Mississippi, a secret provision of the 1762 Treaty of Fontainebleau turned over French Louisiana to Spain, and another treaty in 1763 gave Spanish Florida to Britain. But barely any Spaniards or British came to settle. Yet again, political control decided upon at European conference tables did not mesh with the demographic facts.

As for Americans in Transappalachia, the scattered cells were growing. Benjamin Franklin knew how fast. In 1751, a quarter century before the Declaration of Independence, the Philadelphia polymath wrote a brief tract that he called *Observations concerning the Increase of Mankind, Peopling of Countries, &c.* Its immediate purpose was to talk Britain into allowing more manufacturing in the colonies, and to do so Franklin provided this first serious survey of colonial population. He estimated that the English colonists numbered "upwards of One million" and were fast growing; that the growth was coming from natural increase rather than immigration; that boys and girls married younger than they did in Europe and had twice as many children. The peculiarly American result was a doubling of population "every 20 years." Franklin was a little off, but he had the right idea. He surely remembered population pressure when he was negotiating peace in Paris thirty years later.

As a sheer demographic reality, however, Transappalachia was not American in 1782 (or 1776 or 1763). It was not truly French, British, or Spanish either. After France lost the Seven Years' War (the "French and Indian War" in Yankee terms) and turned over its North American pos-

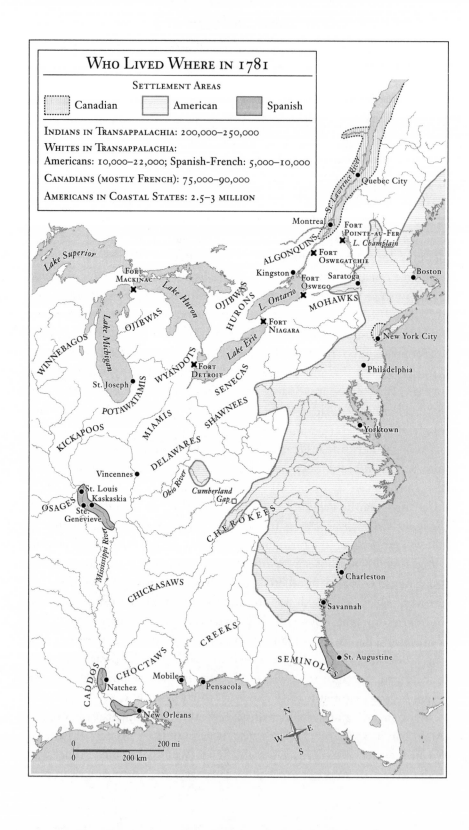

WHO LIVED WHERE IN 1781

SETTLEMENT AREAS

Canadian   American   Spanish

INDIANS IN TRANSAPPALACHIA: 200,000–250,000

WHITES IN TRANSAPPALACHIA:
Americans: 10,000–22,000; Spanish-French: 5,000–10,000

CANADIANS (MOSTLY FRENCH): 75,000–90,000

AMERICANS IN COASTAL STATES: 2.5–3 MILLION

St. Lawrence River

Quebec City

Montreal   FORT POINTE-AU-FER
ALGONQUINS   *L. Champlain*
FORT OSWEGATCHIE

Kingston   FORT   Saratoga   Boston
OSWEGO

Lake Superior

FORT MACKINAC

OJIBWAS   *Lake Huron*   HURONS   *L. Ontario*   MOHAWKS

WINNEBAGOS

Lake Michigan

OJIBWAS   FORT NIAGARA

New York City

St. Joseph   WYANDOTS   FORT DETROIT   *Lake Erie*

POTAWATAMIS   SENECAS   Philadelphia

KICKAPOOS   MIAMIS   SHAWNEES

DELAWARES   Yorktown

Vincennes

St. Louis   *Ohio River*   Cumberland Gap
Kaskaskia

OSAGES   Ste. Genevieve

Mississippi River

CHEROKEES

Charleston

CHICKASAWS

Savannah

CREEKS

CADDOS   CHOCTAWS   Mobile   SEMINOLES   St. Augustine

Natchez   Pensacola

New Orleans

N
W   E
S

0   200 mi
0   200 km

sessions to Spain and Britain in the 1762 and 1763 treaties, no new migration replenished them, and many *habitants* intermarried with Indians or English-speakers. Outside of the St. Lawrence Valley and the New Orleans area, the settlements gradually lost their French identity. Scarcely any presence remained in another generation or two except a few mispronounced place-names.

Spain was even thinner on the ground. New Spain north of central Mexico had always been chronically underpopulated. This fact was central to why Spain and then Mexico would lose Texas and the Southwest. After 1763, the Spanish were hard put to make any appearance in Louisiana when they became France's legatee west of the Mississippi. A military squadron's successful but very brief capture in February 1781 of Fort St. Joseph near the eastern shore of Lake Michigan had no permanent effect. Even by 1803, when Spanish authorities at New Orleans momentarily gave Louisiana back to France (which promptly turned it over to the Americans, who had just bought it), Spaniards were scarce anywhere east or north of Texas, and hardly a massive presence even there. The young Spanish governor at New Orleans, Bernardo de Gálvez, swept the British from the lower Mississippi and West Florida in 1780 and 1781. But while that hurt the British and helped the Americans, it did not entice more Spanish settlers to Transappalachia. Franklin was not the only American aware of the demographic vacuum. His soon-to-be colleague on the American peace team, John Jay, had observed to the French and Spanish representatives in Philadelphia in December 1778 that Louisiana (i.e., the area west of the Mississippi) would soon attract more than 20,000 Americans, and Spain would be hard put to "hold the territory against this human flood."[8]

English-speakers had begun to slip west of the Appalachians long before 1782, even before 1763. Virginia created a county west of the Blue Ridge in 1745 and obtained royal and colonial charters in 1748–1749 for the Ohio Company of Virginia, a speculation covering most of the present state of West Virginia. Other incorporations followed. Hardly anyone went there, but every such act, even if nothing

Keep in mind that the area shown as American in 1781 was thinly populated. Except for the very few towns (and New York, Charleston, and Savannah were still in British hands), almost none of it contained more than six persons per square mile. Note also that even those "settled" areas comprised well under half of the national territory awarded in the 1782–1783 treaties. Yet the areas shown as Spanish and British occupied far less area and many fewer people. Overwhelmingly, the peoples of Transappalachia were Indians, of many tribes.

but a dream on paper, firmed up the conviction that Transappalachia would soon be a frontier sighing seductively for settlement. By the time the crown drew the Proclamation Line of 1763, the edge of settlement already almost touched it from southwestern Pennsylvania to north-western North Carolina. When the Revolutionary War began a dozen years later, the line had been reached or breached from New York north of Albany all the way to Georgia. By 1775 settlers were filtering through the Cumberland Gap, at Virginia's southwestern tip, and turning north into Kentucky. At the headwaters of the Ohio they were congregating at Fort Pitt, and in New York they were chafing to move west along the Mohawk. To coastal authorities, British before 1776 and American thereafter, these unrestrainable migrations were a nuisance, a liability, and a taxpayers' expense because they constantly produced conflict with Indians. Yet settler surges also meant opportunities for investment. Before 1763, when Franklin and other colonists still thought of them-selves as fully British, the defeat of France and Britain's acquisition of New France were a joy. The Proclamation Line tempered that joy. When the Quebec Act in 1774 swallowed up everything north of the Ohio and called it Canada, it seemed "intolerable" to the Americans, another grievous crown outrage.

The distant western cabins and lean-tos of Americans scarcely pierced beyond the Appalachians when Lexington and Concord erupted in April 1775. From the Maine coast migrants crept west to include southern New Hampshire and Vermont within the New England back-country, and they passed Albany by sixty miles or so into the Mohawk Valley before serious Iroquois resistance interdicted their progress. They then tiptoed south through the Catskills in the general direction of New York before turning west again in northern New Jersey and fol-lowing Forbes' Road (just opened in the French and Indian War) past Fort Pitt. Coursing down the Ohio River (though taking care to stay on the southern, less Indian-defended side), settlers edged back inland to the Great Valley of Virginia, where they could follow an already well-worn path toward the Cumberland Gap. Some (though not yet many) were poised along the rivers flowing westward from the Smokies into Tennessee. They finally dribbled down into Georgia and reached the Atlantic again near the Georgia-Florida border.

None of this settling seriously crossed the mountains except in two places. Virginians began filing into the Monongahela Valley in far western Virginia and southwestern Pennsylvania in the late 1760s, moving toward the Monongahela's junction with the Allegheny to form the Ohio River. In the spring of 1775 Daniel Boone led a settler group *through* the Cumberland Gap, turned sharply north, and started what were soon four small "stations" with a fluctuating population of fifty to three hundred men, women, and children. They were essentially isolated from neighbors by nearly two hundred miles of trackless forest, and from coastal America by far more than that. To look at a map of 1775 or 1780 and find "American influence" or even more egregiously "American settlement" in Kentucky is to put cartography at the service of myth.

At the onset of the Revolutionary War, then, there were effectively almost no Americans in Transappalachia. This changed fast. Settlers scurried into the region all through the war. The greatest increase, truly an invasion, lifted Kentucky's settler population from the few hundred of 1775 to somewhere between 10,000 and 20,000 in 1780. By 1782 and treaty time, seven years after Boone's incursion, seven years after Lexington and Concord, Americans had pushed across the Mohawk Valley to Lake Ontario, no longer stymied by Iroquois. They were paddling up the Connecticut River into central Vermont and New Hampshire, which became bonanza frontiers in the 1780s and 1790s. They floated their flatboats down the south shore of the Ohio to its falls near Louisville, and down westbound mountain rivers into eastern Tennessee. With crown authority gone, the westward pressure and location of population—whites pressing Indians—negated forever the earlier fact that Americans were a coastal people, or only that. They were on the verge of becoming continental as well. The negotiators at Paris knew this—even John Adams from the Massachusetts shore—and they were constrained to act accordingly, even though Transappalachia's numbers in no way justified their adamancy.

But let us not get carried away. Despite the recent increase, the American population of Transappalachia was under 25,000 by November 1782, when the negotiators were deeding it to the United States. The settlers were scarcely 1 percent of the total national population, nearly all of whom were living within a few score miles of the Atlantic, and they were a fraction of a still much greater Indian population. The United States did not acquire Transappalachia because of any overwhelming ethnic presence of its own. There was none.

What Did the United States Conquer
in the Revolution?

Wars in the eighteenth century, as in other times, were fought over territory. Naturally, when the fighting was over, whoever had lost or won territory largely determined who finally kept it. The American Revolutionary War was an exception, because the United States was awarded Transappalachia without conquering it, or even having it under military control when the war ended. Not only did Americans not live there, they did not capture it.

After the first battles at Lexington and Concord in April 1775, patriotic ardor swelled. In the fall of 1775, an American army bivouacked its way north through Lake George and Lake Champlain and effected a "genteel liberation" of Montreal on November 13.[9] Some troops stayed in Montreal while the rest proceeded downriver to join another American force coming up from Maine to lay siege to Quebec on December 30. British forces under Sir Guy Carleton drove them off in May 1776. The American commander in Montreal, General David Wooster, brought off a negative public relations coup when he forbade the Quebecois to attend Catholic Mass at Christmas, adding to the Montrealers' suspicions that they were better off under the British. The Continental Congress sent three delegates, led by Franklin, on a perilous late-winter expedition to Montreal to persuade the Quebecois to join the rebellion. After twelve fruitless days in April, Franklin and companions returned home. On June 15, 1776, the American invaders retreated south. Canada was not going to become the fourteenth rebellious colony, and the 1775–1776 invasion marked the farthest American reach into Canada ever.

The American invasion of Canada failed because London had finally resolved to suppress and overwhelm the rebellious colonists. At the same time that the Continental Congress was signing the Declaration of Independence, massive British forces were landing at New York. In August, 32,000 ground troops invested the city (population 25,000), supported offshore by 10,000 seamen. George Washington arrayed 23,000 underprepared troops and minutemen against them and lost the battle of Long Island. He managed to escape to New Jersey, but the British remained in New York City and its environs throughout the war.

The war soon settled into near stalemate in the north. A concerted

British attempt to split off rebellious New England from the other colonies failed in the fall of 1777, when American generals Horatio Gates and Benedict Arnold forced the British surrender at Saratoga, New York. France, now satisfied that the rebellion was serious, signed treaties of alliance and commerce with the United States in February 1778, and French financial and military aid became welcome and indeed essential to American victory. New England remained solidly in rebel hands, the middle colonies were under mixed control, and the South became the active war zone from late 1778 until Yorktown three years later. The British, not without evidence, hoped for a Loyalist uprising across the South to aid the armies they were sending there, but only sporadic support materialized. When General Charles Cornwallis led his army to the Yorktown Peninsula in northern Virginia, George Washington rushed southward. Combining 8,800 Americans with 7,000 French troops under Lafayette and Rochambeau, with the French navy sealing off escape by sea, Washington forced Cornwallis to surrender on October 19, 1781. In early 1782, as serious peace negotiations were about to begin, Britain held New York City, Charleston, Wilmington (North Carolina), and Savannah, along the Atlantic seaboard, with more than 20,000 troops. The Americans held New England and the interiors of the other rebellious colonies.

As for Transappalachia, the only sustained American military activity against the British west of the mountains during the war was that of Virginians led by George Rogers Clark. (The mid-1779 campaign of John Sullivan in southern New York wrecked the Iroquois but not the British, at least directly.) Clark's exploits, much celebrated later as having won the West, did not in fact cover much territory. Bernardo de Gálvez's capture of British West Florida for Spain in 1779–1781 benefited the United States more, in the short and the long runs, than Clark's efforts, valiant though they were.

Clark led a few score soldiers on a daring, difficult march in early 1778 down the Ohio and cross-country to the former French outpost of Kaskaskia on the Mississippi, capturing it in July. He then backtracked east to take Vincennes on the Wabash. His plan was to head north and take Detroit, but he lacked the men and resources. Detroit, and the entire Great Lakes and the forts on them, remained in British hands at the end of the war.

There is virtually no evidence that the American negotiators in Paris in 1782 were even aware of Clark's activities, or Sullivan's crushing of the Iroquois, or the battle of Blue Lick in August 1782, ten months after Yorktown and after the Paris peace talks were well under way. At Blue Lick a force of almost one thousand British troops and Indians from various Ohio tribes crushed 180 Kentuckians, killing 72, including a son and a nephew of Daniel Boone, who escaped. The American presence in Transappalachia was feeble to nonexistent. The only evidence that the American team was aware of activity in the region is a letter to Franklin in April 1779 from a man in Louisiana, telling him that Clark had captured Vincennes, then lost it, and might retake it.[10] None of the records of the 1782 negotiations refer to this letter, or in any other way to Clark and his backcountry victories or the Blue Lick disaster. Had the Americans captured Detroit they might have had a strong claim to the Great Lakes. They did not do so, however. Americans' hopes to annex Canada—that is, Quebec and Nova Scotia—so strong in 1775–1776, were dead by 1779, put to rest by the tides of the war and British immovability from New York, Halifax, and Quebec City. Franklin resuscitated the idea of Canadian annexation in 1782, but without result.

As it had always been, the struggle to occupy Transappalachia was much more a fight between whites and Native Americans than between French, British, or Americans. The 1782–1783 negotiations gave it to the Americans—among the white powers. It would take decades for them to push out the Indians, by force and by treaty.

Four Boundary Options

By the time the peace negotiations reached their final phase in October and November 1782, over a year had passed since Yorktown and over half a year since the British Parliament recognized that the war was lost. In that half year and in those fast-moving final weeks of negotiations, the four contending parties—France, Spain, Britain, and the United States—all jockeyed for maximum achievement of their specific war aims. They confronted four essentially different options with regard to territory and boundaries for the newly independent nation. France, Spain, and Britain were by no means of the same mind on where the Americans' boundaries should be. Should they get Transappalachia? Or any of it? Or any or all of Canada?

The first option was to "keep what you've got"—or, in the era's diplomatic language, *uti possedetis*. In 1780 and 1781, before Yorktown

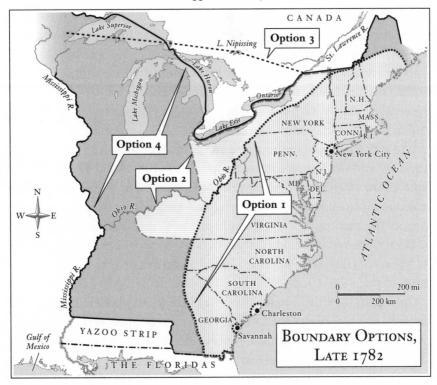

The treaty negotiators proposed several options in late 1782. Option one was minimal and would have confined the United States between the Atlantic and the western Appalachians. New York City, Charleston, and Savannah were still British-occupied and could have remained so. Option two, preferred by the French and Spanish, would have split Transappalachia, giving most of it to either Britain or Spain and keeping the United States well east of the Mississippi River. Option three would have given everything south of the "Nipissing Line" to the United States. Option four, basically the Great Lakes and Mississippi border, actually resulted.

and when the American cause looked weakest, this was murmured about in French and Spanish circles. It would have been highly disadvantageous—even a disaster—for the United States. New York, Savannah, and Charleston on the coast (together with Halifax and St. Augustine, the entire Atlantic seaboard), as well as the forts along the Great Lakes and much of the surrounding country, would have remained British. For how long, and whether Britain would have reinforced and held its possessions, is impossible to say. But Transappalachia, at least the northern part of it, would not have become American. Fortunately for the United States, France and Spain rejected this option after Yorktown, because it would have left Britain too strong in the western Atlantic and the Caribbean, where France and Spain had island possessions and significant trade.

The second option was to split Transappalachia, assigning most of it to Britain and Spain, with both of them quite possibly serving as "protectors" of the native Indians. This was more dangerous for the United States than the first option, because it was much more likely. It fit very well the objectives of both France and Spain. It came close to becoming the final version, because it was supported as late as mid-October 1782 by the Aranda-Rayneval agreement of that moment (Conde de Aranda was the Spanish minister in Paris, and Gérard de Rayneval was the deputy of the French foreign minister, the Comte de Vergennes). Several variations of it surfaced in the diplomatic cross fire of the early fall of 1782; all would have kept the United States out of Transappalachia, or most of it.

In one version, the area north of the Ohio River would have remained British, as it was under the Quebec Act of 1774. Spain would have gotten everything south of the Ohio except for Kentucky and northern Tennessee, where American settlers had already seeped in. Another version would have confined the United States to the coastal area east of the 1763 Proclamation Line. In either case, Spain would have controlled both banks of the Mississippi and navigation and trade on the river as far north as it wished, as it already did from Natchez to the Gulf.

Had that occurred, one wonders whether Spain could have withheld the onrush of American settlers into Kentucky, Tennessee, and beyond. Even if they had come, Spain might have persuaded them to accept its rule and separate from the United States. Spain had chronic difficulties in enticing enough colonists to populate areas it already held. But for a time, at least, Transappalachia would have been divided and the Mississippi would have been Spanish. Louisiana would have then been beyond America's reach when the chance arose in 1803 to buy it. Nevertheless, in 1782 some such line splitting Transappalachia reflected the actual status of population and forces.

A third option—that of the Nipissing Line—was radically different, by hundreds of thousands of square miles. It has rarely been mentioned in American narratives of the outcome of the Revolutionary War. For a brief time in the fall of 1782, this option was on the table, and its collapse at the crucial moment "reflects badly on the Americans, particularly Jay."[11] The Nipissing Line would have followed the southern boundary of "Canada"—that is, Quebec—as it existed before the 1774 Quebec Act. It was then a line running from the point where the forty-fifth parallel (the northern border of New York State) meets the St. Lawrence River out to Lake Nipissing (at present North Bay, Ontario) and continuing west across Lake Superior. What soon became southern Ontario, from Cornwall to the Georgian Bay, including present Toronto, London, Windsor, and all the rest, would have become American. Even fewer Canadians, British, or Loyalists actually lived in the region than Americans did in Kentucky. There would never have been an Ontario, except the nonfarmable reaches north of Lake Huron and Lake Superior. The fact that the United States had utterly no population or forces north of the Great Lakes, or even north of the Ohio, was not why the negotiators in Paris decided against the Nipissing Line. Their agreement on option four, which gave the United States much more than option two (Aranda-Rayneval) and much less than option three (Nipissing), resulted from diplomatic infighting quite independent of who was where.

The fourth option is how things actually ended up. Transappalachia, all of it, became American. Ontario did not.

The Peace Negotiations before Yorktown, 1774–1781

Peace efforts began even before the Declaration of Independence. Prior to the great French-American victory at Yorktown in October 1781, they went essentially nowhere. Had a peace been concluded before then, it would have been much less favorable to the United States than what eventually emerged. A basic problem in the negotiations was the wildly divergent British and American views of the rebellion. In Britain, Lord North's ministry, with the full backing of the king and probably the people, saw the rebels as a contumelious rabble led by a few elite adventurers, without legal or moral justification. They believed that a hard line—military force, not just tough laws like the Quebec Act and the "intolerable acts" of 1774—would restore the rightful order.

As the quagmire deepened, the hard line softened—but only somewhat, and only by the force of financial exhaustion and military stalemate. When the peace treaty was finally concluded in late 1782, the British people agreed to it, although they did not like it. In America, on the other hand, "natural rights," as broadcast everywhere, from the Declaration of Independence to Thomas Paine's pamphlets and Samuel

Adams's rabble-rousing, justified throwing off the authority of both king and parliament.

With such "rights" on their side, American leadership in Congress, the press, and elsewhere confidently expected to win. To start, they sent those two rather inadequate armies north into Quebec, hoping that the French province would race to become the fourteenth state. Instead, rejection. But it is striking how unflaggingly American negotiators, Franklin above all, stuck to their initial positions regarding unqualified independence and extensive boundaries. The boundaries, Franklin insisted, must include Transappalachia, and should include all of Canada. From time to time, during the war, the Continental Congress wavered on boundary issues, but almost never did its negotiators in Paris do so. Had there been a transatlantic cable, or satellite communication, Congress might well have overridden them, and lost the West.

American assumptions that Transappalachia was indivisibly part of their territory went far back in time to the colonial charters. They also rested on cultural attitudes about English Protestant civilization's superiority to Catholic French and Spanish pretensions and, more to the day-to-day point, to Indian "savagery." By the 1740s, as already noted, the lands over the mountains beckoned as investment opportunities for—choose your word—speculators or developers. Colonial governors (though they weren't supposed to), Franklin himself and the movers and shakers of Philadelphia, the Livingstons and Jays of New York, Washington and other Virginia planters, even some investors in New England, dabbled and planned and chartered land companies of huge extent in the Ohio Valley. Washington considered his western holdings the cornerstone of his wealth, more so than Mount Vernon.[12] John Jay's wife, born Sarah Livingston (she was a cousin of Robert Livingston), had a sister who was married to John Cleve Symmes, who in 1788 persuaded Congress to grant him two million Ohio acres to sell at a profit to settlers. He failed to do so, but not for want of trying. A partner of Symmes's was Elias Boudinot, onetime president of Congress. There were many others as highly placed.

The American romance with Transappalachia included land-grabbing and moneymaking, but it was hardly just that. It involved patriotism, and even more, many thought, the fulfillment of the plans of God and Nature for America. Diverse American voices—religious, cultural, and economic—converged in the assumption that Transappalachia was and had to be American. A few decades later such a notion would exfoliate into "manifest destiny." This belief had its source as far back as the Puritans' conviction that America was "exceptional," chosen by Providence—Nature's God—to occupy, settle, and exploit the great expanses of North America. Even if the coastal elites had objected to western settlement, they knew—and Franklin's 1751 *Observations on Population* affirmed it—that they could not stop it. The king had tried with his Proclamation Line of 1763 and was ignored. The Indians put up a stiff and constant resistance to the loss of their homelands, yet white numbers simply overwhelmed them. From all sorts of sources, the American assumption that Transappalachia was naturally theirs was already unarguable by 1776.

Not as many Americans looked upon Canada in the same way (i.e., as eventual American territory). Yet some did, arguing that geopolitics, security needs, and economics (mainly the fur trade) required it. Congress originally believed that Quebec and possibly Nova Scotia would join the American cause. It sent two armies, a verbal invitation, and that diplomatic team composed of Franklin and Catholics Charles Carroll (one of Maryland's signers of the Declaration) and his cousin John Carroll (a Catholic priest who became America's first bishop). The armies were repulsed, the invitation was ignored, and the envoys were politely refused.

Franklin, however, continued to covet Canada (i.e., Quebec) as part of the eventual peace settlement. In 1776, he also suggested Nova Scotia, Bermuda, the Floridas, and the Bahamas. In December 1777, he still sought Canada and the Floridas. Two months later, when France recognized the United States and signed the treaties of commerce and aid, the Continental Congress rejoiced in the thought that this would deliver all of Canada as well as a western boundary at the Mississippi River. In May 1778, Congress sent new instructions to Franklin in Paris to claim Nova Scotia and both banks of the St. Lawrence and the Great Lakes as well. Again, in late 1779, Franklin let it be known in Paris that if Britain wanted peace it should offer Canada and Nova Scotia. When Congress sent John Adams to Paris in September 1779 it instructed him to insist first, of course, on independence, but next on a northern boundary at essentially the Nipissing Line (Quebec too if possible) and a western one at the Mississippi. John Jay went to Madrid at the same time, charged to negotiate the Mississippi boundary and free navigation (i.e., no customs duties) on the river, and free access to a port or ports on the lower river, although that area was entirely in Spanish hands.

The hopes for Canada evaporated, and those for Transappalachia progressively faded, as 1779 turned into 1780. Congress's instructions to its negotiators remained firm, but they were hardly entertained in Europe. Adams in Paris and Jay in Madrid got nowhere. Neither France nor Spain favored an America that included much of anything west of the mountains, certainly not a Mississippi boundary, nor "free navigation" on the river. Both allies were already doing plenty to help the American cause in very material, even lifesaving, ways—loaning money, providing ports to America's privateers and its tiny navy, joining the French fleet's operations on the Atlantic coast, and diverting Britain by war-making in the Mediterranean, the West Indies, and the Gulf coast. From New Orleans, Governor Bernardo de Gálvez not only gave an American agent, Oliver Pollack, more than 60,000 pesos to supply George Rogers Clark in the Illinois country, but he threw the British out of Baton Rouge in August 1779, Mobile in February 1780, and Pensacola in the spring of 1781, thus removing Britain from West Florida and the Gulf of Mexico. A Spanish ground force captured the British post of Fort St. Joseph beside Lake Michigan. Though it quickly withdrew, it affirmed Spanish "rights of conquest" well north and east of the Mississippi. France and Spain were helping the Americans tremendously. That did not mean they wanted a new North American republic to exist from the Atlantic to the Mississippi.

In fact, in European eyes and in reality, the United States from mid-1779 well into 1781 was surviving on French and Spanish lifelines. When Congress in October 1780 reaffirmed Jay's instructions to negotiate free navigation on the Mississippi "desde y hasta el mar"—from and to the Gulf—it maintained that the river had been "the boundary of several States in the union and their citizens while connected to Great Britain and since the revolution [had] been accustomed to the free use thereof in common with the subjects of Spain."[13] This stretched reality beyond recognition. Spain claimed its exclusive right to Mississippi navigation based on its presence on the east bank up to the thirty-first parallel and on the west bank to the river's source. France's able representative in Philadelphia, the Chevalier de la Luzerne, made clear in early 1780 that France expected the western boundary of the United States to be the 1763 Proclamation Line, far from the Mississippi and consequently without any navigation rights on it.

The French and Spanish stances were clear and consistent. They were not the Americans' positions. Spain did not want the United States near the Mississippi. It would deliver money and matériel to the Americans, but not Transappalachia. France had no claims on or aims at territory in North America, and it kept sending not only money but troops and ships to help the Americans. But it supported its Bourbon ally's control of the Mississippi and Transappalachia. The divergence with the Americans was clear, and in early 1781 Vergennes made it clearer: he suggested a truce in the North American war on the basis of *uti possedetis* with the boundaries reflecting exactly who held what at that moment. Transappalachia north of the Ohio River would stay British except possibly the southern halves of what are now Ohio, Indiana, and Illinois. Spain would get the region south of the Ohio down to the Florida border, except possibly for the American settlements in Kentucky.

This was the nadir of the American territorial cause. Luzerne told Congress in early June 1781 that France might have to agree to a truce based on *uti possedetis*, which at that moment would have excluded South Carolina and Georgia from the union and allowed Britain to keep New York, Charleston, Savannah, the Great Lakes forts, and miles of countryside. Congress wavered for the first and only serious time. It appointed a new peace team in Paris that included Franklin, Adams, and Jay.[14] They were to keep to earlier instructions regarding boundaries, but their only absolute demand was full independence. On other points (including boundaries) they were to "secure the interest of the United States in such manner as circumstances may direct"—that is, get what they could— and, a very major restriction, "undertake nothing . . . without [France's] knowledge and concurrence." That summer Franklin sent a letter to the Earl of Shelburne—a good friend of his since 1767, when Franklin was the agent of Pennsylvania in London—suggesting that Britain cede Canada to the United States in order "to avoid further friction" and to compensate America for war damages inflicted by Britain and its Indian allies. Franklin could make the most outrageous claims in such a way as to establish a remote base point in negotiations, yet not antagonize his correspondent. The suggestion went nowhere, but option one, "keep what you've got, and no more," did not resurface.

THE PEACE NEGOTIATIONS AFTER YORKTOWN

It was a godsend for the Americans that the Yorktown victory came when it did. The French, Spanish, and American positions on territorial boundaries hardly budged in the year or so from then until October and

November 1782. France and Spain, despite wanting to help the Americans defeat Britain, had no interest in conveying Transappalachia to them. Spain in particular would thereby (and soon) face an aggressively growing power along its thinly populated North American imperial borders of Louisiana and Florida. The Americans aimed to acquire as much as they could: Transappalachia, the right to sail the Mississippi, and possibly Canada. The various Indians were not present at the peace table nor were they consulted, but their best chance (since whites would not leave them alone) was to maintain friendly ties with Britain in the north and Spain in the south, keeping the Americans as far away—and for as long—as possible.

Politics, stakes, personnel, and positions in Britain reacted to Yorktown as to an earthquake. To begin with, on December 8, 1781, George III and his ministers, still led by Lord North, agreed to send no more troops to America. That did not mean, however, that British opinion felt anything but humiliation or that it acquiesced at all amicably in American independence. On January 1 the *London Chronicle* still had "expectations of a reconciliation between the mother country and her colonies."[15] At that same time, Robert R. Livingston, Congress's foreign secretary, wrote from Philadelphia to Franklin urging him to keep pressing for the most extensive boundaries he could get, on the basis of the colonial charters "and more particularly by the Settlements of People who are engaged in the same Cause with us," whether in the West or in Canada.[16]

But Canada was where people decidedly not "engaged in the same Cause with us"—the Loyalist refugees—were heading. Franklin and Adams despised Loyalists. Franklin's only son, William, formerly the royal governor of New Jersey, remained loyal and was living in England. Franklin never communicated with him again. In backcountry New York, where Mohawks and other Indians allied with and fought beside the British in the hope of retaining some control over their lands, settlers blamed the British for Indian "savagery" and scorned any idea of restitution to Loyalist neighbors who fled north to Canada. In Britain, many people claimed that simple honesty required colonists to pay any debts they had incurred before 1775 and to indemnify the confiscated property of those who had honorably remained loyal to the king. On this, British and American public opinion were far apart. They never closed, and as a result the forthcoming peace negotiations continued almost without hope of pleasing both sides.

That said, British politics shifted quickly after Yorktown to a new framework and new players who made negotiations possible. In the closing days of February 1782, the House of Commons agreed that the war in America was effectively over (although the war against France and Spain continued), and on March 5, Parliament voted for peace. Two weeks later Lord North, the hard-line prime minister since 1770, resigned, and the Marquess of Rockingham replaced him on March 27. The Earl of Shelburne became colonial secretary and over the following months, despite serious opposition, he moved stepwise toward an American peace. Every realist in London agreed by then on the same agenda: divide the Americans from France, end the war in North America, and then conclude a more advantageous peace with France and Spain.

Shelburne faced a bankrupt treasury as well as a war-exhausted country. The colonies be damned, but the colonies were gone. Call them whatever they wished—the United States of America, if that had to be. At least prevent them from cementing in any way their alliance with France. Because of the common language and culture, they might relax, relapse, or revert to some sort of amicable relation with the mother country. Splitting them from France—and making a separate peace?—would be much the best alternative.

In Paris, Vergennes also faced major money problems and—the mirror image of Shelburne in this respect—was ready to employ any means at hand (loans? troops? ships? *land*?) to keep the United States faithful to its treaties with France and, he hoped, to a mutually supportive relationship for years to come. In Madrid, King Carlos III had approved substantial aid to the United States. But he had not recognized its independence or signed any treaty with it. A republic directly abutting the three-hundred-year-old Spanish Empire in North and South America was grossly undesirable; ideas of independence and self-rule traveled too easily. Spain had given money to the United States in the dark hours of the war. In the Caribbean, one of its admirals raised 500,000 pesos in Havana for the Americans just before Yorktown, and he safeguarded French possessions so that the French fleet could sail north and checkmate Cornwallis. Spain's representatives in Madrid and Paris correctly sensed ingratitude, and soon worse, from one of the American negotiators in Paris in 1782. It was not Franklin, whose "prudent intelligence" a Spanish historian recently contrasted with "the rash excitability of John Jay."[17]

The peace process truly began in late March 1782, almost as soon as

Shelburne took over the Colonial Office. A certain Lord Cholmondeley, visiting Franklin in Paris, volunteered to carry a note to Shelburne. Franklin was glad to oblige: "I embrace the opportunity of assuring you of the continuance of my ancient respect for your talents and virtues, and of congratulating you on the returning good disposition of your country in favour of America, which appears in the late resolutions of the Commons." Franklin hoped for "*a general peace*, which I am sure your Lordship with all good men desires, which I wish to see before I die, and to which I shall with infinite pleasure contribute everything in my power."[18]

The Treaty of Alliance of February 1778 bound France and America not to "conclude either truce or peace with Great Britain without the formal consent of the other first obtained." But, Franklin could reason, who was concluding anything? These were only expressions of esteem and hope. True also, Congress had instructed Franklin and the other commissioners in 1781 not to negotiate with Britain without the "knowledge and concurrence" of the French. But whatever his self-justification—too good an opportunity to miss?—he went ahead. Anyway (he could argue), the British started it. And with the approval of the cabinet and the king, Shelburne sent Richard Oswald, an elderly Scottish businessman, to Paris. Franklin and Oswald, both in their mid-seventies, got along well. Franklin nevertheless took a tough and consistent position, proposing that Britain cede Canada (i.e., Quebec) and Nova Scotia in order to avoid future frictions. Shelburne's "response was crisp": he "rejected the proposal out of hand," in the words of two British historians.[19] Nor would the cabinet or the king—or Vergennes, had Franklin informed him—have agreed either. It was at least a start. Did Franklin keep asking for Canada to give himself a fall-back position (the Great Lakes line) and to keep the Mississippi River in the picture? His lust for Canada was so consistent for so long that it may not have been such a stratagem at all. But it probably served as such.

Oswald made two more trips in May to see Franklin, and notes criss-crossed with no great result. On July 1, however, Shelburne became prime minister. Oswald visited Franklin again, and on July 9, Franklin gave him "a few hints or articles." Some were "necessary for them to insist on; others which he could not say he had any Orders about, or were not absolutely demanded, & yet such as it would be advisable for England to offer for the sake of Reconciliation, and her future Interest."[20] The "necessary" articles were four: first, "full & complete" independence "& all troops to be withdrawn"; second, "A settlement of the boundaries" of the states and the loyal colonies; third, Canada's boundaries to be "what they were, before the last Act of Parliament, I think in 1774 [the Quebec Act], if not to a still more contracted State"; and fourth, fishing and whaling rights off Newfoundland. The "advisable" articles—also four—called for war damages; an apology for "distressing [the States] so much as We had done"; free trade; and "Giving up every part of Canada." Franklin also warned Oswald that reparations to Loyalists would be "impossible to make," though some might deserve "compassion." Any reparations were up to the states, not the central government.

The "necessary" articles became the embryonic first version of the peace agreement. Shelburne was willing to entertain them, putting him and Franklin on the same wavelength. Pulling back the boundary to where it was before 1774 (the Quebec Act) implied that it would not be the Ohio River and that Transappalachia, possibly more, would become American. Franklin's "necessary" articles did not mention the Mississippi at all, but he probably assumed that Shelburne would see that the river went with the package: wherever the boundary of Canada was to be, it would be a boundary with Transappalachia, not just New York and New England. Thus Shelburne reduced any threat of France or Spain aggrandizing themselves in the middle of North America.

Up to this point, mid-July 1782, discussions had been going on between Franklin on the American side and Shelburne (via Oswald) on the British. In that month, Britain evacuated Savannah. On July 25 Shelburne commissioned Oswald to negotiate a peace agreement based on Franklin's "necessary" articles. The process seemed to be moving along.

Then two matters interrupted it from late July for another eight or nine weeks until late September. One was the start of John Jay's active role. Congress had appointed Jay and Adams to join Franklin in Paris, but until late July Franklin was the only active negotiator. Jay arrived from Madrid on June 23 but was sick with influenza for another month. Adams had earlier aggravated Vergennes so much that the foreign minister refused to meet with him, and Adams traipsed around Europe trying to make himself useful, ending up in the Netherlands with recognition of American independence and a loan. He returned to Paris only on October 26.

Jay began functioning in late July. In September and most of October, it was nearly a solo performance, because the seventy-six-year-old

Franklin took his turn at unavailability, becoming laid up with kidney stones. Jay's (and his wife Sally's) two years in Madrid had been extremely unhappy, unproductive, and uncomfortable. Their antipathy for the Bourbon courts, and, frankly, for Catholic Europe, did nothing to ease his discussions with the French. In fact, he soon tried to undercut the Spanish, despite their abundant aid, by proposing to help Britain recover West Florida.

The second perturbation, an extremely serious one for the boundaries question, was the incompatible divergence of Spanish and American claims to Transappalachia. On July 26 Jay began arguing about the region with the Conde de Aranda, the Spanish minister in Paris. While Jay was not giving up "a furlong," Aranda argued Spain's much better claims, based on military occupation and treaties, to formerly French Louisiana (including the Illinois country), West Florida, and the Mississippi itself.

To Vergennes fell the unpleasant task of trying to reconcile the irreconcilable claims of France's two allies.[21] On July 30, Aranda met briefly with Vergennes and at more length with Gérard de Rayneval. Spain wanted the United States nowhere near the Mississippi. France agreed that the United States had no persuasive claims other than, perhaps, a few settlements. The colonial charters, Jay's only case, were dismissed by the Europeans. Aranda and Rayneval assumed that Britain would retain the Ohio River as the southern boundary of Canada as the Quebec Act provided. The region south of the Ohio would be divided, Spain keeping most of it and the United States obtaining just the Kentucky settlements.

Jay met with Aranda from August 3 to September 10, when their negotiations broke off. They did not budge on mutually irreconcilable proposals—Spain claiming much of Transappalachia, the United States claiming all of it out to the Mississippi, as well as rights of navigation on the river and duty-free ports near the Gulf. No fewer than five French and Spanish boundary proposals, none satisfactory to Jay, passed across the table in those weeks. Vergennes drew a line well west of Aranda's, taking into account that American settlements already existed in Kentucky and Tennessee. But his line still ran considerably east of the Mississippi. George Rogers Clark's activities were "ephemeral." Vergennes regarded the American claims based on the colonial charters as "foolishness," as the charters came from the very monarch against whom the Americans had rebelled; and moreover, that monarch—the one now reigning—had redefined the western boundaries of the colonies in the 1763 Proclamation Line and the 1774 Quebec Act. West of it the Americans had no British rights to succeed to. The Americans, from Vergennes' standpoint, were getting a gift if they ended up with anything more.

This, then, was option two: the lines of Aranda and Rayneval, splitting Transappalachia. Most of it south of the Ohio River would have gone to Spain, while north of the Ohio would have remained British. Option two was a distinct possibility in August and early September 1782. Spain had excellent claims on the region and Aranda argued the Spanish case well. Vergennes refused to accept the extreme American claim all the way to the Mississippi (nor free navigation and duty-free ports). If the American negotiators obeyed their instructions and proceeded with the "knowledge and concurrence" of the French, then Transappalachia would have become partly Spanish, partly British, and only partly American. The American claims to it, to Canada, and to the Mississippi were in their gravest jeopardy in those weeks up to September 10.

In August, however, Jay turned to "the extremely risky, though necessary" alternative of making a secret deal with Shelburne, behind Vergennes' (and of course Aranda's) back, and for some time, even Franklin's.[22] Franklin had not changed his views. Writing to Livingston on August 12, he warned that Aranda wanted to "coop us up" between the mountains and the Atlantic, and he hoped Congress would not waver on the Mississippi boundary and free navigation. A few days later, Oswald told Shelburne that Franklin continued to believe that both America and Britain would ensure "peace and good neighborhood" if the West (Transappalachia, and Quebec too) went to the United States. But Jay was running the American show just then.

On August 29 the British cabinet, the king concurring, agreed on new instructions for Oswald. "We are ready as Mr. Jay desires to Grant the Independence of the 13 Provinces in the preliminary or First Article of a Treaty either of Peace or Truce," irrevocably, unconditionally. And "we will settle the Boundaries of the Provinces and Control the Limits of Canada as desired by Dr. Franklin." Just what that included was perfectly explicit. Oswald could assume that he should be conciliatory (his natural wont anyway) and generous. The British were committing themselves that these points, together with clauses about a clean evacuation of British troops and American rights to North Atlantic

fisheries, would become preliminary articles for a general treaty whenever the Americans wanted. Essentially, they were Franklin's four "necessary" articles of early July. These instructions reached Oswald on
September 4.

Franklin, though still suffering from his kidney stones, was agreeable.
But the lawyerly Jay was insisting that Britain agree to independence
prior to a treaty, rather than in the opening article. In other words,
Britain had to recognize American independence, by act of Parliament
or royal proclamation, as a precondition of negotiating. Oswald pointed
out that these were either beyond the English constitution or politically
out of the question. Technically Jay had a good point, but as a practical
matter he delayed matters quite probably to the great territorial disad-
vantage of the United States, though we can never be certain. Oswald
asked Jay to lay out whatever language he thought best, and it was
accepted in London, though not for a few more weeks.

Jay had become sufficiently certain by September 10 that agreement
with Britain was simply a matter of time. He broke off his monthlong
talks with Aranda. Neither Aranda nor Rayneval had budged on
Transappalachia. In fact, Rayneval sent Jay a note on September 6
(received September 9) that stated again that the 1763 Proclamation
Line was the proper western limit of the States, that Spain had rights to
everything east of the Mississippi south of Natchez by conquest, and
that north of that "is either independent or belongs to England. Neither
Spain nor the United States has any rights of sovereignty over the Indians in question."[23] The Indians could be awarded a buffer zone, possibly
under Spanish "protection." With that, Rayneval concluded by noting
that he would be out of town for a few days.

Jay learned, also on September 9, that Rayneval's out-of-town trip
was to London to talk to Shelburne. The talks lasted until September
18. Jay, badly shaken, as highly suspicious of Rayneval and Vergennes as
he was of anything Spanish, sent an envoy (Benjamin Vaughan) to dis-
suade Shelburne from any rapprochement with the French. Such a thing
could have happened: Shelburne might have made some sort of deal
with France. He could have accepted the French and Spanish position
on Transappalachia, given away none of Canada, indeed nothing north
of the Ohio River, and left the United States "cooped up" along the
Atlantic. Had Shelburne gone along with Vergennes at that point, "there
can be little doubt," writes the Oxford historian Vincent Harlow, "that
the future Dominion of Canada would have included what are

now . . . Ohio, Indiana, Illinois, Wisconsin, and Minnesota"[24]—and, *a fortiori*, Michigan: all of the Old Northwest.

Vergennes' real object was much simpler: slow down the Americans' progress with the British, keep the war going, maybe win Gibraltar for Spain, maybe split Transappalachia as Rayneval and Aranda had been insisting it be. Above all, discover whether Shelburne really was serious about a peace agreement (which he was). But Jay did not know that. If he had moved more inventively in those hours he might not only have kept Transappalachia but gained most of future Ontario (option three, the Nipissing Line) as well.

He also was unaware that the British cabinet was not pleased with his pettifogging on treaty language. Nor did he know that the British fleet decisively defeated a large-scale Spanish assault on Gibraltar on September 13–15, news of which reached London on September 30. On top of British admiral Sir George Rodney's victory over the French that summer in the West Indies, Shelburne could be sure that the Bourbon powers' navies were no longer so threatening. He could think of closing out the war on favorable terms. Yet Rayneval had presented Shelburne with too many unpalatable proposals relating to their war in Europe, matters unrelated to North America but of grave concern to Britain. Shelburne could not miss the obvious split between Jay on the one hand and Vergennes and the Spanish on the other, and he exploited it. His policy for some time had been to break up the Franco-American entente, and here was his chance. None too soon: Parliament was scheduled to reconvene in a few weeks, and it was urgent that the ministry have a treaty to present. Therefore the tactic was to humor the Americans and accede to their demands—though not quite all of them.

During the first days of October, Jay drew up a draft treaty whose main points resembled Franklin's "necessary articles" of early July. After obtaining approval from the still-ill Franklin, Jay gave it to Oswald on October 5. Oswald recommended it almost without change to Thomas Townshend, Shelburne's colonial secretary, on October 7. The opening sentence cleared up Jay's problem about recognition: the agreement would be between "His Brittanic [*sic*] Majesty" and "the Commissioners of the United States of America." The first article acknowledged the thirteen United States to be "free, sovereign, and independent," with the northern boundary to run from where the Connecticut River meets the forty-fifth parallel due west along that latitude "Streight to the South end of the Lake Nipissing and then Streight to the Source of the

River Mississippi." On the west the boundary would proceed down the middle of the Mississippi to thirty-one degrees latitude, and finally on the south along the northern boundary of the Floridas to the Atlantic.

This spelled out option three, the Nipissing Line. It gave up Franklin's old desire for all of Canada and Nova Scotia. Instead it proposed that the U.S. boundary with Canada follow the pre-1774 frontier of Quebec, rather than the post-1774 Ohio River boundary more than seven hundred miles to the south. Except for future Ottawa, North Bay, and Sudbury, the whole of the Ontario Peninsula, now including every significant town or city from Kingston to Windsor, would have become American rather than Canadian.

In these discussions, as Oswald wrote Townshend on October 2, Jay "repeated his wish that the Spaniards might be dislodged from West Florida" and asked why the British kept so many troops inactive in New York City and Charleston "when they could be recovering West Florida."[25] Jay wanted Britain, not Spain, to occupy the east bank of the lower Mississippi. His draft included "free navigation" on that and any other rivers in the world controlled by Britain or the United States.

Jay was being more than two-faced. He was encouraging his enemy, Britain, to go after a country that had fought and aided his country and cause. A British historian recently called Jay's move "both foolish and dishonourable," the result of "quite inappropriate vindictiveness."[26] Though Oswald enthusiastically urged the deal to Townshend, it went nowhere, and as events turned out—the final treaty ceded both West and East Florida to Spain as a sop for Britain keeping Gibraltar—it would have been fruitless. And, looking ahead twenty years, it would have been highly inconvenient for the United States if Britain rather than Spain had controlled the east bank of the lower Mississippi when the opportunity of the Louisiana Purchase came along. It remains true, however, that no negotiator for any of the countries involved made a proposal as treacherous as Jay's was against Spain.

The British cabinet considered Jay's draft on October 17. It did not accept the Nipissing Line and instructed Oswald and Henry Strachey (a tougher-tongued envoy sent to stiffen Oswald) to insist on the Quebec Act's Ohio River line. But—Shelburne added on October 20—"if nothing of this can be obtained after the fairest and most strenuous trials," Strachey was to accept the American proposals. Between October 30 and November 4, Franklin, Jay, and Adams (who had finally returned to Paris a couple of days earlier) worked out a second draft with Oswald and Strachey. They took up the boundary question first. Their new boundary clause receded slightly from the Nipissing Line, instead following the forty-fifth parallel all the way to the Mississippi, but that still left nearly all of future southern Ontario in American hands. If that proved unacceptable, the Americans proposed as an alternative a line beginning where the forty-fifth parallel hits the St. Lawrence River, then following the river and the Great Lakes: in other words, option four.

Here was the essential and final compromise on boundaries, and the American team, Oswald, and Strachey agreed to it in the final revision, dated November 7. Strachey, as late as October 29, fresh from London, still talked of lines something like Aranda and Rayneval's. Jay wrote in his diary, however, that "I told him if that was insisted upon it was needless to talk of Peace, for that we would never Yield that point."[27] On November 8 Strachey transmitted to Townshend and the cabinet the draft with the line-of-lakes boundary on the north and the Mississippi on the west.[28] Shelburne received it on November 10. The prime minister was far too eager to wrap up the treaty before Parliament reconvened to let the talks collapse. His goals remained clear: to divide the Americans from France (and obviously from Spain) through a separate peace, and to lay the basis as far as he could for a British-oriented rather than a French-oriented America, whatever shape that orientation might take. To do so, the western boundary was not to be a deal killer. The final treaties repeated the November 7 boundary clause with no material change.

Could the Americans have held out for option three, the Nipissing Line or the forty-fifth parallel? Opinions differ. "Patriot historians" such as Samuel F. Bemis and Richard Morris, extollers of the wisdom and virtue of the American team, either thought not or skidded past this question in their treatments written in the mid-twentieth century. Vincent Harlow, also writing at that time, implied that after the October 17 and mid-November cabinet meetings, option three was not a possibility and that Shelburne "had no intention at any time of giving away the fruits of Wolfe's victory on the Heights of Abraham [in 1759]. . . . There was never any question from the British side of a surrender of Canada."[29] But by Canada did Harlow mean Quebec—no argument there—or future Ontario, which is the real area in question? More recent writers, American and British, believed that Shelburne would have agreed (kicking and screaming) had Jay and Adams pushed harder.[30] But the two Americans' suspicion that Vergennes and Aranda were working with the British behind their backs scared them into agreeing to the line-of-lakes option.

Without verbatim transcripts of Shelburne's conversations and the cabinet's meetings, and being obliged to rely on their and the Americans' correspondence, we will never know definitively. But the cabinet was so distracted in those moments away from the wild and distant interior of North America and so fixated on winning fishing monopolies, collecting prewar debts, and securing reparations for the Loyalists, that they might have given away the future southern Ontario. Had they done so, the heavy going that the treaty, even with the line-of-lakes boundary, soon confronted in Parliament from December 1782 to February 1783 suggests that an even greater giveaway would have been defeated. Nonetheless, the British wanted fervently to end the war. They might have agreed to Nipissing. We are left to wonder if they would have, if pushed harder.

The cabinet met on November 14 and 15. They were unhappy with the draft's provisions on prewar debts owed British merchants; on fishing rights (with respect to which Adams discoursed learnedly and lengthily on the migration patterns of fish); and, most of all, on compensation for the Loyalist refugees. That almost did derail the negotiations. Meeting again from November 25 to 29, neither side would budge, until Oswald produced an acceptable compromise: that Congress would "earnestly recommend" to the states (which the American team insisted bore responsibility if any existed) to consider awards to the Loyalists. The British realized this probably meant no awards at all, but it at least acknowledged some responsibility somewhere in America. It was a fig leaf for domestic consumption.

On November 30 the two sides signed "preliminary articles"—preliminary because the Americans were bound not to conclude a final treaty without France. Technically they had not. But one historian has called Franklin's architecture "a marvel of Jesuitical evasion," ending the war with Britain yet not formally contravening the treaty of 1778 with France.[31]

The British, king to commoner, were disgruntled with the treaty. Oswald wrote Shelburne on November 30 that he and his colleagues bowed to "the inflexibility of uncommon circumstances."[32] He meant the impending convening of Parliament on December 5, which had not been in session since the previous spring, before Shelburne's ministry took office and before serious negotiations began. But Parliament was marginally more opposed to continuing the war than it was to any treaty Shelburne might lay before it, and the mood of the country ran parallel. Fortunately for the Americans' territorial claims, Parliament, and presumably the people, were far more concerned with the debts, the Loyalists, and even the fisheries than they were with the Great Lakes or the Mississippi, and they put little pressure on the negotiators or the cabinet about the boundary clause.

Vergennes had gotten wind of the Americans' behind-his-back dealings with the British. He had sent Rayneval to talk to Shelburne in early September, to be sure, but unlike the Americans, he was under no instructions or obligations not to do so or to inform them. He was surprised by the "astonishing result" for the Americans, and he wrote to Rayneval that "the English have bought peace rather than made it; their concessions, in fact, regarding the boundaries as well as for the fisheries and the Loyalists exceed everything I thought possible."[33] He had his own peace treaty to negotiate, and he immediately pressured Aranda and Spain to forgo Gibraltar and instead accept from Britain the island of Minorca and East and West Florida. Aranda agreed, and so the United States bordered for the next twenty years on Spanish territory—the Floridas to the south as well as Louisiana to the west.

Franklin, Jay, Adams, and the late-arriving Henry Laurens sent the treaty to Robert Livingston in Philadelphia on December 13. They argued that, despite many a claim by Britain and Spain to the "Western Country" and the Mississippi, and efforts by France and Spain to frustrate America's hopes, the results "leave us little to complain of, and not much to desire." Franklin got the ticklish job of informing Vergennes, and four days later he wrote to him. Franklin admitted that in dealing with the British his team had failed to keep the French government informed (the Americans had for months violated their instructions to do so), but he asked Vergennes to overlook what he painted as just a breach of etiquette. And Franklin actually asked for a further loan of 30 million livres. What Franklin labeled misbehavior others might have called treachery, and the loan application outrageous. But Vergennes obliged in February with 6 million. Franklin had nowhere else to turn for money; Vergennes had no alternative but to lend it, lest the American government, however duplicitous its diplomats, collapse financially.

Congress approved the treaty in late March. By then, on January 20, 1783, Vergennes, Aranda, and the British envoy Alleyne Fitzherbert signed the French and Spanish preliminary treaties, Franklin and Adams witnessing. A week later the British ministry presented the pacts to Lords and Commons. Protests were loud and many. "Everything of value" in Canada had been sacrificed; a "rabble" had been rewarded; Florida was "surrendered"; Indians "had been basely deserted"; the Loyalists "betrayed."[34] Shelburne countered that the treaty was the best anyone could have extracted; that it ended the expensive, hopeless colonial war; and—he insisted thunderously—it created the basis for future good and productive relations, especially trade relations, with the United States.

None of this saved him. Parliament swallowed hard and approved the treaty, but it did not have to put up with any more of Shelburne. On February 24 his government fell. Peace prevailed, but not cordiality.

Postmortem: Why Did the United States Gain So Much?

To summarize the territorial gains and losses in the 1775–1783 war between Britain and its former colonies, and the 1779–1783 British war with France and Spain:

France gained or lost no territory. She hoped to see an independent United States on the western coast of the Atlantic, and did so.

Spain won back Florida, did not recapture Gibraltar, and found itself with a large, robust, and generally hispanophobic neighbor bordering on Louisiana and Florida. Despite all the aid Spain had given it since 1779, the neighbor was by no means friendly. Furthermore, it was a republic, and its very existence stood as a destabilizing example to Spain's American empire.

The Indian nations south of the Ohio River lost their erstwhile ally and protector, Britain, and faced the tender mercies and proven aggressiveness of American frontier invaders. Indians north of the river could fear their future for the same reason. The Indian tribes would become the biggest losers, although the Indian-British connection continued north of the Ohio until the Americans won the battle of Fallen Timbers in 1794. Even after that, western Indians retained hopes of British support well into the nineteenth century, without result.

Britain lost the thirteen colonies but avoided losing Canada— Quebec, Nova Scotia, and future Ontario. Colonials who had remained loyal to the British crown were persecuted, injured, burned out, and run off by the rebels. There may have been as many as 50,000 such Loyalists, and they (as well as thousands of slaves who escaped and joined the

British) retreated—some to Britain, some to the West Indies, and many to Nova Scotia and (very soon) the previously uncolonized St. Lawrence Valley upriver from Quebec, there to pioneer what was soon called "Upper Canada" and ultimately Ontario.

The Americans were the big winners: independence and a vast area they had not won militarily, had scarcely populated except for parts of Kentucky and Tennessee, and had no solid legal claim to, prior to the peace treaty. Measured in square miles, the treaty added an immense expanse. The original rebelling thirteen colonies comprised about 384,000 square miles. Of that, about 120,000 were west of the Proclamation Line, reducing the original United States to about 264,000 square miles *if the French and Spanish position in late 1782 had prevailed.* But the new nation not only kept the 120,000 square miles, but also gained another 540,000—the areas of the ten-plus states eventually created out of Transappalachia.[35] Of the total U.S. land area created by the 1783 treaty, which was roughly 900,000 square miles, fully 70 percent was west of the Proclamation Line of 1763.

How, in the final analysis, did the United States make such a killing? Or rather, how did the negotiating team in Paris do so—since Livingston and Congress were not in touch with them from June 1782 until well after the signing, and even if they had been, their instructions from 1779 to 1782 demanded less? One apparent answer is the consistency and stubbornness of Franklin. As far back as his days in London before the war and in Paris during it, he wrote and said, time after time, that Canada (Quebec) should become American and that the Mississippi boundary was not negotiable. This was outrageously out of line with the facts on the ground, but Franklin stuck to it. His persona as an Enlightenment sage and scientist and the great respect in which he was held in both France and England, and his exceptional skill in face-to-face relations, allowed him to get away with such grotesqueries. Jay and (for the month he took part) Adams proved even harder to budge on anything; they were legalistic and long-winded; Strachey complained that he never saw "such quibblers."

Were they brilliant? Franklin certainly was, as a person. But the team's conduct was not brilliant. It was underhanded when it dealt with Britain behind Vergennes' back, and downright treacherous when Jay encouraged the British to push the Spanish off the Gulf coast. They were above all lucky. Shelburne was prime minister only from July 1, 1782, to February 24, 1783. Other British politicians, had they been running the government, might have cut some sort of deal with the Americans. But only Shelburne, almost certainly, would have given them so much. The Americans seized the Shelburnian moment when it presented itself. Lucky, too, that the American struggle coincided with a volatile period for Britain, France, and Spain. As others have pointed out, the Spanish colonies in contrast timed their forthcoming independence struggles toward the close of the Napoleonic Wars or just after, when they could provide no power a helping hand in European conflicts or play off one or two of them against Spain. The Americans were also fortunate that they had Vergennes to deal with, an honorable monarchist who really wanted the United States to be independent, and who supported it with money, ships, and troops to a degree detrimental to France itself.

Settlers continued to surge into Transappalachia in the early 1780s, but no one could say that the region was anything like fully settled by Americans. Even Kentucky and Tennessee would not be for a good forty years, and the farther reaches like Wisconsin and Minnesota took another hundred. American arms had not conquered it. George Rogers Clark's zigzags did not even come up in the peace discussions. Seven British forts along the St. Lawrence and Great Lakes remained British for almost fifteen more years—the excuse being that the Americans had done nothing to indemnify Loyalists and therefore had reneged on their treaty obligations, giving Britain every right to continue fur trading with the Indians.

Demography did not win it either. French and Spanish aid kept the United States from going under on the battlefields or financially. Stubbornness, conviction that the West belonged to them, and a willingness to double-cross their allies helped the American team greatly. Idealism in rhetoric, realism in policy: from the start, this was the American contradiction. This deep belief that America *had a right* to all that land—the sense that America was exceptional—was already in the minds not only of the negotiating team but of many of their countrymen.

But above all, luck, in several forms—those whom they perforce dealt with, the moment when they did so, and the circumstances in which those others happened to be—answers more of the question than any other reason.

Even so, an even luckier land opportunity, the luckiest ever in American history, was still ahead, just twenty years away. Expansion beckoned again, and Jefferson and his countrymen were ready.

Chapter Two

Louisiana, 1803: Second Good Luck

We have lived long, but this is the noblest work of our whole lives.
—Robert R. Livingston, upon signing the
Louisiana Purchase Treaty[1]

You have made a noble bargain for yourselves & I suppose you will make the most of it.
—Charles-Maurice de Talleyrand-Périgord,
French foreign minister[2]

The French Surprise

On April 30, 1803, at Napoleon Bonaparte's headquarters at St.-Cloud, near Paris, Robert Livingston and James Monroe for the United States, and François Barbé-Marbois for France, signed the treaty conveying Louisiana from France to the United States. The borders were indefinite except for the eastern one, the Mississippi River, but it was understood to include the entire watersheds of the Mississippi and Missouri, Platte, Arkansas, Red, Canadian, and any other rivers flowing into them, not just the present state of Louisiana.

The transfer surprised everybody. Even the man who proposed the sale, Napoleon Bonaparte, had decided on it only a few weeks before. It roughly doubled the size of the United States. It removed all American vexations about trade and travel on the Mississippi and its tributaries. It cost $15 million plus interest (although $3.75 million of it went to pay Americans for ships and cargoes wrecked by French "corsairs" in the late 1790s). It was no small sum; the federal budget at the time was under $10 million. But Louisiana was no small place nor was Napoleon's offer any small opportunity.

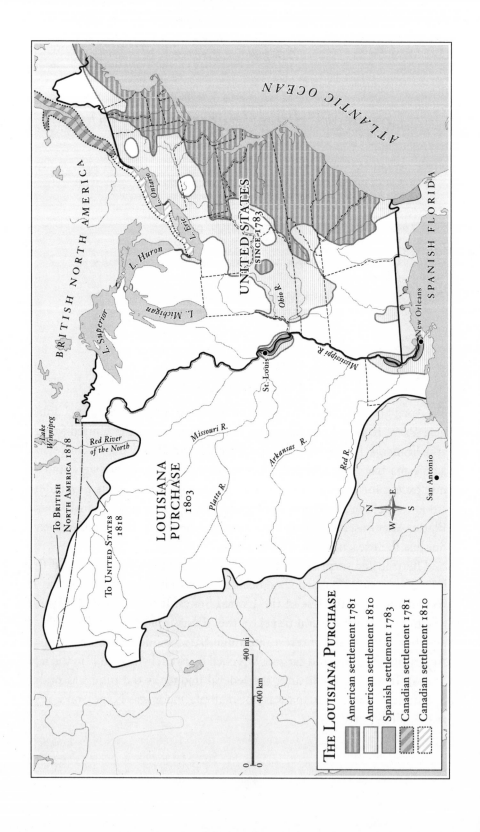

THE LOUISIANA PURCHASE

American settlement 1781
American settlement 1810
Spanish settlement 1783
Canadian settlement 1781
Canadian settlement 1810

LOUISIANA
PURCHASE
1803

UNITED STATES
SINCE 1783

BRITISH NORTH AMERICA

SPANISH FLORIDA

ATLANTIC OCEAN

To BRITISH
NORTH AMERICA 1818

To UNITED STATES
1818

Red River
of the North

Lake
Winnipeg

L. Superior

L. Huron

L. Michigan

L. Erie

L. Ontario

Missouri R.

Platte R.

Arkansas R.

Red R.

Mississippi R.

Ohio R.

St. Louis

New Orleans

San Antonio

N
W   E
S

0   400 mi
0   400 km

Transappalachia Transformed

Much had changed in the twenty years since the 1783 Treaty of Paris awarded Transappalachia to the United States. In that rambunctious region, time had hardly stood still. Transappalachia, as well as Vermont, New York, and Georgia, filled up with hundreds of thousands of fast-moving, fast-breeding young Anglo-American men and women and, often, the black slaves they brought with them. They fought, battled, murdered, and pushed aside Indians in northern Ohio, central Indiana, and western Kentucky and Tennessee. They so overwhelmed the natives that Vermont, Kentucky, Tennessee, and Ohio—where white settlers had hardly stepped in 1780—were all states of the union by the year of the Louisiana Purchase. Moreover, they were states with just as much sovereignty and independence, and the same relation to the federal government, as Massachusetts or Virginia or the rest of the original thirteen.

In Transappalachia, as the Anglo-Americans rode in, the Indian nations living there found themselves under severe aggressive pressure. The 1783 treaty awarded Transappalachia to the United States, not to Spain or Britain, but it said and did nothing about the real inhabitants. Anyone assuming an Anglo-American advance to be righteous or natural could not also assume that the Indians would stay in place. Perhaps they could be "civilized," that is, taught to farm, weave, and spin; but as long as they hunted, fished, and quarreled with one another and with whites, they would have to be dealt with—perhaps moved farther west. As Henry Knox, secretary of war, observed in 1790, "the Indians held the right of soil and could choose whether or not to sell their lands, [but] this concept of free choice broke down under the pressure of the frontier advance."[3] Federalists sought to restrain it, Jeffersonians to promote it,

The Louisiana Purchase included the watersheds of the Mississippi River and all of its east-flowing tributaries including the Red, Arkansas, Platte, Missouri, and many smaller streams. Texas is south and west of these watersheds and hence was not part of the purchase, nor was any part of the Floridas, which were east of the Mississippi.

The Purchase included some land north of 49° but not the larger area drained by the northward-flowing Red River of the North, which flows into Lake Winnipeg. The Anglo-American Convention of 1818 sliced through these watersheds and set the boundary at 49° as far west as the Continental Divide in the Rocky Mountains, to the advantage of the United States.

and south of the Ohio even more than north of it, the frontier advance was a free-for-all.

Conflict between whites and Indians had a long history. Troubles dated back to Jamestown's with Powhatan and the Massachusetts colonists' with the Pequots, and earlier yet to Walter Raleigh's abortive Roanoke colony of the 1580s. Jefferson, in the Declaration of Independence, listed incitement of "merciless savages" among the offenses of George III. Before that, English colonists called the North American phase of the Seven Years' War the "French and Indian War," and Anglo-biased history has kept that name. Whatever they were called, conflicts between whites and Indians were nothing new.

A pattern of Indian-white relations emerged quickly by 1790, after the states ceded their western land claims to the central government and after the Constitution created a stronger one. The westward flight of settlers was massive and fundamentally uncontrollable. It could be slowed or hastened by federal land law; it could be bent in one or another geographical direction depending on federal investment in roads or, later, in railroads; and it could be protected or left to its own devices by the level of military force Washington sent to protect settlers or pave their way. But the flight was too strong to stop. As it continued into Kentucky and Tennessee during the Revolutionary War and through the 1780s, it brought them statehood in 1792 and 1796. It began buzzing north of the Ohio River in the late 1780s, then swarmed there in the 1790s.

At first Indian resistance was effective. Detachments of General Josiah Harmar's Ohio River army were ravaged by Miamis (under Little Turtle), Shawnees, Delawares, and others in 1790 near future Fort Wayne. The U.S. Army suffered its worst defeat ever from Indians in November 1791 when a confederation of more than a half-dozen nations wiped out more than six hundred of General Arthur St. Clair's troops in present western Ohio. That victory bought the Indians time until 1794. On August 20 of that year, however, Anthony Wayne's army decisively defeated them at Fallen Timbers on the Maumee near present Toledo. In the subsequent Treaty of Greenville of 1795, Indians surrendered title to three-fourths of what became the state of Ohio only eight years later. They assumed that Greenville set the boundary. For the Americans, however, the real boundary was the Mississippi, and the following years brought treaty after treaty with tribe after tribe, ceding ever more pieces of land, ever farther west.

That became the pattern: settler incursions, Indian resistance, arrival of the military to protect the settlers, whose political noise grew louder with every newcomer. Sooner or later, the Indians fell back, if not right away then on the second or third try. Then came the signing of a treaty, extracted or extorted, by whatever "chiefs" the federal government could find who looked to be in authority. The signed treaty would convey title not only to the land but also to hunting and visiting rights, all going to the United States in perpetuity. The land would subsequently be absorbed in every way, including legal and political, becoming officially a U.S. territory.

The die was cast. Indians did not vote. Tribal traditions divided them. To compete they needed technology as good as the Americans', and tried to obtain it as well as money and troops from the British. This, however, put their fate in others' hands. Their stories did not make the American press, nor did the Indians publish widely read atrocity and captivity tales, as whites did. Settlers, on the other hand, had the ear of the media of the time and of politicians, who, except for a dwindling band of East Coast Federalists, were enthralled with the ideology of expansion and, in Jefferson's famous term, an "empire for liberty."

The worlds of the Indian nations began to crumble. What the Pequots and Wampanoags and Mohegans had experienced in colonial New England, as had the Aztecs in central Mexico and the Inca Empire in Peru in the 1500s—demographic decimation, military defeat, and cultural oblivion—began happening in Transappalachia in the 1790s and in Missouri and Louisiana following the Louisiana Purchase. It happened also to the Miamis of central Indiana and western Ohio, who were led by an astute and vigorous statesman-general-chief named Little Turtle. The Miami case is instructive; it displays most of the important elements of the repeating white-over-Indian supplanting, and it happened early, between the acquisitions of Transappalachia in 1783 and Louisiana in 1803. The elements are: first, the demographic decimation; second, the material disadvantages; third, the search for allies, either other Indians or the British, to counter the American military push; and finally, the cultural crumbling despite Little Turtle's excellence as hero and leader.

Transappalachia underwent a massive population shift (element one). When Europeans—French, British, then Americans—entered Transappalachia, Indians outnumbered them by a wide margin. But the Americans, in particular, kept coming and coming, relentlessly and by the thousands. Kentucky exploded from several hundred settlers in 1780 to 74,000 by 1790 (according to the census, which probably undercounted them seriously) and upwards of 250,000 by 1803. Kentucky, Tennessee, and Ohio were home by then to well over 350,000 non-Indians, of whom at least 50,000 were African-Americans, nearly all slaves. During those same twenty years, the Indians not only failed to match such increase but either maintained their stable birth and death rates or actually declined in number, either from further deadly military engagements or from European diseases. There is no way of knowing the exact numbers, but there is also no denying the basic point: that American intruders (black and white), initially far fewer than the Indians, greatly outnumbered them in the space of two or three decades, both from their own rise and from the Indians' fall.

Element two, the material disadvantages of the Transappalachian Indians compared to the Americans, is even simpler to state. Indians did not infect Americans with debilitating or lethal diseases, but Americans donated to Indians such "gifts" abundantly, above all measles (deadly in a nonimmune population) and smallpox. Indians fashioned their own clubs and tomahawks, but they could not manufacture their own muzzle-loaders or cannons. These tools of war, which had become essential, had to be bought, bartered, captured, or stolen from the nearby British or from Americans themselves. Indians of course produced their own food, clothing, and housing. Thus, when a raid by white settlers or militia burned or trashed villages and crops in the field, the Indians were hard put to fight on or even survive. They had no backups coming from farther east. Not only were their populations shrinking in relation to the invaders, but their resources for resistance became less and less dependable as well. Without standing armies or central governments, the whole population had to be involved in war, and do its hunting, gathering, and winter provisioning at the same time.

The third element, the search for allies, was nothing new. From time immemorial, Indians had always looked for allies from less threatening quarters in order to hold off the more threatening. Prior to European contact, for countless centuries, Indians fought, allied, and made peace with one another. Warfare and treaty making were just as present in pre-contact North America as in ancient and medieval Europe and Asia. From the mid-1600s a century-long set of accommodations with French fur traders and missionaries, together with the French thinness on the ground, ultimately sutured the "French and Indian" alliance to confront the aggressive British colonists before 1763.

After 1783, Indians of northern Transappalachia, soon to be named the Old Northwest, relied as best they could on the stingier British. Britain still held forts along the Great Lakes and inland, despite the peace treaty, as a counterweight to the aggressive American frontiers-people. Little Turtle of the Miamis, then about forty years old, forged an armed confederation of a dozen or so hitherto standoffish nations, an achievement resembling those of Pontiac before him and Tecumseh later. In the early 1790s, British commanders at Fort Niagara and Fort Detroit refused to allow Americans seeking intelligence on Indian whereabouts to sail across Lake Erie, despite the boundary line that supposedly ran down the middle of it. By doing so they backed the Indians. But in 1794–1795 the British in Detroit, to avoid conflict with the United States, refused to provide Little Turtle with troops and slammed the door of Fort Miami on him when his retreating confederates sought refuge there after the fight at Fallen Timbers.

Britain was at war with Revolutionary France and needed commerce, not trouble, from the United States. London had already restricted American trade with France, and was not in a mood to further outrage Americans for the sake of any Indians. A few months later, Britain agreed once more, in Jay's Treaty of November 1794, to leave the forts (Niagara, Detroit, Mackinac, Miami, and others on Lake Ontario and the St. Lawrence) that they had promised to abandon in 1783. They had remained, on the valid ground that the United States had never done anything for the Loyalists.

The British evacuation from the forts was peevish and reluctant. Some British policy makers wanted to stay, and lobbied for an Indian neutral ground, or "buffer," that would have kept the Americans well away from the Great Lakes and the St. Lawrence indefinitely. This idea lingered until the War of 1812. The British settled for a large hand in the fur trade for some years. In 1810–1811, when Tecumseh rallied the Northwest's Indians to stop the American advance, Indians hoped again for British help, and again were left in the lurch. But that is a later story. The search for allies, whether from other Indian nations or from whites, was simple realpolitik. Sometimes it worked, usually it didn't. Years later, in the early 1830s, Black Hawk of the Sac and Fox made the last attempt to confederate the nations of the Old Northwest—by then pushed to the western edge of Transappalachia, along the Mississippi—and rally them in armed struggle against the Americans. Black Hawk even hoped, as traditionally, for British help, but that had become unrealistic long since. So had any likelihood of stopping the Americans at the Mississippi. The northernmost reaches of Transappalachia, in Wisconsin and Michigan, gave way to white settlement only slowly, but by then Indian resistance seldom stopped it, British assistance never.

Fourthly, the cultural element. The "world of Little Turtle," as one historian trenchantly called it, crumbled against the onslaught of the Americans' relentless advance, better armed, less disease-prone, and fully confident that they had the momentum. "The new republic," he writes, "had a difficult time seeing a role for Indians. Either they would become like Americans or they would be removed. It was as simple as that." The American stance reflected "not inherent racism . . . but a completely different sense of purpose about the place itself."[4] The Indian cultures of Transappalachia had already changed, by 1790, from over a century of white contact, most of it with the French and then with the British and Americans.

The cluster of villages around Kekionga, called Miamitown (near present Fort Wayne), were not that socially or visibly different from white settlements along the Ohio, or more aptly, the French towns of Kaskaskia or Vincennes farther southwest. The Transappalachian Indians did not live in tepee clusters, chase the buffalo, or wear war bonnets. They had their own lineages, their nations, their customs, their mythologies, as did the Europeans. But those would disappear, just as surely as the Aztec Empire succumbed to Cortéz and the Incas to Pizarro in the 1520s and 1530s. The Miamis, the Potawatomis, the Piankashaws and the Wea, like the Shawnees and Delawares a little earlier, would be defeated militarily and eroded culturally, and in the late 1830s what was left of them would be physically removed "out of harm's way" to remote regions well west of the Mississippi.

Spain's Beleaguered Mississippi

South of the Ohio the Transappalachian frontier had a head start. Although bloody skirmishes continued in other parts, central Kentucky and Tennessee were no longer seriously contested between whites and Indians by 1783. Frontier settlements and stations along the rivers flowing west toward the Mississippi multiplied to the extent that, as we have seen, rights of navigation on the great river were an American demand in the 1782 peace negotiations. With every fresh settlement came corn and other produce, flatboats to take it downriver, and more pressure to keep the river safe for American sellers. Before 1800, the central government played little role in the area, and the Kentucky Resolutions of 1798 nearly declared western independence.

Through the 1790s and up to 1807, plots, rumors, and conspiracies, associated with names like General James Wilkinson and Aaron Burr, threatened the separation of the southern part of Transappalachia from the United States. The Southwest was politically volatile and far from Washington's effective control. One way for the central government to secure the Southwest was by quieting Indian titles to lands along the Mississippi. This became a priority of the Jefferson administration after 1801. Pressure increased on the Choctaws and Creeks who lived astride the south-flowing Tombigbee and other rivers that could take American produce directly to the Gulf, even though the Gulf ports like Mobile were in Spanish territory. In 1796 Tennessee became a state, and Americans began filling up the land along the east bank of the Mississippi, more eager than ever to ship goods down the river and to deposit them, duty-free, at New Orleans for transshipment to foreign markets.

In the 1780s, Spain refused to consider the American river traffic. In 1795, she reversed herself and decided to capitalize on it rather than fight it. Why the shift?

Spain had been anything but enthusiastic about American traffic on the Mississippi and through New Orleans ever since American flatboats started appearing around 1780. As the boats and their rowdy crews multiplied along the lower river and its ports, Spanish administrators tolerated them to some extent while realizing that their presence violated fundamental, long-standing policies: mercantilism, the economic theory that colonies existed to benefit the mother country; defense, which mandated that foreign powers never infiltrate or even get too close; and culture and social order, which foreign elements—non-Spanish-speaking, non-Catholic, non-*simpático*—would seriously disrupt. Three hundred years of Spanish colonial experience taught these things. They were long-settled matters. Spain never had any considerable number of settlers in Louisiana and never would. New Orleans and the other French-founded towns like St. Louis and Ste. Genevieve were growing, but at nothing like the rate of Kentucky and Tennessee. Bernardo de Gálvez, when governor of Louisiana around 1780, not only drubbed the British forces at Mobile and Pensacola but also helped American agents in New Orleans send supplies to George Rogers Clark's Illinois campaign. But Gálvez's substantial aid in support of American independence came because in the long or short run it hurt Britain, Spain's antagonist. Conversely, Clark and the Americans in Kentucky bore no deep love for Spain, although they were glad to have its help at that moment.

Gálvez was promoted to viceroy of Mexico in 1785, and his aide and successor as governor in New Orleans, Esteban Miró, solidified alliances with the Indians on the eastern side of the Mississippi. Miró parried approaches by James Wilkinson and other Americans who connived at splitting off from the United States and joining Spanish Louisiana. Prudently, Miró did not trust them, and he firmly maintained Spanish control of the river and lower Transappalachia. This entirely satisfied King Carlos III and his administration in Madrid. Two years of negotiations in Philadelphia between the Spanish minister, Diego de Gardoqui, and John Jay, in which Jay sought to open the river to Americans, ended in 1786 with Jay renouncing American rights on the river. Appalled, southern congressmen condemned and defeated the draft Jay-Gardoqui treaty.

The Spanish, in both Madrid and Louisiana, were perfectly aware of the population imbalance. Carlos III in July 1787 instructed his officials to do everything they could to encourage immigration of Catholics into Louisiana and the Floridas, the "strategy of opposing population to population [being] the best defense." Strengthening Indian alliances and fostering creation of an Indian buffer state between Spanish territory and the Americans had been objectives since the 1760s. The king regarded Choctaws, Seminoles, and others as "the best demographic recourse for defending the inviolability of Louisiana and the Floridas, as well as how to guarantee the security of the Provincias Internas of New Spain [Texas especially] and the Viceroyalty of Mexico itself."[5] If the Americans won Louisiana and the Floridas, the Spanish feared, where would they stop? The silver mines of Mexico were essential to the entire Spanish imperial economy. Inventive measures were needed, and the Spanish developed them.

In 1786–1787, Miró in New Orleans, Gardoqui in Philadelphia, and King Carlos in Madrid were all giving a firm no to American appeals for Mississippi River shipping privileges. But in 1795 the Spanish said yes. What changed? The Spanish hold on Louisiana became more and more vulnerable, and demonstrably so. Miró's nervous successor in the early

1790s, Baron Hector Carondelet, constantly feared a British or American invasion down the river, warning his superior in Havana that the enemy could overrun him before enough troops or even the bad news arrived to stop them. His fears were well grounded. George Rogers Clark, with support from Edmond Genêt (the French reign of terror's minister in Philadelphia), started organizing just such an expedition until Genet and his support were sent packing by the Washington administration. And Clark's threat was not the only one from Americans.

Carondelet, looking at the longer run, saw something that Europeans, whether in Madrid or Paris or London, had difficulty grasping. The fundamental American threat was not military but demographic. When Aranda (by then foreign minister) asked Carondelet in June 1793 for a report on conditions in Upper and Lower Louisiana, the governor sent good news and bad news. Since the British had left, production of indigo, cotton, sugar cane, rice, corn, wheat, furs, and other goods had become "very vast." Louisiana, however, now contained "40,000 industrious and warlike people"—Americans—with "unmeasured ambition . . . vigorous, hostile to all subjection, and who have been uniting and multiplying in the silence of peace . . . with a remarkable rapidity." Transappalachia south of the Ohio had slight European population in 1780, but now, only thirteen years later, it had more than 50,000 and was growing fast. "This vast and restless population," Carondelet continued, "driving the Indian tribes continually before them and upon us, is endeavoring to gain all the vast continent occupied by the Indians between the Ohio and Misisipi [*sic*] Rivers, the Gulf of Mexico, and the Appalachian Mountains . . . [and] their ambition will not be limited to this part of the Misisipi . . . [but] in time [will include] the possession of the rich mines of the interior provinces of the very kingdom of Mexico."[6] This was no false alarm. Did Madrid fully understand or believe the governor? It went against the European grain.

The Americans' rate of population increase was beyond anything known in Europe for hundreds of years, if ever. It was difficult to comprehend and almost impossible to plan for. Europe's populations had been more or less stable since the Middle Ages, dropping after the Black Death of the mid-1300s and slowly recovering, picking up only in the late 1700s in newly industrializing areas. T. R. Malthus was reflecting at that very time (the first edition of his *Essay on Population* came out in 1798) on Europe's gloomy future. He predicted with arithmetical starkness that population would outrun food supply. America, however, was an exception, Malthus wrote, because there, land and its product were inexhaustible. America was a "new habitat" where biologically maximum reproduction could continue indefinitely. It had already been doing so, at over 3 percent a year, a rate utterly beyond European experience. The causes are uncertain, but among them were the encouragements of abundant land and good nutrition. Americans came, and as Carondelet warned, they would keep coming. The king's instruction of 1787 certified that he understood the demographic threat. Yet if he really believed that immigration of Catholics and an Indian buffer state would end the threat, he grossly underestimated it.

Carlos III likely had Indian welfare also in mind. The Spanish never aimed to displace or remove, much less annihilate, the Indians. They had no uncontrollable flood of new settlers to placate. For Spain the encouragement of Indians as buffers not only would protect its own territory but would also protect the Indians. The Spanish had no problem with that. Quite the reverse: they believed that justice required that Indians had a right to be where they were, as they were (except missionized). Anglo-Americans seldom believed that. Indians were to be brought up to the level of white society and should look like it, through removal if necessary—being "put out of harm's way," that is, warfare with whites—and the passage of time. In any event they were to be displaced so that their land "could be made better use of"—farmed or mined rather than hunted on.

What the Americans of that time (and most American historians since) regarded as Spanish "intrigues" to foment Indian depredations, the Spanish regarded as helping themselves by helping Indians stay in place. The immigration-cum-Indian-buffer policy was a way to do that, though obviously risky, which the Spanish realized. We as Americans (historians or otherwise) are so programmed to think of frontier expansion as inevitable that it is a wrench to think like Carondelet and other Spanish administrators, responding to conditions confronting them. They saw, if imperfectly, the force and magnitude of American expansionism even though they recognized clearly the demographic challenge they faced. When Americans fought the "great nations" (the Cherokees, Choctaws, Creeks, and Chickasaws) whom the Spanish were recruiting, they were attacking Spanish interests at one remove. Could a permanent "Indian buffer" have been constructed in what is now Mississippi and Alabama? Before 1763, quite possibly. By 1800, almost certainly not. But Carondelet cannot be blamed for trying. It was his only plausible resort.

Spain was hugely overextended. Its North American empire alone ran from Canada to the Gulf, including everything west of the Mississippi, and along the California coast through Mexico and Central America. Add South America except Brazil, and the Philippines: Spain's empire was a stunning achievement of the sixteenth and seventeenth centuries, remaining viable for most of the eighteenth. Even the rise of Britain after the destruction of the Spanish Armada in 1588 and the incessant British privateering and warfare failed to lay the Spanish Empire low. But along the Mississippi, the American advance, fueled by fecundity and immigration, made hard-line resistance fruitless. There would never be a Spanish migration to offset it. There would hardly be enough troops to defend it. Accordingly, in 1795 Spain decided to accommodate the Americans in ways over which it had at least some control for the near and perhaps middle future.

The European power situation figured in Madrid's thinking more strongly than Carondelet's message. Spain was a European power and (as in the late 1770s) affected, and was affected by, what went on with France, Britain, and other nations on the Continent. In 1788 Carlos III died, and his son Carlos IV, less wise and resolute, succeeded him. Despite the guillotining in 1793 of his cousin Louis XVI, the French member of the Bourbon "family compact," Carlos IV decided he needed France more than Britain. He concluded that improved relations with the United States could also help as a counterweight against Britain. Thus Carlos and his chief minister, Manuel Godoy, undercut Carondelet and the ancient defensive policy along the Mississippi, and they began to suggest that Spain would give back Louisiana to the French if the price was right. It took until 1800 to do that, but in the meantime, Carlos and Godoy did the United States a big favor.

At San Lorenzo de El Escorial, the king's summer quarters northwest of Madrid, on October 27, 1795, Carlos IV signed a treaty with Thomas Pinckney, the American minister. It gave the United States virtually all it had been seeking since the Paris peace talks of 1782. Specifically, the treaty allowed Americans free, unhindered navigation of the Mississippi. It granted a privilege of duty-free transshipment of goods (the long-sought "right of deposit") at New Orleans for three years, renewable there or at another port after that. And—something Spain had not agreed to in 1782–1783—it recognized as American territory the south-western part of Transappalachia, from the Ohio River to the thirty-first parallel. This included Natchez and the rest of the east bank of the Mississippi, which the Spanish evacuated shortly thereafter and which in 1798 became the Territory of Mississippi. Finally, it committed Spanish officials to moderating Indian hostility to Americans along the lower Mississippi.

Unlike Jay's Treaty a year earlier, which barely passed the Senate, the Treaty of San Lorenzo (known also as Pinckney's Treaty) sailed through unanimously. Freedom to run goods and people up and down the river was finally achieved after more than a decade of strenuous resistance from Madrid. As was true of the British retreat in the Northwest, however, the agreement did not mean that all Spanish officials were enthusiastic about it. Negotiated in Madrid with European exigencies in mind, it completely undercut Carondelet's resistance policy, his treaties with the "great nations," and the fortifications he had built. It landed like "una bomba," as a Spanish historian called it, in New Orleans. It opened the river and its ports to Americans, giving them "full liberty of action within the Spanish colonies." Consequently, "by the Treaty of San Lorenzo, the Mississippi ceased to be a frontier of Spain."[7] Spain had tried everything it could to maintain the U.S.-Spanish boundaries of 1783. These measures failed. As for the advancing frontierspeople of Kentucky and Tennessee, they regarded the opening of the river as simply their just due, a long-awaited step in their inevitable advance southwestward, another triumph over the Spanish. The privilege once gained quickly became, in their minds, a right. Any future rescinding of it would seem outrageous.

LOUISIANA, GREAT AND SMALL

In 1796, just after the Treaty of San Lorenzo, a census counted about 1,100 persons in and around St. Louis, and another 1,150 at Ste. Genevieve and New Madrid—all told, about 3,100 in Upper Louisiana. In 1803, about the time the United States took over, a New Orleans writer gave 6,028 as the population of "Illinois, St. Louis, &c." Thus it nearly doubled in those years, much of it from Shawnees, Delawares, as well as Americans (white and black) who were pushed out of Kentucky for one reason or another. Daniel Boone and his family and followers were among them. We know little about most of these migrants, except statistically: they were young (the U.S. median age in 1790 was just under sixteen), married young, and averaged about eight children per family. They also behaved like young people. Scores of distilleries turned boatloads of corn into hundreds of barrels of whiskey, and though no settler understood that it killed germs, everybody knew that it was usually safer to drink than water, and drink it they did; only a young population could have consumed such quantities.

We do know something about the famous Boones, who were among the migrants welcomed into Spanish Upper Louisiana because of the pro-immigration policy following the Treaty of San Lorenzo. Daniel Morgan Boone, old Daniel's son, moved in 1797 from Kentucky with his family and four slaves to a valley on Femme Osage Creek, upriver from St. Louis. Lieutenant Governor Zenon Trudeau provided him with an unusually large land grant and promises of more for any families he brought in. The law mandated that grantees be (or become) Catholic, but Trudeau and his successor, Charles Dehault Delassus, promised not to enforce it. Old Daniel followed a year later. Kentucky was no longer sufficiently frontierlike; he had had a lot of legal troubles over land; he was ready for something new. Delassus met Boone and the fifteen families he brought with him at St. Louis and created him "syndic" of the Femme Osage district. Boone thus became a Spanish *comandante*. His children and grandchildren settled down to farming, or in some cases to hunting. Not surprisingly, their neighbors, the Osage, often objected, just as the Shawnees had objected, to Boone's incursions in Kentucky a few decades earlier.[8]

The New Orleans writer François-Xavier Martin gave the 1803 population of Lower Louisiana as about 25,000. About 15,000 lived in New Orleans and adjacent Tchoupitoulas, 6,600 in parishes a little upstream toward Baton Rouge, 1,500 in Baton Rouge itself, and 1,600 over in Natchitoches. Another (roughly) 25,000 lived in Upper Louisiana, that is, everything upstream including St. Louis. Forming this total of 50,000 were whites, slave blacks, free blacks, French, Spanish, Indians, and any combination thereof. The visitor might hear French, Spanish, English, or Indian languages on the same street. A head count of Indians was only guesswork, but Martin and the Kentucky traveler Hugh Brackenridge estimated that about 60,000 lived in proximity to whites in Lower and Upper Louisiana.[9]

All told, the several dozen nations probably totaled around 100,000, from the mouth of the Mississippi north and west to the source of the Missouri River in present Montana. Brackinridge pointed out that "from the fatal ravages of the small pox, the present Indian nations of Louisiana, particularly on the Missouri, have not the tenth of the numbers which they had near thirty years ago"—that is, around 1780, before the whites invaded Transappalachia and when the Spanish presence was small.[10] Then there were at most 5,000 Americans in Transappalachia. By 1800, the census counted 387,000 and there were no doubt well over 400,000 in reality. At the time of the Purchase, Louisiana already had a non-Indian population larger than Transappalachia had when the 1783 peace treaty was signed. Louisiana, French or Spanish—and in truth, anywhere west of it—was indeed indefensible. It was certainly true that the decision to sell Louisiana to the United States was Napoleon's, and his alone. He decided to sell it because it could not be defended. But *why* could it not be defended? Because of that American 3 percent annual increase, by which "the miracle of compound interest," which works just as well for people as it does for money, caused frontier populations to double roughly every twenty years.

The Treaty of San Lorenzo spurred a rush of Americans and their produce-laden flatboats downriver. The Spanish tended their Indian alliances as carefully as they could, but they turned over Natchez and the east bank of the Mississippi south to the thirty-first parallel in 1798, making that line the actual (not just treaty) boundary between the United States and Spanish Florida. Spain's new, comparatively open policy enriched those in New Orleans and suited those in Madrid. The turmoil of the French Revolution, meanwhile, threw up Napoleon Bonaparte as "First Consul" and military dictator, and Napoleon brought with him elaborate dreams of a resuscitated French Empire, worldwide and certainly including North America.

Spain Retrocedes, Napoleon Stews, Jefferson Sweats

Even before Napoleon took power, the ruling Directory in Paris instructed its ambassador in Madrid to persuade Spain to give back Louisiana, which France had ceded in 1762. The French argued that they would make a much better barrier than Spain against British aggression or American encroachment—which, ultimate horror, might eventually include even Mexico. That planted a seed in the mind of Carlos IV and his queen, María Luisa. Napoleon watered that seed, because it meshed with his plan to reestablish France in the West Indies and in Louisiana.

In July 1800, Napoleon told his foreign minister, Charles-Maurice de Talleyrand-Périgord, to revive the idea of regaining Louisiana from

Spain. Queen María Luisa of Spain had a brother, Ferdinand, who was Duke of Parma in northern Italy. Greater things might be had for him or, as it turned out, his son Prince Louis of Parma, with French help. And so Carlos IV, ever uxorious, agreed to give Louisiana back to France if Napoleon would see to it that the duke acquired Tuscany and other Italian territories and became "king of Etruria." Napoleon also wanted Spain to give the Floridas to France, but Carlos IV balked at that. Louisiana was reward enough, and on October 1, 1800, France and Spain signed a treaty at San Ildefonso, outside Madrid, promising to retrocede—give back—Louisiana to France. Before that happened, Napoleon was to set up the Duke of Parma as king of Etruria *and* persuade the powers of Europe to recognize him as such. Spain also provided France with six warships (instead of Florida). It was a straight-up swap: Louisiana would go back to France, provided that Carlos's brother-in-law became a king in northern Italy. Louisiana was defined as having "the same extent" as when France last held it in 1762.

Napoleon and Talleyrand further assured Carlos—verbally—that France would never transfer, sell, or alienate Louisiana to a third country. (Only Britain and the United States were remotely possible candidates.) The Spanish dawdled about the turnover, in part from nervousness about the third-country possibility. In the summer of 1802 the Spanish prime minister, Pedro Cevallos, asked that the guarantee be put in writing. In July the French ambassador to Madrid, Gouvion St.-Cyr, provided Cevallos a note "in the name of the First Consul" agreeing "that France will never alienate it."[11] Carlos authorized the transfer in October. Another year went by before Spain turned over Louisiana to France, and by then Napoleon had reneged on the oral and written promises. France never held clear title.

Lucien Bonaparte, Napoleon's brother, signed a treaty on behalf of France at Aranjuez, near Madrid, on March 21, 1801, confirming terms of the San Ildefonso treaty of the previous October. The Aranjuez treaty was secret to reduce the chance that either Britain or the United States might invade and conquer Louisiana before the exchange took place. But, as a French historian wrote, "It did not remain a secret very long. The United States quickly learned of it."[12] They did not learn fully or certainly what was in the treaty, however. For another two years Talleyrand kept the treaty under wraps, and the question remained open whether Spain had also transferred the Floridas.

Napoleon's geopolitical plan was to reacquire Louisiana as a grand supply base for his key object, St.-Domingue (now Haiti) in the West Indies. Along with Guadaloupe and other French islands, it was the fount of the sugar and coffee production of the Western world. By the end of the summer of 1801, he signed a peace treaty (the Peace of Amiens) with Britain, giving him a breather during which he could concentrate forces on St.-Domingue. The colony had been wracked since 1791 by a gruesome internal struggle among its 60,000 white and mulatto slaveholders and its more than 500,000 black slaves. France in 1794, during the Revolution, had abolished slavery throughout its empire including St.-Domingue, and the emancipated, led by the charismatic Toussaint L'Ouverture, had taken over the colony. Napoleon needed to reassert French control, and without announcing it until after the fact, to reenslave the people. With the ink barely dry on the Peace of Amiens, he appointed his brother-in-law, the capable general Charles Leclerc, to command a force of more than 40,000 troops bound for St.-Domingue.

The fleet arrived on January 29, 1802. Then began a war without quarter, thousands killing thousands. Leclerc captured Toussaint in June and shipped him to France, where he died in prison in early 1803. The news that France was reinstituting slavery in the nearby colony of Guadaloupe ended all pretense of benevolence. The war accelerated. Yellow fever became an equally effective enemy of Leclerc's forces. The massive army melted away to about 2,000. The general notified Paris that he had lost 24,000 and would lose more.[13] Leclerc himself died of yellow fever on November 2, 1802. Ten thousand reinforcements arrived in the fall but did nothing except keep the death toll rising until, in late 1803, Toussaint's successor Jean Dessalines drove what remained of the French army completely off the island. An estimated 350,000 Haitians and more than 50,000 French had died. The Republic of Haiti came into being on January 1, 1804. (The United States, fearful of encouraging slave uprisings at home, avoided recognizing it until the late nineteenth century.)

Napoleon had outfitted yet another army in 1802 that was to proceed to Louisiana, under the assumption that all would go well in St.-Domingue. Nothing went well. That army assembled at a small Dutch port called Helvoetsluis at a mouth of the Rhine and was supposed to leave in the fall, as soon as Spain signed the retrocession agreement. Delays put off departure until late December, then January. By that time the port had frozen. When it became ice-free in mid-March, a British fleet was offshore boxing it in. And Napoleon had given up on Louisiana.

Through all this, from his inauguration in March 1801, Jefferson turned his mind to events as best he could learn them. Word trickled in of the secret French-Spanish treaty from American diplomats, first from Madrid and then from London, but they did not know what territory it included or even, for sure, if it existed. Because the United States was engaged in an undeclared naval war with France during the turbulent late 1790s, it had no minister in Paris who could find out. Soon after Jefferson took office, he appointed Robert R. Livingston, who arrived that December. Owner of vast estates along the Hudson, future financier of Robert Fulton's steamboat, chancellor of the state of New York, former friend but by then political opponent of John Jay and the Federalists, Livingston did an excellent job in the next two years in discovering what Napoleon and Talleyrand were doing, and why, and how the United States could benefit.

Jefferson and Secretary of State James Madison had reason to be concerned about the machinations of France and Spain. In April 1802 Jefferson wrote a private letter to Livingston. One of that great writer's best and most often quoted, it went directly to the point:

> The cession of Louisiana and the Floridas [which had not happened] by Spain to France, works most sorely on the United States. . . . We have ever looked to [France] as our *natural friend,* as one with which we could never have an occasion of difference. . . . [But] there is on the globe one single spot, the possessor of which is our natural and habitual enemy. It is New Orleans, through which the produce of three-eighths of our territory must pass to market, and from its fertility it will ere long yield more than half of our whole produce, and contain more than half of our inhabitants. France, placing herself in that door, assumes to us the attitude of defiance. . . . The day that France takes possession of New Orleans . . . we must marry ourselves to the British fleet and nation.[14]

The president and Madison kept after Livingston, as well as Rufus King in London and other American diplomats, for exact information on the retrocession. The important question of whether Florida was included remained unsettled until the Purchase took place a year later.

But at the same time that Jefferson sent his letter to Livingston, hand-carried, he also entrusted his friend Pierre Samuel du Pont de Nemours to take a verbal message to the French authorities. In it, he hinted that the United States might be willing to buy New Orleans and West Florida (now the Louisiana panhandle) as well.

Livingston worked slowly but deftly through the rest of 1802. He laid out the possibility that France could sell the United States all of Louisiana—west of the Mississippi, the first time that was broached—and north of the Arkansas River, with navigation rights south to the Gulf. When Talleyrand gave him the runaround, Livingston opened a back channel of much more candid conversation with none other than Joseph Bonaparte, Napoleon's brother, who was sure to deliver any message of Livingston's to the First Consul.

By late 1802 the actual transfer from Spain to France had still not happened. The St.-Domingue bloodbath was taking place but the result was not yet clear. Napoleon had no reason to jump at, or even notice, the American approach. Within a week of General Leclerc's death in Haiti, however, another *bomba* dropped in New Orleans itself. The Spanish acting intendant, or civil administrator, Juan Ventura Morales, abruptly closed the port to American traffic on October 16. The news sped upriver to Natchez in two days, to Kentucky in ten, to Washington by late November, and Europe soon after. The uproar in the Ohio Valley and Tennessee, wherever American goods were moving downriver, was deafening. Congressmen and senators felt the pressure immediately and directed it at Jefferson and Madison: open the port and river, or Americans would take New Orleans by force.

Through the winter, westerners clamored for war. The Kentucky legislature sent Congress a vigorous complaint and an urgent demand for action. Jefferson and Madison feared it could not be turned aside, but they tried diplomacy first. Jefferson gave Louisiana only the briefest mention in his annual message to Congress in December 1802. Madison wrote to both Livingston in Paris and Charles Pinckney in Madrid that the closure was explosive. Kentucky's downriver shipping in the first half of 1802 alone was worth $600,000, and much of it "is now, or shortly will be, afloat for New Orleans." The House, he wrote Pinckney on January 10, 1803, "has passed a resolution explicitly declaring that the stipulated rights of the United States on the Mississippi will be inviolably maintained," and many congressmen wanted "to give to the resolution a tone and complexion still stronger."[15] The crisis mounted; protests splashed over the administration "from every quarter" of the Union. On January 15, Federalist senator James Ross of Pennsylvania entered a resolution authorizing the president to send 50,000 troops to capture New Orleans.[16] A milder resolution to provide 8,000 troops passed in February. News of the Ross resolution went immediately to Livingston, who, when he got it on April 8, told Talleyrand. The American armed threat was real.

Extraneous events, luckily, went Jefferson's and Madison's way. For all the domestic uproar, winter brought a pause. If Leclerc and his army had not collapsed, Napoleon's imperial strategy would have been carried out, including holding Louisiana. If the French fleet in Holland had left before their harbor froze and had proceeded directly to New Orleans, war might have broken out then and there. As harvests ended, downriver traffic slowed.

Why did Morales close New Orleans? The governor himself, Manuel de Salcedo, publicly disagreed, though he could not override Morales. The Spanish minister in Washington, Carlos Martínez, known as the Marques of Casa Yrujo, agreed with Madison that Morales was violating the 1795 treaty. What they did not know was that the order came from Carlos IV himself, on Prime Minister Cevallos's advice. That treaty extended the right of deposit for only three years, renewable if nobody objected. Nobody had until then. Technically Morales had a point and of course he was obliged to follow the king's orders, and did so without implicating the monarch. Very likely he was sick and tired of American smuggling through New Orleans, while Madrid was disturbed by "lack of consideration shown to Spanish sailors in American ports."[17] As for Cevallos and the king, they were asserting, for about the last time, Spain's imperial right to control who traveled through its own territory. Legally they were on solid grounds. Militarily and politically, facing both France and the United States, they were hopelessly quixotic. They soon retreated. After Minister Pinckney protested the closure, the king ordered it lifted, and on February 16 Cevallos did so—but kept the king's involvement secret. On March 1, Cevallos passed the king's order to restore the right of deposit to Morales. He told Casa Yrujo, in Washington, to notify Jefferson immediately, which Yrujo did on April 19. Morales opened the port of New Orleans on May 17 and the pent-up river traffic immediately resumed.[18]

On January 18, 1803, three days after Senator Ross offered his resolution, with the political heat very intense, Jefferson appointed his neighbor and protégé James Monroe as extraordinary envoy to the French government. He was to work with Livingston "to procure a cession of New Orleans and the Floridas to the United States; and consequently the establishment of the Mississippi as the boundary between the United States and Louisiana."[19] Congress appropriated $2 million for that purchase.

Monroe duly arrived in Paris on April 12. But by then much had already taken place. On January 12, at a dinner party shortly after he learned of Leclerc's death and his army's destruction, Napoleon burst out, "Damn sugar, damn coffee, damn colonies." He also knew that his second army, the one iced in port in Holland, might end the same way if he sent it. Even Napoleon shrank from such a loss of credibility. On March 12, at a salon in Paris, he abruptly threatened war to the British ambassador. He and the Spanish court were well aware of the bellicose hostility existing in the United States; Morales had done a fine job of raising the stakes. Napoleon knew that Monroe was on his way with new instructions from Jefferson. The French chargé in Washington, Louis-André Pichon, also informed him that if Monroe had no luck in Paris he was to move on to London and perhaps seek a treaty binding the United States and Britain against France, something to be avoided strenuously.[20] Napoleon had asked Carlos IV for East Florida (the peninsula) but was refused. Demography promised that even if he staked another army to hold Louisiana, the Americans' numbers would overrun the province before long.

For all these reasons, and despite his elaborate and long-held plans for restoring to France a New World empire, Napoleon decided to sell Louisiana to the Americans. Instead of huge costs, the sale would raise cash for his war with England. Instead of the United States supporting Britain or fighting on her side, the Americans would be at least neutral and preoccupied, and perhaps grateful and even helpful.

Livingston did not know Napoleon's mind (nor did anyone) in February and March 1803. But he wrote Madison on February 18 that "France is fully impressed with the nullity of her possession in Louisiana unless she has some port in the Gulf"—which the loss of St.-Domingue precluded. Livingston continued to impress on Talleyrand and Napoleon the idea of selling Louisiana north of the Arkansas, or better, ceding New Orleans and West Florida (thinking France had them). It could only benefit France, Livingston argued, to do so, and the sale would "rivet the friendship of the United States" to France. With accuracy, he anticipated Monroe's instructions.[21]

SWINGING THE (DIRTY) DEAL

Abruptly, on April 11, Talleyrand asked Livingston "whether we wished to have the whole of Louisiana." Caught off guard, Livingston replied, "I told him no; that our wishes extended only to New Orleans and the Floridas." He reiterated that France should "give us the country above the river Arkansas, in order to place a barrier between them and Canada." But, said Talleyrand, without New Orleans "the rest would be of little value; and that he would wish to know 'what we would give for the whole.'" Livingston mentioned "twenty millions, provided our citizens were paid," referring to Americans' claims against French privateers for damages during the 1796–1798 naval war. Talleyrand told Livingston to think it over for a day and added that "he did not speak from authority, but the idea had struck him."[22]

He did not speak from authority because Napoleon had asked François Barbé-Marbois, whom he trusted more than Talleyrand not to take a cut, to do the negotiating. But the idea itself was authoritative. On the previous day, April 10, which was Easter Sunday, Napoleon met after Mass with Barbé-Marbois, his minister of finance, and Admiral Denis Decrès, minister of marine. "I know the full value of Louisiana," said Napoleon, "and I have been desirous of repairing the fault of the French negotiator who abandoned it in 1763." Despite that, he continued, "I have scarcely recovered it [from Spain] when I must expect to lose it" to the British. "I have not a moment to lose to put it out of their reach. . . . I think of ceding it to the United States. . . . They only ask of me one town in Louisiana, but I already consider the colony as entirely lost, and it appears to me that in the hands of this growing power, it will be more useful to the policy and even to the commerce of France, than if I should attempt to keep it."[23]

What did the two ministers think? Decrès favored keeping the colony and empire. Barbé-Marbois said let's sell what we will probably lose anyway. Napoleon took these conflicting views under advisement. Early the next morning he called in Barbé-Marbois. Pointing out that Britain was making "naval and military preparations of every kind," Napoleon declared, "I renounce Louisiana. It is not only New Orleans that I will cede, it is the whole colony without any reservation. . . . I renounce it with the greatest regret. To attempt obstinately to retain it would be folly. I direct you to negotiate this affair with the envoys of the United States. Do not even await the arrival of Mr. Monroe; have an interview this very day with Mr. Livingston." He told Barbé-Marbois to ask 50 million francs as the price, to keep him informed "hour by hour," and to "correspond with M. de Talleyrand, who alone knows my intentions."[24]

James Monroe landed in Le Havre on April 8 after twenty-nine days at sea. He made it to Paris on April 12. Livingston wrote Madison that he spent the day with Monroe going over papers, "and while he and several other gentlemen were at dinner with me, I observed the Minister of the Treasury walking in my garden." Livingston invited Barbé-Marbois to come in for coffee, which he did, but said that "as my house was full of company, he thought I had better call on him any time before eleven that night. He went away, and a little after, when Mr. Monroe took leave, I followed him." When Livingston returned home at midnight he immediately sat down and wrote Madison a detailed account. Napoleon wanted to sell all of Louisiana to the United States for 100 million francs (Barbé-Marbois had doubled Napoleon's figure, so that whatever he ended up with above 50 million was bound to please his leader). But 80 million (60 to France, 20 to settle the American claims), thought Livingston, ought to do it.[25]

Only then was Monroe informed. Livingston had not done so on the ground that Monroe had not formally presented his credentials, and, true enough, Napoleon could be a stickler. On April 14, Livingston introduced Monroe to Barbé-Marbois. Over the next two weeks, they discussed the price, how it would be paid, and the American claims. The sale itself was agreed to in principle at the start. On April 30, Livingston, Monroe, and Barbé-Marbois signed the treaty by which "The First Consul of the French Republic . . . doth hereby cede to the United States in the name of the French Republic for ever and in full Sovereignty the said territory . . . in the Same manner as they have been acquired by the French Republic" in the 1800 Treaty of San Ildefonso with Spain—"with the Same extent that it now has in the hands of Spain, & that it had when France possessed it."

Further articles transferred all public buildings and archives; provided that "the inhabitants shall be incorporated in the Union of the United States and admitted as soon as possible [to] all these rights, advantages and immunities of citizens of the United States" and are assured of "the free enjoyment of their liberty, property, and the Religion which they profess." French and Spanish ships would have exclusive duty-free rights for twelve years. The price, how it would be paid, and the claims by Americans were dealt with in two "conventions" appended to the treaty and also dated April 30.[26] In dollars, $11,250,000 would be paid (with 6 percent interest) to France directly, and $3,750,000 to American claimants, clearing off France's liabilities.

Napoleon approved the texts the next day, May 1. He never consulted the Corps Legislatif as constitutionally required. The $15 million was larger than the U.S. government's entire receipts ($11 million) and expenditures ($7.9 million) for 1803, and the envoys had no authorization beyond $2 million for New Orleans itself. But they surmised correctly that Jefferson and Madison would approve, get it through Congress, and pay it over several years via the subscribing banks (Baring's of London and Hope's of Amsterdam). On May 13 they transmitted the treaty to Washington.[27] Jefferson had it in hand on July 3 and was delighted to announce America's good fortune on Independence Day, July 4.

The nation was astonished. Jeffersonians were elated, Federalists nonplussed. Virtually no one had opposed the acquisition of New Orleans, and Pennsylvania's Senator Ross, who had urged taking it by force, was a Federalist. Soon, however, the treaty began to gain critics, both from Federalists (particularly New Englanders) who foresaw the isolation of their region, and from strict-constructionist Jeffersonians who worried about the absence in the Constitution of any federal right to acquire territory. The treaty "shall be ratified . . . in the Space of Six months after the date of Signature," according to its final article, or in other words, by October 30, 1803. Congress would not normally reconvene until December, but Jefferson circulated the treaty in late summer to members and asked Congress to convene on October 17. It did so. In two days the Senate ratified it by a 24–7 vote (one Federalist, Dayton of New Jersey, joining the Jeffersonians in support). The House of Representatives was responsible for appropriating the money to effect the purchase. The Jeffersonians had to do considerable arm-twisting, winning the first of several votes only by 59–57 on October 24.[28]

The critics in Congress complained about several aspects. Was this or any purchase constitutional? Was it too much money? Was it proper to grant citizenship (as the treaty apparently did) to the French, Spanish, and *free black* people of New Orleans, so foreign and so unacquainted with democratic government? Was it just to uproot the Creeks and other Indians east of the Mississippi and remove them to the "howling wilderness" of Louisiana, as some were advocating? Should the French and Spanish receive duty-free access, which seemed to favor Louisiana's ports over other states'?

All these questions were settled, hushed up, or overridden. Jefferson himself had concerns about the constitutionality of such a purchase, and he went so far as to draft a constitutional amendment before Madison and others persuaded him that approval and ratification would take far longer than the October 30 deadline. As others have remarked, he struggled with his conscience and won. As was often the case with the Sage of Monticello, expedient necessity prevailed.[29]

There was one objection, however, that was impossible to argue down convincingly, even by that most astute political theorist, James Madison. Did Napoleon have the right to sell Louisiana? Did he (and France) have clear title? A century later the historian Henry Adams, great-grandson of President John Adams and grandson of President John Quincy Adams, said no: "The sale of Louisiana to the United States was trebly invalid: if it were French property, Bonaparte could not constitutionally alienate it without the consent of the Chambers; if it were Spanish property, he could not alienate it at all; if Spain had a right of reclamation, his sale was worthless."[30]

Napoleon never presented the sale to his legislature and defied even his own brothers when they took him to task for not doing so. The question remains whether Spain still had a decisive claim. The answer is yes. The Treaty of San Ildefonso of 1800 was the document of retrocession, and Napoleon and his American purchasers violated it in several ways. One, the transfer depended on Napoleon's creating the kingdom of Etruria in northern Italy and seeing to it that the Duke of Parma, or his son, became its king. France continued to garrison "Etruria" and thus had not allowed the new king to rule. Two, Napoleon had promised, as a condition, to persuade the major governments of Europe to agree to Etruria's creation and the new king's title. He extracted this agreement from Austria but not Britain or Russia. That condition was unfulfilled. Three, and most important, Spain had an oral promise, confirmed in writing in late 1802, that France would never sell or otherwise alienate Louisiana to a third party. Napoleon obviously knew this, and so did Jefferson and Madison, and so did the Congress during the October 1803 debate.

When the Spanish learned of the sale, they were outraged. Cevallos pointed to the treaty's violations of San Ildefonso, the Aranjuez agreement of March 1801, and St.-Cyr's pledge of July 1802, and raged that "the cession endangered Spain's entire empire," which, in time, it certainly did.[31] Spain's minister in Washington, Casa Yrujo, sent a note to Secretary of State Madison on September 4, 1803, insisting that "the mere reading of the paragraph which precedes [St.-Cyr's pledge] will convince you, as well as the President of the United States, that the sale of Louisiana which France has lately made is a manifest violation of the obligations contracted by her with His Catholic Majesty [Carlos IV], and that France wants [lacks] the powers to alienate the said province without the approbation of Spain." Madison did not respond. On September 27 Casa Yrujo sent him another note, even more blunt:

> It is evident that the treaty of sale entered into between France and the United States does not give to the latter any right to acquire and claim Louisiana, and that the principles of justice as well as sound policy ought to recommend it to the Government not to meddle with engagements as contrary in reality to her true interest as they would be to good faith, and to their good correspondence with Spain.

He was sending these notes, he emphasized, on the king's orders.[32]

Madison replied on October 4 that he had laid Yrujo's notes "before the President," and remarked that "the repugnance manifested in these communications on the part of his Catholic Majesty . . . was as little expected, as the objections to the transaction can avail against its solidity." After reiterating that friendship existed between Spain and the United States, Madison quoted a letter of May 4, 1803, from Prime Minister Cevallos to Charles Pinckney, the American minister at Madrid. The key sentence read, "The United States can address themselves [*podra dirigerse*] to the French government to negotiate the acquisition of territories which may suit their interest."[33]

Whether this constituted permission to buy Louisiana is doubtful (a letter cannot override a treaty). Whether "territories which may suit their interest" included all of Louisiana is not clear. That Cevallos spoke for Carlos IV must be thought probable. That Cevallos could or did let France off the hook of San Ildefonso is not defensible, and regardless of what he wrote Pinckney in May, he "denounced the sale as illegal" in the fall.[34] Casa Yrujo responded on October 12 to Madison's note of October 4, pointing out that "Spain having made the retrocession of Louisiana to France, under certain conditions and modifications, Spain has the *indubitable right* to claim their execution. Of this nature was the stipulation, that France should not sell nor alienate Louisiana in any manner whatever." Yrujo also noted that the French promise "is much older" than Cevallos's letter and still held. Thus, with "reason and justice" the king denounced "the ratification of a treaty founded upon a manifest violation of the most solemn engagements entered into by France."[35]

Madison never responded to Casa Yrujo's October 12 note. But on that same day, he wrote Pinckney in Madrid that he was changing Monroe's instructions. Monroe was to go to London, not to Madrid, as previously ordered, to talk about acquiring West Florida. There was no point, Madison said, in "attempting, at present, to procure from the Spanish Government the residuum of territory desired by the United States [West Florida, because of] the ill-humor shown by that Government."[36] The French also suggested to Monroe that a visit to Madrid might be imprudent just then. A week later Congress convened and quickly ratified the treaty.

Napoleon's sale was "a base betrayal" of Spain.[37] Barbé-Marbois himself, years later, wrote that Spain's assent to the sale was "undoubtedly necessary" because of the 1800 San Ildefonso treaty, but haste was essential. The Madrid government "complained bitterly . . . and for nearly a year it was impossible to obtain from that court an approbation of the treaty. Its complaints were well grounded."[38] Finally in February 1804, a few weeks after the actual American takeover, Carlos IV acceded to the sale in the wan hope of promoting good relations with the United States. French pressure as well as a suggestion from Pinckney that the United States might take New Orleans by force (if Spain still held it) persuaded Carlos IV to "abandon [Spain's] strategically weak but legally strong position," in the hope "that a graceful acquiescence might earn enough good will to save the Floridas and Texas from Jeffersonian expansionists."[39]

France sold Louisiana without a clear title and the United States knowingly bought it with the title still cloudy. The temptation, the opportunity, was too great for even Madison the constitutionalist and Jefferson the arch-democrat. Imperialism trumped honesty.

Opening the Louisiana Package

The question remained just what had been bought and sold. What were the boundaries of the Louisiana Purchase? The simple answer—for France and the United States, though not Spain—was that Louisiana included the Mississippi, its tributaries (including the Missouri), and the watersheds of those rivers, from present Montana and Minnesota south to Oklahoma and Arkansas. The southernmost tributary of the Mississippi is the Red River, which is now the Texas-Oklahoma boundary. No river in Texas flows into the Mississippi. If watersheds mattered, and they did, the Purchase included no part of Texas (or, obviously, of the Oregon country or California, as they were west of the Rocky Mountain continental divide).

According to the treaty, the Purchase included all of Louisiana just as France was receiving it from Spain and as Spain had received it from France in 1762. When Livingston pressed Talleyrand for some precision, the foreign minister famously told him, "I can give you no direction; you have made a noble bargain for yourselves & I suppose you will make the most of it."[40] Livingston tried hard to get the French to agree that all of West Florida was included. Madison and Jefferson, no less insatiable, also pressed that point. But that was a very heavy straw, and all perceived that it would finally break the Spanish camel's back. So the Americans backed off. Seven years later, however, the part that is now the Louisiana panhandle was simply overrun and absorbed. Spain had been dealt with shabbily by the United States, as in 1782–1783, and would be again.

The boundaries certainly included New Orleans. The transfers of the city and the territory, whatever it was, from Spain to France and then from France to the United States duly took place in late 1803. On November 30, Governor Salcedo and the French prefect Pierre de Laussat presided over the lowering and raising of flags in the Plaza de Armas, or Place d'Armes, now Jackson Square. Three weeks later, on December 20, Laussat and the newly appointed American governor, William C. C. Claiborne, watched the tricolor come down and the Stars and Stripes go up.[41] On March 9 and 10, 1804, similar ceremonies in St. Louis turned over Upper Louisiana officially to the United States.

What, now, did the United States govern? In New Orleans, more than 8,000 people, of whom half were white and mostly French Creoles, a third slaves, and a sixth (1,335) free blacks and mulattoes. About 120 Americans were in the mix, plus a few hundred Spanish officials, militia, and their families.[42] In the entire territory up through St. Louis, the 50,000 of 1803 doubled to 97,000 in the 1810 U.S. Census, of whom 76,000 were in the "Territory of Orleans," shortly to become the state of Louisiana, and 21,000 farther north. The Orleans population was 45 percent white, 45 percent slave, and 10 percent free people of color.[43] Africans had been slaves in Spain and its New World empire for centuries. But its brand of Catholicism treated slaves, however lowly, as humans. Spanish law regarding slaves took effect in Louisiana by 1769, and under it came manumission and self-purchase. By 1803, when the Americans took over, nearly four thousand African former slaves had either bought their own freedom or been manumitted, creating a significant element of free blacks.[44]

These figures did not include the tens of thousands of Indians not far west of New Orleans, St. Louis, or the Mississippi generally, or east of it in future Alabama and Mississippi. New Orleans in 1803 also soon gained upwards of ten thousand white and mulatto refugees from the race war in St.-Domingue.[45] All in all, the population in and around New Orleans was as unfamiliar and untypical as Americans farther east were saying it was. The provision in the treaty that gave citizenship and all its rights to the people of New Orleans caused grave misgivings across the country, not just in Congress and the slave states. Slaves were familiar enough, but French, Spanish, free people of color, mulattoes, and Catholics were all suspect and foreign. Imperialism's path could be thorny, and by no means democratic. From the Louisianan's point of view, could they be annexed without their consent? Could Washington-appointed officials, as happened for several years, rule them without providing any avenues of self-government? Territorial status similar to provisions of the 1787 Northwest Ordinance (except to allow slavery) soon followed, however, as did statehood in 1812.

French historians have never been happy with the loss of Louisiana. "Imagine French prestige," wrote one, "if all those lands had kept French liberty and French language; half of the United States would now speak and think French." For money to make war, "Bonaparte cheated the Spanish and sold against their will French land and without consulting the desires of the people." The British would never have captured it; Jackson's victory over them at New Orleans in 1815 proved that.[46] More realistically, wrote another French historian, Bonaparte realized that France could not effectively exploit "this immense territory" and understood that the expanding United States "would never accept its westward expansion being blocked. . . . The dream was over, certainly grand, but it was effaced by new geopolitical realities of the nineteenth century."[47] As in 1782, the depth of conviction by the Americans then in power—Franklin and others then, Jefferson in 1803—that the United States could, should, and would expand, a conviction constantly reinforced by demographic increase at a world-record rate, made that expansion virtually irresistible. The great powers of Europe could not hold their colonies against it, though Britain came closest to doing so.

The Native Americans, as numbers of whites and the technologies of both peace and war shifted against them, were overwhelmed with even greater ease and less compunction. Jefferson thought of removing those east of the Mississippi into the nearer reaches of Louisiana such as present-day Arkansas, but dropped the idea as he realized the inexorability of the white frontierspeople's advance. The removal took place under his successors the Jacksonians. They adopted Jefferson's removal idea and its "philanthropic" basis—get the Indians out of harm's way until they rise to the level of white civilization—but carried it out with more ruthlessness.

By the time of the Purchase in 1803, the Miamis and other tribes living between the Ohio River and the Great Lakes had progressively withdrawn from their lands, by treaty or by force. Gone were the days when they could maintain themselves as a buffer between French and English, British and Americans. Simultaneously, since the Spanish started encouraging immigration following the 1795 treaty, the Osages, who had ruled the scene along the Missouri River, found themselves encroached upon by whites from Kentucky like the Boone family as well as by Shawnees, Delawares, and other Ohio Valley Indians. White Hair, the outstanding leader of the Osages, like Little Turtle of the Miamis a decade or two earlier, saw what was coming and negotiated and fought to retain trade relations as long as possible.[48] West of New Orleans, along the new border between American Louisiana and Spanish Texas, Chief Dehahuit played the leading role in creating a "Neutral Ground" for his Caddos. He played it well until, again, the demographic tide swamped the Caddos by 1815.[49]

Blind luck played a greater role in the Louisiana Purchase than in any other major acquisition. As Livingston pointed out to Madison, France in 1801 was run by one man, who had reduced all his ministers to clerks. Without Napoleon's decision to sell, either nothing would have happened or westerners would have pressured Jefferson into taking New Orleans by force. St. Louis would have followed. Whether or when the entire Missouri basin—into which Jefferson was already planning to send Lewis and Clark—would have become American is conjecture, but probable. Yet in the peaceful way the Purchase took place, in its huge extent and its suddenness, Napoleon's abrupt decision was crucial. Contributing factors included Livingston's ability to see an opportunity and press for it. The utter lack of doubt on the part of Jefferson, Madison, and the public, whether Jeffersonian or Federalist, that the United States must have New Orleans (and the rest later), underlay American diplomacy. A willingness to bend if not break rules allowed Jefferson to squelch the constitutional objection in his own and others' minds. It also allowed Napoleon to ignore the French constitution and his treaty obligations to Spain. The numerical weakness of the Spanish, and the increasing imbalance of whites against Native Americans, opened the way for the Americans to take over the Mississippi River all the way to the Gulf. Expanding at the maximum biological rate, frontier settlers were breaching the Mississippi.

The next acquisition would be the Floridas. Before that took place, the United States aggressively tried to acquire another neighbor. Uniquely, however, that attempt failed.

Chapter Three

CANADA, 1812–1814:
FAILED AGGRESSION NORTHWARD

The acquisition of Canada, this year, as far as the neighborhood of Quebec, will be a mere matter of marching, and will give us experience for the attack of Halifax the next, and the final expulsion of England from the American continent.

—Thomas Jefferson to William Duane, August 4, 1812[1]

A THREE-FRONT WAR

In 1942, shortly after the United States entered World War II, appeals on American radio networks for people to buy war bonds informed listeners that "the United States has never lost a war. But neither has Japan." The United States did win that one, but it did not win the War of 1812. It achieved none of its announced war aims; the enemy invaded and burned down the major public buildings of Washington; the country was lucky to get out of the war without any loss of its territory. The Canadian-American War of 1812–1814 was one instance when aggression, combined with demography and diplomacy, did not gain new territory. One reason was that the American government bungled its war-making, but a better one was that the opposition—the British and Canadians—was too determined and powerful. Had the United States encountered similar resistance later from Spain or Mexico, its southward moves might have been thwarted as well. Its northern opponents, to the contrary, did an excellent job of defending themselves and their turf.

Expansion was not the only American objective, and indeed not the immediate one. But it was an objective. The War of 1812 was actually three wars. One was triggered by events at sea and took place on the

Atlantic. It concerned "neutral rights," the trade that Americans might have with Britain and France, then the most powerful nations of Europe, locked in the final phases of the Napoleonic Wars. As a by-product, American shippers and the Jefferson and Madison administrations were also concerned with "impressment," the British practice of stopping and boarding American vessels and carrying off seamen who were British-born, following their theory that once a Brit, always a Brit, whatever naturalization a person may have undergone. The second war took place in what is now Alabama and Mississippi and into both East and West Florida, and ended at the battle of New Orleans in January 1815. In that phase, Andrew Jackson of Tennessee commanded forces that invaded the lands of the Creeks and other Indian nations as well as Spanish territory. This war was essentially separate from the other two, except for the battle of New Orleans. Since this southern war culminated in the American acquisition of the Floridas, it will be discussed in the next chapter.

The third war was Canadian-American. It began in the Old Northwest, in what is now northern Indiana and Ohio, southeastern Michigan, and the lands around Lakes Huron and Michigan. Most of this war took place on the north and south banks and on the waters of the St. Lawrence River, Lake Ontario, and Lake Erie. It happened, in other words, along the shaky boundary between the United States and British North America set in the 1782–1783 peace negotiations. British garrisons did not evacuate several forts on the American side of that boundary until 1796, as a result of Jay's Treaty of 1794. The British maintained active military contact—many Americans called it "incitement"—up to 1812 and beyond with Indian nations well south of the boundary. Within this third theater, American forces tried to capture Upper Canada (now Ontario), and then, they hoped, Lower Canada (now Quebec), with the ultimate goal, as expressed by Jefferson, of conquering the rest of present Atlantic Canada as well. The Americans failed to accomplish any of this and were thrown back in all but a few instances. The peace treaty signed at Ghent in Belgium on Christmas Eve of 1814 reaffirmed the 1783 boundary, and agreements in 1817 and 1818 reaffirmed and extended the border permanently. American aggression northward had been stopped and would not be repeated. After 1815, annexing Canada was rarely more than wistful rhetoric, though it surfaced time and again even into the twentieth century.

O, Canada

The fascination of many Americans with the possibility of absorbing Canada and extending the blessings of American-style liberty to the North Pole—or at least down the St. Lawrence—was nothing new. As we have seen, the Continental Congress appealed in 1774 and 1775 to "Canadians," then nearly all French, to join the thirteen English colonies' resistance to Britain. Two American armies invaded Quebec in 1775–1776 and were thrown back. In the late 1770s and in mid-1782, Benjamin Franklin included Canada on his list of war aims. In the 1782 peace talks, Britain came very close to giving away southern Ontario along the Nipissing Line, but settled instead for the Great Lakes–St. Lawrence boundary, which it continued to control.[2]

By 1812, however, kinship and commerce tied New England to the Atlantic provinces. New England's quarrels with Britain were over maritime issues, not about Canada. The clamor for war and annexation came from the "War Hawks" of the West and South. Yet the American yearning to absorb Canada was long-standing. In 1811–1812 it became part of a grand strategy. Since the United States could not possibly defeat Britain at sea and resolve the maritime issues by naval force, the idea was to invade and possibly annex Canada (or threaten to), so that at the very least the United States would hold Canada hostage until Britain gave in on impressments and neutral shipping rights. As in a pesky nuisance lawsuit, Britain would thereby hastily settle things with America and get on with its main preoccupation, Napoleon. (Whether the Americans would then give back Canada was one step beyond such thinking. It seems extremely unlikely.)

Why was annexation popular? Land hunger was part of it. American border businessmen who wanted to control Great Lakes trade encouraged it. The northwestern third of Ohio and the northern two-thirds of Indiana had not yet been reached by American settlers, nor, basically, had Michigan (but for the forts) or northern Illinois. Northern Vermont was the heaviest-settled area along the Canadian-American border in 1810, and from there settlers were spilling over into neighboring Lower Canada. They were no vast horde, however, no denser than twenty or twenty-five per square mile. As one American politician remarked, "Lord knows we already have more than enough" land. Some Americans

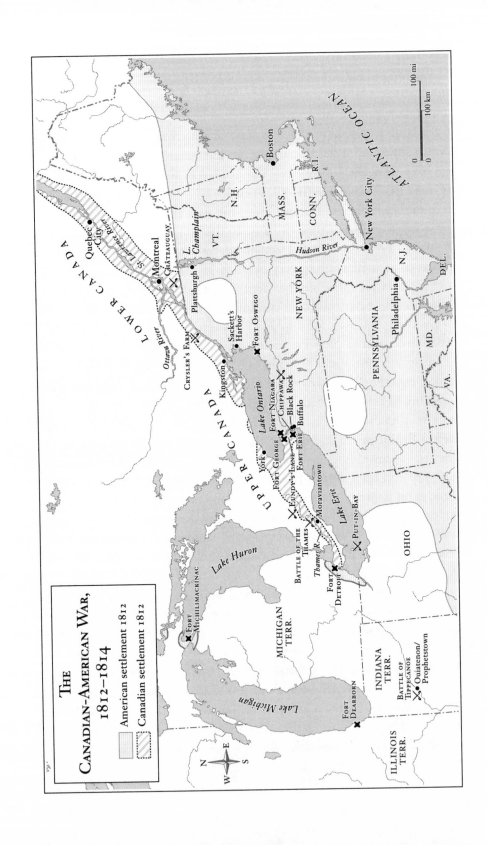

THE
CANADIAN-AMERICAN WAR,
1812–1814

American settlement 1812
Canadian settlement 1812

N
W E
S

100 mi
100 km

ATLANTIC OCEAN

Boston

New York City

N.H.
MASS.
CONN.
R.I.
VT.
N.J.
DEL.
MD.
VA.

NEW YORK

PENNSYLVANIA

Philadelphia

Hudson River

L. Champlain

Plattsburgh

CHÂTEAUGUAY

Montreal

Quebec City

St. Lawrence River

Ottawa River

LOWER CANADA

CRYSLER'S FARM

Sackett's Harbor

FORT OSWEGO

Kingston

Lake Ontario

FORT NIAGARA
CHIPPAWA
Black Rock
FORT ERIE
Buffalo

York

FORT GEORGE

LUNDY'S LANE

Moraviantown

BATTLE OF THE THAMES

Thames R.

Lake Erie

PUT-IN-BAY

UPPER CANADA

Lake Huron

FORT MICHILIMACKINAC

MICHIGAN TERR.

FORT DETROIT

OHIO

Lake Michigan

FORT DEARBORN

INDIANA TERR.

BATTLE OF TIPPECANOE

Ouiatenon/ Prophetstown

ILLINOIS TERR.

did go to Upper Canada from northern New England and New York, and even joined Canadian militias in 1812–1814. More often, northeastern American migration aimed for central and western New York and beyond. The attraction of the land across the border in Canada was not so much to provide farms for settlers but rather to produce, and profitably sell, grain—either down an American-controlled St. Lawrence or to New York City, after some canal-building across New York State.

On the Canadian side of the line lived thousands of ex-American Loyalists who had taken up farms in Nova Scotia and future Ontario after 1784. They had fled the thirteen colonies during or after the Revolutionary War, often at the loss of their property and at the expense of indignities or injuries. These were the people that, according to the 1783 peace treaty, the Confederation Congress would "earnestly recommend" to the states for restitution. The states did nothing, as expected, and it fell to the British crown to give Loyalist land grants, including some along the north bank of the St. Lawrence and the northern and western shores of Lake Ontario. They retained bitter memories of their treatment in the United States and taught their children accordingly. More migrants from the northeastern United States continued to arrive right up to 1812. Where the loyalties of these ex-Americans would lie was anyone's guess: Would they welcome an invasion or would they support their new neighbors?

Canada's population, like the United States', was overwhelmingly rural. Its cities were small. The largest, Halifax, Quebec City, and Montreal, were all under ten thousand, and Kingston, the "redoubt" at the eastern end of Lake Ontario, which the Americans shrank from attacking, had just over one thousand inhabitants by 1812. At that moment, Canada's population had reached about 525,000, two-thirds of them French-speakers in Quebec. The English-speakers were divided between the Atlantic coastal provinces and the St. Lawrence–Great

---

"Settled" areas in Upper and Lower Canada and on the American side of the border were often very sparsely populated. The main areas of land combat were (1) around Detroit, which the British and Canadians captured (along with Fort Michilimackinac) in July and August 1812, and which the Americans recaptured together with southwest Upper Canada in the fall of 1813 (the only territory that the United States gained), and (2) the Niagara frontier from Fort Erie north to Fort Niagara, essentially a bloody standoff from late 1813 to late 1814. The American land invasion from Sackett's Harbor and down the St. Lawrence was stopped at Crysler's Farm in November 1813. The Americans' naval victory on Lake Champlain in September 1814 prevented a British/Canadian drive to New York City.

Lakes settlements. Fewer than 100,000, perhaps only about 75,000, populated Upper Canada along the northern shores of the St. Lawrence, Lake Ontario, and Lake Erie. The U.S. population, by contrast, had reached 7,500,000. Despite the Jeffersonians' dislike of standing armies, the country had about 12,000 troops to send against half as many defenders of Canada, mostly British regulars with local militia support. Compared to the huge surge of people into Kentucky and Tennessee, and by 1812 into Missouri and southern Indiana, Americans' migration into Canada was a small affair. A critical mass of pro-American infiltrators did not exist (as it would in Texas a few years later), which was one reason why the annexation failed.

Though land in itself was not the chief American object, other things were. One was to overawe the Indians of the Northwest and separate them from British commercial and military influence. The Miamis, Potawatomis, Shawnees, and others had "bothered" the new settlers of Ohio and southern Indiana and necessitated outposts such as Fort Wayne, Fort Detroit, and Fort Dearborn. In 1810–1811, the great Shawnee leader Tecumseh and his half brother Tenskwatawa ("the Prophet"), with British help, forged an alliance for what proved to be the final serious effort by Indians to interdict the Americans' frontier advance. But in November 1811 an American force under William Henry Harrison stopped the combined Indians at Tippecanoe in northern Indiana and burned their nearby settlement, Prophetstown. From then on Tecumseh and his cohorts were less an independent force than adjuncts to British campaigns, hoping for autonomy with British protection.

A second reason for occupying and possibly annexing Canada was economic. Canada was Britain's major source of ships' masts and other materials of war; President James Madison and his supporters hoped to deprive Britain of that. They also wanted access to the North Atlantic via the St. Lawrence. In time—specifically, by 1825—the opening of the Erie Canal provided migrants and shippers along the Great Lakes with a much better route to the Atlantic, ice-free and all-American. This excuse for capturing the St. Lawrence thus disappeared later, but it was high on the agenda in 1812.

The third objective was less measurable though deeper-rooted. The underlying, long-lasting, gut reason for Americans to invade Canada was—to use the phrase of thirty years later but whose spirit was already mature—manifest destiny. Many Americans at the time of the Revolution and again in the 1812 era believed firmly that the United States was destined one day to rule all of North America. The opportunity was being handed them, or so it seemed in 1812. If not then, when? As Jefferson wrote to William Duane in August 1812, just after the war began: "the acquisition of Canada . . . as far as . . . Quebec will be a mere matter of marching."[3] And the Canadians, the Jeffersonians assumed, would welcome the invaders with open arms.

President Madison and the War Hawk Congress

Thus several reasons led the United States to declare war on Britain in 1812. Tecumseh and his Indian followers in the Northwest objected, often violently, to the continuing push of white settlement. Settlers, traders, and politicians wanted something done about the Indians. Canada, sparsely settled west of Montreal, seemed ripe for the taking; and taking it would, so it seemed, solve the Indian "problem" and hit Britain where she presumably hurt. Britain was interfering drastically with American shipping in the Atlantic, impressing sailors from American ships, besmirching America's national honor, and treating the United States as a disloyal postcolonial upstart. Britain could protect herself only by ruling the waves, and impressments were essential, at least at that moment. Americans from President Madison to Congress to newspaper editors, however, regarded impressments as attacks on "American honor and sovereignty."[4]

Would the United States have declared war on Britain solely to stop her intrigues with the Northwest Indians? Or solely to invade, capture, and annex Canada? Almost certainly not. The national interest lay chiefly in opening trade, stopping impressments, and ending insults to the nation's honor. But how? The obvious answer: declare war on Britain, take Canada (or at least Upper Canada), and force Britain, then busy fighting Napoleon, to capitulate on the maritime issues. The northward aggression was largely a means to an end. To some Americans along the border and in what was then the West, however, it was an end in itself. If the invasion worked, it would deprive the Northwest Indians of their British benefactor and ally; it would gratify long-held dreams of driving Britain out of North America and making it all American (except for Spain's possessions, easily dealt with later); and it would open the St. Lawrence. Tactically, in theory, the idea made great sense: instead of confronting Britain in the Atlantic, where the United States could pit only a few dozen ships against Britain's several hundred, the battles would take place on land. There American armies were bigger, and reinforcement from a nearby and much larger population than Canada's was presumed to be easy.[5] All it required was that larger army on land, and a few warships and privateers to harass Britain at sea.

On November 4, 1811, the Twelfth Congress convened and began clamoring for war. For several years British ships had been stopping and raiding American vessels. An infuriating example was the attack in June 1807 by the British ship *Leopard* on the frigate U.S.S. *Chesapeake*, leaving three dead and eighteen wounded and carrying off four others. From then to 1811, President Jefferson in his last two years in office and Madison in his first two responded to British and French interference with American shipping mainly by restricting who (including Americans) could enter or leave American ports. Nothing worked. As incidents continued, the clamor for war grew shrill and loud practically everywhere except in Federalist New England. This Congress, elected in late 1810, rode in on a wave of war fever. By the time it took office in November 1811 the fever was higher. The young Henry Clay of Kentucky, a freshman in the House of Representatives (though he had served briefly in the Senate), was elected Speaker, and he filled the foreign affairs and military committees with war hawks like himself. When President Madison opened the session with a belligerent annual message, Clay and his cohort were ready to oblige.

Speaker Clay appointed Peter B. Porter of Black Rock, New York, now part of Buffalo, chair of the Foreign Affairs Committee. (Not incidentally, Porter was one of those border businessmen materially interested in Upper Canada's economic potential.) On December 6 Porter presented to the House the committee's report recommending war as the only reply to repeated insults. Privateers would help, but the main effort against Britain would be to "deprive her of her extensive provinces lying along our borders to the north." For most of December, House members spoke long and eloquently in support of the Porter committee's recommendations. Only a few, most notably John Randolph of Virginia, opposed them. Good news of William Henry Harrison's November engagement at Tippecanoe and Prophetstown on the Wabash was trickling in, and it rekindled talk of

the influence of British agents in keeping up Indian hostility. . . . The 9th of November will not be forgotten, and time shall only brighten the fame of the deeds of our army, and a tear shall be shed for those who have fallen. . . . the widow will mourn her disconsolate situation; the orphan shall cry for the return of his father in vain; and the mother carry her sorrow to the grave.

So spoke Richard Johnson of Kentucky, who later took credit for killing Tecumseh and rode that claim (and a belt said to be made of Tecumseh's skin) into the vice presidency in 1836.

Felix Grundy of Tennessee, another war hawk, proclaimed that driving the British from North America would end intrigues with the "ruthless savage." "I am willing," said Grundy, "to receive the Canadians as adopted brethren." Johnson had "no doubt" that Canadians, French, English, or even "the refugee tories of the revolution . . . are sound in their morals and in their politics, and would make worthy members of the United States. . . . They . . . only want an opportunity to throw off the yoke of their [British] taskmasters." No one, not even those leery of a war, doubted "our ability to make a conquest" of the Canadas. John Calhoun of South Carolina, like Jefferson, hoped "to see the day when the British will have no Halifax on this continent."[6]

Few spoke against the war measures, and no Federalist even bothered. Those opposed implied that there was more to the proposed invasion of Canada than simply hitting Britain at her one soft spot. Supporters stayed clear of overt land grabbing, painting Canada simply as a means of resolving the maritime issues and stopping "intrigues" with the "ruthless savage." Randolph of Virginia, however, laid bare what he saw as the war hawks' hidden agenda:

Gentlemen from the North have been taken up to some high mountain and shown all the kingdoms of the earth, and Canada seems tempting in their sight. That rich vein of Gennesee [*sic*] land, which is said to be even better on the other side of the lake [Ontario] than on this. Agrarian cupidity, not maritime right, urges the war. Ever since the report of the Committee on Foreign Relations came into the House, we have heard but one word—like the whip-poor-will, but one eternal monotonous tone—Canada! Canada! Canada! Not a syllable about Halifax, which unquestionably should be our great object in a war for maritime security.[7]

Not every Jefferson-Madison Republican congressman supported Porter's resolutions. Adam Boyd of New Jersey pointed out that "it is an easy matter to go to law or war, but it is a hard matter to get out of it." The hard-core war hawks numbered perhaps two dozen, mostly from the South and the Transappalachian West plus a few (like Porter) from districts along the Canadian border in New York, Vermont, and New Hampshire. Ohioans were divided, some fearing that a war would bring more Indian trouble, not less.[8] From January to April 1812, the House considered a series of measures to raise taxes, build frigates, increase the army, and reinstitute an embargo on imports. Votes were often close, though generally supportive of the move toward war. Even Porter realized in April that the United States was woefully unprepared to invade Canada at that moment, though he continued to urge doing so, and after taking it, to annex Upper Canada. Porter understood as well as anyone that the land north and west of Lake Ontario had just as much crop and livestock potential as his own district in western New York.[9] Why let these riches slip down the St. Lawrence to England?

Efforts to persuade Britain to repeal the Orders in Council (its restrictions on U.S. shipping) or discontinue impressments failed in the spring of 1812. Madison found himself compelled to send Congress a war message on June 1. The president elaborated on the maritime issues exclusively, except for one paragraph on "the warfare just renewed by the savages on one of our extensive frontiers—a warfare which is known to spare neither age nor sex and to be distinguished by features peculiarly shocking to humanity." Because the "tribes [are] in constant intercourse with British traders and garrisons," Britain must be held responsible. Madison never mentioned Canada. Yet the recruitment of soldiers and the commissioning of officers pointed almost entirely that way. The House passed the war declaration three days later by a less than overwhelming 79–49 vote. The Senate debated, largely on procedural obstacles thrown up by opponents, for nearly two weeks before agreeing, 19 to 13, a margin well below the two-thirds that a treaty would have required. Seven of the twenty-eight Republican senators voted against Madison and the war, and two others who were absent probably would have.[10] On this flimsy basis, the president declared war on June 18. Two days earlier, Britain had suspended the Orders in Council, nullifying the chief cause of hostilities (without them, impressments could not happen). Madison did not know that, of course. By the time the news reached Washington, the war was on. "True patriotism" required that it continue, without a reason—except to invade and annex Canada? So it did, for almost two and a half years.

"A Mere Matter of Marching"

Thus the United States went to war against Britain, the world's foremost naval power and the chief opponent of Napoleonic France. The British-Canadian aim was simply to keep out the American invaders, maintain good relations with the Iroquois and their other Indian allies, and continue to control the Great Lakes and the St. Lawrence all the way to the sea. The strategy, in other words, was to defend North America successfully for as long as the Napoleonic War continued. The American strategy was to invade Canada, not at its strongest points (Quebec City and Halifax) but farther west in several places, with the initial major thrusts directed at Montreal and Kingston. After taking them, Upper Canada along Lakes Ontario, Erie, and Huron would wither on the vine because that region could no longer be supplied through the St. Lawrence.

This grand plan was almost immediately modified by events (defeat at Detroit) and incompetence (political leaders failed to raise enough well-trained troops and military leaders failed to use them effectively). At the outset of hostilities, in July 1812, American fecklessness and unpreparedness were doubly manifest when a British and Indian contingent captured Fort Mackinac without a shot, before the lieutenant in command knew that war had been declared. At Detroit, General (and Michigan governor) William Hull attempted an invasion across the river into Canada, then pulled back. Fearing a massacre by British-allied Indians, he surrendered Fort Detroit on August 16 to a considerably smaller force under British major general Isaac Brock. A day earlier, Hull's order to evacuate Fort Dearborn, at the foot of Lake Michigan, resulted in the killing of sixty-eight Americans by Potawatomi Indians despite a pledge of safe conduct from friendlier Miamis, an action known as "the Fort Dearborn Massacre." Potawatomis, Winnebagos, and other tribes firmly controlled everything west of Fort Wayne.

American thrusts toward Montreal did not come until late in the war and did not get far. Kingston always seemed too strong to risk attacking head-on. Seesaw fights, hard-fought and bloody, went on along the Niagara in 1813 and 1814, but the British successfully defended the Niagara frontier. Jefferson's "mere matter of marching" had been wildly optimistic.

On Lakes Erie and Ontario, American sailors won some naval and amphibious encounters. Sailing west from Sackett's Harbor, their base on the eastern end of Lake Ontario, they overran, sacked, and burned York, the capital of Upper Canada, on April 27, 1813. They fought off a retaliatory attack on Sackett's Harbor on May 29. Under Oliver Hazard Perry's command, they defeated a smaller British fleet at Put-In Bay on Lake Erie on September 10, 1813, cutting off British forces in and east of Detroit. That permitted the one clear American land victory of the war, the battle of the Thames, on October 5, where Tecumseh was killed. But no American fleet left Sackett's Harbor to capture Kingston, only twenty miles north; Sackett's ended the war under blockade by a strengthened British fleet.

From that small base also went two armies. The first, under General Jacob Brown, one of the few competent American commanders, headed west to the Niagara battlefront. Brown captured Fort Erie on July 3, then defeated the British at Chippawa on July 5. Both sides regrouped and met at Lundy's Lane (now within the city of Niagara Falls, Ontario). In the bloodiest battle of the war, two thousand were killed, and it ended essentially in a draw. The Americans withdrew, and in November abandoned badly damaged Fort Erie. The other Sackett's-based army proceeded down the St. Lawrence under General James Wilkinson, avoided Kingston, and ended in ignominy at Crysler's Farm a few miles upriver from Cornwall on November 11, 1813. That encounter, together with an American defeat at nearby Chateauguay two weeks earlier, collapsed the only serious American offensive against Montreal in the whole war.

The Americans' Niagara campaign also failed. There too, the "mere marching" along the north shore of Lake Ontario to Kingston and on to Montreal never happened. The Americans won some stirring single-ship naval engagements in the Atlantic and their privateers harassed British ship movements, but Britain succeeded in blockading much of the American Atlantic coast. Its ships sailed up the Chesapeake and burned the public buildings of Washington (in retaliation for the burning of York) in August 1814. To all intents and purposes Britannia ruled the waves. The British and Canadians achieved far more of their defensive aims than the Americans did of their offensive ones. The outcome—above all, staving off American invasion and probable annexation—contributed powerfully to the creation of Canadian national identity.

Along the border in northern New York and Vermont, healthy prewar commerce simply continued as wartime smuggling. At the western end of the Canadian-American front, Ohio and Michigan frontierspeople continued to fear Indian attacks more than to evince eagerness to defend "maritime rights" or even to acquire Canadian territory. Indians greatly helped the British and Canadian defense efforts.[11]

As the military standoffs went on, so did talk of annexing Canada, though it grew less loud and insistent as the unsatisfactory war proceeded. Ten days into the war, Jefferson wrote Revolutionary hero Tadeusz Kościuszko that "the *cession* of Canada . . . must be a sine qua non at a treaty of peace." The Jeffersonian congressman Matthew Clay of Virginia avowed on January 2, 1813, "I am not for stopping at Quebec or anywhere else. . . . We must take the continent from them." In December of that year, House Speaker Henry Clay warned that Canada, once conquered, "ought never to be surrendered." The Federalists, as impotent as later antiwar House minorities would be in 1846 and 1898 and 1968, railed fruitlessly about the pointless bloodshed, but annexationist talk continued. It muted considerably in 1814, and was laughed at in Canada.[12] Every one of the American invasion attempts—eastward from Detroit, westward across the Niagara River, across Lake Ontario to York, and down the St. Lawrence and Lake Champlain—resulted in some minor, transient victories, but overall failure. The American invasions of Canada in 1812–1814 gained no more land than those of 1775 and 1776.

A FORTUNATE PEACE

On August 8, 1814, three British and five American peace negotiators sat down at Ghent, in Belgium, to talk terms. The United States had made motions toward peace as soon as the war began, but despite Britain's mortal combat with Napoleon, no serious progress resulted. At that point, the positions of British and American forces were not very different from what they were in June 1814, or for that matter in June 1812. And no significant territorial changes came later, despite several major battles in late 1814: Fort Erie, August 15 (Americans repulse British); Bladensburg, Maryland, August 24 (British repulse Americans); Washington, August 24–25 (British torch the Capitol and the White House); Plattsburgh and Lake Champlain, September 11 (Americans win); Baltimore, September 13–14 (standoff); and the postarmistice battle of New Orleans, January 8, 1815 (Andrew Jackson wins). In fact the only lasting, solid British conquests in the entire war were their occupation of much of eastern Maine, their captures of Fort Mackinac and Fort Dearborn in the opening days, and, with their Indian allies, their taking of what is now Wisconsin, upper Michigan, and other parts of the Old Northwest. For the Americans, gains were limited to the southwestern Ontario peninsula across the Detroit River for about sixty-five miles eastward to Moraviantown where in October 1813 they won the battle of the Thames.

In sheer acreage, Britain had much the better of it. Raids, counter-raids, and skirmishes took place at many points in Indiana, Michigan, along the Niagara and the St. Lawrence, and on Lakes Huron, Erie, and Ontario. Except for southwestern Ontario, the Americans conquered nothing in Canada, and the British and Canadians successfully defended it. The Americans' overwhelming population advantage was never brought to bear, because of an almost ludicrous combination of civilian-military disagreements, arguments among generals, inept and inadequate logistics and transport, an inability to neutralize Britain's alliances with several thousand Indians, and a general failure to think things through, from President Madison on down.

The peace talks should therefore have resulted in territorial or other chastisements of the United States. That they did not was largely a consequence of Britain's nearly complete absorption in cleaning up Europe after the defeat of Napoleon. The British foreign secretary, Viscount Castlereagh, one of the era's most brilliant diplomatic statesmen, was present and preoccupied at the Congress of Vienna. To the peace conference at Ghent went second- or third-stringers for Britain; but, as in 1782, the Americans sent a very able team. Admiral Lord Gambier, leading the British, and the lawyer William Adams were errand boys for Castlereagh, and Henry Goulburn, the young and bristling third member, unfailingly set Americans' teeth on edge with his profound conviction, constantly evident, that they were merely upstart colonials. The American team of five, in contrast, included John Quincy Adams, experienced in diplomacy since his childhood and currently American minister to Russia; Albert Gallatin, for thirteen years secretary of the Treasury for Jefferson and Madison; Speaker (and war hawk) Henry Clay; Jonathan Russell, the American representative in London; and Senator James Bayard of Delaware, a moderate Federalist. The Americans squabbled, as the presence of an Adams almost assured they would; yet they came home with all that seemed possible, and more.

Peace moves had actually started before the war began, when Castlereagh annulled the Orders in Council in June 1812. That news, of course, took some weeks to reach North America. By then hostilities had begun, and the prospect of "merely marching" through Canada was still a vivid hope. In September 1812, Czar Alexander I of Russia, facing invasion by Napoleon and eager to free his British ally of the American annoyance, offered to mediate. Nothing happened over the winter, and by spring 1813 Castlereagh declined the czar's offer and refused to relent on impressment. By the summer of 1814 the American team was finally in place at Ghent, and the British team appeared in early August. The talks began on August 8.

When the British opened with demands that would in effect have reversed the 1782 acquisition of northern Transappalachia, the negotiations nearly collapsed. As a sine qua non, or what would now be called a nonnegotiable demand, Britain asked the United States to turn over virtually everything west of the 1795 Greenville Treaty line as far as the Great Lakes to form an "Indian buffer zone." Britain asked additionally for territory from Lake Superior west and southwest to the Mississippi, and much of Maine. They also wanted Canada protected by permanent naval disarmament on the Great Lakes. The buffer zone would have included northwest Ohio, most of Indiana and Illinois, and all of Michigan and Wisconsin. It was meant to insulate Canada from American aggression, reward and protect Britain's Indian allies, and continue European control of the Great Lakes fur trade that dated to the days of New France. Most serious of all, but following the usual custom that a treaty ending a war nullified all previous treaties between the contracting parties, the British maintained that the 1782–1783 peace treaties were abrogated. All boundaries and other agreed-upon points, and perhaps even the recognition of U.S. independence, were at risk.[13]

On August 24 the Americans said absolutely no, and made plans to walk out. Their own demands, notably the end of impressments of seamen and the other maritime issues that led the United States to declare war in the first place, hardly reached the table. The buffer zone idea would have given up effective American sovereignty over the Northwest and therefore any foreseeable chance of American settlement there or displacement of its Indians.

Touchy and tentative contacts followed for several weeks. Britain gradually climbed down and the talks went on. Madison published the British demands, which reawakened patriotic and bellicose spirits in the

United States. They seemed unreasonable even to many in Britain. In due course the British team retreated from the buffer zone demand, proposing instead that the United States recognize all Indian rights as of 1811 (pre-Tippecanoe). The Americans accepted this offer on October 13.

Britain then waited for good news "from the front." It arrived; the Royal Navy had burned Washington. The British team offered, as in 1780, a peace based on *uti possedetis*, the principle that each side would keep what it had at that moment. With Napoleon confined on Elba, some British voices urged that the Duke of Welllington lead forces released from Europe to Canada and then occupy goodly stretches of U.S. territory. But the Iron Duke, then and later the nation's foremost military hero, rejected that idea: Europe remained unstable, he believed (and indeed Napoleon did return on March 15, though briefly), and, in his unchallenged opinion, Britain had "no right . . . to demand any concessions of territory" from the United States. News of American victories at Baltimore and on Lake Champlain swung the peace talks toward the status quo *ante bellum*, which the Americans proposed on November 10. It became the basis for the treaty.

The Indian buffer zone dematerialized into a wispy phantom. The United States would simply recognize the Indians' rights as of 1811. Britain would withdraw from Wisconsin and elsewhere south of the Great Lakes and cease her protection and alliances with the Indian nations that went back to 1763. American officials could resume their Indian treaties and American settlers their encroachments. Eventually the Indians of the Northwest would be forcibly removed. Britain's Henry Goulburn finally understood "the fixed determination which prevails in the breast of every American to extirpate the Indians and appropriate their Territory."[14] Britain thereupon abandoned its Indian allies and a European modus vivendi regarding Indians that had operated since the mid-seventeenth century, first with the French and then with the British. Great Lakes Indians, for the first time in 150 years, were orphaned from a European ally. The United States would keep pushing westward, just as it had been doing. It continued to rid Transappalachia of Indians. It evaded and ignored the treaty's status-quo-ante clause as it applied to Indians. Ghent removed the possibility of an outside power fortifying Indian resistance to American expansion (though some Indian leaders refused to give up the hope).[15]

A number of stubborn points between Britain/Canada and the United

States were either left unresolved or were remanded to future discussions. Impressment was the most obvious; North Atlantic fisheries were another; the Maine boundary with New Brunswick and the U.S.-Canadian border west of Lake Superior were a third; naval and military control of the Great Lakes, or their demilitarization, was another. The Treaty of Ghent, signed on Christmas Eve 1814, left all of these open. Yet it ended the Canadian-American War, the American attempt at northward expansion by aggression, on the basis of where things stood when the war began. In the peace negotiations, if the British had won their opening demands, and the United States had received what it deserved for starting the war and conducting it so badly, it would have lost most of the Old Northwest and any significant role in the St. Lawrence–Great Lakes waterway. Such a result would not have been surprising or unjust. But as in 1782, luck held for the Americans. What they lost on the field, they preserved at the conference table—exactly the opposite of the long-held American popular myth of a valiant military undercut by bumbling diplomats. The war hawks (and Jefferson) failed to win what they hoped for. The United States squeaked by because of the able diplomacy of Gallatin and his colleagues and British exhaustion after years of fighting Napoleon.

The leftover issues were gradually settled over the years. In 1817 the Rush-Bagot agreement began the process of naval disarmament on the Great Lakes and St. Lawrence. Land disarmament and subsequent reduction of military bases followed, though not until the Treaty of Washington in 1871. The "Convention of 1818" solved the decades-old fishing rights problem and also drew the Canadian-American boundary along the forty-ninth parallel from the Lake of the Woods as far west as the continental divide in the Rocky Mountains. It thereby followed a line that went back to the early eighteenth century to demarcate the Hudson's Bay Company domain from the French. This geographers' line trumped hydrography: the northern reaches of the Mississippi watershed that came with the Louisiana Purchase went to Canada, and the drainage area of the Red River (now the Minnesota-Dakota boundary) that flows northward to Lake Winnipeg became American. Since the latter was considerably larger, the United States was lucky again. The anomaly of the northwest corner that appeared in the 1783 treaty out of geographical ignorance was also resolved. The boundary of Maine, however, was not agreed to until 1842, and the extension of the forty-ninth parallel boundary to the Pacific not until the 1846 Oregon treaty (see Chapter 6). The impressment problem that exploded into war in 1812 simply faded away, because Britain's purpose in it and other maritime restrictions, to blockade France, disappeared along with Napoleon.

MEMORIES OF 1812

The war deepened and solidified Canada's sense of herself as a nation. Although the original Loyalist settlers of the 1780s and 1790s in Upper Canada had become outnumbered by more recent American immigrants, the War of 1812 became, by the 1820s and 1830s, thanks in part to Canadian mythmakers like John Strachan, a great Canadian victory over the overweening bully United States. Out of the war experience "there arose a sense of community among all Upper Canadians."[16] Beyond that, the conflict brought "bitterness" to Canadians, who were invaded, injured, and their property destroyed for no reason other than that they "were near at hand . . . British . . . [and] considered weak and vulnerable. . . . The War of 1812 . . . would become a pivotal event in a developing Canadian nationalism."[17]

As most wars do (construably victorious ones, anyway), the Canadian-American War of 1812–1814 provided both sides with icons that aided each in developing their respective nationalisms. American schoolbooks and patriotic occasions have looked back with awe and gratitude to Captain James Lawrence's "Don't give up the ship" as his U.S.S. *Chesapeake* was captured on June 1, 1813; to Oliver Hazard Perry's "We have met the enemy and they are ours" on September 10, 1813; to Francis Scott Key's penning *The Star-Spangled Banner* at the siege of Baltimore a year later; and to Andrew Jackson's postbellum victory at New Orleans in January 1815. Canadians revere General Sir Isaac Brock and renamed a St. Lawrence River town after him. They venerate Laura Secord, the housewife who ran twenty miles through the Niagara swamps and thickets on June 22, 1813, to warn the British-Canadian forces of American attack plans she overheard from loose-tongued officers who had commandeered her house. They remember the "crucial and resounding victory over 4,000 Americans by an Anglo-Canadian force of just 800" at Crysler's Farm.[18]

Most of all, Canadians pride themselves in having beaten back an invasion by the armies of a country a dozen times larger than theirs and thereby teaching that invader not to try it ever again. Although it took at least a generation for the events of 1812 to consolidate into a nationalist story, it became "one of the great myths of Canada as a nation."[19] A Canadian history of the war published in 1864 began: "1812 . . . is a sign of solemn import to the people of Canada. It carries with it the virtue of an incantation. . . . They are inscribed on the banner and stamped on the hearts of the Canadian people—a watchword, rather than a war-cry."[20] A school text of 1886 pointed out that Upper Canada had only 75,000 people and 1,500 regular troops to defend a 1,500-mile border against an invading nation of about eight million. Yet it observed:

> Such was the spirit of her sons that, hopeless as seemed the undertaking, she did not hesitate to take the field at the first sig-nal of danger. . . . [By war's end] the country had been devas-tated, innumerable homes made desolate, and thousands of lives sacrificed, in an inglorious attempt by the American people to subjugate Canada, and supplant the Union Jack by the Stars and Stripes.[21]

American hopes that the French-Canadians were "disaffected" and would help them overthrow "British tyranny" were dashed as voltigeurs (light infantry) and other units of French-Canadians rallied to fight the invaders, notably under Charles-Michel de Salaberry at Chateauguay on October 26, 1813. Quebecois were cemented to the British-Canadian cause by the trashing that New Englanders and other Americans dealt their language and religion, and by knowledge that the French Revolu-tion and Napoleon had been enemies of the Bourbon monarchy and the Catholic church and were therefore their enemies. Neither they nor the second-generation Loyalists who populated the upstream banks of the St. Lawrence to Cornwall, Prescott, Kingston, and on west were likely to welcome an American invasion. Canadian historians agree as unanimously as historians ever do that "the war of 1812 was crucial in creating a firm sense of Canadian identity."[22] That identity included "First Nations"—the native peoples—and the Quebecois as well as Anglo-Canadians, whether bloodline United Empire Loyalists or later immigrants from Britain, Ireland, or the United States. On both sides, the mythic heroes and events emerged. On both sides they were as pow-erful, and as unrepresentative of the historic truth, as myths often are.

Spread-eagle shouts that all of North America should by nature and by rights be incorporated into the United States continued for over a hundred years. They became especially loud during the heyday of manifest destiny in the 1840s but lasted well beyond. In 1889, for instance, a Chicago newspaper noted the covetous eyes with which American railroads regarded Canada's western prairies, just then opening up to settlement. It asked in a headline, "Will Canada Join Us? Strong Drift toward Annexation."[23] Other examples are legion.

In 1993 a Canadian professor of law and psychology named Floyd W. Rudmin published a small book called *Bordering on Aggression: Evidence of US Military Preparations against Canada*. His argument was that Fort Drum, in northern New York, along with other bases near the border, was being prepared as a launching pad for an invasion of Canada. The book read, as such tracts often do, as plausible although a bit paranoid—until President George W. Bush announced that the United States could deploy armed force where and when it wanted, without asking anyone's permission, and did so in Iraq in 2003.[24] The American desire for Canada began before Benjamin Franklin. The notions that conquest would be "a mere matter of marching" and that American forces would be greeted as liberators, not occupiers, were argued in 1812. Because people did not know this history, these presumptions were repeated almost verbatim in 2003.

In 1814, as in 1782, the United States had good diplomats, an adversary (Britain) distracted elsewhere, and tremendous luck. In 1782 it gained much more land than it should have; in 1814 it held on to much more than it deserved. Demography did not award Canada to the United States, because Upper Canadians were already entrenched. It helped that they were culturally similar, neither Indian nor French. Demography (as well as aggression and the adversary's weakness) would, however, help the United States in its next move, the three-stage acquisition of Spanish Florida.

Chapter Four

FLORIDA, 1810–1819:
SOUTHWARD AGGRESSION I

Power tends to corrupt and absolute power corrupts absolutely.
—Lord Acton, 1887[1]

THE WOES OF SPAIN

How the United States acquired Florida could be told in a sentence. Americans invaded the area, annexed the western part of it, chased out the Indians, overran what was left, and gave a distracted and defenseless Spain no alternative but to agree to relinquish the rest by treaty in 1819. That, however, is too brief a telling. There's a lot more to it.

The heart of the story runs from 1810 to 1819, yet it needs a longer perspective. By 1810, Florida had already been a Spanish colony for nearly three centuries, beginning with Juan Ponce de León's voyage around the peninsula in 1513. The Spanish founded St. Augustine in 1565 as the capital. It remained a defensive outpost of the captaincy-general of Havana. In the peace settlement of 1762–1763, Spain lost Florida to Britain and was awarded French Louisiana instead. Britain split the colony at the Apalachicola River into East and West Florida, with capitals at St. Augustine and Pensacola. The present Florida pan-handle, and a little more, became West Florida, while the peninsula became East Florida.

Spain had enticed few real Spaniards to Florida; by the late eighteenth century it amounted to only a handful of trading posts and forts along the Gulf coast and around St. Augustine. The population included five thousand to seven thousand Europeans (Spaniards, British, and, after 1776, a batch of American Loyalist refugees) and a far greater number of Creeks, Choctaws, Chickasaws, Seminoles, and other Indians.

Britain's sovereignty lasted only twenty years. The next Treaty of Paris, the one that recognized American independence in 1783, transferred East and West Florida back to Spain. The new United States was thereby bounded by the Spanish Floridas to the south as well as Spanish Louisiana to the west. Of the British who had come to Florida during those twenty years, many left for the Bahamas and other British refuges, though some stayed. So did the firm of Panton, Leslie & Company, which the British had licensed to trade with the Creeks. The American takeover began in 1810 in far West Florida, now the Louisiana panhandle. Over the next few years it rumbled eastward, piece by piece: first the rest of West Florida, then East Florida for a moment in 1812. In 1813–1815 it got caught up in a war with the Creeks and the tail end of the War of 1812 with Britain. Finally American forces overran every Spanish location except St. Augustine itself.

An astonishing range of people contributed in one way or another to the takeover. On the American side, it included five presidents starting with Jefferson and continuing all the way through Madison, Monroe, and John Quincy Adams to Jackson. It involved the Emperor Napoleon and two kings of Spain. The half-Creek confederator Tecumseh, King Payne of the Seminoles, and leaders of other Indian nations played important parts. A grab bag of insurrectionists, rabble-rousers, slave-holding planters, and officials both honest and knavish intervened at crucial moments to push Florida toward the United States.

On the Florida frontier itself, the cast of characters included Indians great and small, who were all to lose their homelands. Ostensibly upstanding citizens like Fulwar Skipwith, John Rhea, and the obstreperous Kemper brothers fomented an uprising against the Spanish at Baton Rouge in 1810. When their armed rebellion threatened to spread to Mobile, federal judge Harry Toulmin repeatedly warned President Madison how hard it was to enforce the U.S. neutrality law, not suspecting that Madison was undermining it himself. A semiliterate old Revolutionary warrior, General George Mathews, became Madison's cat's-paw in the self-styled "patriot war," which tried to capture East Florida in 1812. This effort failed when Major Jacint Laval, another Revolutionary veteran, refused to commit U.S. regulars to Mathews's filibuster without direct orders from Washington—orders Madison could not give without openly committing an act of war. In the final phase, in 1818, the

British intriguer Robert Ambrister and the elderly Scots trader Andrew Arbuthnot paid with their lives for getting in the way of Jackson's storming of East Florida. Adventurer-pirates Gregor McGregor, a Scot, and the Frenchman Louis Aury claimed cover under the flags of nascent Mexico and Venezuela when they briefly took over Amelia Island in East Florida in 1817.

The takeover wrapped up unfinished business in several ways from the American standpoint. The division of Spanish Florida into East and West by Britain, which the Spanish retained after they returned in 1783, sowed the seeds of argument: Was West Florida ever part of Louisiana, and therefore part of America's Louisiana Purchase in 1803? Also, where was its northern boundary? Spain had never defined it, and in the absence of settlers, never needed to. Britain in 1763 defined the boundary as the thirty-first parallel of latitude, and in 1764 added an area northward to 32°28', where the Yazoo River meets the Mississippi, so as to include Natchez. Louisiana, as it was transferred from France to Spain in 1762, was entirely west of the Mississippi except for the town of New Orleans itself and Lakes Maurepas and Pontchartrain adjacent to it. Thus, everything else on the east bank of the Mississippi to a little beyond Pensacola was West Florida. So it was when Spain regained the Floridas in 1783.

After the 1783 treaties, Spain did not recognize the Mississippi as its boundary with the United States, as did Britain and France. It retained its traditional claim to the "Illinois country" east of the Mississippi and north of the Ohio River. Britain still considered the thirty-first parallel to be the northern boundary of the Floridas, a view the United States naturally preferred. But Spain had good arguments, based on seventeenth-century French explorations that Spain inherited as well as its capture during the Revolutionary War of British positions as far north as present St. Joseph, Michigan.[2] These claims, never backed up by settlement, bedeviled relations between Spain and the United States from 1783 until 1795, when Spain agreed to the thirty-first-parallel boundary.

By then, Kentucky had become a state and Tennessee was about to. More and more American flatboats loaded with western produce crowded down the Mississippi toward the Spanish port of New Orleans. In 1794 the United States concluded Jay's Treaty with Britain, removing the British from the Great Lakes forts they were supposed to have left in 1783, but doing little else. It had, however, one favorable, unforeseen consequence. It frightened Carlos IV of Spain and his functionary, Manuel Godoy, into thinking that the United States and Britain were on the verge of a great rapprochement. Therefore it behooved Spain to settle differences and promote friendship as best it could with the United States.[3] The upshot was the Treaty of San Lorenzo de El Escorial, which Americans called Pinckney's Treaty, signed in 1795. Spain gave up its claims north of thirty-one degrees and permitted Americans to sail freely on the Mississippi and deposit ocean-bound goods duty-free at New Orleans (see Chapter 2). That was the famous "right of deposit" that Americans had been arguing for—in modern terms, the right to ship and transfer goods "in bond." In 1798, accordingly, the Spanish governor at Natchez turned the town over to the United States.

To Americans west of the mountains, this seemed a natural and inevitable solution to festering disputes—an attitude that characterized, one way or another, the whole Florida story. To Madrid the treaty seemed an expedient and generous move. To Spanish colonial administrators in New Orleans like Governor Hector Carondelet, Godoy and the king had trashed years of hard work by himself and his predecessor, Esteban Miró. They had tried to stave off American incursions by making treaties of friendship and commerce with the Choctaws, encouraging immigration, and, as far as possible, building forts and creating a "human frontier" between the colony and the ever expanding Americans. Later Spanish historians considered the 1795 treaty a disaster, the removal of any barrier to American expansion, the first great step that led to the final loss of Florida in 1819, and of northern Mexico later on. "From that time on," wrote one, "the Floridas would be reduced to a narrow strip of practically indefensible land, which irremediably would fall into the hands of the Americans. . . . Unpopulated, without money or troops, and affected by the crisis in Spain resulting from the Napoleonic invasions, they would be occupied little by little from left to right until they would be given up by the Treaty of 1819."[4] Down the slippery slope went Florida, beginning in 1795.

It received another shove when France retook Louisiana and sold it to the United States, isolating Florida all the more. The Spanish governor at Natchez warned Godoy in 1797 that if Louisiana was lost, ultimately the United States would take Mexico as well.[5] More immediately, the American acquisition of Louisiana and New Orleans in 1803 bore repercussions for Spanish Florida in two ways. It laid the lower Mississippi Valley completely open to American traders, troops, and settlers. In they poured—not all of them remaining chastely on the west side of the Mississippi opposite West Florida, or in New Orleans itself. Some ventured into Baton Rouge and other land south of the thirty-first parallel. So an incursion of American population began, exactly what Miró and Carondelet had tried to prevent in the 1790s. Second, the treaty of purchase between the United States and France was vague on just what had been purchased: "the same extent that it [Louisiana] now has in the hands of Spain, & that it had when France possessed it" up to 1762. Did that include West Florida or any part of it? Jefferson, Madison, and (once the Louisiana Purchase treaty was signed) Monroe maintained that it did. French, Spanish, and British authorities said it did not.

In the long view, then, the American conquest of the Floridas began with the peace treaties of 1782–1783, placing the new nation next to Spanish Louisiana and Florida. It went on for almost forty more years until the final ratification of the Adams-Onís treaty in 1821. After the peace of 1783 came the Treaty of San Lorenzo in 1795; then the Louisiana Purchase; and finally the War of 1812 and the Creek War in 1814. From the American standpoint, then and since, all of this was a natural and inevitable process. It was one essential step toward filling out Jefferson's "empire for liberty." In reading almost any American account of it, one senses a certain inevitability: that Spain would lose Florida and the United States would gain it. Yet prior to 1795 or 1800 there was no such inevitability. Events conspired after 1800, in a near-perfect storm, to end Spain's imperial control.

Through these events, the Spanish lost a colony that had lasted, except for the brief British phase, for three centuries. It was a loss that threatened or foretold even greater losses in Mexico and farther south. There is a Spanish saying, *mi casa es su casa*—"my house is your house"— expressing gracious hospitality. The much-revered Virginia dynasty of Jefferson, Madison, and Monroe, which oversaw the Louisiana Purchase and the piece-by-piece engorgement of the Floridas, reversed it. For them, *su casa es mi casa*—your house is my house.

That house, to be sure, fell upon a run of bad luck as the eighteenth century closed. Spain's worldwide empire, begun by Columbus, was still holding its own when Carlos III died in 1788. English-language histories of Spain often leave the impression that Spain was done for after the defeat of the 1588 Armada, but in truth, it remained a major power in Europe and the New World around 1780, when Bernardo de Gálvez chased the British out of the Gulf Coast. Nevertheless, if Spain was still strong in the Americas in eighteenth-century terms, it was vastly over-extended in nineteenth-century terms, just as France had been in Canada and Louisiana in the Seven Years' War. An entirely new phenomenon suddenly confronted them both: the unprecedented population growth of the United States. The frontier Americans of the South and West were surging against Spain's Louisiana and Florida borders by 1800, outnumbering Spaniards everywhere.

Spain was then abruptly cursed by bad luck and terrible leadership. Carlos IV, succeeding his father in 1788, was amiable, indecisive, and uxorious, "less prepared by aptitude, upbringing, education, and experience to confront the far more difficult decades after [his father's] death."[6] Dominated by his queen, María Luisa, who has flatly been described as "lascivious," Carlos IV allowed policy making to be controlled by a young guards officer, Godoy, who became first minister in 1792. His intrigues and bad decisions, unchecked by the bedazzled monarchs, coincided with the reign of terror in France, including the beheading of Carlos IV's cousin, Louis XVI, and his queen, Marie Antoinette. Spain declared war on republican France, was invaded but then made peace with France, and thereby became an enemy of Britain. The Royal Navy cut off Spain's traffic with its colonies, most harmfully stopping the flow of silver from Mexico, Spain's crucial source of income. The naval contest climaxed with Britain's great victory at the battle of Trafalgar off Cádiz in 1805.

By then Napoleon was ruling France. From his standpoint, Spain was becoming more albatross than useful ally. In March 1808 the crown prince of Spain overthrew his parents and became king as Fernando VII. Godoy barely escaped a lynch mob. But a fed-up Napoleon forced both kings to abdicate, and installed his brother Joseph Bonaparte as king of Spain, backed up by a French army. Britain counterattacked, and the ensuing Peninsular War continued until Napoleon's defeat in 1814. Spanish authority dwindled to a regency ostensibly loyal to Fernando. Holed up in Cádiz, this regency drew up a limited-monarchy, liberal constitution in 1812 in Fernando's absence. When he returned, he rejected the 1812 constitution and reascended his throne as absolute monarch. From then until 1820, when liberals forced him to accept the 1812 constitution, Fernando ruled as an intemperate autocrat, replacing ministers and reversing policies without warning or good reason.

The significance of this woeful Spanish tale is that no one, no king and not the Cádiz regency, enforced, implemented, or even devised any consistent policy toward Florida or any other colony. In Mexico and across South America, independence movements flourished. Florida was but one of the many colonies—indeed, all those in Central and South America—that Spain lost in the 1810s. Still a major power in 1792, Spain was reduced permanently in just over two decades of French Revolution and Napoleonic Wars to lower status in Europe and the world. The United States, its North American neighbor, could not help but benefit. Lord Acton was right. Absolute power corrupted absolutely. But Acton did not say how fast it could happen.

THE FIRST NIBBLE: WEST FLORIDA, 1810–1813

By 1810, the Louisiana Purchase was seven years old, and Anglo-Americans clearly dominated the government, commerce, and population of New Orleans, St. Louis, and the riverine settlements in between. The U.S. Census in that year found 77,000 diverse people in the Territory of Orleans (soon to become the state of Louisiana). Thousands of white Americans, their black slaves, and eight thousand to ten thousand white, free black, and slave refugees from war-shredded Haiti and Santo Domingo swelled the city and the land around the great river as far north as Natchez and beyond. In adjacent parts of the United States, the 1810 census counted 262,000 in Tennessee, 407,000 in Kentucky, 252,000 in Georgia, and 40,000 in the Mississippi Territory, which included present Alabama—and none of these figures included Indians. The Creeks alone numbered over 15,000, most of them living along the Alabama and Chattahoochee Rivers.

The whites and blacks, moreover, were newcomers. Georgia and the Mississippi Territory, Tennessee and Kentucky, and, west of the river, Louisiana, Arkansas, and Missouri were all places where slavery flourished and where the influx of settlers multiplied state populations by three, six, even twelve times in a decade. These were frontiers of settlement, southern-style, filling up with new people at speeds unknown in Europe since the Middle Ages, if ever. Whoever was already there was under severe pressure to get out of the way. There was no time for assimilation and in any case it was not wanted, since the "whoevers" were Indians and free blacks, and, in the Floridas, the Spanish.

The governors and garrisons of Spanish Florida had been aware of this population onslaught since at least the 1780s. Before the 1795 Treaty of San Lorenzo gave the United States all Spanish claims north

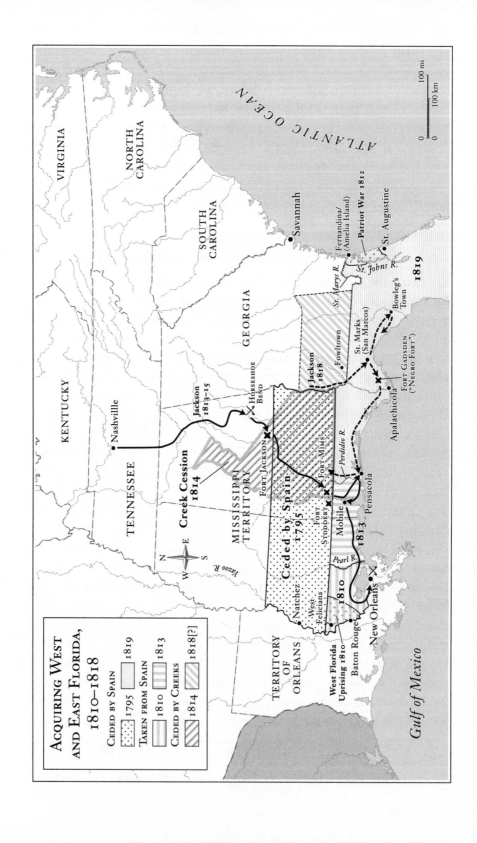

ACQUIRING WEST
AND EAST FLORIDA,
1810–1818

CEDED BY SPAIN

[:::::::] 1795   1819

TAKEN FROM SPAIN

1810   1813

CEDED BY CREEKS

1814   1818[?]

VIRGINIA

NORTH
CAROLINA

SOUTH
CAROLINA

GEORGIA

KENTUCKY

TENNESSEE

Nashville

MISSISSIPPI
TERRITORY

TERRITORY
OF
ORLEANS

Creek Cession
1814

Ceded by Spain
1795

Jackson
1813–15

HORSESHOE
BEND

FORT JACKSON

FORT MIMS

Natchez

West
Feliciana

Baton Rouge

West Florida
Uprising 1810

1810

New Orleans

Pearl R.

FORT
STODDERT

Mobile

1813

Pensacola

Perdido R.

FORT GADSDEN
("NEGRO FORT")

Apalachicola

Bowleg's
Town

1819

St. Marks
(San Marcos)

Fowltown

Jackson
1818

St. Johns R.

St. Marys R.

Fernandina/
(Amelia Island)

Patriot War 1812

St. Augustine

Savannah

ATLANTIC OCEAN

Gulf of Mexico

Yazoo R.

N
W   E
S

100 mi
100 km
0
0

of the thirty-first parallel, Governors Miró, Carondelet, and Gayoso de Lemos at New Orleans and Natchez had tried to encourage immigration and create a white "human frontier" loyal to Spain while also promoting the Choctaws, Creeks, and other Indians as buffers against the Anglo-Americans. Godoy's treaty reversed those efforts. Britain had been trying the same thing in the Old Northwest, giving up the idea only after 1814. Spain could never export enough people to fill Florida, nor could it fill Texas, which soon was also under demographic siege. In stable demographic times, Spain's trade with the Indians could go on, if not altogether smoothly, at least profitably to each side. Naval and military garrisons sprinkled along the coasts were sufficient defense against unfriendly Europeans. But when the United States' exploding population began pressing against it, Florida confronted something new. Quite aside from ambition, expansionist ideology, military force, and the catastrophes that befell Spain after 1792, the demographic handwriting was on the wall.

When Spain recovered the Floridas in 1783, West Florida consisted of the present Louisiana panhandle, the Natchez area, the Gulf coasts of present Mississippi and Alabama including Mobile, and the western part of the present Florida panhandle. It was a hard-to-defend coastal strip whose main and almost only settlements were Natchez, Baton Rouge, Biloxi, Pascagoula, Mobile, and Pensacola. With about one thousand residents and a garrison of three hundred to four hundred in 1810, Pensacola was the largest. The whole province, according to a census in 1795, had 8,390 people, and it may have had several thousand more by 1810–1813, as Anglo-Americans supplemented the chiefly French-Creole colonial population.

East Florida had even fewer. Censuses counted 4,700 in 1793 and about 5,000 in 1810–1816, more than half in and around St. Augustine. The only other significant towns were Fernandina, sixty miles north,

American uprisings took place in part of the present-day Louisiana panhandle in 1810 and in present-day northeast Florida (the "patriot war") in 1812. Much of what is now Alabama was extorted from the Creeks in the Treaty of Fort Jackson in August 1814. Lines trace the routes of Andrew Jackson's two ethnic-cleansing expeditions: in 1813–1815 against the Creeks, Spanish, and British, culminating in the Battle of New Orleans on January 8, 1815, and in 1818 into East Florida against the Spanish and the Seminoles.

Spain surrendered the Yazoo strip (the lower third of Mississippi and Alabama) in the Treaty of San Lorenzo of 1795. Americans invaded and occupied Spanish West Florida from the Mississippi to the Pearl River in 1810, and from the Pearl to the Perdidido in 1813.

with a few hundred; St. Marks (San Marcos), on the Gulf, with 189 people (only three of them women) in 1803; and Apalachicola, hardly more than a warehouse for Panton, Leslie, the Indian traders. St. Augustine was truly a mix of Spaniards, free blacks, and black slaves, and north of it to the Georgia border lived Anglo-Americans and black slaves, and hardly any Spanish. Surrounding them all were thousands of Indians, chiefly Mikasukis, today often called (along with Muskogulges) Seminoles. Outside the capital and the garrisons, Spain was so thin on the ground as to be invisible. Yet West and East Florida were Spanish territories, by treaty, international law, and historic tradition.

Florida's borders, everyone agreed, were the Atlantic, the Gulf of Mexico, and (on the north) the thirty-first parallel and the lines and rivers forming the Georgia-Florida border. To the west, however, everyone did not agree. Was anything else east of New Orleans really part of Louisiana? The French had governed the strip from New Orleans east to the Perdido River from New Orleans for convenience, but turned it over to Britain in 1762 because it was part of West Florida, never part of Louisiana.

When President Jefferson sent Monroe to join Livingston in Paris in the spring of 1803, he instructed them to buy New Orleans and West Florida if the French would sell them. Before signing the 1803 treaty of purchase, Livingston wrote Secretary of State Madison that West Florida was not part of Louisiana and could not have been ceded to Spain because in 1762 France had ceded the Floridas to Britain. Madison clearly knew this, since he told Monroe in March 1803 (again, prior to the Purchase) to go to Madrid and buy West Florida from Spain if Spain still owned it—which it did, having taken Pensacola, Mobile, Baton Rouge, Natchez, and the surrounding area by conquest from Britain in 1779–1781. France was nowhere around.

In June, however, within days after signing the treaty, Livingston and Monroe were claiming that West Florida was part of the Purchase. Jefferson and Madison were also saying that by August. If so, why did Monroe then prepare to go to Madrid, as he had been authorized before the treaty, to buy the Floridas? The French dissuaded him, telling him that the Spanish were not eager to discuss it (in fact they were furious about the Purchase). Jefferson "insisted on receiving from Spain a territory which that power claimed it had never sold and which France denied having bought."[7]

From the fall of 1803 onward, Jefferson and his followers maintained that West Florida belonged to the United States, despite the U.S. position prior to the Purchase and despite explicit contrary statements from Paris, Madrid, and even London. Jefferson's then-loyal supporter in the House of Representatives, John Randolph, introduced a bill in November 1803 annexing most of West Florida to the Mississippi Territory and authorizing the president to create a customs district for it. This bill, called the Mobile Act, passed Congress and Jefferson signed it on February 24, 1804. It was a splendid case of unilateralism and fact denial. Spanish garrisons existed at Baton Rouge, Mobile, and Pensacola. The French governor who turned over New Orleans, Laussat, made clear that West Florida was not included. Barbé-Marbois said it was not. In a note of February 24, 1804, the Spanish government intended "to destroy the pretensions of the United States . . . to situate the eastern limits on the Rio Perdido" (i.e., east of Mobile), confirming that "it is beyond any doubt" that the eastern limit of Louisiana was the Mississippi and the lakes near New Orleans, and "that Spain possessed Florida as Florida and not as Louisiana."[8]

On December 21, 1804, Talleyrand, still foreign minister, categorically denied that West Florida had ever been part of Louisiana. "There could be no room for doubts," he said, "because after 1762 West Florida was publicly and officially known as a distinct territory from Louisiana." The United States acknowledged this in the 1795 San Lorenzo treaty when it agreed that its boundary with Spain was the middle of the Mississippi River.[9] In February 1805 the French and Spanish ministers in Washington, General Louis-Marie Turreau and the Marques de Casa Yrujo, told Secretary Madison that Napoleon wanted Madison to know that the 1800 retrocession of Louisiana (and therefore the 1803 Purchase) included "only Louisiana, with the eastern limits traced by the Treaty of Peace of 1763," as modified by the 1795 Treaty of San Lorenzo, and also that "West Florida should remain in its entirety within the hands of Spain which had obtained it by conquest, and by the Treaty of 1783 with England." Talleyrand, on Napoleon's orders, dismissed the U.S. pretension to West Florida as "without foundation." Casa Yrujo added that his king "did not have the intention of extending the limits of Louisiana to the east of the Mississippi, Iberville [River], and lakes Maurepas and Pontchartrain out to the sea."[10] Casa Yrujo, on learning of the Mobile Act early in March 1804, protested to Jefferson and Madison that it was "an outrageous libel."[11] It could not have been plainer. Everybody except the Jeffersonians agreed that West Florida was West Florida, not Louisiana, and that the United States had not bought West Florida in 1803.

Nonetheless, Jefferson and his officers, though they backed off from occupying anything south of the thirty-first parallel, soon set up a customs office just north of that line at Fort Stoddert on the Mobile River. The administration, as well as U.S. major general James Wilkinson and Governor William C. C. Claiborne in New Orleans, continued to claim West Florida. Americans in the area took them at their word. On August 7, 1804, the brothers Nathan and Samuel Kemper, with thirty men, tried to capture the Spanish fort at Baton Rouge, a largely Anglo town by then. The defenders under Captain Carlos Grand-Pré held them off. U.S. regulars (Wilkinson's troops) detained the Kempers, thus ending the uprising, but did not turn them over to the Spanish authorities.[12] This first filibuster set the pattern for the next six years: local Anglo rebels attempting to take the area from the Spanish, but being held off; nearby American authorities neither supporting nor prosecuting the rebels; verbal support, but nothing stronger, coming from Washington. Material support would clearly have been an act of war, as Jefferson and Madison realized. They were eager, however, to accept any territory that came their way without it.

By 1809, Madison was advised that five-sixths of the people of West Florida were living at Baton Rouge, and that nine-tenths of them were Anglos. The garrisons at Baton Rouge, Mobile, and Pensacola were undermanned. The Spanish governor at Pensacola since 1795, a fifty-year-old Catalan named Vicente Folch y Juan, visited Louisiana governor Claiborne at New Orleans several times in early 1809 to discuss peaceful coexistence or a gradual American accession, though without result. In August Folch warned his superior in Havana, Captain-General Salvador de Muro y Salazar, the Marques de Someruelos, that several thousand Anglo-Americans were coming downriver to New Orleans on flatboats every year, and many of them were staying in Baton Rouge, Mobile, and even Pensacola instead of returning north. Rather than clamp down on them or leave them to incite nearby Indians, Folch recommended that they be welcomed.

Claiborne had listened noncommittally to Folch but apparently concluded that capturing West Florida would be easy. In April 1810 he visited Madison (by then president) in Washington. As soon as he returned to New Orleans (June 14), he asked Colonel William Wykoff to lead an insurrection near Baton Rouge. On June 20 Secretary of State Robert

Smith gave congruent instructions to Governor David Holmes of the Mississippi Territory to ready his militia in case civil disturbances erupted in either West or East Florida.[13] "The American government," wrote the first historian of these events, "was now ready to abandon oblique diplomacy for underhand intervention. . . . Some finesse, to use no uglier word, seemed necessary. A revolt, or at any rate, a united representation, exhibiting every appearance of spontaneity, would best serve the purpose."[14]

Although the United States could not send regular troops into West Florida (despite the Mobile Act and repeated claims that it was part of the United States) without committing an act of war against Spain, the settlers in and around Baton Rouge—most of them Anglo-Americans— were eager for independence. The militias of Orleans and Mississippi Territories would back them up as long as war did not result. At that moment, early in the Peninsular War, Spain simply did not have a government that its colonial administrators could trust. Someruelos in Havana was focused on insurrections in Venezuela and Mexico, not West Florida. Isolated in Pensacola, Governor Folch therefore began to hint at ceding the area. Florida was once described by an acquisition-minded American as a pistol whose barrel pointed at New Orleans. The Spanish could have reversed the metaphor and called Florida—once it fell into U.S. hands—a pistol pointed directly at Cuba.

On June 23, 1810, a reported five hundred settlers met at a plantation north of Baton Rouge. They complained about anarchic conditions in the area, and then struck "the first blow for liberty" by inviting the Anglos in neighboring districts to meet with them to elect a common council. For the next several weeks, they constantly declared their loyalty to Fernando VII and hoped—publicly—for his return to power, while effectively taking control themselves. The governor of the district, Charles Dehault Delassus, approved of the meetings as long as they observed, and preserved, Spanish law. How disingenuous they were, and how unrealistic the governor was, is unclear from the sources; subsequent actions suggest both.

On July 8 to 10, Baton Rouge joined in. On July 25 delegates from several districts met at St. John's Plains (moving soon to Baton Rouge) as a constitutional convention to create a legislature and appoint other officials for themselves, while remaining ostensibly loyal to Spain and the governor. This convention stayed in session until August 29 and was "more in the nature of a revolutionary congress than of a convention for . . . framing a new government."[15] It is remarkable how faithfully, in fact legalistically, the delegates clung to the forms of Anglo-American law, as displayed throughout the convention proceedings. They were no mudsills or peasant rabble, but rather the larger planters, the merchants, the colonels and captains of militia: in short, the upper crust. (The rumbustious Kempers were neither delegates to this convention nor office-holders within it.) An Anglo-American elite was replacing a Spanish elite and what was left of a French Creole elite. If any element of class conflict was present, it lay in the promise of more draconian control by the Anglos over slaves, fugitive slaves, and Indians.

On July 27 the convention sent a remonstrance to Delassus referring to "the existing grievances and dangers to which the people and their property are exposed." They proposed to exercise executive, legislative, and judicial functions as a committee to protect public order—with the governor's "intire approbation" and as "part of the Dominions of our beloved King Ferdinand the seventh." They even offered to pay Delassus's salary.

The governor, of a Flemish family that had lived in Louisiana since the early eighteenth century, was in his late forties and had been a military officer for over twenty years and governor of Baton Rouge for seven. He well knew that he could not squelch the uprising, which in no way conformed to Spanish law. Without help from Someruelos in Havana his sole option was to temporize politely. He replied how "tranquilizing and satisfactory to me" it was to be assured of the convention's loyalty to the king, which he "did not doubt a moment." He was sure they had nothing to do with the "seditious pasquinades" and "false rumors which are spread in the different Districts," and he was "persuaded that every thing which you announce to me will be without doubt conformable to the laws under which we live so happily." He thanked them for their "generous testimony to support my salary at your charge," but was "very satisfied & honoured by the pay I receive from the King."[16]

By late August this minuet spun into the convention's creation of four militia regiments, complete with officers chosen from among themselves. Delassus accepted even this, with some small changes. He continued his politely benevolent acquiescence well into September. But he sent a message through a loyal Anglo to Governor Folch, his superior at Pensacola, admitting that he had an insurrection on his hands and asking for forces to put it down. The insurgents intercepted the letter and agreed on the "futility of continuing their mock allegiance to Spain" and their need for "a quick, decisive blow for liberty."[17]

Early on Sunday, September 23, eighty insurgents overwhelmed the fort at Baton Rouge, killing commander Louis Grand-Pré and another soldier. The convention deposed Delassus and asked Governor David Holmes of the Mississippi Territory, based nearby just east of Natchez, to be on guard to prevent a possible slave revolt like St. Domingue's (a continuing nightmare among American planters in both Floridas). Holmes told the U.S. Army colonel in the area to send troops to pacify Baton Rouge. The conventioners declared "this Territory of West Florida to be a free and independent State" on September 26, and they pledged themselves to support it "with our lives and fortunes" (but not adding, as the signers of 1776 did, their "sacred honor"). On September 28 they sent a copy of their declaration to Holmes asking him to forward it to President Madison in the hope that the United States would "take the present Government and people of this State under their immediate and special protection, as an integral and inalienable portion of the United States."[18] Holmes obliged on October 3, adding that the uprising, the declaration of independence, and the annexation request meant that "the views of our government have been in great measure realized."[19] Madison's and Secretary Smith's instructions of June had borne fruit.

On October 27 Madison issued a proclamation, annexing West Florida as far east as the Pearl River to the United States as part of the Orleans Territory. It became the panhandle of Louisiana when the state was admitted to the Union two years later. Madison's proclamation insisted that the rebels had nothing to do with this annexation except to make available what was already U.S. territory, because West Florida had been part of the Louisiana Purchase—the Jeffersonians' consistent line since May 1803.

The Baton Rouge insurgents, led by their new governor, Fulwar Skipwith, expected to be admitted as a state of their own. They "fumed" and "resented" Madison's attachment of them to Louisiana. They even threatened armed resistance. But Claiborne's arrival with a few dozen U.S. regulars put an end to that, and by early December, the Baton Rouge district became effectively American. A local chronicler later admitted that "Madison had authorized, by a few strokes of his pen, the seizure of territory belonging to 'a just and friendly power.' " The president also "sent a sharp message to the Conventionalists through Governor Holmes, to the effect that their independence was an impertinence, and that their designs on public lands were something worse."[20] (The insurgents had made clear in their declaration that they felt entitled to such spoils.)

On December 5, President Madison informed Congress that West Florida had been occupied in accord with his proclamation of October 27. On December 7, with Governors Claiborne and Holmes present, the American flag replaced the insurgents' despite Skipwith's promise to resist to the death. On December 18, Senator William Branch Giles of Virginia introduced a bill to incorporate West Florida into the Territory of Orleans. Senator Timothy Pickering of Massachusetts opposed it. He produced Talleyrand's letter of December 21, 1804, to General Armstrong, the American minister in Paris, flatly denying that West Florida was part of the Louisiana Purchase. The letter had been kept secret by the Jefferson and Madison administrations. Instead of admitting that, the Madison-friendly Senate on January 2, 1811, censured Pickering for making it public.[21]

As a final bit of mendacity, Secretary of State Smith—who had instructed Governor Holmes on how to support the insurrection—told the French minister, Turreau, on October 31 that Madison's annexation proclamation was simply a response to Britain's occupation of Pensacola (which had not happened) and was essential to prevent the British from marching on to Baton Rouge (a fictitious threat). "I swear, General," said Smith, "on my honor as a gentleman, not only that we are strangers to everything that has happened, but even that the Americans who have appeared there either as agents or leaders are enemies of the Executive."[22]

And so the soon-to-be Louisiana panhandle was annexed to the United States in late 1810. Yet Madison's proclamation claimed all of West Florida, which extended east beyond Pensacola. Getting it took some time, however. The effort began immediately after the Baton Rouge insurgents declared independence and before Madison proclaimed the annexation. On October 10, the Baton Rouge leaders invited "the people inhabiting the Mobile and Pensacola district" to join the uprising, and on October 28 they authorized two commissioners to go and persuade them. One of the two was the firebrand Reuben Kemper, who "hated them [the Spanish] as much as any man is capable of hatred" and whose two brothers had led the 1804 uprising at Baton Rouge.

On October 24, 1810, Kemper arrived at Fort Stoddert, just over the border above Mobile. He must have been dismayed to learn that Folch had reinforced Mobile and that the chief federal officer at Stoddert, District Judge Harry Toulmin, was warning local Americans not to filibuster into Spanish territory.[23] Toulmin had come to the United States in 1792 from England with Joseph Priestley, the discoverer of oxygen, and through him became known and trusted by Jefferson, who appointed him federal judge for the Tombigbee District of the Mississippi Territory in 1804, and by Madison. He served until 1819 and, during the strife of 1810–1811, he largely succeeded—sometimes at the risk of his life—in dampening the lawless zealotry of the Americans around him who were hell-bent to march on Mobile. Toulmin also reported to President Madison each week's events, stressing his efforts at restraining his neighbors from breaking the neutrality laws. He did not appear to realize that Madison tacitly and secretly supported settler aggression in the Floridas.

Throughout October and November Toulmin reported that some "rash act" might touch off a general conflict. Folch, he wrote, might make a deal, which would short-circuit a coup by the insurgents, which would have undercut American as well as Spanish civil authority. At that moment they numbered only between sixty and two hundred, but they kept claiming that one thousand more were on their way from Baton Rouge. Those reinforcements never showed up, and when Kemper and his associates threatened to march on Mobile early in December, Toulmin arrested them. On December 22, U.S. captain Edmund Gaines with fifty men asked the *comandante* at Mobile, Cayetano Perez, to surrender the plaza and fort. Perez replied that he was not authorized to do so, and needed to consult Folch. Perez also talked down Colonel Thomas Cushing, who arrived off Mobile Bay on January 2, 1811, with five gunboats and 250 men. Toulmin defused Cushing, and the threat of armed takeover receded.[24] Mobile remained Spanish in 1811.

The diplomatic offensive continued, however. While Toulmin was doing his best to restrain the filibusters north of Mobile, Folch told Someruelos at Havana that if no aid arrived by January he would have to turn over West Florida to American officials. Better them than Kemper's mob. On December 2, Folch sent a letter to Secretary of State Smith through Colonel John McKee, the U.S. agent to the Choctaws. Folch offered to transfer West Florida *on two conditions:* if he had received no help from Havana or Mexico within a month, and if no diplomatic negotiations had begun. On January 3, 1811, Madison sent a secret message to Congress, enclosing Folch's letter, asking for a joint resolution authorizing the United States to take any part of the Floridas if Spain agreed to it, or if a "foreign power" (i.e., Britain) threatened to seize it. Congress obliged on January 15, authorizing a takeover if the "local authority of said territory" approved it. "Local authority," of course, could mean the Spanish governor or it could mean insurgents, if the United States chose to recognize them as such "authority."

The more immediate possibility was Folch's offer of December 2. After discussion with Madison and the secretary of state, McKee replied to Folch that his offer was accepted and the United States would proceed immediately to occupy the rest of West Florida—completely ignoring Folch's two conditions. On January 30, 1811, Governor Claiborne announced West Florida as taken, except for Mobile itself.

The Spanish did not quite see it that way. The Regency Council—the rump Spanish government in Cádiz loyal to Fernando VII—instead was discussing whether to declare war. The Spanish minister in Washington protested vehemently and frequently. A Spanish historian, echoing the documents, called it a usurpation, and said that Madison had resorted to "intrigue, subornation, seduction by force."[25] On February 27, 1811, Folch told McKee that Someruelos and the viceroyalty of Mexico *were* helping him, that he had been ordered to hold West Florida "at all costs," and that he would follow those orders. On March 3, Congress forbade publication of its January 15 resolution. It did not become public until April 20, 1813, when the Mobile-Pensacola front heated up again. Folch apologized to Someruelos on April 5 for having made his December 2 offer. He reported on April 22 that American forces were massed against Mobile, and that he would sooner give it to them than to Kemper and his crowd. Someruelos said no. Kemper and company did "occupy and plunder" Biloxi and Pascagoula, and Americans took Dauphin Island, opposite Mobile harbor. Claiborne considered attaching them to the impending state of Louisiana. Then he realized how hard it was to "find enough literate citizens to fill the public offices."[26] Thus Mississippi and Alabama gained their Gulf coasts thanks to their liberators' illiteracy. For the rest of 1811 and until early 1813, despite periodic threats and passing gunboats, Mobile and Pensacola remained Spanish.

EAST FLORIDA AND THE "PATRIOT WAR" OF 1812

Balked in West Florida, the Madison administration and border filibusters refocused their efforts on East Florida. The strategy was similar: inspire a local uprising; do not commit the United States officially or publicly; rely on local governors, militias, and private citizens rather than U.S. regulars as far as possible; when the uprising succeeds, recognize it as the "local authority"; then annex the supplicant territory to the United States. On the face of it, the job seemed simpler than the conquest of West Florida, because East Florida was a smaller place—not geographically, but practically. Although it included the entire peninsula, the Spanish settlements were almost all confined to what is now the extreme northeast corner of the state of Florida, from the Georgia line where the St. Marys River meets the sea to just south of St. Augustine. This was a strip about one hundred miles long and twenty miles wide, from just west of the St. Johns River to the ocean. Two-thirds of the population of a few thousand lived in St. Augustine, the 250-year-old capital, and were Spanish-speakers. North of the capital lived a chiefly Anglo and African population on plantations and at the settlement of Fernandina, on the northern tip of Amelia Island. More than 150 miles west, on the Gulf coast, lay San Marcos (St. Marks), a tiny outpost; a further one hundred miles west was the trading post at Apalachicola; and still another hundred miles west was Pensacola. St. Augustine could defend itself, but the other places were almost unreachable, given the difficulty of overland travel and the time required to reach them by sea. Such was the small and scattered European population.

Outside of St. Augustine the people included more blacks than whites, and more Indians than either. Planters in Georgia had reason, from their viewpoint, to seek change in East Florida. They distrusted the Spanish, hated the Indians, and feared the free blacks, many of them fugitives from their own plantations who had taken refuge with Indians and whose very existence kept alive fears of a slave revolt. Haiti was ever in their minds. No immediate population pressure pushed Georgians and Tennesseans across the Florida border. But the pervading sense of the rightness and inevitability of American expansion and the injustice of Spanish rule and religion underpinned an aggressive stance among the border planters as well as among militia leaders and politicians in both Georgia and more distant Tennessee.

How to justify a takeover? Not even Jefferson and Madison claimed that East Florida had ever been part of Louisiana and therefore of the 1803 Purchase. They could only declare that East Florida, especially after parts of West Florida became American, was of no use to Spain, and that Spain still owed damages to Americans for closing the port of New Orleans in late 1802. With these almost frivolous arguments the Spanish scarcely agreed. But with the Peninsular War tearing up their country, and with political and imperial authority divided between the intruder king, Joseph Bonaparte, and the loyalist regency in Cádiz, they were in no position to defend themselves. Nevertheless, they managed to do so for several more years.

Concrete American steps against Spanish East Florida began with Madison's January 1811 secret message to Congress, followed by Congress's obliging passage of the January 15 "no transfer" resolution. It authorized the executive to take any part of the Floridas, if Spain or whatever "local authority" controlled it would let it go, or if a foreign power threatened to capture it. The only likely such foreign power was Britain and, until Napoleon fell in early 1814, Britain made no thrust at Florida or the Gulf Coast. (Later in 1814 would be different.) But if a "local authority" appeared and invited the Americans in, then the "no transfer" resolution gave Madison a pretext—first to support that authority (i.e., foment its insurgency against the Spanish), then to ensure its control (using nearby American military and naval assets), and finally to annex the area as he did the Baton Rouge district in October 1810.

On January 26, 1811, eleven days after the "no transfer" resolution passed, President Madison had a conference with General George Mathews, a veteran of the Revolutionary War and a former governor of Georgia, and Colonel John McKee, the Choctaw agent. Madison gave Mathews instructions—some written, some not—to explore any discontent among American citizens living in East Florida (the planters) and to support their desires for a change in government. Exactly what kind of support? Mathews was assured of such military, naval, and financial backing as he might need. On paper, those assurances were vague, and what was not on paper was vaguer still. Moreover—and this was typical of the miscommunications that chronically characterized the Madison administration's conduct of the War of 1812—the secretaries of war and the navy were either not fully informed of the president's plans or were out of touch with Mathews at crucial times.

Mathews's instructions covered West Florida as well as East, and he and McKee first visited Governor Folch at Pensacola. They found that Folch's spine had been stiffened by orders from Captain-General Someruelos at Havana. Folch was not, after all, prepared to turn over the rest of West Florida to the Americans, as he had offered conditionally on December 2, 1810. The United States had not met his conditions, Someruelos had supported (or threatened) him, and the Americans backed off. Mathews and McKee therefore turned their attentions to East Florida.

On June 9, 1811, Mathews returned to St. Marys, Georgia, across the river from Amelia Island and Fernandina. Both towns were commercially vigorous, but while St. Marys chafed, at least nominally, under American trade restrictions in place since Jefferson's administration, Fernandina was virtually an open port. Mathews met with leading citizens of the St. Marys area, including planters James Seagrove and William and Lodowick Ashley, militia general John Floyd, and wealthy John Houston McIntosh. Capture of Fernandina would be good for business. More important to them, it would (they hoped) rid them not only of the Spanish but also the fugitive slaves and the threat of a slave rebellion. Mathews's orders also provided that participants in the "local authority" would be rewarded with land grants. On the Spanish side of the border, however, Mathews found that large planters and small farmers alike, as well as the commercial people (and smugglers) of Fernandina, were happy with things as they were. When Mathews proposed going to St. Augustine to persuade Enrique White, the Spanish governor, to turn over the province, one of the Florida planters warned him that "as sure as you open your mouth to White on the subject, you will die in chains in the Moro Castle [in Havana], and all the devils in hell can't save you."[27] Mathews dropped the idea and rode back to Georgia.

Despite the lack of enthusiasm he found in East Florida, on August 3 Mathews wrote Secretary of State James Monroe (who had replaced Smith in March) that East Florida was ripe for revolt. He needed two hundred guns and fifty swords from the local U.S. Army commander to arm the rebels. By late November Mathews had heard nothing from Monroe and had not succeeded in suborning Spanish soldiers or officials or in recruiting East Floridians. Yet he kept working on the Georgians around St. Marys and on nearby U.S. Army and Navy commanders. Colonel T. A. Smith of the army and Commodore Hugh Campbell of the navy both asked Washington for instructions. Neither heard back. By March 10, 1812, Mathews had not quite seventy men at hand, of whom only about nine were really Floridians. With them he intended to take St. Augustine. Colonel Smith left for a few days and the officer in charge, Major Jacint Laval, flatly refused to put troops under Mathews's command or provide matériel without explicit orders from Washington. Campbell waffled. Mathews had to back off from his St. Augustine plan and instead went after Fernandina. Campbell's gunboats blocked Fernandina harbor on March 15, and two days later entered it. The Spanish commander, Lieutenant Justo López, assumed their hostile intent. With only a token force and literally under the gun, he surrendered Fernandina and Amelia Island to McIntosh, Lodowick Ashley, and 250 insurgents. On March 19 Mathews and Colonel Smith arrived and accepted the "cession" of Fernandina to the United States.

The next step was to march on St. Augustine. Nearing the capital and its fort on March 26, the insurgents demanded surrender from Acting Governor Juan de Estrada (White had recently died), but he refused. The insurgents managed to capture a nearby deserted structure called "Moosa Old Fort" on April 11, but three days later a Spanish schooner hit them with a twenty-four-pound shot and they beat a retreat. Mathews reported to Madison and Monroe on April 16 that he had captured East Florida except for St. Augustine.

As yet unknown to Mathews, however, on April 4 the president and secretary of state had publicly disavowed him and his mission. The administration had just been exposed for buying a packet of fake spy letters. The Federalists in Congress, not quite yet a spent force, were splenetic. Mathews's whole adventure was about to become a further diplomatic embarrassment. It was unquestionably an act of war, against which the British and Spanish ministers had been protesting vehemently for months. Mathews was repudiated.

But Madison and Monroe were not through. On April 10 Monroe asked Governor David B. Mitchell of Georgia to take over American forces in East Florida, withdraw them (as tardily as possible, consistent with appearing to evacuate), and ask the Spanish governor to grant amnesty to the insurgents. On May 27 Monroe added that he did not expect, "if you should find it proper to withdraw the troops, that you should interfere to compel the patriots to surrender the country, or any part of it, to the Spanish authorities." Thus, "no better way of continuing Mathews's work could perhaps have been devised."[28]

On June 10, Sebastian Kindelán y O'Regan took over as governor at St. Augustine from Acting Governor Estrada. On June 11 Kindelán demanded of Mitchell and Colonel Smith that they pull U.S. forces out of his province within eleven days. Mitchell replied with excuses and repeated the request for amnesty. Kindelán commanded, for once, a superior Spanish force—not only the garrison and fort at St. Augustine, but also serious and effective help from the Seminoles. They also armed free blacks, which of course shocked the Georgians. The "patriot army" began falling back. A militia colonel up in Georgia named Daniel Newnan began gathering forces to back up the "patriots." In late September, he invaded Seminole territory. After winning an initial skirmish, Newnan's militiamen found themselves under siege and had to be rescued by Mitchell and Colonel Smith.[29] The Seminoles had helped slaves escape Georgia plantations, and now the former slaves helped them defeat Newnan.[30] Throughout the entire Florida story from 1810 to 1819, race conflict was always present, and the Creek and Seminole wars, about to erupt, would be the bloodiest episodes of all.

During the summer and fall of 1812, the Indian and black forces broke Smith's supply lines along the St. Johns River, terrorized insurgent sympathizers, and sent the Georgian invaders flying back home across the St. Marys. They "accomplished all that Kindelán hoped for," reducing the invaders to "an ineffective rabble."[31] The siege of St. Augustine was over, reported Kindelán on August 9. In October, Monroe transferred authority in East Florida from Mitchell to Major General Thomas Pinckney, but with orders not greatly different from Mitchell's (i.e., withdraw as slowly as possible and demand amnesty from Kindelán). On January 13, 1813, Monroe informed Pinckney that reinforcements were coming that would empower him to take St. Augustine. Monroe's excuse now was that since the United States was at war with Britain (and had been since June 18, 1812), and since Britain and Spain were allies, Florida was as good as British. Therefore the United States had to invade East Florida in order to beat the British to it.[32] On February 2, however, the Senate again—as it had the previous July—defeated an authorization to invade. Despite that, Pinckney was ordered to continue in East Florida. During February his and Colonel Smith's forces chased Seminoles around East Florida and burned many Seminole villages, including the main one, King Payne's Town.

Only on March 7 did the secretary of war inform Pinckney that since the Spanish government approved the amnesty for the insurgents, Pinckney should pull his troops from East Florida, including Fernandina, if Kindelán agreed. Kindelán did agree on March 31. On May 6,

1813, he took back Fernandina for Spain. East Florida was free of American insurgents or armies for the first time since March 1812, and it would remain so until December 1817. Outside of St. Augustine and Fernandina, however, the colony was devastated. The insurgents had become essentially marauders. They had pillaged virtually every plantation, farm, and outpost around St. Augustine, killed or run off cattle, and dispossessed settlers. Claims against the United States for supporting the insurgents were not settled for another forty years, and then often unfairly.[33] Quietly surreptitious conversations in Washington had led to blood all over the ground of East Florida.

As the "patriot war," so styled by its perpetrators, disintegrated into anarchy in late 1812 and early 1813, West Florida heated up again. Armed men gathered at New Orleans and in Tennessee with the object of taking Mobile, Pensacola, and finally St. Augustine. Andrew Jackson stepped on the Florida stage at this point, not to leave it until 1821.

Jackson once wrote to Governor William Claiborne, "I hate the Dons."[34] He certainly behaved like it: contemptuous, volatile, always aggressive toward Spain. With two thousand militiamen at Natchez, he was eager to march. But after the Senate defeated the East Florida authorization on February 2, 1813, Secretary of War John Armstrong told him to disband his troops; General Wilkinson's regulars in New Orleans would handle West Florida. On April 11, 1813, in the very week that Pinckney was leaving East Florida, Wilkinson arrived at Mobile with six hundred troops and five gunboats. Comandante Cayetano Perez had seventy men, unpaid and on the verge of starvation. Disobeying orders to fight to the death, he surrendered Mobile's Fort Carlota and evacuated to Pensacola (and was later court-martialed for doing so, but cleared). It was "the most flagrant U.S. attack on Spanish territory up to that time,"[35] and it was done by regular forces, not by filibusters. If Spain had had the power, the regency in Cádiz would probably have declared war. Months later, when it ordered the viceroy in Mexico and the captain-general in Cuba to mount a squadron to take Mobile back, the captain-general replied that it was impossible.[36] Mobile remained American from that point on, illegal though the occupation was.

The results of early 1813 for the United States were, then, evacuation of East Florida but capture of Mobile. The United States had annexed the western segment of West Florida, from the Mississippi to the Pearl River, under Madison's proclamation of October 1810. The middle segment, from the Pearl to the Perdido, including Pass Christian, Biloxi,

Pascagoula, and Mobile—now the Gulf coasts of Mississippi and Alabama—were captured by Wilkinson in April 1813. Although "it was an act of war to do so, whatever her [the United States'] claims," the occupation in American eyes simply fulfilled federal legislation of April 1812 declaring the area part of the Mississippi Territory.[37] The only part of Spanish West Florida still in Spanish hands was the easternmost strip from the Perdido, just west of Pensacola, to the Apalachicola, about 170 miles to the east. In practical terms that meant Pensacola itself. Bernardo de Gálvez had led a Spanish army out of New Orleans and pushed the British out of Baton Rouge in 1779, Mobile in 1780, and Pensacola in 1781, taking West Florida for Spain. In 1810–1818, however, war-wracked Spain could provide no resources to defend it from the Americans.

THE CREEK WAR, 1813–1815

The next phase of the Florida story was a devastating dismemberment of the Creek nation, and it flowed seamlessly from the "patriot war" in East Florida. There were several contributing causes: the Seminoles were already deeply involved; Americans kept coming into Creek country north of the Gulf coast; and the Creeks were divided among themselves. As was true of British-Indian alliances around the Great Lakes, the system of alliances that Spain had constructed with the Creeks and other tribes had fractured as American pressure and presence increased. Some Indians chose to be friendly and cooperative, others resistant. The great confederator Tecumseh and his brother Tenskwatawa the Prophet were outstanding resistance leaders. They are often thought of as Shawnees and hence northern Indians. But the two were Creek on their mother's side. In October 1811 they and twenty-four companions lectured five thousand Creeks at Tuckabatchee in Alabama on the forthcoming inevitable battle with the Americans. Many young Upper Creeks, known as Red Sticks because they painted their weapons red, and some Seminoles were inspired by Tecumseh's message. After the "patriot war" the Seminoles needed no advice on who their enemies were, nor did the Creeks. They were ready to assist their Spanish friends, but far more, they were prepared to fight for their homelands—much of present Georgia, Florida, Alabama, and Mississippi—and their ways of life. Initial aggressiveness in the summer of 1813 seemed to pay off.

American pressure of all sorts—unrelenting settlement advance, a new road from Georgia straight through Creek country to Fort Stoddert, the spread of slave-based cotton agriculture—brought out the divisions common to so many Indian nations over whether or how much to accommodate encroaching whites. By the early nineteenth century, black and Indian mixing had been going on for generations, and many "Creeks" or "Seminoles" were in fact black. As such, in the eyes of the advancing whites, their very existence inspired slaves to rebel or run off. The Creeks' trade with the British and Spanish was disrupted after 1810. The harangues of Tecumseh and the Prophet whipped up the traditionalism of many younger Upper Creeks while others, Upper and Lower, clung to the hope of peaceful relations with the Americans. The Creek nation split over these issues to the point of civil war; in early 1813 border encounters degenerated into murderous battles.

On July 27, 1813, Upper Creeks beat back whites at Burnt Corn Creek north of Mobile and Pensacola. It was only a skirmish; two Americans died and probably several Indians. Yet it sparked a much larger battle on August 30 at Fort Mims on the Alabama, a few miles west of Burnt Corn and less than ten miles from Fort Stoddert. A thousand Red Sticks cut down about 250 whites—soldiers and settlers, men, women, and children. It was a great victory for the Red Sticks. Never, however, was a victory more Pyrrhic. Vengeance, led by Andrew Jackson, was swift, repeated, thorough, and devastating to the Creek nation.

On October 12, Jackson, a major general of Tennessee militia (his regular army commission at that rank did not come until June 1814), led 3,500 volunteers into northern Alabama. Pouncing on one Creek village or party after another, by the close of winter they had killed more than 700 Indians while losing 200 Georgia militiamen and fewer than 50 Tennesseans. On March 14 Jackson's army, by then 4,000 strong, arrived opposite the elaborate Creek fort at Horseshoe Bend on the Tallapoosa and faced more than 1,200 Creeks. The decisive face-off took place on March 27. The Americans lost 47, along with 23 Creek and Cherokee allies, while the Creeks suffered (by American estimate) 900 killed and 300 taken captive. This broke the Creeks. Since October probably 2,500, more than half of their effectives, had been killed or put out of action, while another 1,000 retreated into East Florida. They were through as a fighting force, and nearly through as a nation. No longer could the Spanish count on them. Britain, about to land thousands of guns at Apalachicola for the Creeks, was abruptly deprived of them as allies. Jackson's demolition therefore affected not only the Creeks. It also dented British objectives to recapture the Gulf Coast and New Orleans, and laid Pensacola and East Florida open to him, if he chose to ignore international boundaries and compound Wilkinson's act of war at Mobile. He so chose.

First he dealt with the Creeks. Determined to end their independence permanently, he met with their leaders at the newly built Fort Jackson, on the Alabama just north of present Birmingham, on August 1, 1814. A week later, under pressure, they signed a treaty requiring them to give up 23 million acres, about two-thirds of present Alabama and a third of Georgia. It was the bulk of their land. The signers represented about 8,200 Creeks who were not Jackson's Red Stick enemies—what was left of them had escaped to Florida—but his allies. As his biographer observed, "Jackson converted the Creek civil war into an enormous land grab. . . . [It was] the beginning of the end not only for the Creek Nation but for all Indians throughout the south and southwest." In Jackson's mind there was no other way. Sixteen years later, as president, he would sign the Indian Removal Act, which took the dispossessed Creeks well beyond the Mississippi.[38]

The dissident Red Sticks, numbering perhaps one thousand, regrouped around Pensacola. There, on August 5, Britain's Colonel Edward Nicholls landed with three ships and two hundred soldiers, with more to come, invited by Governor Mateo González Manrique as protection against an American attack. Spanish officials were almost as reluctant to welcome the British into the Floridas as they were the Americans, but González Manrique decided they were the lesser evil.[39] Nicholls's forces then set out to drive the Americans out of Mobile. Jackson left the treaty scene, hurried south, and reached Mobile on August 22. On September 15, Nicholls arrived from Pensacola by sea and attacked the fort. One of Nicholls's ships, the *Hermes*, sailed too close, and shore fire demolished it. The attackers returned to Pensacola. Jackson pursued by land with three thousand troops and arrived there on November 6. Nicholls evacuated after blowing up Pensacola's fort. The body count was seven dead and eleven wounded Americans; fourteen dead and six wounded Spanish. The Creeks and Seminoles who had hoped to join the Spanish and British were pushed eastward to Apalachicola, on the coast, and then to Prospect Bluff, fifteen miles upstream. Also known as Negro Fort, it had been created by British lieutenant George Woodbine the previous May after he captured Apalachicola. By December as many as three thousand Indians—women and children as well as warriors—were clustered there.[40]

Jackson evacuated Pensacola almost immediately, on November 9, and returned to Mobile. On November 22, he pulled back to New Orleans. During the next six weeks American detachments pursued Indians around Pensacola, British naval and military forces arrived off Lake Borgne, just east of New Orleans, and Jackson prepared for the climactic battle. On January 8, 1815, two weeks after the Treaty of Ghent ended the War of 1812 (though no one around New Orleans was aware of it), Jackson, with 4,500 troops, mostly militiamen—for once, fewer than his opponent—defeated General Sir Edward Pakenham's 6,000 seasoned veterans. Britain's strategic plan had been to win the Gulf Coast and New Orleans, then proceed up the Mississippi Valley and link it to Canada, which once again would have encircled the United States on the west, much more firmly than France or Spain had ever done. This plan was nullified at New Orleans.[41]

JACKSON VERSUS THE DONS, 1815–1818

Spain's hold on the Floridas was in greater jeopardy than ever. The British had invested Apalachicola in May 1814, built Negro Fort at Prospect Bluff, and occupied Fernandina in July 1814. They proceeded to their Chesapeake campaign and the torching of Washington, and then returned to their Gulf Coast–New Orleans offensive. Defeated there, they left in the spring of 1815, and also evacuated Prospect Bluff.[42] Creeks, also defeated, had fled Alabama and western Georgia for Florida, increasing its Indian population to perhaps six thousand. Tens of thousands of white Americans and their slaves swarmed in behind them; the great western Georgia and Alabama land rush, the "flush times" of the Old Southwest, began. Article IX of the Treaty of Ghent provided that lands lost by Indians during the War of 1812 should be restored to them. That did not happen in the Northwest when the British did not insist on it, and Jackson refused to honor Article IX in the Southwest. To the contrary: the War Department named Jackson a commissioner to negotiate treaties with the other tribes; from 1816 to 1818 he wrestled millions of acres in land cessions from the Choctaws, Chickasaws, and Cherokees, essentially dispossessing those tribes, just as the Treaty of Fort Jackson had already dispossessed the Creeks. The

Cherokee and Choctaw treaties involved swaps whereby they received land along the Arkansas River in return for ceding it east of the Mississippi.[43] The path to removal of the southwestern Indians was clear.

After the withdrawal of the British and the ongoing dispossession by treaties of the four major tribes, only the Spaniards, the Seminoles, and refugee Creeks in East Florida remained in the way of American capture of the Floridas. In 1815 Spain still held Pensacola and East Florida, the first at risk of a return of Jackson at any time, and the second (except St. Augustine and St. Marks) close to anarchic devastation in the wake of the "patriot war." At Prospect Bluff—"Negro Fort"—on the Apalachicola, more than three hundred fugitive slaves comprised "the largest Maroon [runaway slave] settlement ever to threaten the peculiar institution of the South." It was a major irritant to Georgians and even to the Spanish at nearby St. Marks because of raids from it. In a rare joint venture, Americans and Spanish decided to take it. On July 27, 1816, an American gunboat fired a hot cannonball that happened to strike the fort's ammunition magazine. It exploded violently, killing about 270 inside the fort.[44] Those still alive headed for Seminole country deeper into Florida.

In 1817 another irritant appeared, this time at Fernandina and Amelia Island. A motley collection of filibusters and pirates led by a Scots adventurer, Gregor McGregor, and then by a Frenchman named Louis Aury, took over the area that spring. McGregor had aided Simon Bolívar's independence movement in Venezuela and Aury claimed to have helped Mexico's, mostly by privateering along the Texas coast. McGregor drummed up support in Charleston and Savannah for his plans to "liberate" Amelia Island. In truth, Fernandina under the McGregor-Aury regime was a nest of smugglers and outlaws, and neither the United States nor the Spanish governor at St. Augustine could put up with it. When Governor José Coppinger tried to recapture it in September, he failed to dislodge Aury, who announced it annexed to "the Republic of Mexico." Thereupon President Monroe sent a land and naval force, which expelled McGregor, Aury, and companions. The United States never relinquished Amelia Island. On January 13, 1818, Monroe told Congress that it had to be kept, and it was.[45]

McGregor and Aury were loose cannons, and thus not to be tolerated. But Jackson was employed by, and theoretically subject to orders from, the U.S. government, and thus legitimate and laudable. In the autumn of 1817 the army, under Jackson and his subordinate General Edmund

Gaines, struck against the Seminoles. Gaines attacked and burned Fowl-town, a Seminole village in southern Georgia, on November 12. The Seminoles retaliated, ambushing a boat on the Apalachicola. Thus began the First Seminole War. It continued through the winter and into the spring of 1818, at first a seesaw affair, but soon favoring the Americans as Jackson's and Gaines's troop numbers increased. Gaines was to chase Seminoles into Florida but not into Spanish posts. On December 26, 1817, Secretary of War John C. Calhoun ordered Jackson to assume command of Gaines's forces and pursue the Seminoles. But how far?

Were Monroe and Calhoun authorizing Jackson to conquer Florida? No direct order has ever been found. Jackson wrote Monroe on January 6, 1818, that East Florida ought to be "seized and held as an indemnity for the outrages of Spain upon the property of our Citizens," and if it were "signified to me through any channel (say Mr. J. Rhea) that the possession of the Floridas would be desirable to the United States . . . in sixty days it will be accomplished."[46] Jackson later and consistently claimed that he was "signified" in just that way by a letter from Washington sent through Congressman John Rhea. Monroe and Calhoun denied giving Jackson such an order. But they knew perfectly well what Jackson could and probably would do, and vague instructions sufficed to encourage him yet preserve their public innocence.[47]

Late that winter, Jackson informed Calhoun that Spain had failed in its treaty obligations of 1795 to control the Seminoles, and on April 6, 1818, he took St. Marks. That seizure turned the Seminole War into aggression against Spanish East Florida. He stormed eastward about one hundred miles to Bowleg's Town, the main Seminole village, found it deserted on April 16, burned it down, and returned to St. Marks. Along the way he captured Robert Ambrister, a former British officer who had been consorting with the Seminoles, and Alexander Arbuthnot, an elderly Scottish trader, and on April 29 he had Ambrister shot and Arbuthnot hanged as spies. Jackson continued west to the site of the destroyed Negro Fort, now renamed Fort Gadsden. With 1,100 men, he moved west toward Pensacola. On May 24 he recaptured the town and on the twenty-seventh its fort, where Governor José Masot, with 218 badly outgunned men, put up only a brief (and verbal) resistance.[48] Having lost Fernandina, St. Marks, and now Pensacola, the Spanish presence in the Floridas was reduced to St. Augustine. Jackson ordered Gaines to seize it as well, but Washington balked at that further and most obvious act of war.

Jackson's grounds for nearly closing Spain out of Florida were "the 'immutable laws of self defence.' " He issued a proclamation creating a civil and military government and setting rules of occupation, with an "arrogance [that] was positively colossal, worthy of the great Napoleon," and then went home to Tennessee on June 2.[49] Observers in northern states were beginning to call him the "American Bonaparte." With Washington's approval, wrote a Spanish historian, Jackson "penetrated Florida, and not satisfied with having quelled the Indians, violated all international laws and without declaring war on Spain, attacked the Spanish forts that . . . could not resist, and seized San Marcos and Panzacola, intending to do the same at San Agustin." It was a "triumph of insubordination, a triumph of military authority over civil, a triumph over the powers of the House and the Constitution of the country." Yet Jackson's invasion forced Fernando VII and his cabinet to settle Spain's quarrels with the United States.[50]

The Bumpy Road to the Adams-Onís Treaty

In the eight years from the summer of 1810, when the Baton Rouge uprising began, to the seizure of Pensacola in mid-1818, Spanish Florida had been periodically invaded and gradually reduced to nothing beyond the capital at St. Augustine. Much had happened elsewhere that bore directly on the withering colony. The Peninsular War in Spain between Joseph Bonaparte and the regency at Cádiz loyal to Fernando VII deprived Spain of anything remotely like an effective imperial government. No one could set or execute a consistent policy toward the Americas. The return of the king in 1814, after Napoleon's downfall, hardly improved things. Fernando hired, fired, and exiled ministers capriciously. Independence movements erupted in Mexico, Venezuela, Peru, Chile, and almost everywhere else in Latin America. The Congress of Vienna, reordering Europe, ignored Spain despite the diplomats' devotion to the principle of monarchical legitimacy. Britain was no help, as Foreign Secretary Lord Castlereagh pursued a policy toward the United States after the War of 1812 of settling outstanding problems and promoting good relations. After 1814, Spain was a derelict among nations, and the Floridas were orphans within the once mighty empire.

Diplomacy never quite died, however. In 1809 the Cádiz regency sent Don Luis de Onís y Gonzalez to Washington as the king's minister, and from then until he left in 1819 after negotiating the Florida treaty with

John Quincy Adams, he served his monarch far better than the king deserved. Forty-seven when he arrived, a Salamancan trained in law and experienced in European diplomacy, he represented his monarch-in-exile for six years without even being recognized officially by the Madison administration. It was afraid to; Napoleon might win, but then, Fernando VII might return, and until that became clear, the Americans could not gamble on accrediting the king's representative. Finally, on December 20, 1815, Madison formally received Onís. Ten days later the envoy presented his first official note to Secretary of State Monroe— who was no doubt unsurprised since Onís had been protesting American incursions and claims through less official channels since the Baton Rouge takeover. Onís asked for three things: the United States should restore to Spain the parts of West Florida occupied since 1810; it should denounce ongoing filibusters into Texas, whose ringleaders came from Kentucky, Tennessee, and Louisiana; and it should not recognize the flags of ships from South America and Mexico that were carrying war matériel from American ports to insurgents there.

Onís left out one of his instructions from Madrid—to insist that Spain did not recognize American occupation west of the Mississippi—in other words, the Louisiana Purchase. Godoy had acknowledged the Purchase in 1804 but Spain had never admitted that the transfer to France in 1800 was legal (which, as shown earlier, it was not). Onís warned Madrid that denouncing the Louisiana Purchase was hopeless, since the state of Louisiana had already been formed from it. Monroe, three weeks later, rejected Onís's other points. He denied that the filibusters had any official backing, insisted that the parts of West Florida that had been absorbed were part of the Louisiana Purchase, and claimed that its western boundary was the Rio Bravo del Norte, that is, the Rio Grande, though the "Rio Colorado" was soon floated as a possibility.[51] Monroe may have been technically correct about the filibusters, but the border claims were false. Yet he kept repeating the old Jeffersonian canard that Louisiana included not only West Florida, but Texas—although neither one was any part of the Missouri-Mississippi watershed. All Onís could do was to consistently deny these assertions.

Throughout 1816 and well into 1817 the two sides dug in, their positions far apart. On April 8, 1817, Onís proposed a treaty that would have fixed the border with Texas at the "Rio Colorado," by which he apparently meant what is now the Red River (the Oklahoma-Texas border), but that the American side understood as the Colorado River in Texas, at the east end of Matagorda Bay.[52] Further proposals crossed desultorily between Onís and Acting Secretary of State Richard Rush and between Foreign Minister José García de León y Pizarro and the American minister in Madrid, George W. Erving. In the summer of 1817 Onís protested American tolerance of the McGregor and Aury operations on Amelia Island. Nothing happened. Onís and his masters in Madrid had virtually no cards to play. Pizarro tried to enlist support from France and England. Neither cooperated. Against the facts on the ground and American aggressive expansionism, state papers and diplomatic notes were weak weapons. On December 10, 1817, Onís wrote Pizarro that it was "incomprehensible that Havana cannot send a frigate with 200 men to re-take Amelia Island. . . . Our Navy must be in a sad [*dolorosa*] condition . . . [if it can't respond to] the repeated insults from this republic and from insurgents."[53]

Two weeks later the United States chased out Aury's gang and took over the island. While Onís protested that unilateral action, he also warned Pizarro on January 8, 1818, that the United States would not give the island back to Spain. One can appreciate Onís's frustrations. They no doubt worsened on January 13, when Monroe sent a message to Congress explaining that the United States had to remain in control of Amelia Island because it was "prejudicial" to the nation for adventurers to hold it. Furthermore, since Spain could not maintain its authority, it "ceased to hold any jurisdiction."[54]

John Quincy Adams returned from England in early December 1817 to assume duties as secretary of state. By then he was America's most experienced and brilliant diplomat, with years of representing the United States in European capitals from St. Petersburg to London. Adams, son of a Federalist president, was nonetheless as ardent an expansionist as any of the Virginia dynasty. From then on, the road to the treaty, while extremely bumpy, pointed toward a conclusion.

In January 1818, Adams reiterated the extreme American position— that Louisiana included West Florida and Texas as far as the Rio Bravo, and that the capture of Amelia Island (and by implication all of East Florida) was essential to keep it from falling into the hands of other nations, Spain (the owner!) among them. Onís kept to his instructions— that West Florida was never part of Louisiana, nor was Texas. Notes sailed back and forth, Adams's "imperious, hectoring . . . vituperative,"[55] and Onís's stubbornly holding on. On April 25, Foreign Minister Pizarro, hoping to avoid American recognition of rebellions in South

America, for the first time authorized Onís to offer the United States a border west of the Mississippi, at the Sabine River (the present Louisiana-Texas line). He also notified Onís that the king had made huge land grants in Florida to three royal favorites, as if Onís needed any further problems.[56]

At that moment Jackson invaded St. Marks and Pensacola. On hearing of it, Onís demanded an explanation. He expected that those violations of international law—actually acts of war—would be censured by Monroe's government and that Jackson would be disavowed, just as Madison had thrown Mathews to the winds in 1812. The president and his cabinet were so inclined. But Secretary of State Adams harangued them into backing Jackson. Adams argued that Spain had failed to prevent Indian outrages and had permitted Ambrister to incite the Seminoles. Jackson had to act in American self-defense and had to be upheld. Otherwise, Adams warned the cabinet that he would lose "the only leverage he had over Onís—the threat of military force."[57]

The leverage was essential, not only to get Spain to turn over the Floridas, but also to agree to another plan of his: a western boundary of Louisiana, a border between the United States and still-Spanish Mexico that would extend to the Pacific. The transcontinental line did become part of the Florida treaty, and many analysts have considered it the most important part. Although it was perhaps implicit in Jefferson's and Madison's expansionism, it was only a remote dream for them. Explicating it and embedding it into an international treaty were John Quincy Adams's achievements.

By July 1817 and into early 1818, Adams and Onís could hardly bear to speak to each other. The French minister in Washington, Jean-Guillaume Hyde de Neuville, served as their go-between. From late July to October, Hyde brokered an agreement that the Sabine would be the Texas-Louisiana boundary. Adams occasionally raised the Rio Bravo specter after that, but essentially he was giving up the American claim to Texas in return for the line to the Pacific. In November, he instructed Minister Erving in Madrid to tell the Spanish government and any diplomats there that Jackson's invasion of Florida was fully justified. Instead of apologizing, Adams demanded that Spain punish its own officers for their "misconduct" in failing to "restrain the Indians," and pay the United States for damages. It was audacious, insulting, and imperialist. It used "half-truths, falsehoods, and powerful rhetoric," as historian William Earl Weeks writes, to "transform the officially unauthorized conquest of foreign territory into a patriotic act of self-defense and the United States from aggressor into aggrieved victim. . . . It was an impressive linguistic feat."[58]

Until January 1819, Onís had virtually no wiggle room. Even Pizarro, perhaps Spain's wisest foreign minister since the days of Carlos III, could not persuade the king and the Council of State to give up their hopeless positions. In September he was sacked and exiled. The new foreign minister (and former envoy to the United States), the Marques de Casa Yrujo, succeeded in gaining approval to allow Onís a free hand to negotiate without checking with Madrid. Haggling continued between Adams and Onís over exact boundaries, but the basic shape of an agreement—Spain cedes the Floridas, the United States gives up claims to Texas, and the treaty line is extended to the Pacific—was in place. Hyde de Neuville continued his good offices. A final draft came on February 20, and on February 22 the Adams-Onís Transcontinental Treaty was signed, with its zigzag line placing New Spain's northernmost boundary at the forty-second parallel. The United States assumed $5 million in claims of its own citizens against Spain dating back to 1802. The Senate ratified the treaty quickly and unanimously.

Yet Spain's ratification lagged. Those three huge land grants made by Fernando VII to his favorites were, Adams thought, nullified by the treaty, which voided any made after a certain date. He was shocked to discover that two of them predated it. The king and the Council of State, and many others in Spain, were disgruntled over the cession of Florida and wanted the land grants honored. The treaty expired, not having been ratified by both sides within the stipulated six months. An internal revolution saved it. In early 1820 constitutionalists in the Spanish army rebelled against Fernando's capricious autocracy and on March 9 forced him to accept the 1812 constitution, limiting his monarchy. In July he swore to uphold it, and in August he finally authorized ratification of the treaty and annulled the land grants in Florida. The Cortes approved the treaty on October 5, and after the American Senate ratified it again, it became final on February 22, 1821. On July 10, St. Augustine passed to the Americans, and on July 17, Pensacola. Jackson was appointed governor of Florida, and remained so until he resigned on November 13, 1821.

During the years leading up to the treaty, one of Onís's difficult jobs was to discourage the United States from giving any support, much less recognition, to rebellions of Spanish colonies in South and Central

America. He did it well, but that soon changed. Florida was not Spain's only loss. From Argentina (1816) to Chile (1818) to Peru and Mexico (1821), and everywhere in Latin America except Cuba and the Caribbean, Spain's colonies declared their independence. On March 8, 1822, Monroe asked Congress to recognize the new republics and authorize funds to open U.S. diplomatic missions there. And in December 1823 he announced to Congress his famous doctrine, warning Europeans not to try anything new in the Western Hemisphere. A Spanish historian asked a century later, "What gave the United States, a people without history, the right to appropriate the new continent?"[59]

John Quincy Adams has justly received lasting credit for the 1819 treaty. It conclusively secured the Floridas; it extended the U.S. territorial claim as far as the Pacific; and it took Jeffersonian-Madisonian expansionist ideology a long step further. Luis de Onís y González has received much less credit, even in Spain, but he was at least the equal of Adams in their negotiations. Having virtually no cards to play, chafing under impossibly inflexible instructions from Madrid until January 1819, having to watch in fury as Jackson, the American Bonaparte, invaded Spanish territory *and was made a hero for doing so* by the American government and people, he gave up only indefensible Florida and some nominal claims to the Pacific coast north of the forty-second parallel. He also saved the equally indefensible provinces of Texas and New Mexico. That Mexico and its northern provinces became independent within two years was no fault of his.

The American demographic onslaught, of course, would overrun Texas and New Mexico and much more within the next thirty years. The Seminoles, who remained unconquered though beleaguered, filtered farther down into the Florida peninsula. The Creeks, Cherokees, Chickasaws, and Choctaws, treatied out of their lands, would soon be removed westward. Mississippi, Alabama, and southwest Georgia opened to a huge land rush, replacing the Indians and their economy with cotton plantations and slavery. Mississippi joined the union in 1817, Alabama in 1819, and Missouri in 1821, provoking raucous arguments about the future of slavery and freedom in the American Union. All joined as slave states, and they were, as well, ethnically cleansed of Indians to all intents and purposes.

Florida thus became part of the United States through a stepwise, nibbling process from 1810 to 1819. As in every instance of territorial acquisition since 1783, no single cause explains it all. The United States benefited greatly from Spain's weakness—in fact, prostration—during the Napoleonic Wars, and did not hesitate to kick the other fellow when he was down. Beginning perhaps with American ingratitude toward Spain's assistance during the Revolutionary War, continuing through the acquisition of Florida, and concluding with helping Cuba, Puerto Rico, and the Philippines disengage in 1898–1899 from what was left of the Spanish Empire, the United States abused Spain worse than it did any other nation except, in sheer acreage taken, Mexico and of course the Native Americans. Hispanophobia and anti-Catholicism, from John Jay to Jefferson and the Virginians through Jackson and John Quincy Adams, suffused the anti-Spanish policies and statements of America's early leaders. The incompetence of Carlos IV, Godoy, and Fernando VII hurt Spain perhaps as much as Napoleon did. A corrupt absolute monarch produced absolute corruption.

Spain's problems, however, were not the whole of the Florida story. Madison and Monroe used chicanery, subterfuge, and bluster in their support of the Baton Rouge insurgents, General Mathews and the "patriots," and Jackson. Official America defended, even extolled, Jackson's Bonapartism in 1818. The United States violated and ignored the laws of nations when it invaded, or promoted insurgency within, the colonies of a friendly foreign power. The president and Congress resorted to secret messages and legislation (today we would call them "classified") and to deniable instructions to agents like Mathews and Mitchell. They went so far as to justify preventive unilateral invasion. Exacerbating everything was a demographic imbalance that was already massive in 1800 and became, perhaps, insuperable by the 1810–1820 decade. Demography would play even more centrally in the next shift of borders, another step southwestward, this time into Texas.

Chapter Five

Texas, 1811–1845:
Overpopulating and Conquering

The danger [in Texas] to Mexico from the United States is in the Settler,
and intrigue and conspiracy, not in their Armies and Navies.

—Charles Elliott, British diplomat, to Foreign
Secretary Lord Aberdeen, June 15, 1845[1]

The Filibustering Decade, 1811–1821

Like the capture of Florida, the taking of Texas had a lot to do with Jefferson's and Madison's exaggeration of the extent of the Louisiana Purchase and their efforts to make their view become reality. The Texas story began in the same way as Florida's. President James Madison and Secretary of State James Monroe, in 1812, continued to claim (as had Jefferson) that the Louisiana Purchase included West Florida *and* Texas. Jefferson and Madison knew better, but whenever contrary evidence— like flat denials in 1804 from Talleyrand and Napoleon (see Chapter 4)—confronted them, they simply ignored the evidence and maintained their expansive view of the Purchase. John Quincy Adams (as Monroe's secretary of state) did so as well, until he gave up the contention in order to secure Florida and the line to the Pacific in the 1819 treaty with Luis de Onís and Spain. Even Jackson agreed with Adams on that. Through the 1820s, however, Adams and Jackson did nothing to inform the American press, preachers, and politicians in the South and West that the contention was in error—just as Jefferson, Madison, and Monroe had aided and abetted the false claim ever since 1803.

Madison and Monroe did not limit themselves to rhetoric. They acted on the claim, fomenting and clandestinely backing not only the West Florida insurrectionists and the George Mathews "patriot war" in

East Florida. At virtually the same time, in a similar tactic, they encouraged and aided a filibuster across the Sabine from Louisiana into Spanish Texas in 1812 and 1813. It was the first of several filibustering invasions of Texas between 1812 and 1820. The last of them, by an American named James Long, was very much on the minds of the Spanish authorities and inclined them to sponsor colonists they could trust: in the beginning, Moses Austin, and his son and successor, Stephen F. Austin, in 1820–1821. A line therefore runs straight from the Louisiana Purchase, to the West and East Florida insurrections, to the 1812–1821 filibusters into Texas, and finally to the Austins' famous empresario grants, which began the large-scale Anglo populating of Texas. That started an irreversible demographic inundation, completely overwhelming the Spanish-speaking population, the *tejanos*, by 1830 and subverting Mexican governance soon after.

Of all the American territorial acquisitions of the nineteenth century, Texas was the purest case of demography determining an area's destiny—not diplomacy, not luck, not even military conquest. The Anglos outnumbered the *tejanos* by 1835, perhaps earlier, by ten to one. An adroit and secure Mexican government might have kept Texas within the Mexican fold, but Mexico's government was neither. Nor should we overlook the role of the true sovereigns of most of the area of present-day Texas until the 1840s: the lords of the Plains, the Comanches. As of 1830 they, along with other Indians both indigenous and newly arrived, may have numbered 40,000, as many or more than the Anglos and *tejanos* combined. They continually defended their land, disrupted the advance of the Anglos, and made life especially difficult for the Mexicans, forcing them into what amounted to a two-front war at the time of the decisive Texan uprising of 1835–1836.[2]

In the spring of 1810, Fernando VII of Spain languished in Napoleonic exile and royal authority was reduced to the regency at Cádiz while British and French troops clashed in the Peninsular War. At Querétaro, in central Mexico, a Catholic theologian and parish priest named Miguel Hidalgo and his companions planned a revolt against Spanish authority. On September 16, 1810—still Mexico's Independence Day—Hidalgo issued his *Grito de Dolores*, a cry for independence.[3] The Hidalgo revolt, the first serious one in Spain's American empire, united tens of thousands of peasants under the rallying cry of "Religion, Patria, the Mother of Guadalupe." On September 28 Hidalgo's force, by then 25,000, marched on Guanajuato. Spinning out of control, it sacked the city. More than 2,000 were killed on both sides. Popular support wavered, then fell away. The viceroy's army prevailed, decisively so at the Bridge of Calderón, between Guadalajara and Mexico City, on January 17, 1811. Hidalgo fled north but was captured and executed later that year. Followers and fellow insurgents, notably Ignacio Rayón and José María Morelos, fought rearguard rebellions until 1815, when Morelos was caught and killed.[4] But others, such as future presidents Vicente Guerrero and Guadalupe Victoria, lived to fight another day.

The Hidalgo revolt flared up in Texas in January 1811, specifically in San Antonio, and next door in Chihuahua. Though it was quickly put down, it became the prologue to a series of filibusters from 1811 to 1821. None succeeded, but they harassed the Spanish into a policy of controlled immigration, beginning with the Austins' empresario grant of 1821.

The first filibuster was led by José Bernardo Gutiérrez de Lara, a Coahuila merchant and Hidalgo follower who later became governor of the state of Tamaulipas, and Lieutenant Augustus Magee, an American ex–army officer.[5] It had American backing at the highest levels. Gutiérrez visited Governors Claiborne of Louisiana and Blount of Tennessee and gained, at the least, their moral support. He then went to Washington in December 1811. A letter of introduction to President Madison bore no immediate fruit because the two had a language problem, but it opened the door for Gutiérrez to meet with Secretary of State Monroe and Secretary of War William Eustis. Gutiérrez wrote in his diary that Monroe promised to send 50,000 American troops to Mexico if war broke out between the United States and Britain. (This happened six months later, but Madison and Monroe by then had far more than they could handle in Canada, so no troops went to Mexico.) More immediately, they promised funds so that Gutiérrez could return to Natchitoches, Louisiana, to raise an armed force. Gutiérrez also left Washington with a supporting letter from the chief clerk of the State Department to Governor Claiborne. Monroe also detailed an agent of his, William Shaler (his cover was "consul at Havana and Vera Cruz"), to sail to New Orleans to meet, aid, and keep an eye on Gutiérrez. Gutiérrez, Shaler, and 130 recruits—including Magee and, turning up like a bad penny, Samuel Kemper of nearby West Florida—moved across the Neutral Zone and the Sabine into east Texas.[6]

On August 12, 1812, the filibusters captured Nacogdoches in east Texas. They proceeded to La Bahía (later renamed Goliad) and took it on November 7. The governor, Manuel de Salcedo, counterattacked; Magee became ill and died; but the filibusters successfully held La Bahía. Gutiérrez and Kemper marched on San Antonio. The only remaining Spanish-controlled town in Texas, it fell to them on April 1, 1813. The insurgents drafted a constitution for the "Republic of Texas" on April 6, and Gutiérrez was proclaimed governor.

The filibuster then fell apart. Gutiérrez intended to keep Texas a liberated province within Mexico, rather than inch it toward the United States, which was the ultimate aim of the Madison-Monroe, Shaler-Claiborne policy. Shaler pulled his support from Gutiérrez, and a royalist army under the efficient and ruthless General Joaquín de Arredondo smashed the insurgents on August 18 at the Medina River near San Antonio. Gutiérrez escaped, and Kemper and 1,200 followers scuttled back to Louisiana. Arredondo reestablished stern viceregal order.

The 1812–1813 filibuster thus failed to liberate Texas for anyone. It was never a settler movement or a typical cattle-stealing border raid or anti-Indian foray. It was an attempt by the Hidalgo survivor Gutiérrez to capture Texas as a base for a republican Mexico. This project was supported clandestinely at the highest levels of the U.S. government, at the same time and in much the same way as Madison and Monroe were backing insurrections against Spain in West and East Florida. No one has found a smoking gun in Madison's or Monroe's hands. Yet there is no doubt that Monroe's clerk provided Gutiérrez with the letter of support, or that Monroe was "running" Shaler.

Although Gutiérrez failed, others kept trying between 1813 and 1821. They included Louis Aury, who after intrusions around Matagorda Bay and Galveston in 1816 went on to his brief takeover of Fernandina Island in East Florida in 1817. The dissident Spanish general Francisco Xavier Mina landed at Galveston and the coast of Tamaulipas in 1817; Arredondo caught him and had him shot.

An American, James Long, led the final filibuster before Mexico became independent. He tried twice to liberate Texas, first in 1819 when with Gutiérrez de Lara and a group of invaders from around Natchez he took Nacogdoches on June 23. Long apparently had no U.S. government support. In the months just after concluding the Adams-Onís treaty, Monroe and John Quincy Adams anxiously awaited Spain's ratification and were satisfied to swallow only Florida. Andrew Jackson, fresh from overrunning East Florida, advised Adams and Monroe to back off from Texas and not risk the treaty. Congress passed another Neutrality

Act in 1818, during the Adams-Onís negotiations, providing fines of up
to $3,000 and prison terms of up to three years for "any military expedi-
tion"—that is, a filibuster—against "any foreign prince or state . . . with
whom the United States are at peace." This time Washington meant it,
and the government abstained from any more such intrigues.[7]

The motive for Americans to follow Long into Texas was their crav-
ing for cheap land. At that moment and for years to come, Texas could
give land-hungry southwesterners more land for less money than they
could obtain from the U.S. public domain. Long failed in 1819, and
Governor Antonio Martínez and General Arredondo chased him and
his people back across the Sabine that fall. Long tried again in 1821,
landing at Galveston Bay and proceeding to La Bahía late in 1821. But
events had overtaken them: Agustín de Iturbide successfully declared
Mexico independent of Spain and himself emperor in February 1821.
Long surrendered to what were by that time Mexican forces on October 8, 1821.

EMPTY TEXAS AND THE BUFFER POLICY

Curiously, while Mexico was putting down Long's final filibuster, it was
adopting a new version of the old Spanish "buffer" strategy. It would
invite preapproved empresarios, Anglos or otherwise, to recruit settlers
who would become loyal Mexican citizens. Thus it was actually welcom-
ing a legal, peaceable Anglo influx, which within ten years became a
much greater threat than the filibusters. Why did Mexico take this risky,
even self-destructive course?

The history of Spanish-speaking Texas ultimately goes back to
Hernán Cortés's conquest of central Mexico for Spain in 1519–1521,
leading to Spain's notional claim to most of North America. In 1598 a
Spanish expedition (made up largely of ethnic Mexicans) marched up
the Rio Grande and established an enduring colony in Pueblo country,
which they named New Mexico. In the 1710s Spain planted permanent
settlements in present-day Texas, first in 1716 at Los Adaes, close to
French Louisiana, and two years later at San Antonio. Texas presidios
and missions were meant to contain the French, who were then arriving
in the lower Mississippi Valley and who founded New Orleans in 1718.
In 1757 the Spanish sent two hundred people to establish a mission and
presidio at San Saba, 120 miles northwest of San Antonio. The Apaches,
who would have none of it, destroyed it within a year. In 1785, Governor

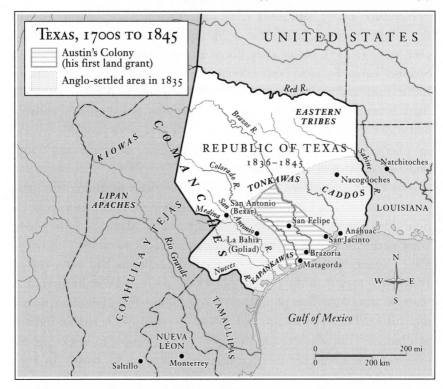

TEXAS, 1700S TO 1845

Austin's Colony
(his first land grant)

Anglo-settled area in 1835

For most of the Spanish and Mexican periods, Texas was part of the province or state of Coahuila y Tejas. The southern boundary of the Tejas segment was not the Rio Grande but the Nueces River, which meets the Gulf of Mexico at Corpus Christi. Stephen F. Austin's first colony lay between the Nueces and the Sabine, the eastern boundary of the province. Later grants to Austin and others were east and west of it and farther inland. As of 1835, Anglos (and their slaves) had settled—rather sparsely—the Gulf Coast from the Sabine to the Nueces and about 150 miles inland. Population then included roughly 32,000 to 35,000 Anglos and their slaves, perhaps 40,000 Indians, and perhaps 4,000 to 5,000 tejanos.

Domingo Cabello signed a treaty with the eastern Comanches, and life in Texas's three towns—San Antonio de Bexar, La Bahía de Espíritu Santo, and Nacogdoches—stabilized, though far from perfectly. After the United States bought Louisiana and after the 1819 treaty finally defined the northern limits of New Spain, the Spanish and Mexicans were still few in number in Texas. The real occupiers were the Comanches on the Plains, the Lipan Apaches in the southwest, the Caddos in the east, and several other sizable tribes along the Gulf coast and elsewhere.

A census of 1777 listed only 3,103 *tejano* (Spanish-speaking) settlers in the whole province. Another in 1785 reported 2,919; another in 1790, even fewer (2,417); and in 1803, about 4,000, the highest ever reached in Spanish Texas. By 1820 Nacogdoches had "nearly expired," partly from Indian raids and partly from banditry from the nearby Neutral Zone. La Bahía was never much more than a river outpost. San Antonio probably had about 1,500 inhabitants at that point. There were probably 20,000 to 30,000 Comanches out on the Plains.[8] They were not shy about retaining control of their homeland.

The chronic problem along Spanish America's northern frontiers, whether in Florida, Louisiana, Texas, or farther west, was underpopulation. The Spanish, and the newly independent Mexicans after them, knew perfectly well that Texas was a demographic vacuum. They were just as aware as the Spanish governors of Louisiana had been before 1803, with regard to the Natchez District and then West Florida, that the exploding American population was invading. Presidios alone would not suffice. The Spanish also had to use any available, tractable Indians as a buffer. They also needed the right kind of people to settle, people who were, or would become, Catholic and loyal to the crown (or after 1821, to Mexico).

The problems with this policy were the same as those of Spain in Louisiana in the 1790s and in the Floridas in the 1810s, lacking only Godoy to make them worse. Not enough of the "right kind of people" were available in Mexico or in Europe. Mexico had to make do with promising-looking Americans. As for the Indians as buffers, the Caddos along the Louisiana-Texas border were largely agricultural and willing to trade and make treaties. They were hardly puppets, however, and they had their own problems with neighbors like the Osages and Wichitas. And west of them all roamed the Comanches and Lipan Apaches, migrant plainspeople, utterly resistant to anyone.

The naturalized Spanish subject Moses Austin of Missouri applied, through the legitimate channel of Governor Martínez, for a grant of Texas land to which he planned to bring settlers. By the time James Long's filibuster ended, Austin had died. His quest for a colony lived on with his son Stephen F. Austin. The approval of Moses Austin's proposal of December 1820 for a colony in Texas was Spain's final expression of the buffer-and-immigration policy. Within two months, on February 24, 1821, Iturbide announced the beginning of true Mexican independence. Independence did not happen everywhere overnight, however. The new government stuck to the same basic policy, proposing generous land grants (though well away from the coast and the Louisiana border) to new settlers, and prohibiting slavery. The settlement process would be farmed out to "empresarios" who would have the right and also the obligation to bring in honest, productive, and loyal people. Governor Martínez in San Antonio regarded Moses Austin as a suitable candidate. Then Moses died in Missouri on June 10, 1821. His son Stephen, who was already in Natchitoches, arrived in San Antonio on August 10. In July, happily enough, General Arredondo wrote Governor Martínez that he could no longer hold the region for Spain, and on July 17 Martínez accepted Iturbide's leadership. In August the last Spanish viceroy, Juan O'Donojú, recognized Iturbide and turned over power peacefully rather than attempting fruitless, bloody resistance.

Stephen Austin's immediate job, then, was to seek formal reapproval from Mexican authorities for his father's proposal. It took months, but he got it. On September 28, Iturbide's control of the country became complete. And not until October was James Long finally arrested and his filibuster snuffed out. No one in authority was unaware of Long's rogue operation, or the need for loyal colonists in Texas.

AUSTIN AND THE EMPRESARIO SYSTEM

Austin's first colonists arrived on the Brazos River, legally and properly, in December 1821. He had picked out his tract in August and then returned to Louisiana to advertise and recruit the first of the three hundred families he contracted to bring. He had attractions to offer. A family could obtain a much larger tract than any legally available in the States. The U.S. land act of April 1820 provided that public land would be sold at auction for whatever it could bring, but no less than $1.25 per acre. The smallest parcel on offer was eighty acres. The act abolished credit purchases, so that a potential farmer needed at least $100 cash down. Land from which Indians had been removed could fetch prices well above that, often more than families, even planters, could pay. As a result, speculators priced many families out of the market.

Austin, on the other hand, offered each head of family 640 acres, another 320 for his wife, another 100 for each child, and 80 for each slave he brought in. When Iturbide reconfirmed Austin's grant on January 4, 1823, settlers received one square league for grazing and a smaller plot for tillage, a huge 4,605 acres all told. They had six years to "improve" the land, but they were not liable for taxes on it or for customs duties on imported implements during that period.

Colonists were expected to become citizens, and therefore Catholics, as Catholicism was the sole religion of the state. There was never, however, any enforcement of conversion, or a threat of deportation for lack of it. They could bring in slaves, although the children of slaves were to be freed when they reached fourteen, and slave trading was forbidden.[9] In this respect Texas's slavery practices fell somewhere between Louisiana's, with its typically southern U.S. chattel-slave system, and Mexico's. There, every revolutionary from Hidalgo through Rayón, Morelos, and Guerrero at the close of the 1820s tried to abolish slavery. Austin, his allies, and colonists struggled through the 1820s to keep it legal, either by having Texas exempted from national laws or by redefining it as "indentured servitude" (for life).

Austin advertised in local papers and recruited settlers in New Orleans, Nashville, and other places in the Southwest, and from the Southwest came most of his takers. He received inquiries from Kentucky, Missouri, Tennessee, Ohio, Illinois, and beyond, and easily recruited his three hundred families. His subsequent grants brought applicants from these states and also Alabama, Arkansas, Mississippi, New York, Ohio, Georgia, Pennsylvania, Virginia, and New England. Most were already west of the Appalachians. The majority were from south of the Ohio. A few were German.[10]

In a day when "land was the barrier, water was the carrier," people steamed or floated down the Ohio and the Mississippi. They then either trudged 250 miles overland or made the two-week sail from New Orleans. By the mid-1820s newcomers already outnumbered Spanish-speakers, and by 1834 there were probably 30,000 of them, plus 2,000 slaves. A census in 1835 stated that nearly 10 percent of households owned slaves—on average, six per white household. As on most settlement frontiers, families were nuclear (few grandparents), young (adults in their twenties or thirties with lots of young children), males more numerous than females. In most respects, life was not much different from life on any southern frontier.[11] In economic position they were perhaps a cut above the average, with at least enough capital to afford the trip to Texas and start-up costs of a homestead or plantation. In religion and culture they were of the Old Southwest: Protestant, accustomed to slavery and convinced that it was necessary and natural. Later colonists, certainly the ones outside the empresario system who crossed illegally into Texas from Louisiana and Arkansas, tiptoed along the edges of literacy, good citizenship, and civility. They bore no loyalty at all to Mexico.

With regard to slavery, nobody—not Austin's colonists, nor other empresarios', nor the thousands of squatters who edged into east Texas in those years—made any promises *not* to import slaves. Austin's first contract explicitly provided that colonists would get eighty acres per slave imported, which openly invited settlers to do so. Slavery of Africans had been part of Spanish law and life since at least 1510–1511, and Spain did not give up the slave trade until 1817.[12]

Yet one of the most consistent positions of Mexico's early patriots, and the utterly clear thrust of Mexican law, policy, and statesmanship beginning in 1810, was to get rid of what slavery there was in the country, and keep out any more of it. Very little existed anyway, and the numbers of slaves had been falling since at least the 1790s. The condemnation was unequivocal. Miguel Hidalgo, the first liberator, proclaimed on October 19, 1810, that masters must free all slaves immediately under pain of capital punishment and forfeiture of all their goods. Ignacio Rayón, his successor, forbade slavery in his *Elementos Constitucionales* of April 30, 1812. José María Morelos, the next liberator, in his *Sentimientos de la Nación*, issued at Chilpancingo on September 14, 1813, decreed that "slavery be proscribed forever as well as distinctions of caste, so that all are equal and only vice and virtue will distinguish one American from another."[13] The colonization law, debated by a congressional committee in the fall of 1822 and signed by Iturbide on January 4, 1823, outlawed the purchase or sale of slaves and freed any children born in Mexico of slaves when they became fourteen.[14] A federal law of July 13, 1824, forbade bringing in slaves; any who did come became free just by stepping on Mexican ground. The new constitution passed in October 1824 did not refer to abolition (it did not need to) and stressed all citizens' equality under the law, much as Morelos had written.[15]

But the *norteamericanos*, at least the kind who came to Texas, were used to slavery and many were slave owners. The U.S. representative to Mexico, Joel Poinsett of South Carolina, began negotiating a fugitive slave agreement with Mexico in 1825, at the behest of Secretary of State Henry Clay (of Kentucky), but Poinsett never quite succeeded. Stephen Austin himself owned at least one slave for a time. While he was no fire-eating slaver, he consistently said that if Texas were to grow and prosper, slavery had to exist there. Every time a law passed restricting it, Austin managed to have Texas exempted, always making his case that the Texas economy and the ability to hold and recruit settlers depended on it. One of the first of Austin's colonists, Jared Groce, brought in ninety in 1822, the largest group but by no means the only one. By late 1825, more than 2,200 people had come to Austin's colony—and 443 were black slaves.[16]

As for the requirement that colonists should become citizens, and therefore Catholics, it was clearly stipulated in Austin's grant and in the laws of Mexico (the Imperial Colonization Act of January 1823 and the constitution of 1824). It went unobserved from the start. Austin himself was never a Catholic. When he recruited colonists he advised them that Catholicism was the sole religion of Mexico and that they should respect it. But he did not enforce conversion in any way, nor did Mexican authorities. The requirement "became almost a dead letter."[17]

Did, therefore, Austin's and other Anglo colonists who came to Mexican Texas after 1821 break any promises about slavery or becoming Catholic? They were not supposed to introduce the first, but they did; and they were supposed to do the second, but they didn't. Yet if a Mexican lawyer, canon or civil, had argued the colonists' case, he would probably have pleaded that a law not enforced is not a binding law.

As for the buffer policy, it worked only too well. Austin fulfilled his quotas as promised and ultimately brought in around 1,200 families. Other empresario grantees were not as successful or efficient, but they too swelled the Anglo population. Besides the grantees, unauthorized migrant squatters kept crossing the Sabine into Mexico. Mexico could no more prevent that than the United States could keep Mexicans from crossing the Rio Grande into the United States 150 years later.

The policy carried the seeds of its own destruction from the start. If the buffers, in this case Anglos from the United States, did not assimilate and become loyal citizens, then they would prove to be the very people the policy was supposed to buff. The uninvited squatters around Nacogdoches were certainly such people. Austin's, and most of the other empresarios' until the early or mid-1830s, remained in their own neighborhoods and did not assimilate in any serious way, but they were generally loyal citizens. Mexican leaders, however, could not shake a well-founded dread of Anglos creating a breakaway revolt followed by American annexation. As early as December 1821, a congressional committee reported that unless Texas imported trustworthy immigrants— possibly Austin's recruits from Louisiana, possibly Mexicans who "would dedicate their lives to save the country from slavery," or possibly

Irish and German Catholics—then the growing United States would "annex Texas, Coahuila, Saltillo, and Nueva Leon like the Goths, Visigoths, and other tribes assailed the Roman Empire."[18]

This 1821 report reflected widespread Mexican opinion about Texas years before the 1835 rebellion. Frontier officials also succeeded in obtaining treaties of peace and commerce with the Caddos, Cherokees, and the Lipan Apaches in the early 1820s, though with just one band of Comanches and only later with the Wichitas. In June 1822, the Foreign Relations Committee approved and sent up to Congress a proposal from Tadeo Ortíz, Diego Barry, and Felipe O'Reilly to bring ten thousand Irish and Canary Island settlers to Texas. These would have been ideal. Congress, however, postponed any action on this until after it passed a general colonization policy, which it did not do until January 4, 1823. The Ortíz-Barry-O'Reilly petition fell by the wayside. That "may have decided the fate of the province of Texas." Ortíz, a follower of Hidalgo's, gained no support for this proposal or for another he made in 1833 to bring in Swiss and German settlers; he died of cholera shortly after.[19]

This delay in late 1822 had another consequence. Iturbide got into a dispute with his military commander at Veracruz, Antonio López de Santa Anna—the political general who would bedevil and disrupt Mexico's peace for the next thirty-three years. Iturbide removed Santa Anna; Santa Anna rebelled and his troops joined him; and in March Santa Anna forced Iturbide out. As for Austin's grant, Iturbide had approved it on February 18, 1822. The junta that succeeded him approved Austin's grant yet again, for the final time, on April 14.

On November 22, 1823, José Anastasio Torrens, Mexico's newly appointed chargé d'affaires in Washington, reported suspicious activity. "Edward Haden" (his real name was Haden or Hayden Edwards) was bringing in Americans, with the ultimate objective of joining the United States. A month later, a report from San Felipe de Austin came to Governor José Antonio Saucedo at San Antonio that two hundred unauthorized families had crossed the Sabine into the Nacogdoches area, and another fifty had done so farther south.[20] Torrens reported again in January 1824 to the secretary of state, Lucas Alamán, that the Americans' ambitions to take Texas knew no bounds. If Jackson were elected president (he wasn't, until 1828), the Florida story might happen again in Texas—infiltration, insurrection, and an American military takeover "to restore order." Torrens met with Jackson, and the general told him with brutal candor that "the best way to obtain territory was to occupy and hold it, then treat for it," as happened in the Floridas. He also admitted that Cuba might be a future U.S. target.[21]

Jackson had accepted the Sabine River boundary in 1819. By the time of the 1824 campaign, however, the lingering fantasy that the Louisiana Purchase had included Texas still infected the minds of the leading candidates: Jackson, who won the most popular votes; John Quincy Adams, who won the presidency in the electoral college; and Henry Clay, who became Adams's secretary of state. No wonder that Mexican statesmen like Alamán had equally lingering suspicions about American aggressiveness toward Texas.

MEXICO'S 1824 CONSTITUTION AND COLONIZATION LAWS

Mexico needed more immigration laws and more follow-through. In August 1824 came a federal colonization law, turning over immigration and colonization to the states. The newly created state of Coahuila y Tejas passed its own law on March 24, 1825. It formalized the empresario system, which would "confer tracts of the public domains upon persons who should introduce at their own expense a certain number of immigrant families."[22] Within months, Austin was not the only empresario. Haden Edwards and Robert Leftwich arrived with settlers on April 15, and two more groups came a little later. These totaled 1,450 families. Though not all of the contracts completely filled up, the number of empresario-led families numbered more than 5,100 by 1831. At a likely average of six persons per family, that meant more than 30,000 Anglos.

When Santa Anna and the army overthrew Iturbide in early 1823, they set up a provisional republican government that included a constituent congress. Its main work, other than securing a foreign loan, was to write and ratify the new federal constitution. It did so in October 1824, and elected a president, the patriot Guadalupe Victoria. He served his full term, but in the following forty years no other president would do so; such were the political upheavals that Mexico was about to experience. The federal constitution recognized nineteen semiautonomous states and five outlying territories, breaking the three-hundred-year hold of Mexico City and its viceroys over the whole country. Reflecting in some respects the American constitution of 1787, with a few sprinkles from the Spanish one of 1812, it created executive, legislative, and judicial branches. It mandated a broad range of civil liberties, though it retained Catholicism as the sole public religion. It thereby followed Spanish and Hidalgoan tradition, which remained until the more liberal (some cried "anticlerical") constitution of 1857. While it did not explicitly outlaw slavery, it proclaimed the civil equality of all Mexicans regardless of race or status. It also preserved the much broader property rights for women (compared to Anglo law) that existed in Spanish law. Less liberally, it continued the clergy's and the military's privileges of being tried in their own courts, so that they literally remained laws unto themselves. But the 1824 constitution was nonetheless truly federal, and generally enlightened.

One of the nineteen states recognized in 1824 was Coahuila y Tejas, distant from the center, vast but underpopulated, and one of the poorest and least self-supporting. Saltillo was named the capital. It was the southernmost major town, 350 miles from San Antonio (traditionally the capital of Texas) and almost 700 from Nacogdoches. The state's boundaries at no point ran along the Rio Grande. They ranged from the Sabine River, the Gulf of Mexico, and the Nueces River, and then far to the south and west, taking in much of the Comanche country of west Texas, meeting the U.S. boundary in the north at the Red River. This was an immense, mostly ungovernable expanse. The great majority of its non-Indian people lived in Coahuila, not Texas. Reflecting that, the state legislature included ten representatives from Coahuila and two from Texas. With most of the space but little money or political power, Texans always resented Coahuila's dominance. They chafed when they had to go to Saltillo to appeal any decision made by the local court in San Antonio, and they felt unprotected against Indian raids. Although Texas could not have managed on its own, its union with Coahuila, lasting eleven years, was a festering grievance.

Coahuila y Tejas's 1825 colonization law preferred Mexican settlers, including Christianized Indians. Foreigners were welcome if they swore allegiance, and they could live tax-free for ten years. This state law was more favorable to immigrants than anything yet. A head of family could receive a *sitio* of grazing land, one league of 4,428 acres, for $30. An additional *labor* (177 acres) of farmland would cost him $3.50 if irrigable and $2.50 if not, with no cash demanded for four years. Newcomers were not to settle too near the Gulf coast or the U.S. border, however. Empresarios who recruited families would receive up to eleven leagues (over 48,700 acres). Several Mexicans became empresarios, including Tadeo Ortíz, the proposer of the Irish colony; a general, José Antonio

Mexía; and Lorenzo de Zavala of Yucatán, later a good friend of Stephen Austin's and in 1836 (for six months until his untimely death) the first vice president of the Texas Republic.[23] Americans dominated, however, with seventeen of twenty-four empresario contracts signed between 1824 and 1832, and they brought in hundreds of American colonists: Edwards, Leftwich, Benjamin Milam, and of course Austin being the leaders.

Edwards's grant was for eight hundred families and was to be located around Nacogdoches. But some of that land was already occupied by *tejanos.* Predictable disputes ensued, degenerating into skirmishes. The area from Nacogdoches eastward to the Sabine, about sixty miles of piney woods country, was closest to the U.S. border and farthest from Mexican federal or state authority. It already held as many as three thousand unauthorized American squatters by 1823.[24] In the summer of 1826 the central government ordered immigration to be cut back, and on October 2 the district governor at San Antonio revoked Haden Edwards's contract. On December 16 an enraged Edwards, supported by some of his colonists along with local Cherokees whose land title was being questioned, declared themselves the "Fredonia Republic," independent of Mexico.

The Fredonia Republic lasted less than a month. Mexican forces from San Antonio actually arrived at Nacogdoches, augmented by Stephen Austin and some of his colonists. They squelched the uprising in January 1827. By the middle of that year, there may have been 12,000 U.S. citizens and only 7,000 Mexicans in the state. Coahuila y Tejas adopted a new constitution in March 1827, keeping the ten-to-two legislative imbalance in favor of Coahuila. It reaffirmed Catholicism as the sole state religion, and declared all children born there of slave parents to be free. No more slaves were to enter, beginning six months after the constitution was published (a crucial breathing space, as it turned out). In September, going further, the state legislature announced it would emancipate the slaves already there. Austin and powerful friends in San Antonio and Saltillo dodged this bullet by making it known that although slavery as such was prohibited, the state would recognize contracts of (lifelong) indentured servitude. The slave plantations that Austin, his colleagues, and officialdom believed were so essential to the growth of the Texas economy would continue. The slaves' lot changed only in name.

The American Demographic Conquest

After the Fredonia escapade was smothered, Austin persuaded the governor to deal leniently with all but the ringleaders. He denounced the uprising, and confidence in his loyalty became more solid yet in San Antonio and Saltillo. The colonization policy seemed to be working. But the Fredonia Republic deeply troubled Mexican authorities farther south. A languishing boundary commission appointed in 1824 under the intelligent and steadfast General Manuel Mier y Terán came alive. Terán, a trained engineer and avid naturalist, was commissioned to undertake a thorough investigation of conditions in Texas. He left Mexico City in early November 1827, but it took him until March 1828 to reach San Antonio.[25] At Laredo, en route, he met General Anastasio Bustamante, then the army commander for the Eastern Interior states and soon to be (from late 1829 to 1832) president of Mexico until Santa Anna overthrew him. Terán and Bustamante traveled together to San Antonio, becoming friends and allies. Terán continued with all deliberate speed to San Felipe to talk with Austin, also to become a respected and good friend, and finally he arrived in Nacogdoches about June 3. There he stayed until January 1829, returning to Matamoros by March 7. He had talked with everyone of significance, Mexican or Anglo, and had taken a painfully long look at the settlements, especially in east Texas.

What Terán saw confirmed his fears that the border area, and perhaps all of Texas, was slipping away. Like other watchful Mexicans, he became convinced that the buffer policy had become the fox-in-the-chicken-coop policy. Austin, on the other hand, loyal though he was, plumped for more and more immigration as the path to an ever bigger and better Texas. As the first and most successful empresario, he saw himself as a moral leader, a paterfamilias, cooperating expeditiously with Mexican friends and officials from San Antonio to Saltillo to, he hoped, Mexico City. Unfortunately, not all empresarios and certainly not all colonists shared his fidelity to Mexican law or his avidity at learning Spanish, and they were not eager to be led by Austin or anybody else, especially Mexicans. In general, they shared the racist and hispanophobic attitudes pervasive in Anglo-American culture.

Beginning in March 1828, Terán reported periodically to the governor of Coahuila y Tejas, the minister of war in Mexico City, and President Guadalupe Victoria. His thoughts appeared first in a draft letter (perhaps never sent) to Victoria from San Antonio, dated March 28, 1828. It reflected his thinking before he even went to the northeastern frontier. He began by pointing out that the population of Texas was "25 thousand savages, eight thousand North Americans with their slaves, and four to five thousand Mexicans."[26] Regarding each, he remarked:

> Alongside these savage men [primarily Comanches and Lipan Apaches] who everywhere assault the Mexican frontier . . . invaders of another kind are seen to arrive carrying the tools of a very advanced industry. Without respect for borders or boundaries . . . they choose the best land. Nature tells them that [it] is theirs. . . . The laws of Mexico have provided for its territorial integrity, prohibiting foreigners from settling within twenty leagues of the frontier or ten from the coast. . . . But in the first place, that line which is the terminus from which the count is to be made is not marked out. Even those farmers operating in good faith would insist that they are not geographers. . . . [And thus] more than two thousand foreigners are living on the best lands on the border.

As for the empresario colonies, he admitted frankly that

> everyone I have talked to here . . . is convinced . . . that these colonies, whose industriousness and economy receive such praise, will be the cause for the Mexican federation to lose Tejas unless measures are taken soon. . . . If it is bad for a nation to have vacant lands and wilderness, it is worse without a doubt to have settlers who cannot abide by some of its laws and by the restrictions that [the nation] must place on commerce. . . . [Better] a wilderness that bit by bit will cease to be so, in the hope of a time not far off when the progress of a population such as Mexico's will spread over its empty lands.[27]

Terán's subsequent reports from Nacogdoches in 1828 added fascinating detail about the land, the Indians, and much else. His basic position did not change, however.

After his return to Matamoros, Terán as an army general was largely preoccupied with fending off a Spanish force of four thousand that landed near Tampico to reclaim Mexico. Santa Anna got most of the credit for the Tampico victory, but he soon appointed Terán *comandante general* of the Eastern Interior states, which included Texas—the position Bustamante had held a year earlier, before he was elected vice president. Based on his expedition to Texas in 1828, and his new responsibilities, Terán sent his conclusive recommendations to the minister of war and navy on November 14, 1829.

The fundamental truth was that Americans occupied the Louisiana frontier, the Gulf Coast, and the mouths of rivers, while the Mexican population was confined to only three places, and "is insignificant compared with the constantly increasing numbers of settlers coming from the North." Prompt measures were essential. The United States was aggressively moving southwest. It was repeating "extravagant claims" that Texas was part of Louisiana, citing the French explorer La Salle's coastal voyage of 1682—an "absurd fiasco," Terán wrote. The Spanish government in 1808 had commissioned a historical analysis of all such claims, and it appeared as a million-word treatise by Don José Antonio Pichardo in 1812. It conclusively refuted them, but Americans kept making them.[28] Garrisons required strong reinforcements, and Terán specified which units should be sent. Coastal trade between Texas and Mexico must be encouraged. New settlers—not American, but Mexican, and at least a thousand families, followed by German and Swiss ones— had to be attracted with loans and bounties. Austin's grants should be revised to keep his settlers away from the coast.

Terán's ideas were further elaborated by his deputy, Constantino de Tarnava, who put them in a letter of January 6, 1830, to the minister of war.[29] With crucial additions, they became the landmark "Law of April 6, 1830." Its contents put Mexico on an ultimately fatal collision course with the United States concerning Texas.

As Terán was fighting off the Spaniards and readying his report, Andrew Jackson became president of the United States on March 4, 1829. A few weeks later he instructed Joel Poinsett, the U.S. representative in Mexico City, to approach the Mexican government about selling Texas. The idea of selling any of its national territory to a foreign power was as abhorrent to Mexicans as it would have been to Americans. Poinsett was given his passports and sent packing. His replacement, an agent of Jackson's named Colonel Anthony Butler, was even less discreet and converted many in Mexico City from suspicion to rage.[30] American aggressiveness came now from Washington, not just from squatter-settlers. Simultaneously, Mexico changed leadership. President Vicente Guerrero, in the tradition of Hidalgo and Morelos, declared slavery abolished completely in Mexico on August 25. José María Tornel y Mendívil, the minister in Washington, encouraged Guerrero to do so, arguing that emancipation would discourage slaveholders from coming to Texas. As before, however, Austin worked with Mexican authorities to keep Texas exempt. This time Ramón Músquiz, the political chief in San Antonio, Governor José Maria Viesca in Saltillo, and his brother Agustín Viesca, then the minister of relations (equivalent to secretary of state), rescued Texan slavery. They suspended the publication of the emancipation decree in Texas and then persuaded President Guerrero to exempt Texas.[31]

In December 1829 a coup put Bustamante in the presidential chair, replacing Guerrero. With his friend at the top, Terán's position and his recommendations regarding Texas strengthened. In January 1830 the young Lucas Alamán became minister of relations, and he quickly codified Terán's recommendations into a bill before Congress. It became known as the Law of April 6, 1830. In almost all particulars it followed Terán's recommendations for Texas. But Alamán made two critical additions of his own. Terán wanted immigration from the United States discouraged and kept from the border and the coast, as before, with preference given to Mexican and European settlers. Alamán's provision (Article 11) forbade "emigrants from nations bordering on this republic [from settling] in the states or territory adjacent to their own nation [i.e., anywhere in Coahuila y Tejas]. Consequently, all [empresario] contracts not already completed and not in harmony with this law are suspended." The other addition (Article 10) accorded with Guerrero's emancipation decree and with Mexican revolutionary thought since Hidalgo: "No change shall be made with respect to the slaves now in the states, but the federal government and the government of each state shall most strictly enforce the colonization laws and prevent the further introduction of slaves."[32] This seemed to allow existing slaves to remain slaves, but it could also mean the end of Texas's earlier exemptions and the subterfuge of "indentured servitude." Thus the April 6 law would have stopped uncontrolled immigration, any new American empresario grants, and eventually slavery. It recognized the supreme demographic threat that

Americans were posing, and it most definitely began a new phase in Texan history, though not the one that Terán, Alamán, Bustamante, and other Mexican patriots intended.

Rumbling toward Rebellion, 1831–1835

Austin was in a terrible spot. He delayed publication of the April 6 law as long as he could, and then portrayed it as aimed at the marauding Plains Indians rather than the colonists. At this he had some success, and the threat of an Anglo uprising simmered down in 1831 and into 1832. But immigration never stopped. Without empresario oversight, thousands of new immigrants were under no one's control, behaving like the rough frontier people they were, picking fights with Indians, causing serious friction with the Comanches, and contemptuous of Mexicans and local government. The April 6 law, either in its military provisions or its border controls, was never fully carried out. Terán, though *comandante* for the region, did not receive the troops he asked for. He tried giving land to cooperative Indians (a vestige of the buffer policy) but the Anglo influx was too massive. All the law did was to deepen divisions and to accelerate Texas's centrifugal spin out of the Mexican orbit. By the time it passed, the Anglo population well outnumbered the *tejanos*, who were clustered in and around San Antonio. Anglos were spread out along the coast and up the rivers, very thickly between the Sabine and Nacogdoches. During the next five years the population imbalance worsened, while Santa Anna further destabilized Mexico's government at all levels. Between those two forces, one demographic and the other political, there was no likely way to keep Texas from becoming independent. Beyond independence lurked the question of whether it would then join the United States.

For nearly two years, Austin labored to keep the April 6 law from operating with full force in Texas. Terán sought more troops to police the border, while Alamán tried to recruit Catholic families from New Orleans; neither succeeded. A settler uprising in Brazoria in December 1831 fizzled out but suggested deep unrest. As 1832 opened, Santa Anna fomented a revolt against Bustamante, dividing the army into factions. Settlers at Anáhuac (near present-day Galveston) had been avoiding the required customs duties, a dispute complicated that spring by a fracas over fugitive slaves. The local army commander, a Kentuckian turned loyal Mexican officer named Juan Davis Bradburn, declared martial law along the coast on May 15. After a pitched fight at Brazoria on June 26–27, the Mexican commander at Nacogdoches, José de las Piedras, arrived, relieved Bradburn of command, and sided with the settlers. Austin did so too.

As loyalties played out, Austin and the settlers found themselves on the side of Santa Anna and against the government. Terán, at his wits' end and seeing the Santa Anna forces taking over the country, ran himself through with his own sword on July 2. In another month, only a few dozen government troops were left anywhere in Texas. Settlers convened at San Felipe on October 1 and asked that the April 6 law be repealed and that Texas be separated from Coahuila. Santa Anna completed his coup in December and in March 1833 became president. The San Felipe colonists convened again in April, again asked for statehood and the annulment of the April 6, 1830, law, and drafted a state constitution. This they sent to Mexico City with a cover letter asking that previous policies be restored along with "your munificence and liberality."[33] The legislature of Coahuila y Tejas announced its intention to declare the April 6 law unconstitutional, and it did so on October 14, 1833. Four weeks later Congress agreed to exempt Coahuila y Tejas from the law—rendering it completely pointless—and Santa Anna approved that act on November 21, 1833.[34]

His stand-in, Vice President Valentín Gómez Farías, decided it was time for another fact-finding survey, somewhat like Terán's. He sent Juan Nepomuceno Almonte, an able English-speaker familiar with Texas. Reporting back in 1835, Almonte urged more non-Anglo colonization and warned that Mexico needed additional troops in Texas. As before: clear thinking, no implementation. Almonte's most lasting contribution was his statistical survey of population, which counted about 4,000 *tejanos* and over 20,000 Anglos in Texas's three departments: San Antonio, the Austin colonies around San Felipe, and Nacogdoches.[35] These numbers quickly became obsolete; Texas may have had 40,000 by 1836.[36] Almonte believed there were also 13,000 Indians, all but 2,700 *bárbaros.*

Austin himself bore the San Felipe settlers' document to Mexico City, arriving July 18, 1833. On the way, he suggested to the San Antonio council that it might declare Texas independent, and soon after he arrived in the capital he told Gómez Farías that Texas ought to be independent of Coahuila—and that it could not be conquered by force. Such candor landed Austin in jail in Mexico City, where he languished until

July 1835. He did not return to Texas until the end of August. By then, he had come around to favoring Texas's independence not just from Coahuila but from Mexico.[37] During his absence the Anglo colonists in Texas had grown increasingly fractious, irked by a "bewildering series" of land laws passed by the Coahuila y Tejas legislature.[38]

These discontents might still have been resolved by wise and sympathetic rule, but the opposite happened. Santa Anna took swift steps toward centralism and personal dictatorship, with no room for tolerating Texan deviations. On May 31, 1834, he dissolved Congress. In October 1835 he abolished state governments, centralizing authority and making the states—including Coahuila y Tejas—no more than administrative districts run from Mexico City. Whatever liberties the Texans had, whatever exceptions or annulments to the antislavery law or even the security of their land titles, were unprotected. By then, Anglo-Texan opinion had coalesced firmly around the idea of the state's independence from the center, a position directly opposed to Santa Anna's. The main division was over means: how aggressive, how resistant to be? Before his confinement in Mexico City, Austin had led the "peace party," those who hoped that diplomacy and gradualism would win them what they wanted. Sam Houston and others had been leading the "war party," those who favored confrontation. By the summer of 1835, as Austin returned, the two groups started closing ranks.

THE WAR OF TEXAN INDEPENDENCE

In late June 1835, at Anáhuac again, thirty armed Anglos seized the garrison, hoping to provoke a widespread uprising. A twenty-six-year-old South Carolina firebrand named William Barret Travis was at the center. In Mexico, Tornel had left Washington to become minister of war, and General Martín Perfecto de Cós, a brother-in-law of Santa Anna's, had become *comandante general* of the army in the Eastern Interior states, Bustamante's and Terán's old job. Despite distractions caused by Plains Indians and an uprising in Zacatecas, Tornel and Cós moved troops into Texas after local authorities failed to apprehend Travis and other insurgents. Austin reappeared in Texas on September 1 and made common cause with the independence leaders. The insurgents fed on many grievances and the fear that if Cós prevailed there could be a slave rebellion—the continuing bogey of Anglo slaveholders from the Georgia-Florida border on west. The insurgents defeated Cós at Goliad on October 9, 1835, and forced him to surrender at San Antonio on December 11.

Meanwhile, in November, the insurgents created a "provisional government" ostensibly loyal to the federalist constitution of 1824 and to remaining a state within Mexico. The profederalists, led by Houston and others, may have included a majority of Anglo-Texans as late as January 1836.[39] But the seekers of root-and-branch independence were strong and vocal, minority or not, and when Austin joined them the war of Texan independence from Mexico became unavoidable. At least two companies of filibustering recruits from New Orleans swelled the insurgent forces; people kept crossing the Sabine into Texas; the imbalance of Anglos over *tejanos* passed ten to one.

And Santa Anna was marching north. The Texans who ran Cós out of San Antonio in December went on the defensive and holed up within the old Alamo mission. Santa Anna arrived on February 23, 1836, with six thousand troops, and the siege began. Travis and another recent immigrant, the Tennessean Jim Bowie—one a hotheaded young extremist, the other a slave-trading sot—shared command in the Alamo. Eleven days later, on March 6, Santa Anna's soldiers moved in and killed the nearly two hundred defenders, at least eight of them *tejano* or Mexican. Shortly before, a constitutional convention at Washington-on-the-Brazos dropped its federalist cover, declared Texas independent, and appointed Houston commander in chief of Texan forces. On March 17 it legalized slavery and decreed that free blacks had no rights and could be sold into slavery.[40]

Houston had ordered Travis and Bowie to pull back from San Antonio and another group under James Fannin to retreat from Goliad, confronted as they were by a far larger army. Neither did, and both were wiped out—Fannin's 340 men executed on March 27 by Santa Anna's order. Militarily the Alamo defenders and Fannin's group contributed nothing, but as symbols of martyrdom they annealed all Anglo-Texans into a united resistance and gained strong support for their cause all across the southern United States. Houston commanded only the remaining eight hundred or so Texan troops, and he prudently retreated as Santa Anna advanced. But an overconfident Santa Anna divided his forces and relaxed. Houston caught them on April 21 at San Jacinto, near Galveston Bay. The battle lasted only twenty minutes. The Texans, who lost eight men, continued slaughtering the fleeing Mexicans, killing 630, a body count well beyond the Alamo and Goliad combined. Santa

Anna and Cós, both captured, promised to make no further war against Texas, to remove all troops from it, and to recognize Texan independence. Made under duress, these pledges were later repudiated by Mexico City. The Mexican army did withdraw south of the Rio Grande, and the Republic of Texas was, in fact, an independent country. Whether it would remain so—or be recaptured by Mexico or join the United States—would take nearly a decade to resolve.

The Path to Annexation, 1836–1845

Early in September 1836, Texans held elections. Houston, who was the hero of the day, defeated Stephen Austin for president by 5,119 votes to 587. The citizenry approved a constitution, and supported annexation to the United States by 3,277 to 91. Austin was no longer popular, because of suspicions of land speculation (unfounded), his varying policies toward Mexican factions (true), and probably his aura of paternalism. Houston nonetheless made him secretary of state; but Austin died on December 27, 1836, aged only forty-three. Before he died he proposed that Texas be annexed as an American state, with the Rio Grande its southern and western boundary from the Gulf to its source in the Rockies and thence to the forty-second parallel, the Adams-Onís line. The Texas Congress endorsed this boundary, effectively annexing the 150-mile coast and the region west of it between the Nueces and the Rio Grande, although the area had never been part of Coahuila y Tejas but of Tamaulipas. This claim would figure centrally in the start of the Mexican-American War in 1846. Migrants continued to stream into Texas. By mid-1836 the Anglo population probably reached 35,000, plus, according to one observer, 5,000 blacks.

In Washington, Andrew Jackson, of all people, hesitated about annexing Texas. On December 21, 1836, he advised the U.S. Congress to delay annexation, and it voted for milder measures: funding a U.S. representative to Texas, and on March 1 recommending that Jackson simply recognize Texas as an independent country. On March 3, 1837, his last day in office, he did so.[41] Many Mexicans and European observers suspected the Jackson administration of complicity in the Texas breakaway, either to extend slavery or to gain more territory. The Adams and Jackson administrations had each offered to buy Texas. Jackson had not worried about other people's opinion when he invaded Florida in 1818. But in the fall of 1836 he almost certainly did not want to jeopardize

Martin Van Buren's election to the presidency, and once Van Buren was safely elected, Jackson still wanted no war with Mexico, which annexation would likely have brought.

Thus Jackson went no further than recognition. Van Buren, a New Yorker, almost immediately confronted an economic panic and depression that lasted throughout his four-year term, putting annexation on hold until at least 1841. President Houston of Texas knocked on the American door in August 1837. But Van Buren's secretary of state, John Forsyth of Georgia, kept it closed for the rather specious reason that the Constitution did not provide for annexing independent countries, and the real reason that the United States did not want to offend Mexico to the point of war. On the Texas side, Houston's successor, Mirabeau B. Lamar, reversed course and opposed annexation while he was president of Texas from 1839 to 1841.

In 1841, Houston returned as Texas president, and the Virginian John Tyler's accession as the U.S. president reawakened annexation possibilities. Tyler avidly supported annexation. He did not press the matter in his first two years. American opinion was polarizing around the slavery issue; southern legislatures were passing resolutions for annexation, while abolition-conscious northern ones passed resolutions against it. In the fall of 1843 Tyler appointed the former vice president and ardent defender of states' rights and slavery from South Carolina, John C. Calhoun, as secretary of state. Calhoun pushed hard for annexation of Texas with Tyler's support. On April 12, 1844, representatives of Texas and the United States signed a treaty by which the United States annexed Texas, took over its public lands and property, assumed its debt, and declared the boundary to be the Rio Grande all the way to its source. Tyler sent this treaty to the Senate a few days later.

One of the great American political battles was on. Former president Van Buren, a Jacksonian from New York and hopeful Democratic candidate for president, announced against annexation. Henry Clay of Kentucky, a slaveholder himself, about to become the Whig candidate for president, wrote a friend that he opposed "immediate" annexation because it would mean war with Mexico. His letter was leaked and also became public.

A Jackson man from Tennessee, James K. Polk, won the much-fought-over Democratic nomination. No one outdid Polk in his ardor for expansion anywhere, including Texas. Clay was distorted into an antiannexationist while Polk ran on a flat-out expansionist platform, calling for the "re-annexation of Texas" ("given away" in the 1819 treaty) and the "re-occupation of Oregon." The Whigs and northern Democrats defeated Tyler's annexation treaty in the Senate on June 8, by 35 to 16. In the fall election, however, Polk defeated Clay by a slight though sufficient margin—170 to 105 electoral votes and 38,367 popular votes out of a total of 2.7 million. On December 3, Tyler's final message to Congress warned that Britain might seduce Texas away from the United States and claimed that the voters had mandated annexation. The American representative in Mexico City, William Shannon, reiterated the hoary falsehood that Texas was part of the Louisiana Purchase.[42]

On January 25, 1845, the U.S. House of Representatives approved admitting Texas as a state, 120 to 98, and on February 27 the Senate passed a similar resolution by 27 to 25. Clearly the two-thirds majority required by the Constitution to approve a treaty with a foreign power was beyond the annexationists' reach.[43] But a joint resolution of the two houses would probably pass, and so it did on February 28, inviting Texas to become a state (though not on quite the terms of the defeated 1844 treaty). Tyler approved the joint resolution forthwith. The aged congressman John Quincy Adams, the only former president ever to serve in the House, called the joint resolution "the apoplexy of the Constitution."[44] On March 4, James K. Polk was inaugurated president of the United States.

From Hidalgo's *Grito de Dolores* of 1810 and the Gutiérrez-Magee filibuster of 1812–1813 to the annexation of 1845, Texas changed and grew radically. By the end of the intervening three decades, the Anglo-Texans, their offspring, and their slaves well outnumbered the Plains Indians, who resisted their advance and harassed Mexicans everywhere they could. President Lamar's policy was no-holds-barred war against all Indians. In 1839 Texas forces burned out and chased out virtually all Cherokees, Creeks, and other Indians from east Texas. The one serious attempt at sitting down with the Comanches, at San Antonio in the summer of 1840, degenerated into a massacre of them that launched years of no-quarter combat on the Plains. The Wichitas suffered the Texans' "murderous force" in the wake of that, while Comanches never let up their raids along, most often, the Mexican frontier. By the fall of 1845 they were penetrating within three hundred miles of Mexico City, all the way to Zacatecas.[45] Mexico's disruptions at the center, with Santa Anna in and out of power, together with these never-ceasing Comanche raids, severely weakened the country's ability to resist Texan claims to the Rio Grande before 1846 and was an enormous distraction during the American invasion from 1846 on.

By the first official Texas census, taken in 1847, the new state had 102,961 whites and 38,753 blacks, nearly all slaves, a total of 141,714. Three years later the 1850 U.S. Census, the first one in which Texas appears, gave the total as 213,000—154,000 white, 59,000 black. (Indians were not counted by the census.) Texas came into the United States by a process somewhat different from Louisiana's or Florida's. More than in any earlier acquisition, demography drove Texas into the union. The never-ending invasion pushed back first the Mexicans and *tejanos* and then the Indians. A rush of throbbing young people migrated to the edges of settlement, reproducing themselves almost as fast as biology would permit. Demography would also drive the next acquisition, Oregon.

Chapter Six

Oregon, 1818–1846:
Fixing the Canadian Border

Petition the Government of the United States, to extend its jurisdiction and laws over that Territory, until the "stars and stripes" shall be unfolded to every breeze, and the Eagle of America shall extend its protecting wings over the entire Continent. . . .

—An American statement, 1844[1]

[As] to . . . the respective pretensions of the three claimants . . . England is considerably superior to Spain, and infinitely superior to America. . . . On the grounds of actual possession . . . England sees not even the shadow of a rival.

—A British statement, 1844[2]

"A Few Miles of Pine Swamp"

The story of how the United States acquired the Pacific Northwest is the cleanest and least dismaying of any of the acquisitions up to this point. There was no double-crossing one's ally, as Jay and his colleagues did to France in 1782. There was no faulty title, as with Louisiana in 1803. No filibustering invasions of Spanish territory, or anyone else's, as in Florida and Texas. The hypocritical double-talk that marred earlier acquisitions was largely absent. An excess of frontier bluster pushed the process along, indeed to the brink of war with Britain. But in the end, a touch of British saber-rattling quickly dissolved differences and produced a treaty in June 1846.

The acquisition of the Oregon country, now called the Pacific Northwest, involved a demographic inundation, as did Texas. It was smaller and quicker, however, and it did not overrun and displace a people of European stock already there. Nor did it tear off part of a neighbor's property. Many Northwest Indians were accustomed to trading with British and Americans, more or less as the Indian nations around the Great Lakes had done. As for slavery, although President James K. Polk was a slaveholder like his mentor Jackson and nearly all other previous presidents, and although most of the Americans who first settled Oregon in numbers were from Missouri, Kentucky, and other slave states, they refused to bring slavery to Oregon (or allow free blacks to settle there either). Nor was free Oregon acquired as a trade-off for slave-state Texas. There was no direct quid pro quo; the two were just the next logical places for an expanding American population to go.

Though the remotest part of the Americas from Europe, the Northwest has a climate like northwestern Europe's. Temperate, well watered (plain rainy, in fact), covered with Douglas firs and other tall timbers along the coast and mountains, the interior gradually becomes a high desert split by the Columbia River. Puget Sound, ringed on the east by the Cascades and on the west by the Olympics, is one of the world's dramatically spectacular harbors. Not many miles north, the sea receives the Fraser River at another fine harbor. Great cities grew up at these points: Vancouver, Seattle, Tacoma, and Portland. Six-foot-long sea otters, worth their weight in silver across the Pacific in China's markets; whales, hunted by Makah Indians off the coast; numberless salmon and other fish—these were nature's gifts to the region. Yet to the Earl of Aberdeen, the British foreign secretary, this region was more a diplomatic nuisance than a strategic asset. He called the Oregon country nothing more than "a few miles of pine swamp."[3] Events proved it far more than that.

There were, of course, native people in the Oregon country, anywhere from thirty to fifty distinguishable tribes. On the north coast and islands lived hunter-gatherers, fierce builders of totem poles, war canoes, and complex societies. The gentler Shoshones on the western slopes of the Rockies supplied explorers Lewis and Clark from their great herds of horses, as did the Nez Percé on the Clearwater. The Jesuit missionary Pierre-Jean DeSmet advised, "The savages who frequent the coast, especially towards the north, are of a much more barbarous and ferocious temperament than those of the interior [where] the natives are of a mild and sociable disposition."[4] DeSmet assured readers that "the white population have little to fear from their attacks," which were indeed rare along the Snake, Columbia, and Willamette, "except on the northern coast, where life is far from being safe."[5] These and the dozens of other groups whose names have sometimes survived—Okanagan, Walla Walla, Cayuse, and many more—probably totaled around

180,000 people at the time that Europeans and Americans first arrived in 1774. From that height they fell sharply to perhaps 110,000 by 1835, 50,000 by 1850, and about 25,000 in 1925, their lowest point.

That catastrophic falloff happened because of the afflictions that had stricken native peoples all over the New World since 1492: wars among themselves, conquest by Europeans, droughts and other environmental calamities, and, worst of all, diseases brought by Spaniards, British, Russians, and Americans, by sea and overland. In the Oregon country the disease toll began with first contact in 1774–1775. The major killers were smallpox, sexually transmitted diseases, pulmonary tuberculosis, measles, influenza, dysentery, and, surprisingly, malaria. Smallpox arrived on a Spanish or British ship between 1774 and 1782, followed by outbreaks around 1801, the mid-1830s, and the 1850s, every time a young, nonimmune generation matured.

Lewis and Clark in 1805 recorded a die-off from smallpox among the Clatsops of the lower Columbia. Another American reported in 1844 that though probably a hundred tribes and over 150,000 people had lived in the region in 1800, "but a small remnant now remain . . . not more than 18,000," and two-thirds of those tribes were "utterly extinct."[6] Dysentery probably from Hawaii struck both Indians and whites on the lower Columbia in 1844. Meningitis, mumps, influenza, and measles hit along the Willamette in a deadly succession from 1835 to 1848. "Depopulation on the lower Columbia was truly fearsome," with die-offs estimated at 85 to 90 percent. All told, from first contact with Europeans in 1774, the population decline in the following century was likely above 80 percent, "or nearly 150,000 people." Cultural disruption and annihilation were inevitable.[7]

A surprise entrant in the killing bee was malaria, then called "fevers and ague." DeSmet noted in his book that "in June, the rivers, swollen by the melted snow, inundate the plains, and increase the stagnant water formed by the rains of winter. The vapors arising from the influence of a meridian sun, cause fever and ague," a disease that returned season after season.[8] Neither DeSmet nor anyone of his era knew that the water hatched out *Anopheles* mosquitoes, whose bites transmitted the malaria. The first carrier was likely an American trading ship, the *Owyhee*, and a sister ship from Hawaii, visiting in August 1829 and July 1830. Whites got relief from extracts of the bark of a tree that we now know contained quinine. Indians suffered "terrible ravages," wrote DeSmet. "Entire camps have been swept away. . . . The savages find themselves attacked by it, they hasten to plunge into the cold rivers, and die immediately." It "carried off nearly two-thirds" of the natives.[9] In the Willamette Valley, more than 18,000 Chinooks and Calapuyans living there in the 1820s dwindled to 2,433 a decade later.

No society suffering that great a loss could survive. The consequence for the American settlers who poured into the area after 1840 was that hardly any Indians were around to stop them. As in 1620s Massachusetts and nineteenth-century Hawaii, entry into Oregon was facilitated by a macabre demographic prelude.[10] Whatever the carrier—American children on wagon trains playing with nonimmune Indian children, horses or beavers, ship crews from the tropics, Indians or white traders coming from exposed areas—ghastly epidemics made safe the path of manifest destiny in the Northwest.

EXPLORING WITHOUT SETTLING: FOUR NATIONS' CLAIMS

Spaniards, then Russians, then Britons, and finally Americans sailed many ships to the Pacific Northwest between the 1530s and 1811. Some followed the coast but never went ashore, and a few hacked out mostly short-lived trading posts, but none settled in the true sense. These efforts were sufficient, however, to establish a tall docket of competing claims. Did first discovery establish sovereignty in the European sense, or was settlement also required? Who actually got there first, and where?

To the Spanish, to whom the pope had given most of the Western Hemisphere in 1493, the entire Pacific coast was available and needed only to be "discovered." Spanish ships proceeded north along California (Cabrillo and Ferrelo in 1542–1543, the Greek known as Juan de Fuca in 1592, Vizcaino and Aguilar in 1596 and 1602–1603). Later, in 1774–1775, Juan Francisco Bodega y Quadra and other Spanish captains made it all the way to Prince William Sound in Alaska. "Quadra" was the Spanish name for Vancouver Island for a time, and "Bodega" is still the name of the lovely bay about fifty miles north of San Francisco.

The English sailor Francis Drake passed by the Golden Gate in (probably) 1579, but did not tarry. No British navigator went ashore until Captain James Cook's third voyage in 1778, when he landed at Nootka Sound on the northwest side of Vancouver Island. Spaniards beat Cook to Nootka by four years. They were so secretive about it that they neglected to leave behind a manned post, however. So the British,

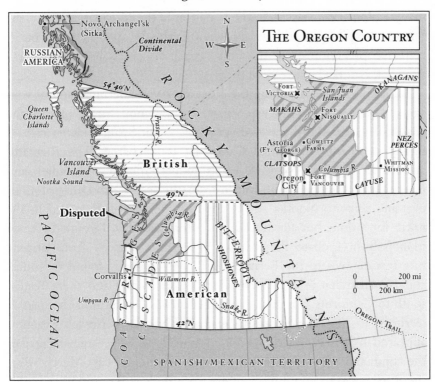

The Oregon country included the region from the Continental Divide along the crest of the Rockies westward to the Pacific. Its northern and southern boundaries were indefinite prior to 1819. Then the Adams-Onís treaty made the forty-second parallel the northern limit of Spanish territory and thus the southern boundary of the Oregon country. British and American agreements with Russia in 1824–1825 set 54°40' as the southern limit of Russian America (which later became Alaska) and thus the northern boundary of Oregon. From 1818 to 1846, by U.S.-British agreement, the forty-ninth parallel defined their border east of the Divide. West of it, sovereignty was shared. The British presence was confined to the dozen-plus outposts of the Hudson's Bay Company, and Americans did not begin arriving in any numbers until 1841 via the Oregon Trail. Almost all of them settled in the Willamette Valley. The British and Americans were greatly outnumbered by the many Indian tribes.

By 1846 the portion south of the Columbia River was tacitly American; the portion north of the forty-ninth parallel was de facto British. Only what is now western Washington was in serious dispute.

unaware of any previous claim, landed and announced that they had arrived first. That led to a scuffle in the late 1780s and then the 1790 agreement known as the Treaty of the Escorial, or the Nootka Sound Convention, whereby Spain did not quit the area but did recognize British rights. This Spanish retreat was the first of Manuel Godoy's many diplomatic disasters. In the Pacific as in the Mississippi Valley, the Spanish Empire was still strong when Carlos III died in 1787, but it retreated precipitously in the next decade at several points in North America, Nootka being one of them.

Russia also appeared along the coast after Vitus Bering's famous voyage of 1741, which, after exploring his eponymous strait, plotted the coast of Alaska. Word traveled very slowly, but Spanish defensiveness finally came into play after Carlos III took charge. The Russians' appearance along the Northwest coast induced him to send soldiers and missionaries to Upper California in 1769 (the year of San Diego's founding) and ships to Nootka and beyond in 1774.[11] Russia stayed to the north for a time, but advanced again after Czar Paul I granted a trade monopoly in 1799 to the Russian-American Company from latitude fifty-five degrees to the Bering Strait. The company founded Kodiak and Novo-Archangelsk (which later became Sitka) and then headed south to California. There it entered what was unquestionably Spanish territory. In 1806 the company's manager, Nikolai Petrovich Rezanov, appeared in San Francisco, and got on so well that he became engaged to the commandant's daughter before returning home.[12] By March 1812, the Russians were hunting sea otters from Bodega Bay and were building Fort Ross—actually, Rossiya—on a tract they had bought from Indians a few miles north.

Americans were the last of the four nations to arrive. Robert Gray and another ship's captain named Kendrick sailed through the Strait of Juan de Fuca in 1788. In May 1792, Gray beat the British navigator George Vancouver to the discovery of the mouth of the Columbia River by a few weeks. That later made possible a persistent American claim to the river and its watershed, as international law and custom then provided.

The Oregon country thus had four nations claiming it before 1800 (not counting, of course, the Indians). The situation bristled with legal arguments and diplomatic deals, but as yet there were no flashpoints (except for Nootka) because so few of those nations were actually there. All of these approaches before 1800, whether Spanish, British, Russian, or American, were voyages of discovery and commerce. Their purposes were limited to trapping or to trading with local Indians who did the actual trapping. They were not intended to establish settlements or plant the seeds for immigrant colonies. They never involved more than a few dozen people.

In 1793 came a prologue to change. The first overland trek from the east to the Pacific shore took place when Alexander Mackenzie of the North West Company made it from the Great Lakes to the Fraser River and finally the Pacific Ocean at 52°20' north latitude. Though he retreated hastily to avoid almost certain annihilation by coastal Indians, he had made himself the first European to cross the North American continent. An exceptional explorer, Mackenzie earlier reached the tidewaters of the Arctic via the river since named after him, proving before Lewis and Clark that there was no practical northwest passage. The first overland crossing of North America therefore was accomplished by an officer of a British fur-trading company in western Canada. The next expedition, however, was American, sponsored by the president: the Corps of Discovery of Meriwether Lewis and William Clark, which reached the mouth of the Columbia in 1805. Six years later John Jacob Astor's trading post, Astoria, arose there.

The United States thus became a player in the Northwest claims stakes, based on the activities of Captain Gray, Lewis and Clark, and Astor's men. The British presence manifested itself not through governmental outposts but in the forts of the Hudson's Bay Company (HBC), the great stock firm founded in 1670 to carry on the fur trade in the interior of North America. The HBC absorbed the more adventuresome but financially shakier North West Company in 1821. It thus controlled and operated fur-trading posts not only in the Great Lakes, in the vast region called "Rupert's Land" (now, basically, Canada's Prairie provinces), but also in the Columbia and Snake River valleys northward into "New Caledonia," the Fraser River country that later became British Columbia. Directed by a "Governor and Committee" in London (many of them Scots) and in North America by a Scot named George Simpson based near Montreal, the HBC was far and away the main European presence in the Northwest from 1824, when Chief Factor John McLoughlin started Fort Vancouver, to the 1840s. Only then did the Americans arrive in force.

The contest between Britain and the United States for the Oregon country would come down to one between a crown-chartered trading corporation intended fundamentally for profits and an increasing population of independent, individualistic settlers imbued with the typical nineteenth-century American ideals of spread-eagle patriotism, personal freedom, and fee-simple landholding.

Two Loose Ends from Ghent

The treaty signed at Ghent, in Belgium, on Christmas Eve 1814 resolved most of the outstanding problems between Britain and the United States. The main thing was to formally end the War of 1812. Two loose ends remained, however.

One was to ensure that another war would not break out along the Great Lakes and St. Lawrence. When hostilities stopped, the United States was constructing two eighty-four-gun warships at Sackett's Harbor. The British were building another at Kingston, apprehensive that Americans might again attack the Canadian side of Lake Ontario and the river. For their own reasons, both sides decided to stand down. In 1817, Acting Secretary of State Richard Rush and British minister Charles Bagot in Washington signed the Great Lakes naval disarmament pact that has henceforth carried their names. Though dented and bent over subsequent decades, it held up reasonably well.[13] As Upper Canada gained people and morphed into the province of Ontario, the long border never erupted into sustained conflict, despite serious flare-ups in the 1830s and 1860s.

The other loose end affected Oregon much more directly. The boundary at the western tip of Lake Superior had been drawn in geographical ignorance in 1782. It was assumed that the Mississippi sufficed as the western boundary of the United States. The Louisiana Purchase changed that; but what were the northern and western limits of the Purchase? International law customarily held that whoever owned a river owned its entire watershed including its tributaries. The river of the Purchase was the Mississippi-Missouri system. One of the purposes of the Lewis and Clark expedition was to discover just what that watershed included. Vast as it proved to be, it logically had to stop at the continental divide along the crest of the Rocky Mountains. A few spread-eagle pamphleteers and mapmakers claimed that the Purchase extended all the way to the Pacific, but most of the world, even American sympathizers, dismissed that assertion. For some years following Ghent, however, no Euro-Americans actually lived west of the Rockies or between the Spanish and Russian coastal posts, except the company "servants" (as the HBC called its employees) in their scattered forts.

Little love was lost between Britain and the United States following 1814, though nothing existed like the hispanophobia and racism with which Americans regarded Spaniards and Mexicans. The British and Americans could at least talk to each other. The disastrous failures of American arms in Ontario in 1812–1814 were considerably redeemed by Jackson at New Orleans. In a much wider arena, Britain had just defeated Napoleon at Waterloo. Her foreign secretary, Viscount Castlereagh, was teaming up with Austria's Prince Metternich and other European conservatives at the Congress of Vienna to restore as much as they could of pre–French Revolutionary Europe. They hoped to reverse and even eradicate the Napoleonic confusions, and to build a lasting if reactionary peace. (They succeeded; their edifice lasted until 1848.) A happy consequence for the United States was that Castlereagh wanted settled issues, not skirmishes, on his American flank. And so Richard Rush accompanied Albert Gallatin, the veteran Jeffersonian, to London. There they met with Frederick Robinson and the Ghent negotiator Henry Goulburn in late August 1818.

Both sides were under the impression that the Treaty of Utrecht of 1713, which concluded the War of the Spanish Succession, set the forty-ninth parallel as the boundary between French Louisiana and British-held Rupert's Land, of which the Hudson's Bay Company had become the trustee. Utrecht did not in fact set such a boundary; it only provided for commissioners to decide how to set it. But several British maps of the eighteenth century, well known to Jefferson, Madison, and Monroe, fixed forty-nine degrees in a century-old tradition. Working from basically the same maps, the four commissioners quickly agreed on forty-nine degrees as the boundary "from the Lake of the Woods to the Stony [Rocky] Mountains." The "northwest boundary gap" left over from 1782 disappeared when they agreed that the boundary should run from the "most North Western Point of the Lake of the Woods" directly along the forty-ninth parallel, if that point happened to fall exactly on that parallel. If not, the boundary should extend "from the said Point due North or South as the Case may be" until it intersected the forty-ninth parallel. The result today is the projection on the map where the Northwest Angle of Minnesota juts up northward about thirty miles into the Lake of the Woods.

Extending the boundary along forty-nine degrees from the Northwest Angle to the crest of the Rockies gave the United States considerably more acreage than it lost. Again, watersheds were the reason. Not much of the Missouri's lay north of forty-nine degrees. But a considerably larger part of present North Dakota and Minnesota were within the watershed of the northward-flowing Red River, which runs from south of Fargo across the border and up into Lake Winnipeg. Britain gave up this goodly chunk of Rupert's Land, while the United States gave up a small fraction of the Missouri Valley. The United States was lucky once again.

Furthermore, the forty-ninth could easily be imagined as a westward-pointing arrow. The commissioners of 1818 could not agree to extend that line, or any other, to the Pacific. Still, it gave the Americans ideas about the future. Early in the War of 1812 the American trading post at Astoria surrendered to a British force, and the HBC took it over as Fort George. In 1817 the ever-acquisitive John Quincy Adams, by then secretary of state, insisted that it should be returned under the terms of the Treaty of Ghent. Adams sent an American sloop of war, the *Ontario*, to the mouth of the Columbia to underline U.S. determination to reestablish itself there. Castlereagh did no more than "regret" the voyage of the *Ontario*, and graciously restored Astoria to the United States, which reoccupied it on November 11, 1818, just four weeks after Gallatin, Rush, Robinson, and Goulburn signed their convention. In that potentially incendiary context, they prudently avoided arguing British and American claims to the Columbia and the northwest coast, and agreed instead that the area would "be free and open, for the term of ten Years . . . to the Vessels, Citizens, and Subjects of the Two Powers." And thus began the "condominium" (really just a recognition of unresolved claims) over the Oregon country.[14]

THE SPANISH QUITCLAIM, THE RUSSIAN RETREAT, AND 54°40'

Before 1819 the Oregon country had been defined only by the various discoveries and claims of Spain, Russia, Britain, and the United States. Soon after, it took the familiar shape seen so often on maps of American territorial expansion.

Spain had been first to arrive and it was the first claimant to depart, leaving another straight line on the map, the Adams-Onís boundary of Spanish California along the forty-second parallel. North of it the United States had a foothold resulting from Captain Gray's 1792 voyage, Lewis and Clark's exploration, and Astoria. Moreover, by the 1819 treaty the United States inherited all prior Spanish claims north of forty-two degrees. British diplomats would argue, wrongly, that the

Nootka Convention of 1790 nullified these. The United States trumpeted these Spanish precedents, since they now fortified the American case. The southern boundary of "Oregon" was henceforth forty-two degrees, and the northern boundary would depend on how successfully the United States could persuade anyone to credit the Spanish voyages. As things turned out, they did not help much.

Russia was next to leave. When the Russian-American Company's 1799 charter came up for renewal, the company pressed the government of Czar Alexander I for more official protection to ward off British and American ships they felt were encroaching on its coastal territory. The czar obliged with a ukase of September 15, 1821, claiming exclusive Russian rights to the coast north of fifty-one degrees and about one hundred miles out to sea. A second ukase of September 25 granted the company twenty years' more monopoly rights. As soon as the British and American governments learned of the ukases, they squealed, and began diplomatic negotiations—at first jointly, then separately—to reverse or limit the Russian claims. Surprisingly, the czarist government backed down, suddenly mindful of its much more urgent desire to induce Britain to support its interests in the Balkans vis-à-vis the Turks. The claim to one hundred miles out to sea was effectively revoked, and the coastal claim withdrawn northward to fifty-five degrees.

This was not enough for Adams and Monroe. When the Russian minister in Washington, a Ukrainian named Pierre de Poletica, presented a detailed exposition of Russia's position, Adams retorted with a claim up to sixty-one degrees, based on the inherited Spanish claims. The British reacted to this in December 1823 by withdrawing from the negotiations. The Americans forged ahead, and on March 4, 1824, Count Nesselrode, the Russian foreign minister, agreed that Russia would accept 54°40'. South of that, Russian ships would not go, and north of it Americans should not go, except to trade at the port of Novo-Archangelsk (now Sitka).

This became the basis for the later American cry of "fifty-four-forty or fight." It completely ignored the British, the only actual presence at that moment between 42° and 54°40', in the form of the Hudson's Bay Company. The Americans accepted, and on April 17, 1824, signed the Russo-American Convention. After protracted talks, the British followed suit, accepting 54°40' as *their* northern limit, as well as recognizing Russian rights to a *lisière*, or coastal strip, north of it. That subsequently became the Alaska panhandle. The British gained their main object, which was to preserve the fur-rich interior for the Hudson's Bay Company. In return for a north-south boundary of northern Alaska at 141° west longitude, about one hundred miles west of where the Russians wanted it, the British signed their own convention with Russia in February 1825. The northwestern boundary of British North America was finally fixed. So too was the boundary that became Alaska's, forty-two years later.[15]

With Spanish claims north of forty-two degrees quitclaimed to the United States, and Russia stopping at 54°40', the limits of the Oregon country were no longer vague. Oregon lay between those two latitudes, from the crest of the Rockies—the continental divide—to the Pacific. The contestants were now narrowed to Britain and the United States. Sooner or later their joint occupancy would have to end. As usual, the competing historic claims to discovery were argued and counterargued. Britain had an edge because the Hudson's Bay Company was actually there, but the United States could claim prior discovery by Captain Gray in 1792 and the spectral Spanish sailors long before that. A permanent division seemed imminent as the ten years of joint occupancy were coming to an end. British interests—really the HBC's fur trading—focused on gaining permanent control of New Caledonia (later, British Columbia), north of forty-nine degrees, and the Columbia River south of it.

The Americans, despite Adams's extravagant feint at sixty-one degrees during the Russian negotiations, proposed to the British in 1824 that forty-nine degrees to the ocean should be the border between British and American territory. Britain counterproposed that the forty-nine-degree line be extended westward from the Rockies, where it then stopped, only as far as the Columbia, and then follow that river to the Pacific. In other words, put simply, the only area *not* agreed upon was what was west and north of the Columbia, the western 60 percent of the present state of Washington. Formal talks proceeded in London in late 1826, with Gallatin again arguing the American case. The British would not concede the Columbia. But since the Americans were really after deepwater harbors along Puget Sound, the British offered them the Olympic Peninsula from the western shore of Puget Sound to the Pacific, which would become an enclave surrounded by British territory. Gallatin declined. The talks led only to an agreement to extend the 1818 line indefinitely, but terminable on a year's notice from either side. "Indefinitely" turned out to be less than twenty-five years.

The Hudson's Bay Company in Sole Possession, 1821–1834

During the first half of that period the HBC's people were virtually the only Europeans in Oregon. After 1834 Americans began trickling in, though few appeared before 1840. As the diplomats dickered in the 1820s, the HBC expanded from a few scattered fur traders to about 458 employees by the mid-1830s in its "Department of Columbia," out of about 1,300 in all of British North America. The 458 included 138 Europeans, 47 "half-breeds," 218 "Canadians" (i.e., French), and 55 Sandwich Islanders (Hawaiians).[16] The company's officers on the ground were called "chief traders," who reported to "chief factors." In the Department of Columbia the chief factor was Dr. John McLoughlin, born in Rivière-du-Loup on the St. Lawrence River, student of medicine in Europe, and faithful officer of the HBC. By the mid-1820s a "servant" of the company, Simon Plomondon, a French-Canadian, became the first permanent white settler on the Cowlitz Prairie between the Columbia and Puget Sound. When other "servants" retired, they and their families often settled on land both north and south of the Columbia, some at French Prairie along the Willamette.

McLoughlin's boss was George Simpson at Lachine, near Montreal. Simpson's rule was "virtually absolute," his personality "essentially amoral" with only "two loyalties—to his company and to himself—and he served both with great ability and complete devotion," though with unblemished honesty.[17] His visits west of the Rockies were few but decisive.

By the 1821 merger, the Hudson's Bay Company took over seven "forts" or posts of the North West Company in the Oregon country, all begun between 1809 and 1818. The posts were arrayed along the Columbia and Snake Rivers, all but one south of the forty-ninth parallel. Simpson closed Fort George (previously called Astoria) and instructed McLoughlin to build a new headquarters eighty miles up the Columbia on its north bank, near its confluence with the Willamette. Named Fort Vancouver, it opened in March 1825. To this string the Hudson's Bay Company gradually added posts above forty-nine degrees, most significantly Fort Victoria at the southern tip of Vancouver Island, begun in 1842.

The HBC fur trading prospered. Nevertheless, Simpson and his London superiors foresaw that when the boundary was finally drawn, the United States was likely to win the Snake River country and the area south of the Columbia (present Oregon). Accordingly, they set out systematically to denude the Snake River valley of fur-bearing animals, as a deterrent to American fur companies that threatened to invade the HBC domain west of the Rockies. The tactic worked; though one hundred to three hundred Americans trapped near the Snake every season in the early 1830s, they remained transient. Trapping in that area thinned out to below the break-even point. In those same seasons, the upper Columbia field proved to be increasingly rich and the HBC's focus slowly shifted northward. British government concern did so as well.

During the 1820s and 1830s, the Columbia River trade and McLoughlin's chief factorship at Fort Vancouver prospered. The few American trappers along the Snake and occasional American trading vessels along the coast did no real damage to the HBC's operations. By the early 1830s, human activity in the Oregon country consisted mainly of thousands of Indians and the few hundred HBC operatives scattered among them. The extension in 1827 of the "joint occupancy" actually favored the United States, since it had no real "occupancy" at that moment.

Yet the British had reason to predict that eventually Americans would appear and would in time outnumber anyone British, whether the HBC or actual settlers. Beginning in 1820, a Virginia congressman, John Floyd, had proposed bills claiming all of Oregon from the forty-second parallel indefinitely north. President Monroe's "non-colonization" message to Congress of December 1823, known later as the Monroe Doctrine, set American policy at least in theory against further British expansion on the northwest coast. In 1830 a New England schoolteacher, Hall Jackson Kelley, published a pamphlet beating the drum for American control of the Oregon country. Kelley reached many ready ears in that expansion-minded Jacksonian day. Kelley asserted that "the American Republic claims a right of sovereignty" from the Pacific to "the summit of the Rocky Mountains . . . and likewise over the country extending . . . to 54–30 [*sic*] north latitude. . . . It was included in the Louisiana Purchase." He followed with a long and tendentious list of American exploratory claims beginning with Gray and Kendrick, as well as the ancient Spanish claims, and he derided "the rights which England set up to this country" as "predicated on idle and arrogant pretensions."[18] Kelley's assertions were echoed in the press, particularly in the upper

Mississippi Valley, then "the West." Editors demanded Oregon, removal of eastern Indians to far frontiers, and support for Texan freedom (from their Mexican hosts). The public was eager to embrace manifest destiny, though the phrase had to wait until 1845. A French observer wrote in early 1846, "The occupation of Oregon by the Americans seems to me today to be not in doubt, but simply a question of time."[19]

Despite the hubbub, Oregon's human population in 1830 remained around 90,000 Indians divided into dozens of tribes and decimated by epidemics, and 1,000 or so French, Anglophone, and "half-breed" servants of the HBC. McLoughlin was operating Fort Vancouver with energy, brilliance, profits, and the confidence of his superiors.

The first crack in this economic and political edifice came in late 1834. Jason Lee, a Methodist missionary from Connecticut, arrived with a nephew and three other men at Fort Vancouver to begin converting Indians, who, they had heard, were clamoring for Christianity. The Lees soon headed south into the nearby Willamette Valley close to a settlement of retired HBC "servants." They found few Indians, since they had been mostly wiped out by the recent malaria epidemic, but the Lees liked the land and began farming. In 1836, led there by American fur traders, Marcus and Narcissa Whitman and three companions arrived in the Snake River country and founded a Presbyterian mission about twenty-five miles east of Fort Nez Percés. Several other missionaries followed in 1838 and 1839, again guided by fur traders. By then the Lees' Willamette settlement included 28 men (10 of them clergy), 6 wives, and 23 Canadian retirees of the HBC.

Three Catholic priests appeared in 1838 to minister to the largely Catholic HBC people and to evangelize the Indians. One was the indefatigable Belgian Jesuit Pierre-Jean DeSmet, whose subsequent book-length report would be widely read, making Oregon known in the United States and elsewhere.[20] DeSmet, like everyone else, gave high marks to McLoughlin. "During this fearful visitation [the epidemics of the early 1830s], which attacked the colonists as well as the natives, Dr. McLaughlin [*sic*] displayed the most heroic philanthropy, in his laborious attention to the sick and the dying." And he continued to do so as "fever and ague" reappeared through 1844.[21] McLoughlin's generosity to settlers became legendary.

Few settlers arrived before 1840; the day of the wagon train was a few years off. But American attentions multiplied. A fur-trading expedition led by Nathaniel Wyeth extolled Oregon. William Slacum, a naval officer sent by Secretary of State John Forsyth to report on local conditions, warned in 1837 that the HBC had to be countered since it stood in the way of U.S. interests south of the forty-ninth parallel. Senator Lewis Linn of Missouri entered a series of bills in Congress baldly declaring Oregon a U.S. territory under American laws and military protection. Jason Lee returned east in 1838 to spread the word of Oregon's attractions. Washington Irving published his romantic travelogue *Astoria*. The Great American Exploring Expedition under Lieutenant Charles Wilkes, sent by President Van Buren to Antarctica and the Pacific, opined that ports on Puget Sound were absolutely necessary. As for settlers, the economic depression that hit the eastern states from 1837 to 1841 made migration attractive, and in 1840 they started arriving. Not all of them were the kind of people whom the missionaries might have preferred.[22]

None of this interest threatened the HBC in any immediate way. Yet the longer-term implications did not escape McLoughlin, Simpson, or the London directors. Simpson and McLoughlin were summoned to London in 1838. The result was the sponsoring of real settlement for the first time. British, Canadian, and American fur traders all knew that "settlement kills the fur trade," and until then the HBC had avoided and discouraged settlers. But when Simpson was in London in February 1839, the HBC board created a subsidiary it called the Puget Sound Agricultural Company. It had three purposes. It would assure more dependable food supplies to Fort Vancouver. It would profitably supply the Russian posts to the north, with which the HBC was sharing control of the coast, shutting out American trading ships more tightly. Finally, it would solidify the company's (and Britain's) presence below forty-nine degrees, filling the area with its own people and preempting Americans from settling there. Land would be opened for settlement at Fort Nisqually, at the southern tip of Puget Sound, and at Cowlitz Farms, about halfway between there and Fort Vancouver. Where to get settlers? First, from the company's retirees, who had headed for the Willamette Valley but would now be encouraged to go northward; and second, farmers from Simpson's and the directors' native Scotland. The terms were leaseholds, with the farmers to keep half the proceeds from the livestock and produce they raised, the company retaining the other half.

A fine proposition—in Scotland. Simpson regarded it as almost irresistible, a terrific deal. But Oregon was not Scotland. Compared to fee-simple homesteads available in the nearby Willamette Valley, the HBC terms were stingy sharecropping arrangements. No Scots ever came, nor did the retirees. The company fell back on recruiting from the problematic Red River settlement (around present Winnipeg), which had struggled along since the Earl of Selkirk had begun it in 1811 and which by 1839 may have had about 700 families. Even from there, only 21 families (116 people) emigrated to Oregon. McLoughlin sent 14 of them, "primarily English half-breeds," to Nisqually, and the other 7, "French Canadians and half-breeds," to Cowlitz. Few though they were, they outnumbered all the Americans in the region in 1841.[23] The Puget Sound Agricultural Company was a failed idea. Before long, the Red River migrants headed south to the Willamette Valley for those larger homesteads, joining the retirees, who had respectfully declined the invitation.

As of 1838 no more than forty Americans lived in Oregon. In 1840 four more missionary couples arrived, led by Joel Walker. In 1841 came the covered wagons of twenty-four members of the group known as Bidwell-Bartleson, half of whom had split off to become the first overland settlers in California. In 1842 another 125 arrived. The Oregon Trail was now clearly marked and fur traders were no longer needed as guides. The Oregon country was on the verge of a major migration.

At this point George Simpson appeared on one of his rare visits. Between the fall of 1841 and spring 1842, he stayed at Fort Vancouver and inspected (without McLoughlin) the company's posts to the north. He decided to shift its main focus from the Columbia to Puget Sound. The decision had consequences much greater than they seemed at the time, large though they were. Many of the functions of Fort Vancouver would move to a new base, Fort Victoria, on the southern tip of Vancouver Island. Although Fort Vancouver remained the HBC's western headquarters until 1849 and was not fully closed until 1860, Lord Aberdeen interpreted this as a relocation of the company's "principal settlement."[24] Certainly it was a major shift in priorities.

Simpson had several reasons for the change. He was irked when his ship's departure from Fort Vancouver was held up for three weeks because it was too dangerous to cross the notorious sand bars at the mouth of the Columbia. Victoria's deepwater harbor presented no such barrier to navigation. Also, the fur yields along the lower Columbia had faded, as they had in the Snake River valley (and in a few years they would dwindle virtually to nothing), while the coast and interior north of forty-nine degrees promised to be richer than ever. From the sheer profit-making viewpoint, the shift was advisable.

Simpson and McLoughlin feared vandalism from American settlers. Few though they still were, Simpson regarded them as "worthless, lawless characters" who, if they were hungry enough, might be tempted to raid lightly defended Fort Vancouver's rich stores. Finally, Simpson worried that the future boundary settlement—there would have to be one someday—would give both banks of the Columbia, maybe everything south of the forty-eighth parallel, to the United States. The company's property along the Columbia might be protected in the boundary settlement, but then again it might not. The steady increase in migrants from the States threatened not only the fur trade but also the "joint occupancy" itself. Better to expand Fort Victoria, Simpson decided, so that it "should by degrees supersede Fort Vancouver as the company's headquarters for the entire region."[25] After Simpson went home, McLoughlin sent James Douglas, his deputy, to Vancouver Island to pick a spot. Douglas reported in July 1842 that Victoria had a fine harbor and nearby crop and pasture land. In March 1843, Douglas and crew began building the new fort.[26]

McLoughlin, Douglas, and Simpson kept a precise count of the American settlers. After Simpson arrived in late 1841, he wrote London that along the Columbia were nine American missions containing about one hundred people as well as more than one hundred others—half Americans, half company retirees—along the Willamette. Almost certainly, more would come. On November 25, 1841, he remarked that "all these people have taken possession of tracts of country at pleasure, which they expect to retain under a good title arising from such possession, whenever the Boundary question may be determined. . . ."[27]

More did come—in 1842 about 140, doubling the American presence. The idea of a provisional government began to spread around the Methodist mission on the Willamette. In May 1843 the settlers created one by a 52–50 vote, 50 of the yeas coming from Americans, the 50 negatives from French HBC retirees. Its "laws" favored the Anglos and not the retirees.[28] Later that year much larger groups arrived, 875 people all told. Their leaders revamped the provisional government and began working cooperatively with McLoughlin, who was extending credit (nearly £7,000) and supplies to the settlers. Simpson and the London directors complained, but McLoughlin, aside from his native generosity, felt he had little choice. The settlers either individually and violently or through the "provisional government" and quasi-legally, were capable of taking over Fort Vancouver itself. American pamphleteers had spread lies accusing McLoughlin and the HBC of instigating Indian raids on migrant trains that resulted in the deaths of hundreds of would-be settlers. Senator Thomas Hart Benton of Missouri made claims nearly as defamatory on the floor of the Senate. Migrants listened to these calumnies and arrived in a hostile frame of mind. McLoughlin's benevolence placated many, though not all.

After the migration of 1843, it was obvious that Fort Vancouver and the HBC had a dim future on the Columbia. Another 1,400 Americans arrived in 1844, and 3,000 more in 1845, bringing the total to around 6,000. They were scattered in farms and in the new town of Oregon City at the falls of the Willamette, about twenty miles upstream from the Columbia. By 1845, the village had about one hundred houses and three hundred people, with a Methodist chapel at the south end and a Catholic one at the north, reflecting its bipolar culture. To compete, McLoughlin opened a trading post there and acquired some land. His personal and policy differences with Simpson, festering since Simpson's 1841–1842 visit, caused London to pension off McLoughlin. He moved to Oregon City in early 1846 and apparently became an American citizen in 1849.[29]

The Willamette settlers emphatically did not include African-Americans. One of the 1844 emigrant parties was led by Michael Simmons and one George W. Bush, who had been employed in the 1820s by the HBC in New Caledonia. Bush was part black. The group discovered that the provisional government banned black people from holding Willamette land. The Bush-Simmons party therefore headed north and settled near the southern tip of Puget Sound at present Tumwater, Washington. The thirty-two people in their community were the only Americans north of the Columbia as of 1845.[30]

MAINE FIRST, OREGON SECOND, 1842–1846

Anglo-American relations had survived some fractious times in the late 1830s—a scuffle along the Niagara frontier, a ship seizure—and both governments desired strongly by 1842 to patch things up. A long-simmering argument clouded the boundary between Maine and New Brunswick, left in cartographical mystery in the 1782–1783 treaties. The king of the Netherlands arbitrated a compromise in 1831, but Maine and the United States rejected it. By the early 1840s American settlers had ensconced themselves in eastern Maine and, from the British point of view, were encroaching. The dispute demanded settlement. If the Oregon boundary could be resolved too, that would be desirable; but "Oregon fever" had not yet become high, and in 1842 Maine was a more pressing problem.

Alexander Baring, a sixty-eight-year-old banker known also as Lord Ashburton, took ship from England in mid-February 1842 as the emissary of Foreign Secretary Lord Aberdeen. Ashburton arrived at Annapolis early in April and proceeded to Washington. Secretary of State Daniel Webster (himself sixty-two by then) and Ashburton sat down to settle their countries' outstanding problems. They were several: the northeastern (Maine) boundary, the lingering slave trade, the extradition of serious criminals, and the Oregon boundary.

Both negotiators were surprised and pressured by local interests that clamored for much more than they reasonably deserved. Washington's heat and humidity were awful that summer, and by July 1, they were bothering Ashburton badly. Hurrying things along, the two reached agreement on the Maine–New Brunswick boundary by mid-July. Quickly they proceeded to agree on smaller boundary disputes along the St. Lawrence and the Lake of the Woods; on the slave trade; and on a few minor American-Canadian irritants left over from the 1830s. Then they took one good look at the Oregon question and decided they could not resolve it in a hurry.

Postponing Oregon, they signed the Webster-Ashburton Treaty on August 9, 1842. The U.S. Senate ratified it forthwith and, after some delay in London because of objections raised by the feisty leader of the Whig opposition, Lord Palmerston, so did Britain. Both negotiators were praised—and also vilified by some—in their respective countries. A latter-day Canadian assessment complained that Ashburton "abandoned more than 2,000 French-Canadian settlers [in the Madawaska district], stranding them on the U.S. side of the Saint John River where they have since been all but assimilated." Another, however, called it "a compromise, but quite a good compromise."[31] But was a good compromise available for the Oregon country? It did not seem so.

Settlers kept pouring across the Rockies and into the Willamette Valley. Indians continued to suffer from imported diseases; and the skins of the Northwest's smaller animals became the beaver hats of bourgeois

Europe. The diplomats relaxed through 1843 and into 1844. The presidential campaign focused on expansion, but the noise was about Texas, not Oregon. Pamphlets and broadsides meticulously and tendentiously traced the respective justifications of the superior rights of Britain or the United States. The most serious American arguments came from Robert Greenhow, a State Department employee, affirming the priority of the old Spanish claims inherited in 1819 and the visits of Captain Gray, Lewis and Clark, and the Astorians. On the British side, Adam Thom, the HBC legal counsel in Rupert's Land, declared that despite all the American settlers on "the Wallamet," they did not reduce "England's original claim of prior settlement" to which "England sees not even the shadow of a rival." The barren wastelands on both sides of the Rockies destroyed the Americans' argument that Oregon was "contiguous" with the United States, and Thom reasserted that nature made the Columbia River the boundary.[32] These were lawyerly briefs. Soon, however, Lord Palmerston and President Polk ratcheted up the rhetoric by introducing dangerously nonnegotiable assertions of "national honor." By early 1846 a real possibility of war existed. On even sillier grounds, it had broken out in 1812.

After Webster-Ashburton, Lord Aberdeen remained eager to settle the Oregon boundary question. The American minister in London, Edward Everett, was on friendly terms with Aberdeen and other key officials, and in early 1844 Aberdeen sent a new minister, Richard Pakenham, to Washington. The Oregon problem could have been settled had the State Department and the president been as frank and eager as Everett and Aberdeen. Pakenham's instructions reiterated the British position of 1826–1827: the forty-ninth parallel west of the Rockies as far as the Columbia, and then downriver to the sea. Aberdeen told Pakenham privately that he could live with forty-nine degrees all the way to the Pacific (excepting Vancouver Island, which juts well south of that parallel), but he could not make that position part of Pakenham's formal instructions because they might cause a political uproar. Later a puzzled Pakenham, then in Washington, felt obliged to stick to his formal instructions and kept that fallback deep in his pocket.

Through the summer of 1844 Pakenham had several talks with the new secretary of state, John C. Calhoun. They made little progress. Calhoun had recently stated in the Senate that the Oregon question should be treated with "masterly inactivity," and he stuck to that approach and to a boundary along the forty-ninth parallel to the ocean, Vancouver

Island excepted.[33] Officially Britain held to the Columbia boundary but would probably have accepted the forty-ninth; the United States would have agreed to it too, although its top officials had let 54°40' seduce public opinion.

While diplomats and politicians parleyed, settlers kept arriving on the Willamette. The "provisional government" claimed more and more authority, jostling McLoughlin and the HBC. In then-western states such as Indiana, Illinois, and Missouri, the clamor for "all of Oregon" increased. Delegates from that region to the Democratic National Convention in June 1844 slid a plank into the platform calling for the "re"-annexation of Texas and the "re"-occupation of the whole of Oregon, that is, as far north as 54°40'.

The "fifty-four-forty or fight" slogan was not broadly shouted during the 1844 campaign, as most eyes were on Texas. But expansionism pleased the voters; the Democratic Party was correctly perceived as the expansionist party; and its candidate, Polk, was expansion's champion. A Tennessean who had been speaker of the House in the mid-1830s, so closely identified with Andrew Jackson as to be nicknamed "Young Hickory," Polk still consulted the old man for spine-stiffening advice. He defeated the Whig candidate, Henry Clay, painted as a waffler on expansion, by a large enough margin to claim a mandate to go ahead not only on Texas, but on Oregon—if not to fifty-four-forty, certainly to the forty-ninth. He would, he proclaimed, "look John Bull in the eye" to get it. His inaugural address was extravagantly bellicose. Polk asserted, "Our title to the country of the Oregon is 'clear and unquestionable,' and already are our people preparing to perfect that title by occupying it with their wives and children. . . . The jurisdiction of our laws and the benefits of our republican institutions should be extended over them in the distant regions which they have selected for their homes."[34] Aberdeen proposed an arbitrator, but Polk repeatedly said no to that, on the ground that agreeing to arbitration meant accepting some portion of the other side's claims. Jackson was urging Polk to take a "bold stance," and the protégé did.

On July 12, 1845, Polk's secretary of state, the future president James Buchanan, gave Pakenham the first American proposal in ten months. It asked for the forty-ninth-parallel line all the way to the Pacific, including the southern portion of Vancouver Island, except for a free port for Britain's use—and no open navigation on the Columbia. While not matching what Aberdeen had privately told Pakenham he would accept, it was a serious starting point. But in a near-fatal blunder, Pakenham turned down the proposal without bothering to refer it to London. Polk became incensed, and withdrew the offer. Buchanan and Pakenham danced around through the fall, trying to find a new start, but Polk refused to budge. In his annual message to Congress on December 2, 1845, he asked Congress to authorize him to give the one year's notice needed to abrogate the 1827 joint occupancy agreement and to extend American law over the Oregon settlers.

Polk was risking a rupture with Britain at the very time that his country was annexing Texas, which was virtually certain to touch off a war with Mexico. As one historian wrote, Polk consistently adopted fairly extreme positions, "positions of strength," from which he could retreat and still gain a great deal. The problem with this tactic is that it is not always easy to retreat without appearing to have been pushed; nor is it easy to talk strongly without goading the other side into stiff resistance. Buchanan and several Democratic senators gradually nudged Polk away from his adamancy. The onetime arch-expansionist Thomas Hart Benton of Missouri, for one, urged Polk to at least listen to a British proposal if one were forthcoming (aside from arbitration, which Polk stubbornly refused).

Polk in his own mind was already thinking less belligerently by Christmastime. His diary reveals that he was far from a rabid fifty-four-forty man at that point. He was willing to listen to a British proposal along forty-nine degrees. If he received one, he wrote, "I would consult confidentially three or four Senators from different parts of the union, and might submit it to the Senate for their previous advice."[35]

Not that he had softened completely. His famous statement that "the only way to treat John Bull was to look him straight in the eye" came on January 4, 1846, in a conversation with a South Carolina congressman. Perhaps he meant to bolster party unity; perhaps he spoke from his heart. Polk may have hoped for a palatable proposal from the British, but did not know how to invite one without losing face (and perhaps territory).

In late January 1846, Polk and Buchanan wrote the American minister in London, Louis McLane. The president still wanted all of Oregon and would not agree to a neutral arbitrator, but he might possibly entertain a proposal rather like the one the United States had made the previous July 12 but which Pakenham had rejected without referring it home: forty-nine degrees to the ocean, British free ports on Vancouver Island.

Polk would transmit it to the Senate without recommendation, and he would consider it if the Senate approved it.[36]

It was by no means certain that Britain would propose much of anything. Palmerston and the press belittled the Americans and their ill-based claims to "all of Oregon." Aberdeen was hard put to persuade Prime Minister Peel that diplomacy could still work. Aberdeen had never cared much about Oregon, and the British government did not regard itself as the handmaiden of the HBC. But it was without doubt the guardian of the national honor. As long as Oregon was chiefly an HBC matter, Aberdeen was very much in charge. If and when it touched on British honor, he was boxed in. The American intransigence was provoking howls among the press and the Whig opposition, forcing Peel and the peace-minded Aberdeen toward a naval buildup—purely defensive, of course—should war break out over Oregon.

When Polk met with the cabinet on February 4, all present were aware that Britain was making "military and naval preparations" in case of conflict.[37] Later that month, the cabinet received a message from McLane, dated February 3, reporting on a conversation he had just had with the foreign secretary. Aberdeen, McLane reported, "would not abandon the desire or the hope that an amicable adjustment might yet be effected, and peace preserved." But he could no longer oppose "measures founded upon the contingency of war" or "preparations which might be deemed necessary not only for the defense and protection of the Canadas, but for offensive operations." McLane warned that the "preparations" would include "the immediate equipment of thirty sail of the line beside steamers and other vessels of war."[38]

This news had an abruptly sobering effect on Polk and his cabinet. It shifted the president from rejecting a British proposal to inviting one. War could break out, and not just with Mexico. On February 26 Buchanan instructed McLane to spell out American receptivity to a forty-ninth-parallel-except-Vancouver-Island proposal. If Aberdeen would make such an offer, Polk intended to ask the Senate for prior approval.

That is what happened. Aberdeen wrote what basically became the treaty, Polk sent it to the Senate, the Senate gave its blessing, and Polk did not have to swallow the words in his December message to Congress about fifty-four-forty. Some months later, Senator Daniel Webster observed that usually "treaties are negotiated by the President and ratified by the Senate, but here is the reverse . . . a treaty negotiated by the

Senate, and only agreed to by the President." But the real author of the treaty was Aberdeen. "The fact was," wrote historian Julius Pratt, "that President Polk had carried his game of looking John Bull in the eye a trifle too far, and John Bull was looking back with menacing glare. Polk's eye wavered."[39]

During those same spring days, the House of Representatives gave Polk the resolution he had requested in December, abrogating the 1827 joint occupancy. The subsequent debate in the Senate occupied several weeks, but while extremists still ranted, the throatiest "fifty-four-forty" talk of January and February receded. The final resolution, which dropped the grossest claims to Oregon, passed by a large margin on April 16. The extremists were clearly in the minority. The Texas annexation and the imminent conflict with Mexico diverted attention from Oregon. In Britain the Peel government was preoccupied with struggles to repeal the Corn Laws (Britain's system of protective tariffs on agricultural products) and to cope with the emerging disaster of the Irish famine. Peel's government, and Aberdeen's Oregon diplomacy along with it, was in danger of collapse. If so, the much more hard-line Palmerston would take over the Foreign Office. Both Washington and London, therefore, were under serious time pressure to agree on Oregon.

Thus Oregon was settled. The forty-ninth-degree line would extend from the Rockies to the Pacific except for Vancouver Island, which, with Fort Victoria, would remain British. The last sticking point—and here Polk dug in his heels—was the right of navigation on the Columbia. The treaty included it but limited it to the HBC, and (in the American interpretation) only until the company's charter expired in 1859. The Senate informally agreed to this on June 13, and after Polk approved it, formally ratified the treaty on August 10, with 41 Whigs and Democrats voting in favor, 14 Democrats opposed.[40] In London the treaty was approved almost simultaneously with the repeal of the Corn Laws. The Peel government and Aberdeen fell as predicted, replaced by Lord John Russell as prime minister and Palmerston as foreign secretary. The finished product had a loose end or two, but the Oregon crisis was over.[41]

WHO WON?

Briefly and bluntly, the winners in Oregon were the American settlers. They got their wish to be incorporated into the United States and on the basis of their own land and tax laws. The U.S. government also won, gaining the Northwest. The losers, once again, were the Indians, reduced by imported disease and treatied out of their land. The Hudson's Bay Company lost too, although its monopolistic days within the British Empire were numbered anyway and its activities along the Columbia had become marginal. McLoughlin retired honorably from the HBC to Oregon City but was forced to fight American settler-legislators for the rest of his life to keep his property. Britain avoided a war, retained a Pacific coastline for Canada, but gave up the area from the Columbia to Puget Sound—in Aberdeen's view, a "few miles of pine swamp," but to others, something rather more valuable.

Could either Britain or the United States have gained more than they did? What difference did the American settler migration make? It is broadly accepted that the HBC, and therefore the British government, made no practical claim after 1826 to anything south of the Columbia. From there south to forty-two degrees, the 1819 U.S. treaty line with Spain, the United States won by default. Conversely, the land north of forty-nine degrees had been conceded (except by the rabid fifty-four-forty men) to the HBC and Britain, practically if not legally, ever since Oregon came on the diplomatic screen in 1818. A rump of expansionists insisted on the "promise" of 54°40' in the Democratic platform of 1844, but this extreme claim proved to be weak, partisan, and sectional in the House and Senate votes of early 1846. Polk and Buchanan became more reasonable when the issue came to a head.

How much those "thirty sail of the line" persuaded them, we cannot know for certain. Polk had been pouting for months after Pakenham declined his July 1845 proposal, thereafter flatly refusing arbitration but hinting privately that he would entertain a new British offer. When it came, it was what Aberdeen, though not the HBC, had been willing to settle for all along. Britain would not go to war for Oregon, unless the issue of "national honor" became too clamorous. In that event, Aberdeen and Peel would have no choice. Fortunately they were not pressed that far. The United States could not have tried for more, "more" being the area between 49° and 54°40', without pushing Britain into a war of national honor.

The Americans no doubt did get more than they deserved, if "deserved" is a function not only of discovery but of settlement. By early 1846 several thousand Americans had arrived in the Willamette Valley south of the Columbia. North of the Columbia, near present Olympia and in the shadow of the HBC's Fort Nisqually, no more than two dozen families had settled, no bother to the HBC.[42] From Fort Nisqually northward for a good 150 miles to forty-nine degrees, there were no Americans at all. Except for the Wilkes Expedition in 1841 and a few other explorations, the United States had no claim, contact, or even knowledge of the Puget Sound area and north of it to 54°40', the southern tip of Russian Alaska. Going to war for Oregon north of forty-nine degrees, or for that matter north of the Columbia had it come to that, would have been absurd.

And foolhardy. Consider what could have happened if war had broken out between Britain and the United States in 1846. Britain had been the world's greatest naval power for generations and would be for more. She would not have needed to send "thirty sail of the line" to annihilate whatever naval force the United States could have opposed to her in the North Pacific. The HBC had for years carried on friendly relations with local Indians, and some in London felt they could count on the Indians in a struggle with American settlers.[43] Britain would have kept the area north of the Columbia, the San Juan Islands, and likely much more. Since the United States was starting a war with Mexico, Britain could have intervened in that conflict or precluded it, and the United States would not have gained what it did, namely, the present Southwest. It might even have had to retreat from Texas; Britain had preferred an independent Texas and might have sent a force to "liberate" it and drive its few thousand slaveholders back into Louisiana and points east. In the Pacific, an eager British admiral had already occupied Hawaii in 1843, and though his own government ordered him to give it up, Britain could have retaken it easily enough. Hawaii, Midway, Guam, and quite likely the Philippines would not have become American either.

So perhaps Aberdeen was too accommodating. He was the second British earl, after Lord Shelburne in 1782, who proved to be extremely helpful to the United States in its quest for territory.

Were the American settlers along the Willamette responsible for the acquisition? Surely not north of the Columbia, for there were virtually none there. Neither did they receive any mention or nods in the official correspondence among Polk and Buchanan, Pakenham and McLane, Aberdeen and Peel. But they were in every negotiator's mind and private correspondence. In an indirect but immediate sense, they were responsible. As Charles Elliot, the British representative in Texas, wrote to Aberdeen in June 1845, the Americans' threat was "in the Settler . . . not in their Armies and Navies."[44] In the same vein, Lord Castlereagh is said to have once remarked to an American diplomat, "You need not trouble yourselves about Oregon, you will conquer Oregon in your bedchambers."[45] They were explicitly seen by Simpson, by James Douglas, and by the London directors of the HBC as threats even as early as 1841. They figured largely in the HBC's decision to move its western headquarters from Fort Vancouver on the Columbia to Fort Victoria at the tip of Vancouver Island. The American settlers had ruined the fur trade along the lower Columbia, had encroached on company land south and north of the river, and were not to be stopped. The company knew from its rueful experience with the Red River settlement (in present Manitoba) that it had no effective way to police settlers, even cooperative and friendly ones, which the Anglophobic Americans were definitely not. And since official Britain at that moment had no great interest in the Pacific coast or in western Canada, retreat by the HBC removed any good reason for Britain to defend those areas—except national honor, if the Americans had foolishly forced that into play.

There was no British equivalent to the Americans' "Oregon fever," no emotional, patriotic pressure to acquire a region it did not inhabit and did not know. That "fever" was the great intangible, not to be quantified, not to be rationalized, but not to be defied. Jefferson, Madison, Jackson, and dozens of lesser voices had proclaimed the justice and inevitability of the United States' westward advance for over half a century. Contrary voices, even moderates like Henry Clay in 1844, could only temper the imperialism, never thwart it. Lieutenant Wilkes had made a good case for why the United States needed harbors on Puget Sound for strategy and the China trade,[46] and Oregon fever was so high that it almost caused a war. But without the settlers the United States would not have come near the forty-ninth parallel west of the Columbia. Demography continued to define diplomacy, not as univocally as in Texas or Florida, but still decisively.

The federal census of 1850 was the first to enumerate the Oregon Territory, which was established on August 14, 1848. The census gives us a fascinating profile. The head count was 13,294 inhabitants, all white but for 207 free blacks and "mulattos." About 8,000 were male and 5,000 female. The age distribution was typical of settlement frontiers: about 41 percent under 15 years old, 48 percent between 15 and 40, and 11 percent over 40. That adds up to a preponderance of children, youthfully exuberant and rapidly reproducing young couples, and unattached males. It had fewer foreign-born, only 7 percent, than most frontiers, in sharp contrast with California to the south. Already, a quarter of the population (the children and youths) were native Oregonians, testifying to a remarkable birthrate. The Ohio and Mississippi Valley states accounted for about two-thirds of the adults, led by Missouri with more than 2,200. The Missouri number may have been swollen by people who "jumped off" from Independence or St. Louis onto the Overland Trail, though they originated farther east. Iowa had a surprisingly high number (452) for a similar reason; many wagon trains left from Council Bluffs.

New York contributed 1,430, more than a tenth, and Pennsylvania 553. New Englanders were well represented, but southerners were not; they could reach Texas much more easily. Oregon as yet had no colleges and few public schools but already twenty-nine private academies enrolling several hundred "pupils," and two weekly newspapers. The territory had 1,164 farms, averaging 372 acres, much higher than in the migrants' typical places of origin; a lot of land could be had, and cheaply. Ten counties had been organized, eight of them in the Willamette Valley as far south as Corvallis, about fifty miles upstream from Oregon City. North of the Columbia were only two: Clark (including the fort and settlement of Vancouver) and Lewis (which included the Cowlitz Farms), together containing only 1,201 people, just 9 percent of the territory's total. The largest village, Oregon City, had about 700 residents.[47]

As a new settlement frontier, the Oregon Territory looked like most others above the Mason-Dixon line as to sex, color, age, rural-urban distribution, and cultural and economic activity. The early Oregonians were rough-and-ready border-state farmers, young and lusty, Anglophobic, Negrophobic, Indian-phobic, and land-hungry. A freehold homestead was their goal. They would be yeoman farmers within a republic that permitted them the maximum individual choice.

In the three seasons after the boundary settlement, 1846 through 1848, about 6,500 more newcomers arrived. At that point the California gold rush erupted, and the stream to Oregon almost flattened. From 1849 through 1860, another 53,000 came to Oregon while more than 200,000 chose California.[48] Along the Willamette, recently the home of several tribes, the Indian population may have sunk as low as five hundred by 1850 (the census did not enumerate them).[49] Settlers gradually ventured north of the Columbia, and on March 2, 1853, the Territory of Washington officially split off from Oregon, thanks to the agitation of settlers at the foot of Puget Sound, for whom the territorial capital in Oregon City was too distant. Washington's statehood, however, was some time in coming. While Oregon entered the union in 1859, Washington had to wait until 1889.

The treaty was silent on whether the eastern or western channel around the San Juan Islands was the true border. Was it the Rosario Strait east of the islands, which would have given them to Britain (and later, Canada), or the Haro Strait west of them, which made them American? Lord Aberdeen told Minister McLane that "the Canal de Arro" was what he had in mind, but he failed to mention that to Pakenham, and so the treaty remained vague. HBC officials pressed Aberdeen, and then his successor, Palmerston, for the Rosario route. In 1849, Douglas, by then in charge at Fort Victoria, set up a fishing station on San Juan Island, but Americans pushed in there as well. Flare-ups followed, as did an armed clash in 1859. Yet neither side wanted big trouble. Diplomatic discussions began, and though delayed by the American Civil War until 1871, the Treaty of Washington then specified the Haro Strait and thus gave the San Juans to the United States.[50]

Local Indians were dealt with more rudely. In 1850 Congress appointed three commissioners "to free the land west of the Cascades entirely of Indian title and to move all the Indians to some spot to the east." Six treaties were concluded in early 1851 and thirteen more later that year. Not one was ratified. Others negotiated in 1853–1855 were "in fact a nearly complete capitulation of the tribes to superior power."[51]

Thus the American empire came to include the Pacific Northwest. The chief rationales were to assuage land hunger and Oregon fever. For probably the first time since Jefferson spoke of the critical strategic need to possess New Orleans, maritime strategy also played a role, if minor as yet: ports on the Pacific were required if the United States was to dominate commercially on the western ocean. Only one large target remained: northern Mexico, including Alta California, which was "ripe for the taking." Polk saw to that.

Chapter Seven

CALIFORNIA AND NEW MEXICO, 1846–1848: SOUTHWARD AGGRESSION II

Generally the officers of the army were indifferent whether the annexation [of Texas] was consummated or not. . . . For myself, I was bitterly opposed to the measure, and to this day regard the war, which resulted, as one of the most unjust ever waged by a stronger against a weaker nation.
      —U. S. Grant, *Personal Memoirs*[1]

Our situation is truly desperate. Everything, absolutely everything, is lost, and judging by the way things are going it is doubtful whether we can save our independence, the last refuge and symbol of our honor.
      —José Fernando Ramírez, 1847[2]

THE LOOK OF THINGS IN 1845

The Oregon acquisition was not small. It included the present states of Oregon, Washington, and Idaho, and large pieces of Montana and Wyoming. But the "Mexican Cession" of 1848, together with its postscript, the Gadsden Purchase of 1853, was twice as large. Add Texas, whose annexation by the United States started the Mexican-American conflict, and the whole area taken from Mexico was larger than the Louisiana Purchase (949,000 square miles versus 827,000). Moreover, the method was much more violent. This was the only acquisition so far that required a war. (The invasions of Canada in 1775 and 1813 were attempts at acquisition, but they failed.) The war with Mexico might well have never happened but for the determination of one man, President James K. Polk. Polk was, to use the terminology of the philosopher-historian Isaiah Berlin, a hedgehog, not a fox. Jefferson, FDR, and Bill Clinton were foxes. Jackson, Polk, and George W. Bush were hedgehogs. Whereas a fox has many ideas, in Berlin's definition, hedgehogs like Polk have one big idea.[3] His was to acquire for the United States the territory west of Texas to the Pacific, most importantly the harbor of San Francisco, but also, maybe, the rest of Alta

(Upper) California and the province of New Mexico, which happened to be en route. He would do this by diplomacy and cash, not to mention bribery, if possible; or by military force, if necessary.

Polk was a man whose interests and intellect were blinkered and narrow. Yet his vision, though tunneled, looked far. He was almost willfully ignorant, but hardly stupid, and he never shrank from using the power of the presidency as he saw fit. Like Jackson, he was a Tennessean. He was a Jacksonian loyalist as Speaker of the U.S. House during Jackson's last two presidential years and Van Buren's first two (1835–1839). He lost a couple of elections in the early 1840s and was considered finished politically. But he captured the Democratic nomination for president in 1844 as the first true "dark horse." After favorites Van Buren and Clay both came out publicly against expansion in May 1844, Polk embraced it—both the "re-occupation" of Oregon to 54°40', and the "re-annexation" of Texas to the Rio Grande. In response, the Democratic Party and the voters rewarded him with the presidency.

In these two claims the "re" was a distortion and exaggeration. But he slipped past Clay, his more illustrious Whig opponent, by 38,367 votes out of 2.7 million, receiving 49.6 percent of the total popular vote and 50.7 percent of the Clay-Polk major-party vote. (James G. Birney of the antislavery Liberty Party got 62,000.) Polk's margin in the electoral college was 170–105. He carried neither his own Tennessee nor Clay's Kentucky. But he did win every other then-western state from Alabama to Michigan except Ohio, and he nearly won there as well. His spread-eagle platform resounded in those parts. He had to back off from the 54°40' claim, as we saw earlier; and he did not have to "re-annex" Texas because President John Tyler and Congress had already done that just before he was inaugurated. But California (and New Mexico with it) were still out there, and Texas's full statehood brought with it the threat of war with an aggrieved Mexico. That war, he could see, was both threat and opportunity.

Polk, like Jackson and Jefferson before him, maintained that Texas had been part of the Louisiana Purchase. The claim was transparently flimsy to begin with, and had been specifically repudiated in the 1819 Adams-Onís treaty. To the Polkites, however, that treaty had "faded away" under the strong light of the American overrunning of Texas. Realistically, Texas had become American, and a few voices within Mexico and among European diplomats urged Mexico to recognize the fact, even though it was political suicide. Piling insensitivity upon intransigence, the Polk policy toward Mexico could only end violently. Before and during the outbreak of war, Polk (like Madison in 1812) employed secret agents, asserted the baseness of the other side's motives and tactics, manipulated the popular mood of manifest destiny, promised more army volunteers than he could deliver, and used other unpretty devices that were not new to presidential behavior then and have become routine since.

At the time Polk took office on March 4, 1845, Upper California (henceforth just "California") had a small population, a shaky and divided government, and an economy built largely on stock-raising and the sale of animal products. The Russians at Bodega Bay and Fort Ross left in 1841. The Mexican authorities were divided between south and north, with Governor Pio Pico futilely reaching northward from his base at Los Angeles to assert control over the autonomy-minded José Castro at Monterey and Mariano Vallejo at Sonoma. Mexico City was as distant as ever from all three. To all intents and purposes, California was an island accessible from the center only by ships from Baja (Lower) California or the west coast of the Mexican mainland. The string of Franciscan missions from San Diego to Sonoma fell into decay and disrepair after they were secularized in 1833, and their Indians had not benefited as planned by the dividing of mission lands. If anything, outlawry—cattle raids, reprisals, kidnappings, and more—were worse than ever, pitting Yakuts, Miwoks, and other never-conquered tribes against Mexican clerics, rancheros, and soldiers. The weakness of the province's defenses became blatant in 1842, when an American navy captain, Thomas ap Catesby Jones, acting on a false rumor that Mexico and the United States had gone to war, landed at Monterey and took it over. He gave it back a few days later when he learned there was no war, but Mexicans, British, and Americans alike could not miss seeing how undefended the province was. A few Yankees had become prominent Californios, notably Jacob Leese in Sonoma and Abel Stearns at Los Angeles; they had learned Spanish well, married into leading local families, and prospered in the hide-and-tallow trade, real estate, and other enterprises. The most prominent American who did not become a Californio was the U.S. consul at Monterey, Thomas O. Larkin, who also served Polk as a confidential agent.

Overland from the east and clambering down the western slope of the Sierras in late 1841 came the first American settlers, the Bidwell-Bartleson party of thirty-two men, a woman, and a child. With great

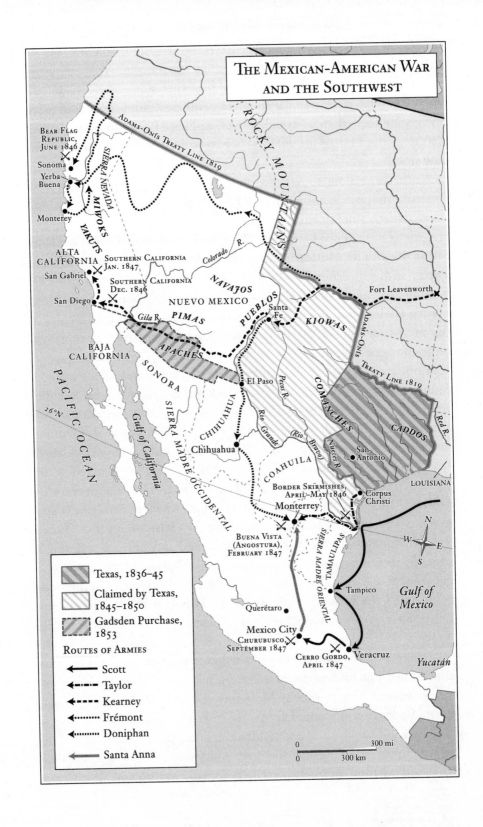

THE MEXICAN-AMERICAN WAR
AND THE SOUTHWEST

ROCKY MOUNTAINS

ADAMS-ONÍS TREATY LINE 1819

BEAR FLAG
REPUBLIC,
JUNE 1846
Sonoma
Yerba
Buena

SIERRA NEVADA

Monterey

MIWOKS

YAKUTS

ALTA
CALIFORNIA   SOUTHERN CALIFORNIA
JAN. 1847
San Gabriel   SOUTHERN CALIFORNIA
DEC. 1846
San Diego   Gila R.   PIMAS

BAJA
CALIFORNIA

Colorado R.

NAVAJOS

NUEVO MEXICO

PUEBLOS   Santa
Fe

APACHES

Fort Leavenworth

KIOWAS

ADAMS-ONÍS

SONORA

El Paso

TREATY LINE 1819

PACIFIC OCEAN

26°N

Gulf of California

SIERRA MADRE OCCIDENTAL

CHIHUAHUA

Chihuahua

Pecos R.

Rio Grande

(Rio Bravo)

COMANCHES

CADDOS

Red R.

San
Antonio

Nueces R.

COAHUILA

BORDER SKIRMISHES,
APRIL–MAY 1846
Monterrey

LOUISIANA

BUENA VISTA
(ANGOSTURA),
FEBRUARY 1847

Corpus
Christi

SIERRA MADRE ORIENTAL

TAMAULIPAS

N
W   E
S

Tampico

Gulf of
Mexico

Querétaro

Mexico City
CHURUBUSCO,
SEPTEMBER 1847

CERRO GORDO,
APRIL 1847

Veracruz

Yucatán

Texas, 1836–45

Claimed by Texas,
1845–1850

Gadsden Purchase,
1853

ROUTES OF ARMIES

Scott

Taylor

Kearney

Frémont

Doniphan

Santa Anna

0   300 mi
0   300 km

though unknowing risk, they had split off from their Oregon-bound group and struggled across the Utah and Nevada deserts and up over the Sierras. No settlers followed in 1842, and only a few hundred in 1844 to 1847. From 1840 through 1845, more than five thousand migrants followed the Overland Trail to Oregon, but fewer than four hundred went to California. During the war years of 1846–1848 Oregon still outnumbered California by 6,500 to 2,350, Anglos and Mexicans combined.[4] A well-conceived but poorly funded plan of 1845–1846 by an Irish priest, Eugene Macnamara, to settle ten thousand Irish famine refugees in California worried the Polk administration (which fretted that Macnamara was a front for a British occupation). The plan fell through, but had Macnamara happened along two or three years earlier he might have succeeded.[5] After 1848 the gold rush changed the population radically, but until then non-Indians were scarce.

By the spring of 1846, nevertheless, some dozens of Americans had arrived around Sonoma, north of San Francisco Bay. They were not technically filibusters like the invaders of West and East Florida in 1812 or Texas in the 1810s, since they did not come to overthrow Mexican authority but to ignore it. Initially, at least, they lacked any contact with U.S. officialdom and not much with Mexican. In 1846, however, they became a homegrown insurgency. They shared the belief so prevalent among Americans of their time that if land was not being put to its most productive use, they knew how to make it so and had a better right to it. Though they were a good three hundred miles inside Mexico, civil and military authority were only sporadically visible. Vallejo at Sonoma,

Zachary Taylor's army proceeded south from Corpus Christi in the spring of 1846 through Mexican territory, running into Mexican units just north of the Rio Grande. These skirmishes set off the war when President Polk claimed they took place on American soil. Taylor marched westward to Monterrey and then to face Santa Anna at the Battle of Buena Vista in late February 1847, where Taylor's campaign stopped. Meanwhile, Frémont roamed east of Monterey (California) and was forced back north, but then returned and joined the Bear Flag uprising at Sonoma in June 1846. Kearney moved west from Fort Leavenworth in mid-1846, captured Santa Fe, and went on to San Diego and San Gabriel in January 1847. Doniphan left Kearney at Santa Fe, marched south to Chihuahua, and joined Taylor at Buena Vista. Scott landed at Veracruz in April 1847 and won at Cerro Gordo and then at Churubusco.

The Treaty of Guadalupe Hidalgo (1848) moved the U.S.-Mexican boundary from the 1819 Adams-Onís line to the Rio Grande, the Gila River, and west to the Pacific. The Gadsden Purchase (late 1853/early 1854) established the present boundary.

Castro at Monterey, and the garrison at San Francisco all functioned without much oversight from either Governor Pico at Los Angeles or from Mexico City. Indians and Mexicans, civilians and soldiers, were constantly raiding and counterraiding. Mexican authorities held the coast securely, but they were hard put to protect the ranchos in the interior hills and valleys.

Into this unstable mix in the spring of 1846 came a U.S. Army scientific and exploratory expedition under the Byronic and well-connected young Lieutenant John C. Frémont. José Castro had grave misgivings: he suspected the explorers were in fact an American military probe. Castro notified Larkin that he wanted Frémont gone. Larkin replied soothingly that he hoped that if the "two parties" met, there would be no "unhappy conclusion." Castro was not to be put off. If Larkin would not order Frémont out of Mexico, Castro warned that "since he entered this Department with an armed force whether through malice or error he must now either blindly obey the authorities or on the contrary experience the misfortunes which he has sought by his crime."[6] Frémont thereupon promised to return to Oregon. Instead he circled back southward. Castro thwarted that move and chased Frémont into a defensive position at Gavilan Peak near San Francisco. The two contingents squared off. Frémont, outnumbered, slipped away under cover of darkness, reaching Upper Klamath Lake north of the Mexican border at forty-two degrees latitude.

Before long, another young officer, Marine lieutenant Archibald Gillespie, brought Frémont a packet of letters from his father-in-law, Senator Benton of Missouri—and from Polk himself. The messages have been controverted ever since. Did Polk instruct Frémont to provoke an uprising of American settlers? Or did he tell Frémont to be ready to take command if an insurgency erupted? More likely the latter, because that was what Polk told his agent, Consul Larkin. In any case, Frémont led his troops back into Mexican territory; joined the Sonoma settlers (though reluctantly at first) as they declared themselves the "Bear Flag Republic" in June 1846; and linked up with Larkin and Commodore John D. Sloat's takeover of Monterey in early July.[7] By then, Mexico and the United States really were at war, and northern California became one of its theaters.

Polk's aggressiveness, California's volatility, and Texas's Rio Grande claims might have gone nowhere if conditions in Mexico had been stable. But Mexico was chaotic and had been so since Texas broke away in

1836. There was an occasional bright spot, such as New Mexico's demolition of an invasion force of Texans who attempted to annex everything east and north of the Rio Grande in 1841. But Mexico's problems were both fundamental and superficial. It had no effective tax-collecting system. It had too many ambitious and feuding generals, preeminently the pop-up dictator, Santa Anna. Political animosities ran deep, more in the nature of competing worldviews than the relatively consensual American partisanship, which was divisive enough. Deep divisions separated clericalists, anticlericals, liberals, conservatives, monarchists, republicans, federalists, centralists—each representing not just policies but ideologies. Compromise and concerted action, even in the face of invasion, loss of territory, or loss of national existence, eluded the troubled country. Mexico was as badly positioned to defend itself and as divided as Spain was in 1808 when Napoleon invaded it. The result by 1848 was national dismemberment. It could have been national extinction.[8]

In this context, Polk the hedgehog held the advantage. On Oregon he had "looked John Bull in the eye," at least until Aberdeen's thirty ships of the line loomed, and he still acquired everything up to the forty-ninth parallel. He could look Mexico in the eye—Santa Anna or anyone— without worrying about any ships of the line. As a result, he did as he pleased, like a true Jacksonian.

POLK'S BRINKMANSHIP

Polk's 1844 platform and March 1845 inaugural speech were thunderously clear about Oregon and Texas. But they never mentioned California. Once in office, however, Polk moved toward his cherished if not yet public project. He had told Navy Secretary George Bancroft in early 1845 that acquiring California was the most important goal of his administration.[9] In October 1845, he told Senator Benton that by "reasserting" Monroe's "doctrine" against allowing European incursions into the hemisphere, "I had California and the fine bay of San Francisco as much in view as Oregon."[10] California was Polk's hidden agenda. Transpacific commercial possibilities, particularly the market potential of China, likely motivated him more than visions of settlement did, but both objectives might be achieved.

President Tyler had done Polk the favor of bringing Texas all but into the Union, after the February 28 joint resolution offering annexation. The only remaining steps were ratification by the Texas Congress and, formally, by the U.S. Congress. The first came on July 4, and the second on December 29, 1845.

Texan statehood meant, of course, a casus belli with Mexico. The Mexican foreign minister had said so bluntly as early as mid-1843. The Mexican minister in Washington, Juan Nepomuceno Almonte, also made that clear. When Congress passed its joint resolution, Almonte told Secretary of State Calhoun that annexation was aggression. He demanded his passports, left Washington, and thereby broke diplomatic relations between the two countries. Any Mexican leader would have agreed that an independent Texas might be barely acceptable but the loss of it to the United States was not. Beyond that, as an issue, were the claims (some well founded, some trumped up) of U.S. citizens against Mexican taxes, customs duties, port regulations, and the like. Even in more normal times the claims issue festered. Polk's position, to the contrary, was that Mexico owed money to Americans; it had no money; it did have sparsely settled land; therefore the claims could be paid off in territory, with some cash going to Mexico as a sweetener.

Texas, from the American standpoint, was no longer on the table, but California would do very well. Polk preferred purchase via diplomatic negotiation to war, though he would go to war "if necessary." Accordingly he sent a Louisiana congressman, John Slidell, to Mexico City in the fall of 1845 to negotiate. Already, however, he prepared to "look Mexico in the eye," and in June 1845 he ordered General Zachary Taylor to proceed from Louisiana to south Texas, and Commodore David Conner to patrol the Gulf coast of Mexico, both to be ready to act if war broke out. Taylor arrived at Corpus Christi (just south of the Nueces River) by early August with eight companies of soldiers and awaited orders.

The "Disputed" Nueces Strip

When Taylor led his troops to Corpus Christi, he arrived at the banks—the southern banks—of the Nueces River. Was he still in Texas, as Texans were claiming, or was he already inside Mexico?

In south Texas, the distance along the Gulf coast from Corpus Christi, where the Nueces River flows into the Gulf, to the mouth of the Rio Grande at Port Isabel, just east of Brownsville, is about 150 miles. Padre Island guards the shore. The Nueces commences in the hills west of San Antonio and wriggles south and east roughly parallel to the Rio

Grande for about three hundred miles. The Rio Grande, much longer, rises in the Rockies, flows south through Albuquerque to El Paso and then southeast to the Gulf. If it were the border, then present New Mexico and west Texas went with it. The Nueces, because it did not flow nearly as far, included none of that vast land.

When the general run of American history books discuss the Mexican-American War, they refer to the strip south of the Nueces and north of the Rio Grande as "disputed." But it had never been disputed until Texans, newly independent in 1836, started claiming it. Earlier, to be sure, Jefferson and his followers purported that, like Texas itself, the strip was part of the Louisiana Purchase. This dated back to the spurious claim that the Treaty of Utrecht of 1713 recognized French rights along the Gulf as far southwest as the Rio Grande. But Spain had been there all along, and after 1821 the region became Mexican. Here as elsewhere the Jeffersonians inflated the extent of their "noble bargain" of 1803 wherever they could. In any case the claim that Texas was part of Louisiana was specifically, and presumably permanently, abjured by the United States in the 1819 Adams-Onís treaty with Spain, which set the American-Mexican boundary at the Sabine, east and north of any conceivable historic part of Texas. The Sabine became, and is now, the border between the states of Texas and Louisiana.

Yet the claim that the Nueces strip was part of the Louisiana Purchase, and therefore part of Texas, resurfaced in the late 1820s when John Quincy Adams sent Joel Poinsett to buy Texas as far south as the Rio Grande. Following its independence in 1836, Texas claimed the Rio Grande boundary. Despite being thrown back by one of Santa Anna's armies at San Antonio in 1842, Texans maintained the claim as they traveled their bumpy road toward annexation. The United States' terms of annexation in 1845 did not explicitly accept that claim, which included not only the Gulf coast but all the land north and east of the Rio Grande to its source and then north to the forty-second parallel. In Congress's annexation resolution the border was left to be worked out over time. The time came very soon.

Clearly, the Nueces strip had never been part of Texas under either Spain or Mexico. So thinly populated was south Texas before 1821 that provincial boundaries were almost pointless, as there were virtually no people or governments there. When the San Antonio missions were founded around 1718, the Medina and San Antonio Rivers separated Texas from the province of Coahuila. By 1767 the Nueces was recognized as the boundary between Texas and Coahuila. As of 1805, Texas's southern boundary ran from the Gulf up the Nueces for over one hundred miles, then north to the Medina (near San Antonio), and then northwest another two hundred miles—none of it anywhere near the Rio Grande. The boundary stayed that way until Texas and Coahuila were made a joint state under the Mexican federal constitution of 1824. They remained a joint state, with the Texas segment consisting of the land north of the Nueces. Stephen F. Austin's empresario maps of 1829, 1833, and 1836 also showed the Nueces River, not the Rio Grande, demarcating Texas from Coahuila.[11]

When Texans defeated Santa Anna at San Jacinto in May 1836, the captured general agreed, with his life hanging in the balance, to sign the "Treaty of Velasco." It withdrew Mexican forces to south of the Rio Grande, implying that the Nueces strip was Texan. But the Mexican Congress repudiated it. Polk, to the contrary, acted as if it were fact. In August 1845, when news came that a Mexican army was about to cross the Rio Grande, Polk asserted that the Nueces strip was "virtually" American and any Mexican crossing "must be regarded as an invasion of the United States."[12] Thus, in his war message in May 1846, he proclaimed that "Mexico has invaded our territory and shed American blood upon the American soil." With that, the war began.

For Mexico, any American troop movement south of the Nueces was an invasion of *its* territory. The coastal strip was part of the state of Tamaulipas, and the inland area belonged to Nuevo León and Coahuila. In an 1847 book, Carlos María de Bustamante affirmed that "sending troops into Mexican territory"—Corpus Christi or anywhere else south of the Nueces—"doomed all moderation, and Mexico was left with no other recourse but to engage in battle. The territory between the Nueces and Rio Grande rivers neither by fact nor by law could have belonged to Texas. Not by fact because it was not populated by [Anglo] Texans . . . nor . . . by law because all this coast, through a territorial division recognized by all the nation and by the Texas colonists themselves, has belonged to the state of Tamaulipas."[13] He was right. No Anglos lived there; the empresario grants did not extend south of the Nueces; and even in 1845 no Texas counties had been organized there. To the contrary, the people living on the north side of the Rio Grande were Mexican, and Mexican authorities had a duty to protect them.[14] Quite unlike east Texas and the region of the empresario grants, there was no demographic argument for the Americans to absorb the Nueces strip. No surge of people occupied it, and the three coastal counties south of Corpus Christi to Brownsville are still the least populated of any on the coast of the Gulf.

RUN-UP TO WAR

Diplomacy ensued, or started to. Word reached Polk in early November 1845 that the Mexican commander on the Rio Grande and leaders in Mexico City were ready to talk, surely a sign that strong words (Polk's preferred tactic) would push the Mexicans in his direction. With cabinet agreement, and at Buchanan's suggestion, Polk sent John Slidell to Mexico City. He was to offer to take over all outstanding claims and buy California and New Mexico. The amount was negotiable up to $25 million, depending on whether Mexico would sell both provinces. As for the claims, Mexico had agreed in 1839 to pay them, made a few payments, then had to stop. Polk was ready to have the U.S. government assume the claims and pay Mexico some cash for its northern states. Did not Mexico need money more than the land? To Polk the answer was obvious. Unfortunately for peace, no one in Mexico saw it that way.

Slidell's credentials from Polk named him "envoy extraordinary and minister plenipotentiary." But the president never asked or received the Senate's confirmation, leaving Slidell in the status of a special presidential emissary. The Mexican government accordingly refused to accept him as fully credentialed. When he arrived in Mexico City on November 29, 1845, the situation was more than usually turbulent. General Mariano Paredes y Arrillaga, commander of field forces, ousted the then unpopular Santa Anna and by early December replaced him as president with another general, José Joaquin Herrera. The foreign minister, Manuel Peña y Peña, a distinguished lawyer and jurist, was a moderate. Peña made clear to Slidell that he would be happy to receive him to discuss his purchase proposal as well as outstanding problems like the claims and borders. But if he recognized him as a new U.S. minister, he would be acquiescing in the Texas annexation, the main reason why Almonte had broken relations the previous spring. This was no quibble—John Quincy Adams would have scoffed if another country had sent someone with Slidell's faulty credentials—but Polk and Buchanan chose to be incensed at the rebuff of Slidell. The president decided that the time had come to move from "diplomacy if possible" to "force if necessary."

Herrera had taken a great risk in allowing Slidell into Mexico at all, and it cost him his job. In late December 1845, General Paredes removed Herrera (in office less than four weeks) and installed himself as president on January 2, 1846. A semicovert monarchist, Paredes followed a harder line: no truck with the United States, no recognition of Texas, certainly no boundary south of the Nueces, and no Slidell. As Polk's biographer states, "the Polk-Slidell policy of combined bullying and bribery was precisely what no Mexican regime could submit to and survive"—Paredes's least of all.[15] Slidell dallied in Mexico City in vain hope. Meanwhile, on January 13, the Polk administration ordered General Taylor to move his forces to the Rio Grande opposite the Mexican coastal town of Matamoros, with Commodore Conner to proceed to the Texas coast for naval support. Slidell informed Polk on March 15 that he was returning empty-handed, and on March 30 he sailed home.

In cabinet meetings through February and March, Polk resisted any further action against Mexico until Slidell reported back. He did not explain why in his diary, but this was the very time when he and the cabinet were absorbing Lord Aberdeen's "thirty sail of the line" remark, and when the abrogation of the 1827 joint occupancy of Oregon was stalled in Congress. Polk paused regarding Mexico until Oregon was clarified. Nevertheless, he had still not received a response from London on the abrogation notice when he learned on May 9 that Mexican forces had crossed the Rio Grande and that several of Taylor's troops had been killed and wounded on April 25. Polk immediately wrote a message to Congress, which received it on May 11. It asked for a declaration of war, a levy of 50,000 volunteers, and $10 million.

Polk was teetering on the brink of a double war as a result of his own blunt diplomacy. He was very lucky that Aberdeen and Peel remained in power long enough to settle the Oregon question amicably, that Aberdeen's "thirty sail of the line" thus became ghosts, and that Taylor's forces were strong enough to win the first small engagements with the Mexicans. Was his stubbornness just tactical? Whatever his private thoughts, he did not admit any wavering, even to his diary. Oregon was not becoming American as a free area to balance slave-state Texas, but because the opportunity played out that way. Polk was not performing a balancing act; to the contrary, he was going to the brink of a double war. (Nor, despite suspicions that lingered for generations, was he or anyone the instrument of a "slave-power conspiracy" to annex northern Mexico to expand slavery. As events transpired, slavery never extended west of

Texas. In fact, antislavery feelings strengthened because of the Mexican-American War; it was no plus for slavery.)

The war message reflects either an invincibly stubborn tunnel vision or enormous mendacity on Polk's part. In it, the president insisted and reiterated, unequivocally, that "the grievous wrongs perpetrated by Mexico upon our citizens throughout a long period of years remain unredressed. . . . We have tried every effort at reconciliation. . . . Now, after reiterated menaces, Mexico has passed the boundary of the United States, has invaded our territory and shed American blood upon the American soil." This was the first, but not the last, presidential call to arms in American history based on a string of false contentions.[16]

On May 12 the House considered the president's requests. His friends attached to it a "preamble" blaming Mexico for invading American soil. The Democratic leadership limited House debate to two hours and much of that was consumed by the reading of supporting documents. The bill passed, 174–14. Some members objected to the preamble, because it put them on record as agreeing with Polk's claims. Yet they did not dare refuse to support the war. Garrett Davis of Kentucky, one of the few allowed to speak, objected to the preamble:

> It recites that war exists . . . and was begun by Mexico. . . . That . . . is utterly untrue. I am decidedly, strongly, in favor of the appropriation of the money. . . . For these purposes, it is sufficient for me that our country is at war. . . . If the bill contained any recitation upon that point in truth and justice, it should be that this war was begun by the President. The river Nueces is the true western boundary of Texas. The country between that stream and the Del Norte [the Rio Grande] is part of Mexico.

Davis nonetheless voted for the bill, as did all but fourteen diehards—all Whigs and abolitionists who abhorred slavery's extension. Forty-eight Whigs voted "yea" to avoid being branded unpatriotic.

Debate in the Senate took another day, much of it centered on who owned the Nueces strip. But the bill passed there too, 40 yea (26 Democrats and 14 Whigs) to 2 nay (both Whigs), with John C. Calhoun and two others not voting.[17] Polk signed the bill on May 13. War was declared.

The now familiar tactic of the chief executive maneuvering Congress into a fait accompli with regard to declaring war was certainly employed by Polk in 1846. It may not have been the first time; Madison came near to doing so in 1812. George H. W. Bush's troop buildup before the first Gulf war and George W. Bush's before Iraq were not novelties. There may be limits on presidential power, but there are no obvious ones on a president as commander in chief sending troops and ships where he wants to. Polk put Taylor's army on the Rio Grande and Conner's navy off the Mexican coast. When the inevitable skirmish happened, congressmen had no option. Either go along, declare war, or be criticized for undercutting the troops. Once American troops were "in harm's way," although Polk placed them there and thereby contrived to have Mexico fire the first shot, it was too late to object. Public opinion soon split on the Mexican War, but at the outset Congress could not buck the belligerent spirit.

As soon as the Senate passed the war bill, and before it even reached Polk for signature, he reaffirmed to Navy Secretary Bancroft that Commodore Sloat and the Pacific squadron should occupy Monterey and San Francisco. The next day Polk sent orders to Colonel (soon General) Stephen Watts Kearny at Fort Leavenworth, on the Missouri River, to head for Santa Fe and secure it. The grand strategy, set at least eleven months earlier in mid-1845, was reaching fruition: try diplomacy (Slidell and money) but position forces (Taylor and Conner). If and when diplomacy failed, send Taylor to the Rio Grande, claim the Nueces strip, provoke Mexico into armed defense of it, and then insist that American blood had been shed on American soil. Congress could not resist that strategy. Meanwhile, make a deal with Britain over Oregon, and forget about the unattainable (and baseless) claim of 54°40'. With war declared, send the army to New Mexico and the navy to the California coast. How it would all end—how much it would cost, how many would be killed, how much of Mexico would be occupied or kept—was not clear at all. But Polk's primary objective, making California American, was nearly in his grasp.

Mexico was prepared for war with the United States only in the strength of its sense of *nacionalidad*, and that existed primarily among its small elites. At the opening of the war, its land area was close to that of the United States, but its population was considerably smaller—about 7.5 or 8 million compared to the States' 17 million. As had been true since Aztec times, most lived in central Mexico. The northern states had always been underpopulated and only distantly connected to the center. The majority of the people were Indians or mestizos, divided in languages, often innocent of Spanish, practicing something close to subsistence farming and contributing little to national product or tax base. Many were Catholics, after more than three centuries of the Spanish presence. Some, however, the *indios bárbaros* of the California interior and the Great Plains, were not only unassimilated but hostile. Comanches and Apaches raided at will many miles south of the Rio Grande, as they had ever since the Spanish pushed north of it. Mexico's preoccupation with the American invasion in 1846 provided the Comanches with further opportunities. As a result, Mexico found itself fighting on two fronts, against both the Americans and the Plains Indians.

Mexico's class structure made a unified war effort difficult. Above the Indian majority were a smaller number of largely mestizo artisans, shopkeepers, peasants, parish clergy, and others, comprising, to stretch a somewhat anachronistic term, a lower middle class. On top were people of European (usually Spanish) stock, the well landed, the upper clergy, military officers, the educated professionals. These Europeans split further into *criollos*, if they were Mexican-born, or *gachupines*, if they were the envied and often disliked Spanish-born. Ideological fissures separated the elites—clericals versus liberals, federalists versus centralists, monarchists versus republicans. Leadership, up to and including the presidency, oscillated among these groups.

Add to all that the epidemic of politically involved generals, including above all the charismatic Santa Anna, with his remarkable ability to raise armies and his ineptitude in leading them; the lack of any effective tax system and, for that matter, anything much to tax; the exemptions of the clergy and the military from the ordinary system of laws and courts; and in 1846, an army poorly paid, fed, clothed, equipped, and armed. The outcome was almost foreordained.

As nationalistic and full of their sense of destiny as the Americans of that day were, the Mexicans were equally so. No one monopolized nationalism in the nineteenth century. Though lacking the illusion that their "destiny" was "manifest," they were just as sensitive to insults to national honor and to threats to the integrity of their national territory. Americans were aggressive expansionists; Mexicans were determined to defend what they had.

The decade prior to 1846 brought Mexico's internal problems and divisions to a boil. Since the defeat at San Jacinto and de facto Texan independence in 1836, politics had never been calm. Santa Anna rode in and out of power, donning whatever cloak—centralist, federalist, liberal, conservative—would bring him back or keep him there. Only one thing was a given: no president or general could alienate any territory, even the lost territory of Texas. If he gave even a hint of that, as Herrera did by admitting Slidell in late 1845, he was ousted by someone more "patriotic." Thus war would surely come, however unready Mexico was. Defeat (and despite all of Mexico's handicaps it was not a certainty until it actually happened) was preferable to dishonor. In the two years beginning in late 1845, *during wartime*, five presidents succeeded one another; finance ministers and war ministers and commanders tumbled after one another; armies coalesced and crumbled. Mexico lost every significant battle of the war. But some were close, and most were valiantly defended. That was a wonder, in view of the country's lack of resources.

A THREE-FRONT WAR

All the land that the United States would ultimately take from Mexico was already in American hands by early January 1847, about seven months after the war began. For more than a year longer, however, fighting, peace negotiations, and clamor about "how much of Mexico to take" continued, until both sides ratified the peace treaty in the spring of 1848. In the process, more than 12,000 American soldiers died, the great majority from disease or accidents rather than combat. Mexico lost more than that, military and civilian, and much of the country was torn apart or torched. The United States found itself faced with the slavery question becoming hotter than ever. Nonetheless, California and New Mexico had become the American Southwest.

How all this happened is quickly told.[18] In military terms, the fighting took place in three almost nonoverlapping theaters: northern Mexico, California, and central Mexico.

The northern front lasted from the border skirmish in late April 1846 to the battle of Buena Vista in late February 1847. Zachary Taylor and his forces moved south from Matamoros and along the Rio Grande in August 1846, and with difficulty defeated General Pedro de Ampudia's forces at Monterrey on September 20–24, 1846. After an eight-week armistice (which infuriated Polk, who wanted Taylor to keep driving) and a winter pause, Santa Anna nearly whipped Taylor in a major battle known to Americans as Buena Vista and to Mexicans as Angostura, which ran from February 21 to 24, 1847. Had Santa Anna not pulled back his troops on the night of the twenty-third, he might well have driven Taylor back into Texas. As it was, there were no further pitched battles, and the northern campaign ended except for raids and skirmishes. Aside from securing the Nueces strip and the Rio Grande boundary for Texas and the United States, it had no direct territorial effects.

The second front began and ended almost simultaneously with the first. In June 1846, as Kearny rode to Santa Fe, the Americans in northern California raised their insurgency. Frémont took command of their Bear Flag Republic, and then linked up with American naval units under Commodore Robert Stockton, which seized San Francisco and Monterey in July. Kearny swept into Santa Fe and captured it bloodlessly on August 18. He left some of his forces there, sent another detachment straight south toward Chihuahua, and led his remaining three hundred troops toward southern California. Stockton and Frémont captured Los Angeles on August 13.

The Californios recaptured southern California in December and *nuevomexicanos* threw over American rule in New Mexico in January, but these counterattacks proved ephemeral. A stronger American force under Colonel Sterling Price of Missouri retook Taos and Santa Fe, and Stockton, Frémont, and Kearny secured San Gabriel and Los Angeles. The second front ended on January 13, 1847, and the Treaty of Cahuenga completed the last Californio resistance. The war with Mexico was not over, but as far as California was concerned, Secretary Buchanan wrote a laconic epitaph to Mexican rule in a letter to Consul Larkin: "You are not to infer that the President contemplates any contingency in which they [the Californias] shall ever be surrendered to Mexico."[19]

A third front was proving essential. By the fall of 1846, it was clear to Polk and his cabinet that Taylor's campaign would be difficult, and that, moreover, Taylor would not permit them to micromanage him. Taylor's Whig affiliation also irritated Polk. The question had become: Could Taylor move south against the Mexicans effectively? Could he march his army the several hundred miles to central Mexico and the capital, over rough terrain and with thinly stretched supply lines, and still be battle-ready? After an abortive attempt to appoint Senator Benton as lieutenant general, outranking Taylor or any other (Whig) general, Polk named Major General Winfield Scott, the senior officer in Washington (but also a Whig), to open the third front by landing at Veracruz and proceeding up through the mountains to Mexico City. On March 9,

1847, Scott landed with ten thousand men near Veracruz, and the final phase of the war began.

First came a no-quarter siege of Veracruz, then a march inland and victory over Santa Anna at Cerro Gordo on April 17–18. By the summer, Scott was closing in on Mexico City. A bitter pitched battle at Churubusco on August 20 was, it was said, Mexico's "finest hour," but it was still a defeat. A two-week armistice ended on September 6, and the next two days saw the worst fighting of the war at Molino del Rey, with two thousand Mexicans and seven hundred Americans killed. Within a week Scott's army stormed Chapultepec Castle, effectively ending the war, despite the patriotic resistance of the military cadets there, celebrated in Mexican history as the *niños heroës*, the heroic children. Scott took over the city and Santa Anna resigned as president (though not as commander of the army) on September 15. The *moderado* Manuel Peña y Peña became interim president. As president or foreign secretary over the next nine months, he would play a key role in persuading Mexican leaders to agree to a peace treaty.

Negotiations had already started. Polk had sent a negotiator, Nicholas P. Trist, with Scott, and after some initial friction Trist and Scott worked very well together. Following the capture of Mexico City, the obvious question was how to wind up the war. It could have ended in March 1847, in theory, since Polk's territorial objectives were satisfied by then. But neither side was ready to stop fighting, and the Scott campaign followed. By the fall of 1847, with the American victory seemingly complete, the question to many Americans was how much of Mexico to absorb. The United States was positioned to take more than New Mexico and California, but should it?

The war had been bloody, mean, and devastating. Before and after September 15, 1847, uprisings against the American army were endemic, and guerrillas harassed it constantly. The supply lines were long and the whole effort hugely expensive in both men and money. Scott's entry into the main square of Mexico City did not mean the end of popular resistance. That continued for some time, draining resources and commitment from the occupier. About 90,000 Americans fought, of whom 59,000 were volunteers on short-term enlistments. Two-thirds came from Kentucky, Tennessee, and other nearby states including Texas, plus another quarter from the expansionist Old Northwest. Only a few thousand were from New England, the middle states, and the Atlantic Coast. This pattern reflected not just the West's louder cries of

Artist Benjamin West's The Peacemakers *portrays the American negotiators of 1782–83. From left: John Jay, age 37; John Adams, 46; Benjamin Franklin, 76. Also, Henry Laurens, who arrived as the talks concluded, and William Temple Franklin, Benjamin's grandson, who served as the team's secretary. West left space on the right for the British negotiators, but they declined to appear. (Library of Congress)*

Sarah (Sally) Livingston Jay (Mrs. John Jay) (Library of Congress)

The following two pages present John Mitchell's 1755 map of eastern North America. The treaty negotiators of 1782–83 used a later but similar edition in their deliberations. The northwest (upper left corner) is obscured by an inset of Hudson's Bay, thereby covering the unknown relation of the source of the Mississippi and the Lake of the Woods. The resulting boundary gap was corrected thirty-six years later. Maine appears as barely a sliver of land north of Massachusetts (of which it was then an outlying part); this too was a festering problem not solved for sixty years. The map depicts the extensions indefinitely westward of the claims of Virginia, the Carolinas, and Georgia based on their colonial charters. Florida is not shown as Spanish or Louisiana as French, though they were at that time. The Great Lakes and many other features are inaccurate; only the Atlantic seaboard from Nova Scotia to Georgia is close to being accurate. (Courtesy of The Newberry Library)

The Count de Vergennes, French minister and secretary of state. He generously provided funds during the Revolutionary War and supported U.S. recognition in the peace talks. (Library of Congress)

The Earl of Shelburne, British prime minister. Shelburne's brief ministry provided a critical window of opportunity for the American negotiators in 1782. (Library of Congress)

The Count of Aranda, Spanish minister at Paris. He hoped (unsuccessfully) to keep the U.S. boundary well east of the Mississippi River. Here he appears with Alleyn Fitzherbert, one of the British negotiators, and Vergennes, as they signed the preliminary peace treaty on January 20, 1783, at Versailles. (Library of Congress)

Bernardo de Gálvez, 1746–86. He helped the American cause by driving the British from the Gulf Coast in 1779–81, as well as providing financing for American resistance to the British in Transappalachia. (Library of Congress)

Little Turtle (Mishikinakwa), leader of the Miamis. He defeated American military thrusts into Indiana and northwest Ohio prior to Anthony Wayne's victories and the ensuing Treaty of Greenville of 1795, which he signed. From then until 1809, he tried to live with the ever-advancing white settlement. He and his people ultimately lost; the Miamis were later removed westward. This portrait is said to have been done by Gilbert Stuart in 1797. (Courtesy, Indiana Historical Society)

Tecumseh, the great Shawnee-Creek confederator and military leader. He organized Indian resistance to white settlement and U.S. control from Michigan to Alabama and allied himself with the British in the War of 1812. He was killed in 1813 at the Battle of the Thames. Painting by Mathias Noheimer. (Library of Congress)

Tenskwatawa, "the Prophet." His religious visions inspired Indian support for his brother Tecumseh's confederation to stop the Americans' advance westward. In November 1811, his settlement on the Tippecanoe, "Prophetstown," was overrun and destroyed by William Henry Harrison, scattering Indian resistance in much of the Old Northwest. (Courtesy, Indiana Historical Society)

Black Hawk (1767–1838), from a painting by R. M. Sully. A chief of the Sauk tribe, he led the 1832 uprising along the Illinois frontier in protest against treaties that extorted lands from his and other tribes. His hopes for British support of the Indians, as in the War of 1812 and earlier, never materialized, nor would they again. (Library of Congress)

Robert R. Livingston (1746–1813), a drafter of the Declaration of Independence and Chancellor (highest judicial officer) of New York State for more than twenty years. In that role, he swore in George Washington as the first U.S. president in 1789 in New York City. He was the principal negotiator of the Louisiana Purchase as U.S. minister to France, 1801–1804. (Library of Congress)

Charles-Maurice de Talleyrand-Périgord (1754–1838), foreign minister of France in Napoleon's government. Talleyrand handled the sale of Louisiana for France. (Library of Congress)

Carlos Mariá Martínez de Yrujo, the Marques de Casa Yrujo (1763-1824), Spanish minister to the United States from 1796 to 1807. He vehemently protested the sale of Louisiana to the United States. His wife, the Marquesa, was formerly Sarah (Sally) McKean of New Jersey. (Library of Congress American Memory)

Major General Jacob Brown, commander of U.S. army forces along Lake Ontario and the Niagara frontier in the War of 1812. Brownville, New York, is named after him. After the war President Monroe appointed him commanding general of the army. As such, he outranked Andrew Jackson. (Library of Congress)

Major General Isaac Brock, who captured Detroit from the Americans. Killed on the Niagara frontier early in the War of 1812, he is nevertheless regarded as the most effective British general. Brockville, Ontario, is named after him. (Library of Congress)

War hawk congressman and militia general Peter Porter of Black Rock, now part of Buffalo, New York. (Library of Congress)

Zebulon Montgomery Pike. His 1806–1807 expedition to the western edge of the Louisiana Purchase resulted in Pike's Peak being named after him, and in his capture by the Spanish in New Mexico. Later posted to Sackett's Harbor, New York, and promoted to brigadier general, he was killed in the American assault on York (later Toronto) in 1813. (Library of Congress)

John Melish's map of 1813 guided the peace negotiators at Ghent in late 1814, concluding the War of 1812. It reveals the uncertain state of geographic knowledge at that time. The Greenville Treaty line of 1795 appears as the effective boundary of northern Ohio. Indiana appears unsettled. Maine angles into

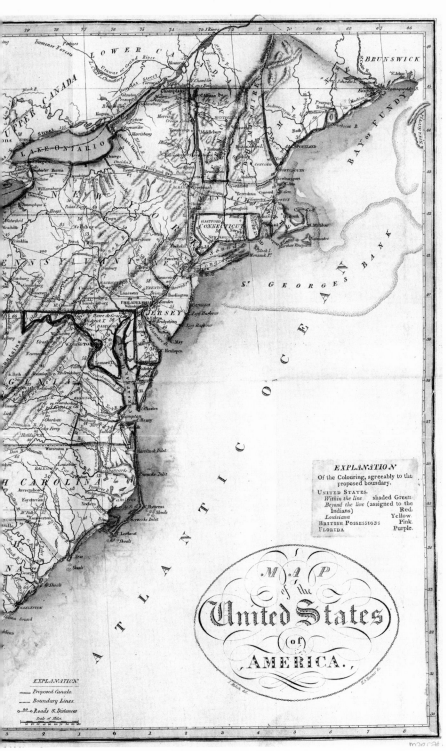

New Brunswick; the Yazoo Strip is incorporated into the Mississippi Territory; Louisiana is not shown as U.S. territory. The
Old Northwest is distorted. In these respects, the map reflects the
realities of 1795–1802 more closely than those of 1813–14.
(Courtesy of The Newberry Library)

Don Luis de Onís, Minister of Spain in Washington from 1809 to 1819, played a losing hand very adroitly in negotiating the Florida/Transcontinental Treaty of 1819 with John Quincy Adams. (Courtesy of The Newberry Library)

John Quincy Adams as he appeared in about 1825, age 58. As secretary of state in 1819 he negotiated the treaty with Luis de Onís that transferred Florida from Spain to the United States, established the northern frontier of New Spain along the 42° line, and thereby gave the United States its first legal claim as far as the Pacific Ocean. (Library of Congress)

Fernando VII, King of Spain from 1808 to 1833. His first six years were spent in exile as Napoleon's captive. After taking power in 1814, he misruled for nineteen years, during which most of Spain's vast empire in North and South America gained independence. (Library of Congress)

Andrew Jackson, invader of Florida, scourge of the Creeks, the "America Bonaparte," and later, president of the United States (1829-37). From a painting by Thomas Sully, about 1820, just after the conquest of Florida. (Library of Congress)

The Earl of Aberdeen. As British Foreign Secretary in 1845–46, Lord Aberdeen oversaw the treaty negotiations that resulted in the acquisition of the Oregon Country south of the 49th parallel by the United States. (Library of Congress)

Dr. John McLoughlin (1784–1857), chief factor of the Hudson's Bay Company at Fort Vancouver, 1825–46. From a daguerreotype in the collections of Fort Vancouver National Historic Site, Vancouver, Washington. (Courtesy of Fort Vancouver NHS, National Park Service)

Fort Vancouver, headquarters of the Hudson's Bay Company in the Oregon Country, from Sketches in North America and the Oregon Territory, *by Henry J. Warre (1848) (Library of Congress)*

President James K. Polk. Daguerreotype done February 14, 1849, just before Polk left the White House. Daguerreotype by Mathew B. Brady. (Library of Congress)

John Disturnell's *1848* map of Mexico. It guided the negotiators of the Treaty of Guadalupe Hidalgo. The Rio Grande is shown as the Texas-Mexico border, i.e., the Texan and American claim despite its lack of historic support. (Courtesy of The Newberry Library)

Nicholas P. Trist, who negotiated the peace treaty with Mexico after Polk fired him. Polk nevertheless accepted the treaty because it gave him his original objectives: Upper California and the Rio Grande boundary. Trist received no thanks (or even his expenses) from Polk. (Courtesy, Monticello/Thomas Jefferson Foundation, Inc.)

Manuel Peña y Peña, president of Mexico's Supreme Court of Justice and interim president of the republic from September 1847 to June 1848. He persuaded the Mexican congress to ratify the peace treaty, despite hard-liners who wanted to continue guerilla resistance indefinitely. (Thanks to Claudia Martínez)

Antonio López de Santa Anna (1794–1876), intermittently president of Mexico and commanding general of its armies from the 1830s to the 1850s. Portrait probably done in the 1830s. (Library of Congress)

Robert J. Walker, Polk's secretary of the treasury (1845–49) and in the 1860s a supporter of Seward's efforts to buy Alaska and other imperial ventures. A Mathew Brady daguerreotype. (Library of Congress)

Secretary of State William H. Seward (1801–72). Another Brady daguerreotype, this presents Seward as he looked in his late forties or early fifties. He was then a U.S. senator from New York speaking frequently in favor of American expansion. (Library of Congress)

Queen Liliuokalani of Hawaii. The last monarch of the Kamehameha line, she and her government were overthrown in the haole coup d'etat of 1893. (Courtesy of Hawaii State Archives)

Edouard de Stoeckl, Russian minister to Washington from 1854 to 1869, who negotiated the sale of Alaska for Russia. From the Brady-Handy Photograph Collection at the Library of Congress. (Library of Congress)

Lorrin Thurston (at right), leader of the 1893 coup, and Sanford Dole (left), first president of the Republic of Hawaii that overthrew the monarchy. (Courtesy of Hawaii State Archives)

The "Sunday proclamation" of Navy Commander Benjamin Franklin Tilley, de facto ruler of Samoa upon the U.S. acquisition. This and other proclamations by Tilley regulated and reorganized daily life in the new colony. (U.S. National Archives)

Emilio Aguinaldo (1869–1964), leader of the Filipino insurrection against Spanish rule, erstwhile cooperator with Commodore Dewey, and then leader of Filipino resistance to American conquest from 1899 until he was captured in 1901. (Library of Congress)

Senator Orville H. Platt (R-Conn.). The 1901 Platt Amendment, which claimed a U.S. right of protection over Cuba and later, by extension, several Caribbean republics, was chiefly written by then–Secretary of War Elihu Root but named after Platt, who presented it to the Senate. (1902 photo, © George Prince) (Library of Congress)

Senator Henry M. Teller (R-Colo.) The "Teller Amendment" to the declaration of war against Spain in April 1898 renounced any future claims to Cuba. It proved highly inconvenient to those who wanted the United States to annex Cuba, but it was effectively evaded by the Platt Amendment. (Library of Congress)

Franklin D. Roosevelt and Winston Churchill at Argentia Bay, Newfoundland, August 1941, where they proclaimed the Atlantic Charter as a blueprint for the post–World War II world. (Associated Press photograph in the New York World-Telegram and Sun *Photograph Collection, Library of Congress) (Library of Congress)*

George F. Kennan, formulator of the containment policy, the U.S. blueprint for conducting the Cold War. (Photo of Nov. 19, 1951, by Wide World, in the New York World-Telegram and Sun *Photograph Collection, Library of Congress) (Library of Congress)*

Secretary of State Dean Acheson (center), flanked by the foreign ministers of France (Robert Schuman, left) and Britain (Herbert Morrison, right) in 1951. With his chief, President Harry S. Truman, Acheson put in place the principal measures of the early Cold War. As the French and British empires went into eclipse, the American empire rose in strength. (Library of Congress)

manifest destiny. Settlers in newly opened areas traditionally came from nearby, not from great distances, and the hope of free or cheap land undoubtedly motivated many volunteers, for whom a farm would be their own private manifest destiny.

Yet life in the army was a dangerous gamble. Killed in battle were 120 officers and 1,429 enlisted men. Deaths from disease, accidents, and other noncombat causes totaled 10,986, or 85 percent of the total of military deaths and about one in nine of all those in uniform.[20] Volunteers were especially ignorant of sanitation, the need to stay dry, and how to avoid needless risks. On all three fronts, men fell from dysentery, diarrhea, yellow fever, cholera, pneumonia, and other diseases. Inadequate tents and uniforms and bad diet weakened their resistance. When they came into towns, boozing and brawling took another toll.[21] This was to be the United States' last premodern war, where such appalling losses took place outside of combat. The forthcoming and much larger Civil War was bad enough, where casualties were about 50 percent non-combat-related. For it, the Mexican conflict was a horrible lesson.

Desertions were high. More than 10 percent of the regulars and nearly 7 percent of the volunteers deserted. Some got away with it, escaping disease as well as combat; some switched from regular to volunteer units. Others joined the Mexican forces, notably the San Patricio battalion, composed principally of Irish and European immigrants. If American troops captured them, they were shot, or, in the case of the San Patricios, hanged, as a particularly vengeful insult.[22] Catholic soldiers who remained in the American ranks confronted persistent bigotry from the press and from their comrades. They also watched comrades loot, burn, desecrate, and mock Catholic churches in Mexico. Anti-Mexican racism was endemic. Volunteers were much less disciplined than regulars, and of all volunteers the Texas Rangers had the worst reputation for tearing up the Mexican countryside and treating Mexicans inhumanely.[23]

Mexican losses included at least an equivalent number of military casualties. Thousands of civilians died from Scott's sieges and the free-booting rampages of volunteers. Mexican crops and property were randomly destroyed. Nevertheless, the defeat of Mexico's organized armies did not end resistance. Although Scott occupied Mexico City, it was by no means clear how the struggle should or could end. The Mexican leaders, divided factionally and defeated militarily, still had choices—or dilemmas. And so did Polk.

POLK'S AND MEXICO'S DILEMMAS, 1847

The Mexican dilemma was whether to round up yet more armies, fight, and probably lose more pitched battles; or to continue a war of guerrilla attrition until the Americans gave up and left; or to accept the losses of California and New Mexico, as well as Texas to the Rio Grande, sign whatever treaty they could, and stop the carnage. A strong faction, the *puros*, wanted to keep going. *Moderados* wanted a treaty. Local independence movements in Yucatán, Oaxaca, and other states threatened to spin off from the nation. How best to keep Mexico together as an independent country, and if that succeeded, should it be federal or centralized? A Mexican pamphleteer beseeched any reorganized government to "direct all its efforts to conserve the principle of *nationality* . . . at all costs." But should it agree, therefore, "to make peace, or to continue the war?"[24]

For Polk the dilemma was whether to continue occupying Mexico, for how long, and for what. The American victories, while hardly overwhelming or even clear-cut in many cases, were trumpeted in much of the press in late 1847 as validation for putting large parts or even the whole of Mexico under American rule. The recent clamor for 54°40' in Oregon was paralleled by cries of "all of Mexico," annexing it as far south as the Isthmus of Tehuantepec, or even extending American rule all the way to Colombia. Since the army was there, why not let it stay?

From Polk's perspective there were good reasons not to. It was expensive. He'd had to plead with Congress for the money to wage the war, and he would have to do so again to fund an occupation. He had faced an antiwar minority from the start—a tiny one in May 1846 when Congress voted to declare war, but a substantial one in 1847. The Whigs won a majority in the House of Representatives in the 1846 election and would take over in December 1847. They would write no large checks for Polk. The 1848 presidential election loomed, and both of the war-hero generals, Taylor and Scott, were Whigs. (Taylor would win the Whig nomination and the 1848 election; Scott was the 1852 Whig nominee but lost to a Democratic general, Franklin Pierce.)

In August 1846, with Congress just hours away from recessing until December, a Pennsylvania Democrat named David Wilmot added a "proviso" to an appropriations bill to the effect that slavery would not be countenanced in any territory acquired from Mexico. No sharper wedge issue existed. The Wilmot proviso did not pass then or in later forms, but it began to split the Democratic Party. Polk confided to his diary on August 10, 1846, that the bill he desired, appropriating $2 million for peace negotiations, had passed the House, but with this "mischievous & foolish amendment. . . . What connection slavery had with making peace with Mexico it is difficult to conceive."[25] He never understood the connection, only that it further complicated ending the war, even threatening his California prize.

But "how much to take"? As early as January 1847, if not before, American occupation of the Nueces strip, New Mexico, and Upper California was an accomplished fact. The United States would not give them back. But what of the next tier of occupied states to the south: Tamaulipas, Nuevo León, Coahuila, Chihuahua, Sonora, and Baja California? What about the Gulf coast to Tampico or Veracruz? What about central Mexico itself, if the Americans conquered it—which they had by September 1847?

Opinions differed in the American public and press, but ambitions broadly surged after the capture of Mexico City in September 1847 and through that fall. The extension of slavery was directly in question, whether Polk understood it or not. It had, however, the surprising effect of moderating territorial demands. The "all of Mexico" proponents never quite answered whether Mexico or its states should become, in time, states of the American union or remain permanent territories. That question provoked argument in 1898, after the United States acquired Puerto Rico and the Philippines. It probably would have done so in 1848 had "all of Mexico" actually been annexed. Proponents resisted any idea that annexed Mexicans would become American citizens with full and equal rights, and they would do the same regarding Filipinos and Puerto Ricans later on.

Yet the temptation was as huge as Mexico was prostrate. Had not Taylor and Scott beaten the Mexicans thoroughly? Was it not the right, even duty, of Americans to spread their culture, religion, and beneficent rule over a lazy, benighted, and degenerate race? Didn't manifest destiny demand taking what could be taken? Wouldn't Providence be insulted if Americans refused this gift? A Boston pamphleteer in 1846 summed up a widespread conviction that "the Mexican republic is politically, socially and morally dissolute. . . . Anarchy is its only domestic rule; treachery its only foreign policy. . . . Her conquest would be practicable . . . her annexation would be a barrier to slavery." The author argued that if

Mexico were annexed into the union as "a series of States of free laboring men," it would "stand as an impassable barrier to the extension of slavery southward." But if Mexico continued to exist, unannexed but supine, "the slavery of Texas will gradually encroach upon the northern Mexican provinces, and its course be indefinite."[26]

From the West and Southwest came loud hyperpatriotic arguments. Eastern newspapers pointed out the need to keep a weakened Mexico from falling into European hands (as indeed happened a few years later when the Austrian archduke Maximilian was made emperor of Mexico). The lure of an Atlantic-to-Pacific canal across the Isthmus of Tehuantepec was strong, and though that did not happen, the idea persisted until the Panama Canal opened sixty-six years later. Westerners, from editors and politicians to army volunteers, coveted Mexican land. The political split on "how much to take" followed the division over the war itself, with Whigs opposed, most Democrats in favor. Abraham Lincoln, elected a Whig congressman from Illinois in 1846, served only one term in large part because he opposed the war, the all-Mexico movement, and Polk himself, whose "mind," Lincoln told the House, "taxed beyond its power, is running hither and thither, like some tortured creature on a burning surface."[27] On December 22, 1847, Lincoln introduced eight "spot resolutions" calling on Polk to answer whether "the *spot* on which the blood of [American] citizens was shed as in his messages declared was not within the territory of Spain [and then] . . . Mexico," and related questions. Lincoln expanded the resolutions into his first major speech, which he gave on January 12, 1848. Polk never responded.[28]

The all-Mexico debate raged in the Senate from December 15, 1847, into February 1848. Southern Democrats, John C. Calhoun most prominently, opposed "all Mexico" because absorbing it would mean expanding nonslave areas—he assumed that Mexico would never reintroduce slavery—and taking on a huge nonwhite population. In a private conversation with Polk, Calhoun "said he did not desire to extend slavery," though he would vote against a Wilmot-like antislavery provision in any peace treaty as a matter of "principle."[29]

Many southerners, however, supported the all-Mexico movement. Among them was the powerful Treasury secretary, Robert J. Walker of Mississippi. Some military men (though not Lieutenant Ulysses S. Grant) favored large, possibly total, acquisition. The always aggressive Commodore Stockton roared in December 1847 that "if the war were to be prolonged for fifty years, and cost money enough to demand from us each half of all that we possess," he would nevertheless be confident that "the inestimable blessings of civil and religious liberty should be guaranteed to Mexico." Walt Whitman, then editor of the *Brooklyn Eagle*, called for "fifty thousand fresh troops" to "make our authority respectable," as "this talk about a peace party is all moonshine."[30] Various generals urged permanent occupation of Mexico north of the Sierra Madre Oriental (it actually runs more north and south, but what they wanted was Tamaulipas and the coast south beyond Tampico). Others coveted the whole country.[31]

Senator Lewis Cass of Michigan, who became the Democratic presidential nominee in 1848, agreed. When John Crittenden, a Kentucky Whig, demanded in the Senate to know why the army needed ten more regiments unless they were to occupy and perhaps annex the whole country, Cass argued that the troops had to be there to produce a "moral effect"—that is, intimidate guerrillas.

The most cogent speech against the all-Mexico idea came from Andrew Pickens Butler, a Democrat and Calhoun's South Carolina colleague. If we persist in "conquering and subjugating the Republic of Mexico," either making it part of "this Confederacy" or keeping it as a dependency, then "it would not be an extravagant proposition for the President to ask for two hundred thousand men to do it with security and safety." In other words, it would be a quagmire. American troops would not be in Mexico to fight, but "to overrun the Mexican states, to disarm the population, to confiscate the public property, to sequester the revenues, and to become . . . armed jailers." Every part of Europe, and many at home, are "a formidable opposition . . . against us."[32]

Heated discussion continued into February, with many nuances worth noting because they reveal the twists of territorial ambition at that time. John Bell of Tennessee opposed strengthening the army and occupying Mexico, because four of the eight million Mexicans are "degraded, vile, addicted to every vice," including "the Romish religion." Annexation would eventually mean "fifty new Representatives [and] forty new Senators, men of this mixed race." Most speakers steered clear of slavery. Southerners were not of one mind, but Calhoun's belief that large-scale annexation would weaken, not strengthen, slavery found support from Senator Jefferson Davis, among others.

As for Polk himself, his initial targets of California and New Mexico expanded after Scott's successes. In late 1847, privately and in the cabinet, he toyed with annexing everything north of the twenty-sixth parallel. His annual message to Congress of December 1847 left the door open for substantial acquisitions south of the Rio Grande. Partly as a result, the all-Mexico sentiment strengthened that winter. On January 2, 1848, he told Secretary of State Buchanan that he would be happy with Upper and Lower California, New Mexico, the Tehuantepec Isthmus, and Tampico.

But the Whig-majority House of Representatives elected in 1846 took office in December 1847 (Lincoln among them). It debated for weeks how much of Mexico to annex. Whigs were not likely to embrace the all-Mexico idea, strong though it was in the press and among the military. New England Whig papers insinuated that the real motive for large annexation was to capture the silver mines of Zacatecas and San Luis Potosí and extend slavery to all of Mexico. It was a way to provide an "outlet for our slaves," who were rapidly multiplying and threatening to overrun the South.[33] Nor were the Whigs eager to finance the army or call for more volunteers.

The all-Mexico debate stopped abruptly when a draft peace treaty from Mexico City arrived and became known in late February 1848, because it limited the gains to New Mexico and Upper California.[34]

Peace Negotiations and the Treaty

Peace feelers had gone out from Washington as early in the war as July 27, 1846 (and if one counts the Slidell mission, before the war started). By November 1846 the decision had been made to send an army to invade central Mexico, and that a peace commission would accompany it. Buchanan was prepared to go himself, but he and Polk agreed that if the Mexicans were not ready to talk, it would be unseemly for the secretary of state to dawdle around Scott's headquarters waiting for them. Buchanan thereupon proposed that "Mr. N. P. Trist, the chief clerk of the Department of State," be sent "with Plenipotentiary powers" to Scott's headquarters.[35]

Nicholas Trist was no simple clerk. He was Buchanan's second in command and had served several times as acting secretary when Buchanan was out of town. A grandson of Thomas Jefferson's, Trist spoke good Spanish and, although he had no great love for Mexicans, he was a skillful diplomat with a mind of his own. Polk and Buchanan provided Trist with a draft treaty—his instructions, in effect—which proposed a boundary from the mouth of the Rio Grande to "where it intersects the Southern boundary of New Mexico," with all of New Mexico, Upper California, and Baja (Lower) California to "be ceded to the United States." The United States would also have rights of passage through the Isthmus of Tehuantepec (though not annexation); it would assume all outstanding claims of U.S. citizens against Mexico; and it would pay Mexico $15 million, even $30 million if necessary.

Trist left for Scott's camp on April 16, arriving on May 14.[36] The Mexican leadership was in turmoil over who should negotiate and on what terms. While Scott's forces approached and took Mexico City, peace talks went nowhere. The existing government proposed on September 5 that Mexico keep the Nueces strip, New Mexico, and California from Monterey on south. Trist knew this had no chance whatever in Washington.

The logjam broke when Santa Anna resigned as president on September 15. Ten days later the *moderado* Manuel Peña y Peña replaced him, and quickly moved the capital to Querétaro, about 130 miles northwest and out from under the occupiers. He also removed Santa Anna from command of the army. The Mexican Congress reconvened in late October, highly divided among *puros* (the hard-line war party, including ex-president Gómez Farías), Santanistas (supporters of Santa Anna), monarchists (including former president Paredes), and—in a narrow majority—the *moderados*, or peace party. The Congress elected Pedro Anaya as interim president with Peña y Peña as secretary of (foreign) relations.

By then, however, Polk was leaning more strongly to annexation of, if not all of Mexico, at least everything north of the twenty-sixth parallel west to the Pacific. He learned from Buchanan that Trist had met intransigence from the war party, the monarchists, and the Santanistas, and also some resistance from the moderates. The all-Mexico wind was blowing harder from several sources, including Secretary of the Treasury Walker, and Polk felt the breeze within the cabinet. His long-time partisan suspicions of General Scott were reinforced by dispatches from the president's confidant, General Gideon Pillow, who was highly critical of Scott's tactics and strategy. With Scott and Trist by then working together, Polk's distrust spilled over onto Trist.[37]

The president was thoroughly misinformed. Not knowing that the peace party controlled the reconstituted Querétaro government and that Trist was in touch with it, he "resolved to-day [October 4, 1847] to recall Mr. Trist as commissioner to Mexico, and requested Mr.

Buchanan to prepare the letter of recall." The cabinet concurred the next day. Polk wrote in his diary that "Mr. Trist is recalled because his remaining longer with the army could not, probably, accomplish the objects of his mission, and because his remaining longer might, & probably would, impress the Mexican Government with the belief that the U.S. were so anxious for peace that they would ultimate[ly] conclude one upon the Mexican terms. Mexico must now first sue for peace, & when she does we will hear her propositions."[38]

Polk's action might be excused by the fact that he had just spent several days in bed with fever and chills and was desperate for news from Mexico. He had less excuse on October 23, having had a report (though not a full story) from Trist as of late September. He told Buchanan to send Trist another recall message anyway. "Mr. Trist has managed the negotiation very bunglingly and with no ability. He has done more. He has departed from his instructions so far as to invite proposals from the Mexican commissioners . . . which [can] never be accepted by the United States" (these were the outdated September 5 terms of the deposed Santa Anna government).[39] Polk not only wanted Trist recalled; he also wanted Scott to prosecute the war and occupation vigorously, levying taxes on occupied areas to reimburse America's costs of the war. It was vintage Polk: hard-line, contemptuous (and ignorant) of the other side's proposals.

Trist learned of his recall on November 16. Anaya and Peña y Peña were cooperating, and on November 22 they appointed a peace commission. Trist agonized. Should he immediately go to Washington and try to explain what was truly happening? On December 4 he decided instead, after urgings from the British chargé, Edward Thornton, and most importantly from his friend James L. Freaner of the *New Orleans Delta*, to continue negotiating. He wrote a sixty-five-page explanation to Buchanan. He informed the Mexicans of his irregular status, but Anaya and his negotiators continued talking, even after Trist told them that the Rio Grande, not the Nueces, was the nonnegotiable border, and that west of it the thirty-second parallel would do. Trist believed that his presence and position provided the best chance to obtain a treaty that would contain Polk's essential instructions and conclude the war. Otherwise the *puros* would take power, the United States would annex all or most of Mexico, and the American army would sink into a bloody, expensive, and interminable occupation. The *moderado* government was shaky; extreme American demands, or even too much quibbling, might sink the process. The war party was willing to fight on. Thousands of Mexican troops and unnumbered irregulars, however ill prepared, were still out there. Talk in the United States of annexing all of Mexico only toughened the *puro* stance. And so Trist stayed, talked, and drafted a treaty.

On January 2, 1847, Peña y Peña became president again, and final negotiations began. They dragged on through January, with San Diego the sticking point. The Mexican commissioners agreed that the boundary would run south of it, giving it to the United States (with Mexico keeping Baja California), but the government did not agree to this for another three weeks. Polk dropped the other shoe and relieved Scott of his command on January 13, news of which arrived three weeks later. Trist expected daily to be ordered home. If he were, the talks would cease. On January 28 he told the Mexican negotiators that he was breaking off the discussions. Moreover, Scott would move to occupy Querétaro and dissolve the government. Whether the threat was real—Trist wrote that very day to Scott to lay back, as the war party was "endeavouring to prevent the formation of a government in order that peace might be an impossibility"—it worked.[40] Peña y Peña told his commissioners to quit nitpicking and sign. On February 2, 1848, late in the afternoon, Trist and the three Mexican negotiators signed the peace treaty in the sacristy of the shrine of Guadalupe Hidalgo. Trist immediately sent Buchanan the treaty, "signed one hour ago at the city of Guadalupe . . . the most sacred on earth" to Mexico.[41]

The remaining questions were obvious. Would Polk accept the treaty? Would the Senate ratify it? And would the peace party prevail in Querétaro and secure ratification by Mexico?

Polk was predictably furious with Trist, and had been since December when it became clear that the envoy was disobeying his recall orders. After reading Trist's long explanation to Buchanan, Polk wrote in his diary:

> His dispatch is arrogant, impudent, and very insulting to his Government, and even personally offensive to the President. [Polk often referred to himself in the diary by his title]. . . . I have never in my life felt so indignant. . . . He has acted worse than any man in the public employ whom I have ever known. His dispatch proves that he is destitute of honour or principle, and that he has proved himself to be a very base man.

Polk, through Secretary of War Marcy, told Scott's replacement, General William O. Butler, to "order him off." In March Butler "reluctantly" escorted Trist out of Mexico, essentially under guard.[42] "This action," in the apt words of one historian, "ranks with the most flagrant examples of presidential ingratitude in American history."[43] Polk cut off Trist's salary and reimbursements from the date of his first recall. Twenty years later, Trist recovered part.

The treaty, carried by Freaner through bandit country and then by fast steamship to Mobile and railroad to Washington, reached Polk on February 19, a record seventeen days after it was signed. Leaving aside his pique, he brought it before the cabinet the next day and sent it to the Senate. Despite the strength of the all-Mexico idea at that moment, and despite his December 1847 message to Congress suggesting maximum annexation, Polk reflected that the treaty's terms were "within his [Trist's] instructions which he took out [to Mexico] in April last. . . . Mr. Trist has acted very badly . . . but notwithstanding this, if on further examination the Treaty is one that can be accepted, it should not be rejected on account of his bad conduct."

Two days later, following cabinet discussion, Polk explained his pragmatic reasoning in his diary:

> If I were now to reject a Treaty made upon my own terms, as authorized in April last, with the unanimous approbation of the Cabinet, the probability is that Congress would not grant either men or money to prosecute the war. Should this be the result, the army now in Mexico would be constantly wasting and diminishing in numbers, and I might at last be compelled to withdraw them, and thus loose [*sic*] . . . New Mexico & Upper California, which were ceded to the U. S. by this Treaty.[44]

Therefore, although Buchanan wanted more territory and Robert Walker still urged annexation of the whole country, Polk settled for striking out only one article (it guaranteed Mexican land titles in the ceded areas) and sent the treaty to the Senate on February 22. Polk's dilemma—to fight on, possibly gaining much more territory but risking an indefinite guerrilla war, or to settle for his original objective of Upper California—was resolved in favor of California. The House Whigs, he predicted, would either defeat or seriously revise his military requests if he asked for them; the Wilmot proviso was certain to resurface at nearly every turn; his party's prospects in the forthcoming election would suffer. Nothing better was likely to develop. He even agreed to withdraw from Baja California despite American control of it, so that Trist's treaty would pass.

The senators debated for eleven days in closed session. Some opposed the treaty because they had always been against the war, others because they feared the extension of slavery, and others because it did not seize as much of Mexico as they wished. But they settled for Trist's treaty almost intact, except for the land-grant article. A proposal from Senator Sam Houston to annex everything south beyond Tampico, plus San Luis Potosí, went nowhere. Jefferson Davis's motion to take most of the northern states (Tamaulipas to Chihuahua) failed, 44 to 11. On March 10, 38 senators voted yea, 14 nay, and 4 did not vote, providing comfortably more than the required two-thirds approval. In the end, senators from all sections and both parties voted for the treaty; they wanted the war to be over. A few Whigs opposed the treaty, as they had opposed the war all along, and a few all-Mexico Democrats from the Northwest thought it did not gain enough territory, just as they had wanted 54°40' two years before.[45] Yet the large majority ratified Trist's "Treaty of Peace, Friendship, Limits and Settlement."

The treaty ended hostilities and blockades and promised removal of U.S. forces within three months after ratifications. It set the international boundary along the Rio Grande from its mouth to the "southern boundary of New Mexico" and then west to the Gila River and then to its intersection with the Colorado River, thence to the Pacific. Thus it gave the Nueces strip, the state of New Mexico, and all of Upper California to the United States, much more than Polk's prayer in 1845 of just the bays of San Francisco and possibly Monterey. Mexicans living in the areas transferred to the United States were "free to continue where they now reside, or to remove at any time to the Mexican Republic, retaining the property which they possess in the said territories, or disposing thereof," without being taxed, and had a choice of Mexican or American citizenship. If they became American, they would "be admitted, at the proper time (to be judged of by the Congress of the United States) to the enjoyment of all the rights of citizens." The United States bound itself to prevent "savage tribes" from "incursions" into Mexico—a provision that proved unenforceable. The United States would pay Mexico $15 million in five installments, and assume the old claims of American citizens against Mexico, up to $3,250,000.[46] Although the treaty transferred a huge and immensely valuable area to the United States, it did not transfer many Mexicans, since so few lived in it except for coastal California and the Rio Grande Valley in New Mexico.

Conversely, if the all-Mexico proponents had won, Mexico would have been an unlikely target for American settlers, while the United States would have adopted several million Mexicans to govern, occupy, and contend with. There was no demographic argument for acquiring all of Mexico. Of the three great acquisitions of the 1840s, Texas was very demographically driven, Oregon somewhat, but California hardly at all. By early 1848 only a few hundred Americans had gone there. Yet the *potential* for many happy and securely landed pioneer families was in the minds of the ardent advocates of manifest destiny. John L. O'Sullivan, who coined the term, wrote in July 1845:

> The Anglo-Saxon foot is already on its [California's] borders. Already the advance guard of the irresistible army of Anglo-Saxon emigration has begun to pour down upon it, armed with the plough and the rifle, and marking its trail with schools and colleges, courts and representative halls, mills and meeting-houses. A population will soon be in actual occupation of California, over which it will be idle for Mexico to dream of dominion.[47]

Settlers already in the Sonoma Valley of course agreed. The freedom lovers were not there yet, but they would soon come, seeking land and, as it happened, the gold of the Sierras.

Mexican ratification was no certainty. Even Polk worried that the excision by the Senate of the article guaranteeing Mexican land grants might break the deal. The fractiousness among Mexican leaders continued. *Puros* wrote that they "preferred a thousand times the most disadvantageous horrors of the war and the disasters of the most frightful anarchy to the loss of national honor [that would be] the immediate consequences of an ignominious peace." A *puro* with a long and honorable résumé, Manuel Crescencio Rejón, who had helped write the constitution of 1824, let fly his "Observations on the Treaty of Guadalupe" on April 17, 1848. He insisted on "America's war guilt" and argued that the treaty made "the maximum concessions."[48] *Moderados* argued that failure to make peace might lose Yucatán (then in rebellion) as well.[49] Both groups were deeply patriotic, but their disagreement was polar as to whether to ratify.

A final, and persuasive, plea came from the veteran *moderado* Manuel Peña y Peña. President once before, foreign minister several times, senior justice on the Supreme Court, and now interim president, he had favored talks with Slidell in 1845, which might have avoided the war entirely. It was he who broke the stalemate in the peace talks in January 1848. He now argued in favor of ratifying the treaty. Fifty-nine in that year, worn down by factional bickering, military defeats, and heavy responsibilities (he died in 1850), Peña held the presidency from January 8 to June 3 during the negotiation with Trist and the ratification process. A serious, sensible, and articulate lawyer, he addressed the Mexican Congress on May 7. "You will be convinced," he said, "that the cession of territory was the least that could be agreed upon, and that it was not possible to hope that in this matter the United States would modify its demands." Without ceding Texas, New Mexico, and Upper California, Peña argued, Polk would "continue the war under the plan as indicated" in his message to Congress of December 6, 1847. The amendments made by the American Senate were most unfortunate, but "not of such an importance that the treaty should be thrown out on their account. . . . It does not consider that a new round of negotiations can be hoped for nor that such a development would result in terms more favorable."[50]

On May 26, 1848, Trist received a message from his British diplomat friend in Mexico City, Edward Thornton, that the House of Deputies had ratified the treaty on May 19 by 51 to 35, and that the Senate in Querétaro had just ratified by 30 to 4.[51] The Mexican dilemma was solved; a guerrilla war would not ensue.

AFTERMATHS

Expansionism did not cease with the Treaty of Guadalupe Hidalgo. In May 1848, just as Mexico was ratifying it, insurgents in Yucatán invited American support or annexation. The Polk administration considered that, but backed off when the insurgency suddenly subsided.[52] Cuba also beckoned. On May 30, Polk and the cabinet, acting on questionable intelligence, decided to offer Spain $100 million for it. The Spanish retorted that they "would prefer seeing it sunk in the Ocean."[53]

Polk turned over the presidency to General Taylor, the victorious Whig, in March 1849. Polk died on June 15, partly from exhaustion; he almost never took a day off and was besieged almost daily with office seekers and beggars, as his diary records. Still, as a footnote to the Mexican Cession, one more expansion followed, rounding out the permanent continental boundaries of the United States except for a few dozen scattered square miles adjudicated later. This final acquisition was the Mesilla Valley of southern New Mexico and the area of present Arizona south of the Gila River—the 30,000 square miles known since as the Gadsden Purchase.

Santa Anna, back in power in 1853 for the last time, decided he needed more money. James Gadsden, a South Carolina railroad builder, had been urging for years that the United States finance a line from Charleston to California. The best route lay through the Mesilla Valley. Jefferson Davis was by then secretary of war in the Franklin Pierce administration, and he agreed with Gadsden, whom Pierce appointed minister to Mexico. On December 30, 1853, Gadsden and Santa Anna signed a treaty trading the land for $10 million. Shortly thereafter, Santa Anna stepped down for the last time, and the United States had acquired the area where the Southern Pacific later built Gadsden's railroad.[54]

Two further aftermaths, one American and one Mexican, were not as felicitous. For the United States, the acquisition of all that territory to the southwest inevitably raised the question of whether slavery would exist within it. Although Polk saw no connection between annexation and slavery, most other people did, either to favor or to oppose it. The Wilmot proviso made the link inescapable. The election campaign of 1848 kept the issue in front of the voters, as former president Martin Van Buren won nearly 300,000 votes as a third-party "Free Soil" candidate. By 1850 the question of slavery extension divided the country. The aged Henry Clay of Kentucky brokered the Compromise of 1850, admitting California as a free state and creating the territories of Utah and New Mexico (which included future Arizona) with the decision on slavery to be left to their citizens when they eventually applied for statehood. For the South, the compromise gave it a much tougher law permitting the chase and capture of fugitive slaves.

The compromise held for a few years, but when the expansionist Illinois senator Stephen A. Douglas pushed through a bill in 1854 providing that the new territories of Kansas and Nebraska could decide for themselves whether to permit slavery—"popular sovereignty," he labeled it—the issue burst forth again. It worsened until South Carolina, followed by ten more states, seceded from the Union in 1860–1861. The Civil War that followed killed more than 600,000 Union and Confederate soldiers, and slavery was no more, in the Mexican Cession or anywhere else.

For Mexico, the aftermath was resentment at the profound injustice of it all, and at the American contempt, cultural and religious, that underlay the process. A group of Mexican intellectuals published a history of the war in August 1848. They began by recalling that Spain's Conde de Aranda, after the 1782 peace talks (remember the Aranda-Rayneval proposal?), predicted that the United States, now a "pygmy," would in the course of time become a giant among nations. The Mexican writers understood that the time had come, and at their country's expense. The "true and effective cause of the war that afflicted us," they wrote, "was the spirit of aggrandizement of the United States of the North, validated by its power to dominate us." Someday, history would reveal how it contravened "all human and divine laws, in a century that calls itself enlightened." The war left "in our hearts a sentiment of sadness for the evils that we underwent."[55] Mexican writers and historians from that day on lamented the war, the loss of territory, the disgrace, the humiliation, but also glorified the valor and justice of the Mexican cause.

To one late-twentieth-century Mexican historian, the history of the Mexican-American war

> is the tale of an unjust act brought about by immoral men in order to satisfy purely material ends. . . . American historians [at least prior to 1970] have written that their forebears were honorable men, men above unjust actions, solely concerned with propagating the blessings of democracy. In doing so these historians have transformed acts of brigandage into acts of patriotism. And they have made heroes of military adventurers, mercenaries, filibusterers, criminals and common gunfighters.[56]

One could disagree that the Americans' ends were "purely material." The frenzy of manifest destiny that suffused Polk's America was a psychological impulse, not a material one. Why did Polk want—insist, connive—so single-mindedly to acquire California? An American historian contended more than fifty years ago that it was to establish the United States on the Pacific, so that it could become a transpacific power.[57] Polk's strong desire to secure rights to cross the Isthmus of Tehuantepec in southern Mexico, presaging the more fruitful effort later to control Panama, also showed an interest in the Pacific. John Quincy Adams's "transcontinental" treaty, with its recognition of U.S. rights along the forty-second parallel to the Pacific, had revealed such a concern three decades earlier. The objective in conquering California was not in any immediate way to provide homes for American settlers, for among all the details in Polk's four-volume diary that motive does not appear (though it does with regard to Oregon). Yet the expectation of a massive westward movement of people underpinned manifest destiny for California. It was a vision in the minds of all these men—Polk, John L. O'Sullivan, Buchanan, Benton, Frémont, Stephen A. Douglas, and the hell-for-leather expansionists in what was then the West, the Mississippi Valley.

The continental United States was complete. It could have been larger, including more, or even all, of Mexico. But at what cost? All but a few expansionists recognized it would be economically and politically too much. As of 1848, there was plenty of "empty" real estate to be filled with democratic people and the blessings of liberty. And there were other ways to be imperial without actually annexing land, as the United States would demonstrate in the next century and a half.

Chapter Eight

POPULATING THE EMPIRE

> *In the United States of America, where the means of subsistence have been more ample, the manners of the people more pure, and consequently the checks to early marriage fewer, than in any of the modern states of Europe, the population has been found to double itself in twenty-five years . . . but we may be perfectly sure, that population will not long continue to increase with the same rapidity. . . .*
>
> —T. R. Malthus, 1798[1]

WHAT WAS REQUIRED TO OCCUPY THE CONTINENT?

Acquiring the continental landmass was one thing. Occupying and settling it was another. Why did the United States succeed?

The expansion was unprecedented. When the United States began its recognized existence as an independent country in 1783, it had fewer than four million people spread over less than 900,000 square miles. All the people and all the territory were east of the Mississippi, south of the Great Lakes, and north of Spanish Florida. Population density averaged fewer than five people per square mile. Between then and 1854, the density doubled, the area tripled, and the population exploded eight or nine times over. Nowhere else in the Americas, even in land-rich Brazil or Argentina or Canada, did population expand at such rates, nor did it anywhere else in the world in recorded times. In this respect, the United States truly was exceptional.

To populate so large a region so quickly, it first had to be acquired. That happened in all the ways already described—by treaty, purchase, filibuster, or outright war, based in various mixes of luck, chicanery, single-mindedness, ideology, aggression, or fecundity. Luck helped in 1782 and 1803; aggression failed in Canada but succeeded in the Floridas and the Southwest; and invasions of settlers led the way in Texas and in Oregon. The losers were usually at a military or demographic disad-

vantage, or they were preoccupied by European or domestic entangle-
ments so that the United States could seize an opportunity.

Besides gaining sovereignty, however, a few more conditions were
required to secure the land. Otherwise it might have remained unoccu-
pied, like New France and New Spain, and might have become as
vulnerable as they proved to be. How could it be safeguarded? Four elements in particular assured the American occupation. None was fully
planned, certainly not by a single prophet, philosopher, or politician; but
all four, together, combined over several decades to produce the result.
Obviously the previous occupants had to go, and over time, the Indians
went. Second, the federal government, as custodian for the people of the
huge landmass, had to devise ways to transfer pieces of it systematically
to individuals. Land policy and the resultant homesteading are so far
back in our history that probably only historians remember them, but
they were crucial to the settlement process and the speed with which it
happened. Third, people had to materialize in large numbers, and so
they did, from a phenomenally high frontier birthrate and from immigration, mainly from Europe and partially from Asia. Finally, Americans
had to believe profoundly that their expansion, public and private, was a
good thing. They required an ideology of expansion. Under various
names—"manifest destiny" served the purpose best, fortified by racist
assumptions of Anglo-Saxon superiority over Spaniards and Mexicans,
and anyone red, black, brown, or yellow—that ideology was seldom
doubted by the mass of white Americans. Until well into the twentieth
century it was supported by the best academic and scientific opinion.
The ideology of expansion was both national—capital-letter Manifest
Destiny—and individual-familial—the sum of millions of small-letter
manifest destinies.

Thus, in addition to acquiring legal sovereignty, the United States'
occupation advanced through Indian removal, land policy, proliferating
population, and self-serving ideology. Most of the elements were present elsewhere, but the combination was unique to the United States. It
would require another book to explain why other New World nations
did not expand as much, and why the United States succeeded in filling
up vast regions where New Spain and New France failed from lack of
population. Among the reasons, Argentina and Brazil did not institute
land policies that provided settlers with secure titles. Neither did they
move their native peoples out of the settlers' way with the thoroughness
or timeliness that Americans did. High mountains, arid deserts, rivers in

the "wrong" places, and lack of usable energy resources inhibited mass settlement elsewhere and at earlier times. By 1790 the die was already cast: young Americans could procreate as fast as biology allowed, in the secure expectation that productive land awaited their many children, an environment that the otherwise gloomy Malthus found unique. Elsewhere, for reasons of policy, economics, topography, and other essentials, that was not true. Young Americans had the means, the motives, and the enticements that others lacked.

Removing the Indians

The North American landmass was never empty, and to make it available, neighbors and other claimants had to leave. The Europeans vacated, one by one—French, Russians, Spanish, British, and Mexicans, in that order. The native peoples were also reduced, removed, repelled, or reconcentrated. Their control or disappearance is an oft-told story (though not, perhaps, told often enough). The more Anglo-Americans who entered an area, the fewer Indians who survived in it. Disease had much to do with that, either killing Indians outright, or making them sick and unfit to resist, or sterilizing potential childbearers. The population balance that initially favored the Indians shifted slowly, and then decisively, toward the Americans. Occasionally pitched battles took place. When (as usual) the whites won, the resulting peace treaty would permanently transfer land title. Indian land may have been communally rather than individually held, but it was still theirs, and they knew it, and quickly learned that once gone it would not be returned. From colonial times to the 1850s, the formality of treaties was observed almost scrupulously, even though the unequal power of the two sides and the inevitable result of Indian departure was known to both. After the wars between the U.S. Army and the Plains Indians from the late 1860s through the 1870s, however, Congress often acted unilaterally and a military takeover ran the Indians off or herded them onto reservations. Sometimes, as in Texas after it gained its independence in 1836, and in California and Oregon, Indians were driven out or often simply annihilated.

In the early nineteenth century, an idea and a policy emerged that was expected to salve white consciences and legal requirements, benefit the Indians, and obviate conflict between the two groups. This was "Indian removal," and its leading early advocate was Thomas Jefferson. In his view, Indians and whites always clashed and, when they did, Indians always lost. Yet they were human beings. Their level of civilization was behind that of whites, the theory went, but given time, they would catch up. To provide a catch-up period, they should be removed from harm's way and resettled well west of the Mississippi in an unspoiled part of the Louisiana Purchase.

President James Monroe, good Jeffersonian that he was, summarized the plan in a message to Congress in January 1825, just before he left office. "The removal of the Indian tribes from the lands which they now occupy," wrote Monroe, "may be accomplished on conditions and in a manner to promote the interest and happiness of those tribes." Removal would "not only shield them from impending ruin, but promote their welfare and happiness." Monroe judged that "it is impossible to incorporate them . . . in any form whatever, into our system. . . . Without a timely anticipation of and provision against the dangers to which they are exposed . . . their degradation and extermination will be inevitable." Thus the United States must convey "to each tribe . . . an adequate portion of land to which it may consent to remove" and provide "a system of internal government which shall protect their property from invasion, and . . . prevent the degeneracy which has generally marked the transition from the one to the other state." By doing that, "we become in reality their benefactors . . . [and] conflicting interests between them and our frontier settlements will cease. There will be no more wars between them and the United States."[2] Uproot them, and thus save them. As the Cherokee Elias Boudinot wrote in 1828, "Where have we an example in the whole history of man of a Nation or tribe, removing in a body, from a land of civil and religious means, to a perfect wilderness, in order to be civilized?"[3]

This policy has been called "Jeffersonian philanthropy."[4] Its ideological generosity and solicitude coincided neatly with the eagerness of frontierspeople and developers to absorb the land of the tribes of the Southeast and the Old Northwest, so much so that many decades later it is difficult to distinguish the benevolence from the rapacity. In any case, the philanthropy could not evolve into policy until settlement approached the Indians' lands and a leader emerged who would effectuate it. By 1829, both conditions were in place. The leader was Andrew Jackson, the newly inaugurated president.

The issue came to a head in Georgia. As white settlers and miners infiltrated, the Cherokees established their own government in 1827, in accord with earlier Cherokee-federal treaties. In 1802 Georgia had agreed to cede its old colonial charter claims extending west to the Mississippi to the federal government, on condition that Indian titles would be "extinguished," in the term of that day, in a reasonable and timely way. Georgia's cession had since become the states of Mississippi (1817) and Alabama (1819). People living there joined Georgians in feeling that the time had come to put the 1802 agreement into effect. Thus Georgia passed laws invalidating Indian titles, nullifying Indian court testimony against whites, and abolishing the Cherokees' government, thus stripping them of both land and recourse.

The Indians fell back on the federal government for help. The Supreme Court saw it their way, and in two decisions, *Cherokee Nation* v. *Georgia* and *Worcester* v. *Georgia*, it voided the Georgia statutes. Chief Justice John Marshall stated that "the acts of Georgia are repugnant to the Constitution, laws, and treaties of the United States." But these decisions came in 1831 and 1832. By that time, unfortunately for the Indians, the other two branches of the federal government—the executive, presided over by Jackson, and the Jacksonian-Democratic-majority Congress—had supported Georgia. Furthermore, the Court's power was limited to the specific issues in the cases before it; it could not order Georgia to drop its anti-Cherokee laws or the Jackson administration to desist from removals.[5]

Jeffersonian philanthropy became law in the Indian Removal Act of 1830, formally entitled "a bill to provide for an exchange of lands with the Indians residing in any of the States or Territories, and for their removal west of the river Mississippi." The Senate approved it on April 26, 1830, by a vote of 28–19. Nearly every New England senator voted against, nearly every southern one voted for, with the Middle Atlantic and northwestern senators split slightly in favor. The debate has a modern ring in many places, and in others, an antique, pre–Civil War tone. Georgia's senators (supported by Alabama's and Mississippi's) asserted an extreme states' rights position that only the Civil War would suppress some thirty years later.

The position more familiar to modern ears emerged in a speech by Senator Theodore Frelinghuysen of New Jersey. He proposed an amendment that the Indians could not be removed unless and until they gave full consent, without "inducements" (bribes), and that they were entitled to self-rule within the boundaries of Georgia. So said treaties, and so federal responsibility demanded. Frelinghuysen pointed out that the federal government had entered into treaties with Indian tribes—

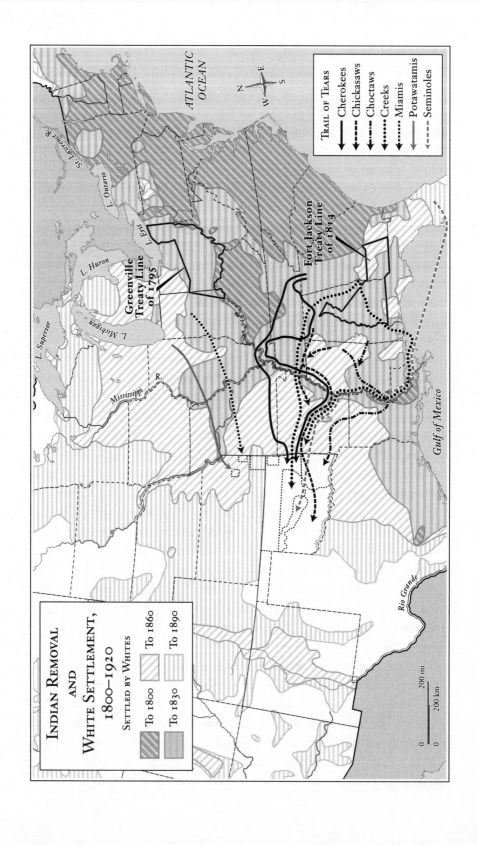

INDIAN REMOVAL AND WHITE SETTLEMENT, 1800–1920

SETTLED BY WHITES

To 1800
To 1830
To 1860
To 1890

TRAIL OF TEARS

Cherokees
Chickasaws
Choctaws
Creeks
Miamis
Potawatamis
Seminoles

ATLANTIC OCEAN

Gulf of Mexico

Greenville Treaty Line of 1795

Fort Jackson Treaty Line of 1814

St. Lawrence R.

L. Ontario

L. Erie

L. Huron

L. Michigan

L. Superior

Mississippi R.

Rio Grande

200 mi

200 km

treating them as sovereign entities—ever since George Washington guaranteed them rights.[6] Indians "by immemorial possession as the original tenants of the soil . . . hold a title beyond and superior to the British Crown and her colonies, and to all adverse pretensions of our confederation and subsequent Union," said Frelinghuysen. State sovereignty, even federal sovereignty, could not override that ancient right.

Senator John Forsyth of Georgia disagreed, insisting that "the United States obtained, by treaty, the power to legislate over the Cherokees, and transferred it to Georgia" in 1802. Georgians' motives "were not formed to suit our interests, nor at all influenced by them." Rather, he claimed, "all [of us] desire to grant more than is justly due for the preservation and civilization" of the Indians, all of whom "would be benefited by their removal beyond the States, to a country appropriated for their exclusive residence." Forsyth asserted that "Indian tribes are not, in the terms of the constitution, foreign nations or states." Therefore treaties with them, even those made by the president with the advice and consent of the Senate, "are not technically treaties, supreme laws of the land." (This flatly contradicted Frelinghuysen, John Marshall, and the language of the treaties.) Since Indians were not Christians aware of "future rewards and punishments," they were unable to swear valid oaths, Forsyth theologized. Hence Georgia had properly banned their testimony in court. They also practiced polygamy, killed horse thieves without trial, and did other uncivilized things abhorrent to Georgians. Therefore Georgians believed they should be removed.

Over the next several days, other senators spoke for and against. The capacity for self-justification and the ability of legislators to find excuses for the outrageous were rarely more evident. Finally, the removal act passed the Senate comfortably, including a $500,000 appropriation to carry it out.[7]

Settlement of the continental United States accelerated from 1800 until 1920, when most of the arable land had become occupied. Rivers were the chief means of access before 1860, railroads afterward. Settlement was sometimes as thin as two persons per square mile at first, and this map does not show gradations of density.

The forced removals of Indians in the 1830s and 1840s, from the Midwest and the southeast to the Indian Territory (later, Oklahoma) and eleswhere, are shown for only seven large tribes. There were a number of others.

The Greenville Treaty of 1795 opened up much of Ohio north of the Ohio River to white settlement. The Treaty of Fort Jackson of 1814 deprived the Creeks of much of their land in Alabama and Georgia.

The House's consideration began on May 13 and continued almost without letup until the final vote on May 24. The arguments resembled those made in the Senate. Georgians insisted that the terms of the 1802 cession of its western land claims to the federal government required federal support for removal. One Georgia congressman, Wilson Lumpkin, declared that if the removal bill failed, "We deny your right of jurisdiction. . . . Our right of sovereignty will not be yielded," and he even hinted at armed resistance should the "General Government" stand in Georgia's way. "We are on the very banks of the Rubicon," warned Georgia's Thomas F. Foster; "cross it, and we may not be able to calculate the consequences. . . . I tell you, sir, Georgia has taken her course, and she will not retire from it."

Several northerners spoke against the bill, notably Henry Storrs of New York and Edward Everett of Massachusetts. They insisted that the Indian treaties were national obligations and, in Storrs's words, that "the observance of treaties, is the law of the whole human family. . . . Our enemies are watching our steps. . . . Passage of this bill will light up joy and hope in the palace of every despot."

Everett cited censuses listing the Indians' cattle, horses, blacksmith shops, schools, and many other evidences of civilization. They are "living as we do, by husbandry, and the mechanic arts, and the industrious trades." Yet "we are going to remove them from these their homes to a distant wilderness. Who ever heard of such a thing before?" Everett pointed out that Indians had never been able to withstand the onrush of white settlers, nor had governments or troops held it back. Settlers will push westward, "boast themselves your citizens . . . extend their jurisdiction over the Indians, and drive them into Texas." They will encounter "numerous warlike and powerful tribes" already living west of the Mississippi. "Ten or fifteen thousand families [will] be rooted up, and carried hundreds, aye, a thousand of miles into the wilderness! There is not such a thing in the annals of mankind. . . . A community of civilized people, of all ages, sexes, and condition of bodily health, are to be dragged hundreds of miles, over mountains, rivers, and deserts, where there are no roads, no bridges, no habitations, and this is to be done for eight dollars a head, and done by contract."

Everett and his colleagues nearly prevailed. On May 24, two votes resulted in ties, broken by the Speaker, and the final one ended 102 in favor, 98 opposed. A swing of three votes would have killed the removal bill. Nearly all of its supporters were Democrats, though many from

Pennsylvania and Ohio defected and voted no. National Republicans—the party of John Quincy Adams and Henry Clay, soon to develop into the Whigs—almost unanimously opposed the bill. Sectionally, the South voted heavily in favor, New England against, with the Middle Atlantic and the West divided.[8]

In due course, through the 1830s, the southern tribes (Cherokees, Choctaws, Creeks, Chickasaws, some Seminoles) were escorted to the Indian Territory (present-day Oklahoma) and northern tribes (Shawnees, Sac and Fox, Potawatomies, Miamis, and others) were taken to what soon became the Kansas Territory—many to be moved a second time, or compressed into reservations, when the line of white settlement again approached, as it did in the 1850s. Thousands died on the way. Everett's predictions came true. Conflict with whites, settlers as well as the army, did not stop, nor did intertribal warfare. Moving the eastern Indians to the edge of the Great Plains intensified strife with the mostly nomadic Plains Indians from Lakotas in the north to Comanches in Texas. Removal was overtaken by white settlement far quicker than the so-called philanthropists of the Jefferson-Jackson era expected.

In 1825, before the removals, the War Department estimated that there were 129,000 Indians within what were then the boundaries of the United States, more than 50,000 of them in Georgia, Tennessee, Alabama, and Mississippi. By 1838, more than 80,000 suffered removal, mostly to what is now Oklahoma, Kansas, and Nebraska. As of 1855, according to the Office of Indian Affairs, 315,000 Indians lived in the United States (much augmented by the 1848 territorial acquisitions) but only 8,500 east of the Mississippi. The southeastern states, together with Ohio, Indiana, and Illinois, were basically Indian-free by 1842.[9]

Following the Civil War, as settlers pushed into the Plains in huge numbers, the U.S. Army fronted for them or came to their "rescue" in the late 1860s and through much of the 1870s, crushing Indian resistance. The Indian wars ended on the southern Plains by 1868, on the northern Plains by 1881, and in the Southwest with the surrender of Geronimo and his Apaches in 1886. By then, the removal policy had long since seen its day, as there was nowhere left to remove people to. But the basic idea of assimilation into white culture, with a fig leaf of beneficence still covering it, persisted in the form of reservations and various devices such as Indian schools and "severalty," which ended tribal ownership and forced individual Indians to behave like white homesteaders.[10] Between 1900 and 1920, American Indians fell to their lowest numbers, partly from warfare, more from diseases. In the twentieth century they became, essentially, just another ethnic minority.

DISTRIBUTING THE PUBLIC DOMAIN

Pushing the original inhabitants off the land had the obvious and intended result of making it available to white settlement. It is probably more accurate to say that the surge of settlers, and the political clout they exercised, did much of the pushing. How land was transferred from public sovereignty and ownership to individual and family holdings is another long story, which, like the reduction of the Indians, need not be detailed here. But a few markers of the astonishingly rapid occupation of the continental landmass are worth noting.

The United States public domain came into existence between 1780 and 1802, when the states with claims to Transappalachian land arising from their colonial charters transferred them to the central government. In 1785, the Confederation Congress passed an ordinance prescribing how the land should be surveyed and sold. There would be a "rectilinear" survey, with the land measured in right-angle blocks of townships and sections westward across the nation's immense surface. This process was both a bane and a boon to settlement: a bane because it took so long and ignored natural irregularities such as mountains and rivers, hills and gullies; but a boon because buyers and sellers knew precisely where the borders of a parcel were. Areas that were settled prior to this system or that remained outside of it, like Kentucky and southern Ohio, were plagued with lawsuits over competing land claims (as Daniel Boone, for example, discovered to his dismay).

From the first, the cash-poor U.S. government regarded the public domain as a moneymaker. The 1785 ordinance provided that farm-sized plots could be sold to individuals. It also allowed sale of whole townships of thirty-six square miles to land companies, which were expected to develop and resell them in smaller parcels as they saw fit. The system did not work particularly well in its early years; it was slow, cumbersome, expensive, and did not raise the expected money. Sizable grants were made outside of it, notably in southern Ohio and later in Texas and elsewhere. Still, the straight lines and sharp corners of counties, townships, and sections gradually crisscrossed Transappalachia, the trans-Mississippi region, and ultimately the Great Plains and parts of the far

West. Congress revised federal land law periodically, almost always in the direction of making it easier and cheaper for individuals and families to gain title to their own farms. By 1862, the original idea of the federal government making major revenue by selling land to companies or individuals had deflated. The famous Homestead Act of that year simply gave away 160 acres to any bona fide settler who would improve them and live on them for at least five years. Cash sales continued, but the main object had become rapid western settlement.

The practice of using companies as middlemen persisted in a large way in the post–Civil War years in the form of railroad land grants. Railroad corporations received massive pieces of the public domain as endowments to assist them in building long-range trackage, particularly transcontinental lines. The first of these was the Union Pacific–Central Pacific railroad from around Omaha to San Francisco, which opened in 1869. It reduced travel time from several weeks to a few days, presumably serving the national interest by binding California to the nation. More land grants and transcontinental railroads followed. They promoted commerce, always a desirable thing, as well as settlement, as they sold off their land holdings to town builders and farmers. Railroads continued to be real estate dealers well into the first years of the twentieth century. In tandem with continued direct government distribution of the public domain through cash sales or as homesteads, the Great Plains from Montana south to Oklahoma filled with eager, hopeful farmers and their families.

Not every area gained people in quite this way. Texas retained its lands when it entered the union in 1845. Both before (through empresario grants) and after (through state sales), Texas often distributed land in much larger parcels than the U.S. public domain usually permitted. Oregon's early settlers received otherwise unheard-of 640-acre units. California revalidated many of the huge land grants made in Spanish and Mexican times, and some have persisted to the present in different but traceable forms, such as the Irvine Ranch Company in Orange County and the holdings of Tenneco and other corporations in the Central Valley. Much of the intermountain West was never opened to settlement, either because it was too arid even for cattle grazing, or it was turned over to mining operations, or because the federal government retained it for national parks, atomic testing, or military uses. But despite these major exceptions, the U.S. government either directly or through intermediaries like railroads managed to transfer hundreds of millions of acres to settlers from 1785 to 1934, when nearly all of the little usable land that was left was closed to homestead entry.

By then—in fact by about 1915 or 1920—farms and ranches covered all of the great continental acquisitions—Transappalachia, the Louisiana Purchase, Texas, Oregon, the Southwest—as completely as they ever would. The peak years of creating new homesteads were the first two decades of the twentieth century. Federal land law up through 1916 gradually increased the acreage that individuals or families could claim, but changes seldom came quickly or generously enough to meet the needs of a hardworking farm family. Forty acres was enough to support an average family in Indiana in 1860, but an entire 640-acre section often proved too dry to live on in North Dakota or Montana in 1915. Water from either the ground or the sky was simply too scarce or irregular, and family farming overreached its natural limit. The law and the railroads enticed great numbers of people too far west and into lives of hardscrabble misery. Parts of the Plains that were heavily settled from 1900 to 1915 reached their peak populations in the 1920 census. After that, America's farm population stabilized for twenty years, and has dropped ever since. The Great Plains states, from Montana and the Dakotas south through Texas, have lost rural population in almost every decade since 1920.

The grandiose Manifest Destiny proclaimed in the 1840s had been completed with the Gadsden Purchase. Continuing, however, were the millions of individual manifest destinies, all the getting, keeping, and living on a small family farm, which were fulfilled family by family and person by person over the next seventy years. This was the legendary westward movement, in which Americans advanced massively into ever farther Wests. Joining them were newly arrived Europeans, Canadians, and Asians. German communities sprouted from Fredericksburg, Texas, to Hays, Kansas, and northward. Immigrants from Scandinavia, the Austro-Hungarian Empire, and the Russias supplemented and often outnumbered the native-born. Dozens of ethnic and religious groups jostled for space on farms, villages, and cities all across the West. The California gold rush of 1849–1852 abruptly pulled a quarter of a million people into that newly acquired state, from Australia, South America, and Europe, as well as the states to the east. Many mining booms followed, some becoming stable communities like Butte, Montana, with its

Irish copper miners, and some merely raucous boomtowns that were as momentary as firecrackers, like Last Chance Gulch or Tonopah.

In all these ways, the territorial acquisitions of 1782, 1803, 1819, and the 1840s filled up. After 1920, almost all of the farmable and ranchable land was taken. The twilight of the settlement frontier had arrived. From then to the early twenty-first century, rural America, with 52 million people in 1920, rose only to 59 million in 2000, while city dwellers and suburbanites quadrupled from 54 million to 222 million. The westward expansion that began in the early 1600s reached its saturation point by 1920. Americans would henceforth do their migrating to cities, suburbs, and metropolises. Land was no longer the prize.

FECUNDITY MAKES FRONTIERS

Besides the reduction of the native peoples and the operation of benevolent land laws, fecundity was essential in making possible this world-historical occupation of a continental landmass. How was it that Americans managed to populate a continental empire, while the French before 1763, the Spanish up to 1821, the Mexicans in the Southwest before 1848, and for that matter the Indians who had been on the land since time immemorial, had not been able to? Aggression against Indians and neighbors north and south were major reasons, as were the land laws. Another one, at the heart of the process, was the frontier Americans' towering birthrate. Lord Castlereagh's prediction that Americans would win their land not on battlefields but in their "bedchambers" does not conjure up images of log cabins and lean-tos, but what went on inside them was the same: procreation. Frontiers were lusty places, and without the love and lust, they would have remained as empty of white people as the far edges of New Spain and New France did.

In the nineteenth century, the process repeated itself generation after generation. A country of young people—the median age in 1790 was about sixteen—married early, very often not long after age twenty. They had more than twenty fertile years ahead of them, and they made full use of them. By their forties, many couples had built a homestead for themselves, and also a family too large to live on it. The oldest children, maturing by then into their own early twenties, headed off for the next unsettled land somewhere to the west. There they did just what their parents had done—they married, had many children, and saw them reach adulthood and leave for a still farther West. Then *their* children repeated the process. This cycle recurred for generations until the land and the water ran out. The birthrate of white Americans in 1800 (and probably black ones too, though statistics are shakier) exceeded that of any country anywhere—Asia, Africa, Latin America—in 2000. The American rate fell gradually, but by 1920 it was still twice what it has been in recent years. Moreover, as native-born fecundity fell, immigration from other countries took up the slack. Prior to 1860 the U.S. population grew by about one-third every decade, and from then until 1920 by about one-fourth. If that high a rate existed today, it would add 80 million to 100 million every ten years, which would be an insupportable catastrophe. In the United States of the nineteenth century, it provided the people to fill the immense and resource-laden spaces of Transappalachia, Louisiana, and the rest.

Malthus was right. From the 4 million counted in the first census in 1790, the U.S. population grew to 63 million by 1890, about sixteen times over, and nearly quintupled from 1890 to 2005.[11] From the "pygmy," as the Count of Aranda called it in 1782, the United States indeed became the "giant" he predicted, exceeded early in the twenty-first century among the world's nations only by Russia, China, and Canada in size, and only by China and India in population.

THE NECESSITY OF MANIFEST DESTINY

Americans' unparalleled growth during the creation of its first, continental empire rested not only on fecundity, the departure of Indians and other people, and favorable land policies. It also required ideology. Americans' expansion across the continent was "a democratic imperialism, a mass-driven force of special character and power," in Donald Meinig's words.[12] Expansion resonated with the people. It meant progress, national glory, and successful stewardship all rolled into one. White Americans were certain that they had the right and duty to take land because they would make it more productive than native peoples, or Spaniards, or Mexicans, had done. They believed they had a right and duty to acquire territory because it would eventually become states coequal with the original thirteen, and thus provide free and democratic institutions, the blessings of liberty, to ever more people. They were convinced, too, that they had a right to defend themselves against outside opponents, even when "defend" crossed over into "push back."

Underpinning the democratic imperialistic urge was the conviction that the American people were, in various senses, exceptional in critical, empowering ways. They believed that, uniquely, they had gloriously abundant natural resources at hand; that the headlong expansion of their space and their numbers were signs of progress and the favor of Providence; and above all, that their ideals, and thus their existence, were morally superior. This conviction dated back to the earliest colonial beginnings. It justified to them their occupation of the continental landmass; the reduction of its original native peoples; the stabilizing of the northern border, first by invasion and, when that failed, by bluster and diplomacy; and the conquest of half the territory of their southern neighbor: until Americans reached the Pacific and governed a coastline stretching from San Diego to Puget Sound.

"The belief that the United States was guided by a providential destiny," the historian Robert Johannsen has written, "that the nation had a preordained, God-sanctioned mission to fulfill, formed a significant element in American Romantic thought."[13] The age of Jackson and Polk was also the Romantic age in music, literature, and poetry. Belief in progress was general and heartfelt. Was it not borne out by the harnessing of steam, freeing factories from the vagaries of waterpower? By the telegraph, which by the early 1850s made communication instantaneous between Washington, New York, and St. Louis, and soon to San Francisco? By railroads, which shrank travel time to a fraction of what humankind had been held to from the beginning of its existence? Those were heady times, with abundant evidence for progress, optimism, exceptionalism, and expansion everywhere anyone might look.

But large groups were either left out of the majority on racial or ethnic grounds, or opted out for social or political reasons. Indians, African-Americans, Asians (about to arrive in the West), and Mexicans were obviously "others," considered inferior to Anglo-Saxons. Irish and German newcomers were gradually and grudgingly admitted to that status; others took much longer or never reached it. The imperialist consensus was not complete: Whigs from New England and other northeastern areas opposed Polk's aggressive expansionism and the Mexican War. Antislavery sentiment sheared off many northern Democrats from their party while abolitionism became a driving issue for Whigs as well. For local, regional, or other reasons, not all Americans approved of the way in which expansion took place. It would be an exaggeration, however, to say that a true and consistent anti-imperialism gained much traction in the 1840s and 1850s. It was not expansion, or even how it was done, that split the Union in 1860. Rather it was the question that inevitably arose from it all: whether slavery was to extend into the newly acquired areas.

The expansion of the United States from 1782 to 1848 was not neatly done nor was it always pretty. Even the most illustrious names, such as Jefferson and Madison, Monroe and John Quincy Adams, certainly Jackson and Polk, were implicated in and even instigators of some underhanded operations and brutal methods. In that they were hardly unique. They were no more—or less—to be censured than Russia as it expanded eastward and southward; than Bismarck when he muscled the German Empire into being by wars against Denmark, Austria, and France; than Napoleon's military dictatorship; than Britain, France, and other European powers in their ruthless conquest and exploitation of Africa and South Asia. Much of that was done in the name of introducing "Western civilization." The American variant was the triumph of "civilization" over "savagery" and "degenerate races."

The expansion of the United States was imperialistic. It was also wreathed in idealistic and exculpatory rhetoric. Americans were not alone in this. The unusual aspect is that nineteenth-century Americans truly believed that their providential mission and destiny permitted, even demanded, that they behave imperialistically; that they were exempted from normal rules against theft or invasion of other people's territory; and that their profound belief in their own racial superiority exempted them from regarding others as equals. What they did then was nothing exceptional. Other nations practiced realpolitik and always had. But Americans, in their insularity, believed they were exceptional. The distance between such noble principles and such self-serving aggressiveness is the measure of hypocrisy.

The transcontinental landmass, Empire I, was complete by 1848 and the 1853–1854 Gadsden Purchase. Yet American expansion was not complete. Still to come was Empire II, the offshore lands around the Pacific and in the Caribbean and Central America, acquisitions that took place in the fifty years from 1867 to 1917. Beyond that lay Empire III, by which the once colonized Americans became the world's greatest power by the year 2000.

Chapter Nine

TO ALASKA AND ACROSS THE PACIFIC

*I see no immediate prospect of the country being settled up. The climate is
too rigid; there is too much rain and too little sun for agricultural purposes. . . . There is comparatively little land suitable for agriculture. . . .
The summer, though pleasant while it lasts, is not long enough for successful farming.*

— Major General George H. Thomas, San Francisco,
September 27, 1869, on Alaska[1]

*It should be the earnest and paramount aim of the military administra-
tion to win the confidence, respect, and affection of the inhabitants of the
Philippines . . . by proving to them that the mission of the United States is
one of benevolent assimilation.*

— President William McKinley, December 21, 1898[2]

THE CONTINUITY OF EMPIRE-BUILDING

Adding the Southwest to the United States' continental landmass in
1848 and 1853 by no means ended the country's outward thrusts. Those
additions completed Empire I, but many other possibilities beckoned
offshore. The expansionists of the 1840s hoped to go right ahead
through the 1850s, and they talked of adding places such as Cuba, Santo
Domingo, Hawaii, Alaska, and (as always) Canada. But the North-South
argument over extending slavery into the western territories stalemated
both sides, as it did almost all other major legislation. The project of a
railroad to the Pacific was also a shared dream, but it never went beyond
the survey stage. It was impossible for North and South to agree on
where it should start—New Orleans, St. Louis, Chicago, or elsewhere—
and therefore whether North or South would connect to it and chiefly
benefit. Similarly, there was no dearth of expansionist plans, even a spate
of filibusters into Central America, but they were overshadowed by the
looming colossal tragedy of disunion and civil war.

Secession came in late 1860, and then the war. It suppressed any serious thought of territorial expansion. After four ghastly years, it ended.

The problem followed of how the conquered South should be "recon-structed." That issue divided people as badly as the war had done. Expansion was still not a priority for most Americans. But in fact, it had never stopped being a priority for William Henry Seward, secretary of state for Lincoln and then, after Lincoln's assassination, for Andrew Johnson. Seward had been expansion-minded throughout his mature career, although less bellicose about it than the Polkites or Stephen A. Douglas. When peace returned in 1865, he was ready to resuscitate long-postponed plans. Any peaceful acquisition would suit him. He vis-ited the Danish West Indies in early 1866 and secured a treaty by which they would become American, but the Senate would not ratify it. He was eager to acquire Greenland and Iceland, if they came his way, but they did not quite do so. He embraced the old idea of a canal across central America—Tehuantepec in 1853, Darien (Panama) by 1869—but that too remained just an idea. Canada, the Dominican Republic, French and Swedish[3] islands in the Caribbean—any would be welcome. He did get Midway Island, an uninhabited atoll at the western end of the Hawaiian group enclosing two little islands, which had been claimed for the United States in 1859. Seward and the U.S. Navy certified the acquisi-tion in 1867.[4]

Alaska—Russian America—proved to be Seward's great success. Knowing that Russia was ready to sell Alaska for its own reasons, he seized the opportunity. There was precedent. There was also continuity: not only had Seward been writing and speaking about expansion since the 1840s, but he was aided on the Alaska and Danish West Indies proj-ects by none other than Robert J. Walker, the ardent fifty-four-forty and all-Mexico advocate who had been Polk's secretary of the Treasury from 1845 to 1849. And Walker was not alone.

Expansion was expansion, whether across the continent or across the water. No radical redirection underlay Seward's capture of Alaska. There were, however, some new features. One was obviously geography, the fact that Alaska (and the subsequent additions around the Pacific and the Caribbean) was not contiguous to the United States. Another had to do with settlement, or rather, the absence of it. Almost no one seriously looked at Alaska as a further frontier of settlement. No one considered it a new Willamette Valley or Texas. Some thousands of native people lived there, a few hundred Russians (most of them soon to depart), and a handful of Americans. Not even mining was expected to flourish, and certainly not the raising of corn, wheat, cotton, or livestock. A major difference between the acquisitions of Empire I and Empire II was that the latter involved settlement by white Americans only in minor ways and small numbers, if at all.

Furthermore, and unlike the episodes of Empire I, the Alaskan acquisition and subsequent ones around the Pacific and Caribbean did not involve the removal and replacement of native peoples. But those peoples—Alaskans, Samoans, Hawaiians, Filipinos, and the rest—though not removed and replaced, were ruled and repressed. In both situations, Anglo-Americans never questioned their own racial superiority.

The final difference was a shift in motive. Settling Alaska with American farmers, as a reason for acquiring it, was low to the point of invisibility for Seward or anyone else. But then what did motivate him? There are several plausible answers, not only for the Alaska Purchase but for all the acquisition attempts both failed and successful from then until the early twentieth century.

Diplomatic historians have proposed, sometimes discarded, sometimes retained, a list of possible motives. A "new manifest destiny" is one, a resurrection of the 1840s slogan, resting on the perennial conviction that the American people and nation are exceptional in their moral ideals, especially that America and its people were duty-bound to spread liberty and freedom to less fortunate peoples. Another motive was popular jingoism, unplanned, unreasoned, and with unintended consequences, most pressingly in the feverish backdrop to the war with Spain in 1898. Cultural historians have begun describing a newly conscious masculinity, a seeking of power abroad (military or maritime) as a kind of chest-thumping.[5] Surprisingly congruent as a motive was the search for expanded commercial markets, notably in East Asia, or raw materials, as in Hawaii, the Philippines, and around the Caribbean. Related to this was the need for naval control of the Pacific, the Gulf of Mexico, and the Caribbean. Rapid growth of industries, mining, and railroad networks in the late-nineteenth-century United States did much to anchor and augment the push across the Pacific toward China.[6]

With personal variations, some combination of these motives propelled Seward and later expansionists such as Presidents Grant, Benjamin Harrison, Cleveland, and McKinley, and Secretaries of State James G. Blaine, John W. Foster, and John Hay, in the years between the Civil War and 1898. Ardent expansionists followed them—Henry

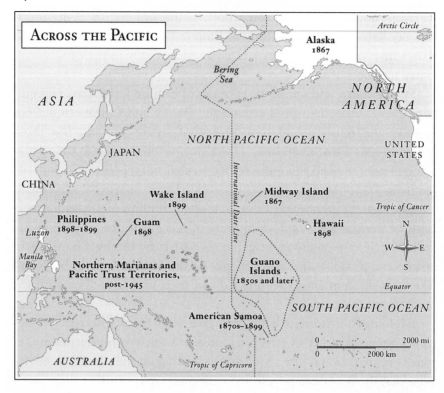

U. S. offshore territories and possessions in and along the Pacific Ocean, 1850–present.

Cabot Lodge and Theodore Roosevelt most prominently, Woodrow Wilson scarcely less so. How these motives combined, however, differed largely according to the target in view.

Since the Alaska Purchase was so completely engineered by Seward before it went to Congress for ratification and funding, and since it was the first chapter in Empire II, it is worth noting how Seward resembled, and how he differed, from previous expansionists. How he justified and celebrated offshore expansion set the tone for the next three decades and beyond. He was no agrarian in the mold of Jefferson, Monroe, or Polk. He did not come from a bucolic preindustrial community like John Quincy Adams's. He was born and raised in a small village in the Hudson Valley, then went to college and studied law upriver in Schenectady. He made his marriage, home, law practice, and political base in Auburn, a small manufacturing and commercial city in central New York not far from the Erie Canal and connected early to trunk-line railroads. He was no frontiersman like Jackson or Stephen A. Douglas. Central New York was also known as the Burned-Over District for its hell-fire evangelicalism, but Seward, who was off in Albany as governor for several years and immersed in the Albany–New York City political-financial nexus, had little to do with revivalism.

The settlement process had come and gone long before Seward arrived in Auburn. It was replaced by a new kind of interconnected economy of which farming and anything related to it was only a part. He was formed instead by a then new America, sparked by town life and technology, by clocks rather than the seasons. Yet he shared with his predecessors a conviction that America was exceptional, that it had developed liberty and freedom and opportunity as no other people or nation had done, and that these virtues could and should be exported. He understood that although the borders of the United States had reached the Pacific, if the union could be held together and slavery stopped from spreading, the country could and should expand into the Pacific and the Caribbean, should build a canal somewhere across Central America, and should develop trade with distant nations, including far-off China, Japan, and Korea.

China, in particular, with its hundreds of millions of people, captivated American manufacturers and shippers with its market potential. Seward himself took a prominent lead in promoting a round-the-world telegraph line, saw Pacific islands as way stations to China, visited there on his world tour after he left office, and lined the walls of his mansion in Auburn with portraits of Chinese dignitaries along with other world leaders. Commerce, not the frontier, engaged him, despite the accelerating migration westward of millions during and after the Civil War. Settlement of the American West would take care of itself, guaranteed as it was after 1848 by sovereignty over Oregon and California. Guarantees of American commercial growth and success, on the other hand, needed the benefit of offshore possessions, including coaling stations to service merchant ships and a protective navy, and new markets.

Seward's position on empire and expansion was clear before the Mexican War. In a speech he gave in September 1844 called "The Elements of Empire," the forty-three-year-old ex-governor of New York predicted, wrongly in those months just before the war, that future acquisitions would not be "by conquest" because Americans believed "that PEACE is more propitious to the ruling passion of empire, than WAR; and that provinces are more cheaply *bought* than *conquered*." He also was wrong in expecting that slavery would be abolished and that secession was unlikely. As for empire, however, he affirmed that "expansive territory . . . inseparably belongs to the idea of National Greatness" and that "the passion of Territorial aggrandizement is universal as well among nations as individuals."[7]

In July 1852, months before the Gadsden Purchase and Commodore Matthew C. Perry's epochal opening up of Japan, Senator Seward introduced a bill to authorize a "survey and reconnaissance of Bhering's [sic] Straits, the Arctic Ocean, and the courses of trade between America and China." The first half of his speech praised the intrepid whaling fleets of New England and their need for better navigational aids in the North Pacific. He then broadened his vision to the entire Pacific and even to world history. "Your mails and passengers," he said to the Senate and beyond it to the American people, "will be carried between San Francisco and Shanghai in steamships." But without this bill, he warned, "you cannot establish a coaling station along the way. . . . Will you leave this survey and its benefits to England?" Also demanded, he pointed out, were a canal across Tehuantepec and, "most important and necessary" of all, a "railroad across our own country to San Francisco." The survey, the steamship, the settlement of California, and much more, he went on, were combining to produce the "sublime result . . . the reunion of the two civilizations, which, having parted on the plains of Asia four thousand years ago . . . now meet again on the coasts and islands of the Pacific Ocean . . . [which] will become the chief theatre of events in [the] World's great Hereafter. . . . Commerce is the great agent of this movement."[8]

In early 1853, Seward reminded the Senate of the nation's march toward "Progress" and "Manifest Destiny." He explicitly rejected armed aggression to achieve these goals. Although he regarded the acquisition of Cuba as ultimately inevitable, he wanted no part of it until slavery disappeared there. (Canada would be another "inevitable" but peaceful acquisition, he thought.) "The commerce of the world," he told the Senate, "is the empire of the world," and it is "on the Pacific ocean, and its islands, and continents" where "the next great Power of the earth" will emerge.[9] After 1865, with slavery gone, Caribbean islands and an isthmian canal also became attractive to him. In his view, however, "Progress" must never be merely material. Instead it must elevate "all mankind as high as possible in knowledge and virtue," and thereby "promote the accomplishment of that great and beneficent design of the Creator of the Universe."[10]

Seward's expansionist ideas were not particularly original. If his private library and his own speeches are good indications, his reading was enormously wide, and he retained most of it. He spoke eloquently, but in the idiom of his day, the early Gilded Age. Not a philosopher but a first-class lawyer and diplomat, Seward wrote speeches, not treatises; advocacy, not analysis. He gave public audiences what they wanted to hear, more elegantly than they could have done, but not much more profoundly. Few questioned the goodness of progress, or manifest destiny, or commerce, the telegraph, railroads, and steam power. Tying the new Pacific Coast states and territories to the existing nation—and why stop there?—troubled no one. What is striking is the continuity of Seward's views and their congruence with those of many other Americans at the time. He did not engineer the Alaska Purchase until 1867. Yet he spoke vigorously about expansion and empire well before the early 1850s, in phraseology very much in tune with the manifest destiny—albeit of the more pacific Whig variety than the screaming-eagle Democratic kind—of the 1840s.

Though his expansionism represented continuity with that of the 1840s, it was surely a redirection, as it had to be in order to justify spreading the American empire offshore. It does not do to overintellectualize Seward and his expansionist ideas. He was not, admits his biographer, "an intellectual force of the first order," even though his "vision, larger than that of [John Quincy] Adams, was of an expansion of American power and place that meant world leadership."[11] But he was not an originator or a theorist, as, for example, Jefferson was. His own justifications for Alaska and other expansions no doubt satisfied him, but it is a pity that no tough-minded philosopher or cross-examiner ever sat him down and made him answer the ultimate question: Why? What did real "progress" consist of? Was destiny truly so manifest?

What would American expansion be based on in the latter half of the nineteenth century, once the country had gained its Pacific coast? Jefferson's argument in acquiring Louisiana, that the Mississippi must be open to the sea for the nation to survive and the West to remain part of it, or Adams's or Polk's contention that more land was required to accommodate an exploding population, was no longer available to Seward. Nevertheless, he found other reasons and reshaped older reasons for inaugurating the expansions of Empire II. Seward was pulled forward into imperialism by "the spirit of the age"—the mid-nineteenth century, so taken with its unprecedented employment of steam power to run factories, sail the seas, and move by railroad faster by far than people had ever, ever done. Urban Americans, together with many in England and western Europe, were understandably proud of themselves and confident that they were the bearers and custodians of human progress as it had never existed before. Put most bluntly, the most obvious difference between the expansionism of the 1840s and earlier, and that of Seward and later, was that the emphasis shifted from settlement to commerce, from peopling an area to controlling its politics and economy. In either case, however, it was expansionism.

THE ALASKA DEAL

Russians had been in North America for over a hundred years, establishing hunting posts as far south as Bodega Bay in California. After the 1824 and 1825 agreements with the United States and Britain, they retreated north of 54°40'. By the 1850s the czarist government was beginning to see that the Amur River region of Siberia was a more promising place to develop, and that Russian America was too distant and logistically difficult to defend. Early in 1853 the governor-general of eastern Siberia wrote Czar Nicholas I that Americans would inevitably overrun all of North America, sped on by railroads, and that the Russian Empire would be stronger if it confined itself to the Asian landmass. Over the next three years, Alexander II succeeded Nicholas, and the new czar was also persuaded that his empire should retire from North America. Defeat in the Crimean War underscored Russian America's vulnerability to invasion by either Britain or the United States, while on the other hand, the central Asian border with China appeared "soft," that is, permeable to Russian pressure.

By late 1857 Alexander had agreed to sell Russian America. The United States was the most likely buyer. The first soundings-out took place when William Marcy, Polk's former secretary of war, was secretary of state in the feckless administration of James Buchanan. But secession and civil war stopped everything. Seward, however, got wind of Russia's approachability.

Not much is known about what the 8,000 to 12,000 native people thought of the Russians pulling out and the Americans coming in. The American military, who ran the property after 1867, "were not in touch" with the inhabitants and "had little notion of who these Natives were." Tlingits at Sitka objected to not being consulted, but to no avail.[12] The

Americans were eager to take over, and the czar's officials were eager to leave. If Russia could get a decent price, a deal could be done.

The longtime Russian minister in Washington, Edouard de Stoeckl, broached the subject with President Buchanan, who was receptive, and with Senator William Gwin of California, who was avid. Stoeckl, a somewhat dandified but effective diplomat, had represented Russia in the United States for over twenty years and was married to an American woman. The czar's ministers, however, decided to wait until the charter of the Russian-American Company expired, which would be soon. But by then Buchanan had left office, Seward had become secretary of state, and the Civil War was raging.[13] Though Stoeckl and Seward were cordially acquainted, the idea of an American purchase had to await peacetime.

When the Civil War ended in April 1865, Russia stood well in American eyes for having welcomed American vessels (Britain decidedly had not), and for the czar's "expressing himself heart and soul in favor of the cause of the Union," as Seward wrote. Czar Alexander again approved the idea of a sale of Russian America, provided that (as stated in Foreign Minister Prince A. M. Gorchakov's instructions to Stoeckl) the initiative appeared to come from the American side. Through a contact—probably Seward's political alter ego Thurlow Weed—Stoeckl managed to elicit not quite an offer but a serious discussion from Seward on March 9, 1867. Further talks followed, and by the end of March the czar, President Andrew Johnson, and his cabinet all agreed in principle to the transfer.

According to Frederick Seward's biography of his father, Stoeckl dropped by Seward's house on Lafayette Square on the evening of March 29 to bring the good news of the czar's approval. Stoeckl said, "Tomorrow, if you like, I will come to the [State] department, and we can enter upon the treaty." Seward replied, "Why wait until tomorrow, Mr. Stoeckl? Let us make the treaty tonight." Stoeckl pointed out that his secretaries and Seward's clerks were long past office hours. But Seward countered enthusiastically, "Never mind that; if you can muster your legation together before midnight, you will find me awaiting you at the department, which will be open and ready for business." And it was. Seward wisely took a moment to tell Senator Charles Sumner (Republican of Massachusetts), chair of the Foreign Relations Committee, as yet noncommittal, what was happening. Seward offered $7.2 million;

Stoeckl agreed; clerks wrote out the treaty; and by about 4 a.m. signatures were on it. By midmorning the document was in front of Sumner's committee.[14]

Over the next several days, Seward extracted a series of testimonials from scientists, Civil War officers, congressmen, and editors to bring Sumner on board. (Contrary to textbook legends about "Seward's Icebox" and the like, press and public generally favored the purchase.)[15] It worked. Gaining Sumner's "early conversion" was "Seward's greatest triumph."[16] On April 8 Sumner brought the treaty before the Senate and delivered a three-hour speech advancing several reasons why the United States should buy Russian America. Sumner, who was then a major figure and the leader of proponents of Radical Reconstruction in the Senate, had been a reluctant expansionist up to that point but was now a vigorous advocate. His reasoning summarizes the best arguments for expansion then being made.

After explaining the text of the treaty, the price, and the international agreements since 1825 that established the boundaries of Russian America, Sumner advanced five arguments that concerned "nothing less than the unity, power, and grandeur of the Republic, with the extension of its dominion and its institutions."[17] First were the "advantages to the Pacific Coast": more accessible freshwater ice (then the best food preservative) from Kodiak Island and North Pacific fishing, and wider commerce with China and Japan. Second, "Extension of Dominion": Russian America was simply the next place in the series that began with Louisiana. "The passion for acquisition, which is so strong in the individual, is not less strong in the community." (Was he reading Seward's old speeches?) "The citizen throbs anew as he traces the extending line."

Third came "Extension of Republican Institutions . . . a traditional aspiration" that, as John Adams wrote, is "destined to spread over the northern part of that whole quarter of the globe." Thus, "even at that early day was the destiny of the Republic manifest," added Sumner. "The present Treaty is a visible step in the occupation of the whole North American continent," and by it, "we dismiss one more monarch from this continent. One by one they have retired; first France; then Spain; then France again; and now Russia; all giving way to that absorbing Unity which is declared in the national motto, *E pluribus unum.*"

Sumner's fourth argument was preemption of rivals. The treaty "anticipates" Britain, foreclosing her from the region. And fifth, the agreement solidifies "the amity of Russia. . . . It is a new expression of that *entente cordiale* between the two Powers," Sumner wrote, referring to "sharers of a common glory in a great act of Emancipation"—Czar Alexander's freeing Russia's serfs in 1861, Lincoln's freeing America's slaves in 1863.

Sumner assured the Senate that the treaty "must not be a precedent for a system of indiscriminate and costly annexation," by purchase or by war. "There is no territorial aggrandizement which is worth the price of blood," he insisted. (He conveniently avoided mentioning the invasions of Canada in 1812 and Mexico in 1846.) Citing a wide array of histories and surveys by Russians, Germans, and others describing the region's virtues, Sumner concluded by suggesting a wholly new name for it. As Captain Cook reported a century earlier, there was a "euphonious name . . . used originally by the native islanders . . . [thus,] following these natives, whose places are now ours, we, too, should call this 'great land' Alaska." The Senate voted almost immediately to ratify the treaty, 27 to 12, and then made it almost unanimous at 37 to 2.

The Senate ratifies treaties, but the House provides the money to make them effective. As opposition mounted to Andrew Johnson and his Reconstruction policies, seen as far too pro-Southern, the bill to pay Russia the $7.2 million languished into the next year. By early 1868, hostility in the House toward the president and anyone associated with him reached a virulent level, and impeachment was just weeks away. The Alaska treaty was in jeopardy. On January 28, 1868, Robert J. Walker, then in private law practice but still close to Seward and members of Congress, published a long letter in the *Washington Daily Morning Chronicle*. In it he set out why the United States must go through with the purchase not only of Alaska, but also of the Danish-held Caribbean islands of St. Thomas and St. John. (Seward had already negotiated a purchase treaty for them but the Senate had not approved it and soon rejected it.)

Walker, originally from Pennsylvania, had migrated to Mississippi in the late 1820s to practice law with his brother, was very successful, and represented Mississippi in the Senate from 1835 to 1845, when he left to become Polk's secretary of the Treasury. He owned slaves for a time, but freed them in 1838; and, when governor of the Kansas Territory in the late 1850s, he resigned rather than accept the proslavery Lecompton constitution. Thus, although he was an "ardent expansionist and imperialist," he was no slaveocrat, and on any expansion possibility he cooperated easily with Seward. While Sumner's expansionism was more muted than Seward's, Walker's was uninhibited; and while all three supported the Alaska treaty, they reflected how that support varied.

Walker's newspaper letter testified to the continuity of American expansionism from the 1840s to the late 1860s. His historical arguments had not been altered by events or evidence. He remained an outspoken fifty-four-forty and all-Mexico man, proclaiming yet again that 54°40' had been the true boundary of Oregon in 1846. In his opinion, Texas should not have been "given up" in 1819, and he was happy that in 1845 it "was again received into the Union." In 1848 California "was ceded to us . . . but with the unfortunate abandonment of the rest of Mexico, which we had conquered and occupied, and should have retained." Had that happened, "the States to be carved out of it would all be free States, because Mexico . . . had abolished slavery" (glossing over the possibility that the United States might have restored it). Thus "the pro-slavery rebellion of 1861 would have been impossible." If only the United States had been more vigorously acquisitive and kept all of Mexico, he was saying, there would never have been a Civil War.

Americans should hope and expect, Walker suggested, to acquire St. Thomas, Cuba, eastern Canada, British Columbia, Hawaii, and more of Mexico. Seward had already negotiated a treaty to buy the Danish West Indies, he noted, as well as one with Colombia to build a canal across the Isthmus of Panama, making "our possession of St. Thomas and St. John an imperative necessity."[18]

Walker and Seward did not succeed with either the Danish West Indies treaty or the isthmian canal pact. The U.S. Senate stopped the first, and the Colombian Senate the second. Both places became American, but not until the early twentieth century. Walker had also discussed with Seward in 1867 "the propriety of obtaining from [Denmark] Greenland, and probably Iceland also."[19] With that, it would have been all the more likely that Canada would fall into the American basket, an American hope dating back to Benjamin Franklin and shared in the late 1860s by Sumner. But when the St. Thomas and St. John treaty ran into trouble, the Greenland-Iceland project disappeared. The political climate in 1868—both the rancorous impeachment fight and nervousness about how to pay the colossal Civil War debt—put even the Alaska project at risk.

The appropriation to pay Russia the agreed-upon $7.2 million finally made it through the House. A whiff of bribery surrounded the bill's passage for decades to come—did Stoeckl pay off influential congressmen to secure yea votes?—but it was never conclusively proved, and a recent and thorough historian of Alaska writes flatly that "no bribery was paid."[20] On July 14, 1868, the House passed the appropriation, 114 to 43. Stoeckl received the money, went home to Russia, and retired. The actual transfer at Novo Archangelsk, renamed Sitka, had already taken place on October 18, 1867, when Captain Pestchouroff, Imperial Russian Navy, on authority of the czar, turned over Alaska to Brigadier General Lovell H. Rousseau, U.S. Army.[21]

Aside from the foot-dragging by the House, it was certainly the smoothest and cleanest acquisition process yet. Russia had clear title and wanted to sell, the United States wanted to buy; no filibusters, force, or false claims marred the transaction. But was it legal and constitutional? At the time, no one claimed publicly that Alaska would ever become a state, and it was not established as a stage-one territory, only as a simple customs district. Seward, speaking on a visit to Sitka in 1869, looked forward to establishing territorial government there, but the U.S. Army and Navy ran it until the 1880s. Also, it was not contiguous, the first acquisition that touched no part of the preexisting United States. Whether Alaska would ever become a state, no one knew, but it might; and therefore "the acquisition . . . probably passes the threshold of plausible candidacy."[22] Unprecedented, yes, but unconstitutional, probably not.

Nevertheless, Alaska differed in a crucial way from Transappalachia, Louisiana, Florida, Texas, Oregon, and the Southwest. Nobody expected it to become a frontier of settlement, a target for young homesteading farm families, another demographic depository.

There may have been 900 residents of European ancestry—Russians, American military, American civilians—in Alaska as of 1867, most of them in and around Sitka. The Native American population may have totaled 30,000 but perhaps many fewer, primarily Tlingits with some Tsimshians and Haida, the tribes that also lived on the Queen Charlotte Islands and elsewhere along the coast south to Puget Sound. Over the next decade the European-descended population fell rather than rose; most of the Russians left, and few Americans arrived. As historian Ted Hinckley explains,

> The Americanization of Alaska was borne northward neither
> by wagon train nor by railroad locomotive, but via the sea.
> Her pioneers yearned for no parcel of unbroken sod on a

crop-producing prairie.... Only an uninformed handful...
visualized a future behind a plow.... Permanency was impossible, insisted her settlers, because the most fundamental of all
pioneer institutions was lacking: America's historic quarter-
section.... Surely nothing was more sacred to nineteenth-
century American society than the yeoman farmer and his
quarter-section of land. [But] not only was the Panhandle unsur-
veyed, its soil was agriculturally uninviting. Finally, what were
hypothetical husbandmen to do with their cash crops if a green
thumb should bless them? Ship their produce to Washington
territory?[23]

General George H. Thomas, in his report to the War Department in
September 1869 on conditions in Alaska, portrayed a very uninviting
scene. The natives around Sitka, he was convinced, "are treacherous,
warlike, and, until recently, discontented with the change of governments. It will be necessary to maintain a large garrison at this place, to
protect the traders from the Indians and preserve order and good behavior among the whites and half-breeds." As for the Aleuts, they too lacked
any "control over their passion for ardent spirits, nor have they very correct ideas in regard to chastity." And his final negative: "I see no immediate prospect of the country being settled up."[24]

Thomas was right about settlement. A new census in 1870 counted
only 391 people in Sitka, and another in 1880 found 157 there, and a
total of 430 whites in the whole district amid 33,426 people of all races.
Thanks to the Yukon and Klondike gold rushes in the late 1890s, the
U.S. Census in 1900 counted 63,592, as the white population soared
from 4,300 in 1890 to 30,500 in 1900.[25] Alaska was made a full territory
in 1912, but the population actually declined somewhat after that, and
statehood was a long time in coming, in 1959. Alaska did not attract people because it had no economy; customhouse duties shriveled from
$21,000 in the first two years after the purchase to $449 in 1870 and
$155 in 1873.[26]

In the 1870s there was talk of making the place into a penal colony, a
kind of American Siberia, though that faded.[27] Congress waited until
1884 to pass an Organic Act creating territorial government,[28] but
Alaska remained something of an orphan within the American system.
When the American settlement frontier halted momentarily during the
depression of the 1890s, some boosters and builders touted Alaska as a

final frontier (as the state's license plate still does). But new ranches and farms never numbered more than a few hundred, while thousands soon appeared from Texas to Montana. Alaska was a frontier, but of mining, oil drilling, and base-building, never of traditional farming and stock raising.[29]

Seward preserved and extended the empire-building of the 1840s beyond the water's edge. To do so he shifted emphasis from settlement to commerce. But it was not crass; rather, it was a mystical commerce that was both end in itself and means to the spread of the American idea of liberty. Sumner shared this view, as did Walker in his more spread-eagle way. So did a great many Americans. The thirty years following the Alaska Purchase brought no new acquisitions of great size, but they did bring some small ones (notably, Pacific reefs and atolls), and many efforts that were near misses. Seward himself almost acquired the Danish West Indies and a canal zone across Panama, and he talked of Greenland and Iceland, the Dominican Republic or part of it, and just about anything that came along and was loose.

He never stopped. A week before he left office he spoke to the incorporators of the Isthmian Canal Company at the home of Peter Cooper in New York, wealthy investors who might participate in a public-private project to build the dream canal. He told them, "We are Americans. We are charged with responsibilities of establishing on the American continent a higher condition of civilization and freedom than has ever before been attained in any part of the world. We all acknowledge and feel this responsibility. The destiny which we wish to realize as Americans is set plainly before us and distinctly within our reach; but that destiny can only be attained by the execution of the Darien ship canal."[30] Civilization, freedom, responsibility, and commerce: hence, expansion. Always more salesman than theoretician, more attorney than philosopher, Seward left public office with more achievements than most secretaries of state, certainly more than others who held office in such difficult times.

FROM GUANO TO SAMOA

American sailing ships had crossed the Pacific to China ever since the 1780s, some to sell New England manufactured goods, some to kill whales and bring back their oil. The navy was there too: Commodore Matthew C. Perry and his squadron forced itself on Japan in 1853 in a legendary voyage that began opening the island empire to the West and its commerce and politics. American ships also visited islands along the coast of Peru to mine guano, a fertilizer much demanded by farmers from New England to the Chesapeake.[31] The Peruvians, however, taxed this sole source of their national income at a level that American farmers did not want to pay.

Responding to popular (farmer) pressure, the secretary of the navy in 1856 ordered the commander of the Pacific squadron, Commodore William Mervine, to inspect the guano-mining possibilities of Baker and Jarvis Islands, some hundreds of miles south of Hawaii.[32] The squadron (the same that had been commanded in the 1840s by the impetuous Thomas ap Catesby Jones) sailed primarily to assist whalers and put down native hostilities to landing parties. Mervine was distinctly un-enthusiastic about trying to land on treacherous shores of volcanic islands and atolls. Bad weather gave him an excuse to lay off Baker, and he skipped Jarvis entirely on his voyage. But public pressure was strong. American ships reported that the islands could be reached, albeit only by skilled sailors. The American Guano Company petitioned the Senate in March 1856 to pass a law authorizing annexation of uninhabited and unclaimed guano-rich islands. The Franklin Pierce administration responded, and on August 18, 1856, Congress passed the Guano Islands Act.[33]

In the next three years, about fifty uninhabited islands were found to qualify, and henceforth "appertained" to the United States. Baker was the first to be annexed, on May 1, 1857. Then came Jarvis, Howland, Christmas, Malden, Phoenix, Johnston, and Palmyra. Occasionally a question arose from the British, but nothing serious, and a dispute with the king of Hawaii over Johnston Island in 1859 did not stop American digging. None of these islands was inhabited, none claimed by another power except as just noted; none had any other purpose than to await guano diggers (for which Hawaiians and other "locals" were imported), except that Baker had also been used as a mail drop for the many American whalers that crossed the Pacific in those years. If manifest destiny was a motive, it was only in the most abstract sense of asserting the right to extend sailing routes and the search for raw materials across the high seas, and that was neither new nor peculiarly American. Nevertheless, the annexations authorized by the Guano Act were indeed annexations, the nation's first ones offshore, since the act preceded the Alaska Purchase by eleven years.[34] By 1903, ninety-four islands had been claimed, mostly by private parties, and many were ratified in the 1930s by executive orders confirmed by Congress.

Most were in the Pacific, but some were in the Caribbean. A few were put to uses other than fertilizer mining; on the eve of World War II a number of them received a few American citizens as a "permanent population," and airstrips were built on them. The Swan Islands in the Caribbean, off Honduras, became a staging base for the CIA's operations against Fidel Castro in 1960 and again in support of the Nicaraguan "contras" in the late 1980s.[35] Only about a dozen islands remained under American jurisdiction by the 1990s.[36] There was never a thought that they would become states or territories in the formal sense, or anything other than "unincorporated territory." With one exception, they had no purpose except to ensure that their one asset, bird dung, was accessible (solely) to American farmers.

The exception was Midway, off the western tip of the Hawaiian archipelago. At first called Brooks Island, it was an atoll containing two large islands and a small one. Captain N. C. Brooks, sailing "the bark Gambia, owned by American citizens, though sailed under the Hawaiian flag," claimed them for the United States in July 1859. Uninhabited and unnamed prior to Brooks's visit, they were first occupied in July 1867, and on August 28, 1867, they were also claimed for the United States by Captain William Reynolds of the U.S.S. *Lackawanna*. The Navy Department called the place "Midway islands." According to the navy, the islands would provide "one of the finest harbors in the world, safe and roomy [to our] naval and merchant vessels." They would also make an ideal coaling station, support "concerted operations between the Asiatic and North Pacific squadrons, especially in the event of a foreign war," speed up mail between California and China, and provide a better mail drop for our whalers. Finally, "if we neglect the prize, other nations will not be slow to grasp it."[37] After hearing the navy's arguments, one wonders how the United States managed for so long without Midway. To be sure, the United States was not the only player in the region; Britain had a strong interest in Hawaii, which was still being called the Sandwich Islands after an English earl; and Japan, of course, would become America's main competitor in the western Pacific in a few more decades.

Thus, under Seward's auspices, Midway became American. It was guano-rich, but it had other virtues too. "Midway" meant midway between San Francisco and China. Commerce with Asia strongly suggested it become American, and it did. The guano islands were a new and limited expansion of empire, but they formed a link through the late 1850s in the expansionist story from Guadalupe Hidalgo (1848), the Gadsden Purchase and Commodore Perry (1853), to Alaska (1867).

America's expansionist agenda soon extended to Samoa. This group of three large mountainous islands and several small ones, about two-thirds of the way from Honolulu to Auckland in the southwest Pacific, received its first American visit in 1839 from the Wilkes Expedition. American interest was limited to the easternmost of the larger islands, Tutuila, which had on its southern shore the best deepwater harbor within hundreds of miles, at a village called Pago Pago. On February 14, 1872, Commander Richard W. Meade of the frigate U.S.S. *Narragansett*, in the by-then-honored seat-of-the-pants tradition of Thomas ap Catesby Jones at Monterey in 1842 and N. C. Brooks at Midway in 1859, negotiated a treaty with the local high chief at Tutuila. This gave the United States exclusive rights to a coaling station at the excellent harbor, as well as the right to use its good offices to cool any disputes between the Samoans and Europeans. When the treaty arrived in Washington, President Grant liked it, but the frugal Senate, which stifled many an executive-branch foreign initiative after the Civil War, did not. The Grant administration nevertheless sent a special agent named Colonel A. B. Steinberger to see to American interests, but his dictatorial tendencies forced him out by 1876.

Samoan native politics were local, familial, and tribal, somewhat like most North American Indian groups. The leadership system was too complex to be described briefly (in fact to an outsider it hardly seems like a "system" at all, with its competing prestige lists, shifting alliances, and overlapping offices). Put roughly, extended family households formed villages, heads of families formed the village council, and these produced two sets of chiefs. Occasionally higher chiefs, descended from gods, might coalesce in an overall ceremonial leader, but only briefly. Suffice it to say that the system did not correspond to American or European ideas of monarchy in any useful way.[38] Yet, as they so often did with North American natives, Americans and Europeans insisted that the Samoans must have an overall monarch or chief who could authoritatively sign treaties and represent his people. In the late 1870s, a towering and genial Samoan from Tutuila named La Mamea filled the bill. Coming to Washington in late 1877, he impressed officials, and the Hayes administration signed a treaty with him on January 17, 1878. It permitted the United States to build a naval station and gave it the exclusive right of "good offices" to mediate any disputes between Samoans and other powers. This time the Samoan treaty sailed through Congress.

Then followed a series of squabbles with both Samoans and the British and Germans, who had interests in coconut oil on the other islands. Few American ships visited Samoa during the 1880s, but as Germany, in particular, pressed for full control of the islands, American official backs stiffened. This was equally true of the Democratic Cleveland administration's secretary of state, Thomas F. Bayard, and the Republican Harrison administration's, James G. Blaine. After a conference in Washington in 1887 failed to resolve differences, German chancellor Otto von Bismarck sponsored another in Berlin in 1889. It resulted, rather confusingly, in a three-power foreign oversight of the local government.[39] This "condominium," predictably, worked poorly, and another treaty of late 1899 (ratified in January 1900) gave the two large western islands to Germany, and Tutuila, including Pago Pago, plus three small islands, to the United States. Britain pulled out at that point, but with the outbreak of World War I in 1914, New Zealand took over the German islands. They were mandated to New Zealand by the League of Nations (and later the United Nations) and finally became an independent constitutional monarchy in 1962, first under the name of Western Samoa and then simply Samoa.

Tutuila, however, has remained an American possession. After the 1899 treaty, the navy took over its administration and imposed naval rigor and routine upon the native culture in a manner reminiscent of, but stricter than, the army in the West in its dealings with the Lakota, Apaches, or other Indians. The Americans brought the gifts of the English language, certain forms of Christianity, and the blessings of private property—come hell or high water. Commander B. F. Tilley, as the first commandant of the U.S. naval station at Pago Pago, was a virtual dictator. In 1900 he issued a series of ordinances and regulations on police, licenses, land acquisition, building construction, mortgages, divorce, possession of firearms, alcohol consumption, Sunday observance, and the duties and role of village chiefs. To understate it, these rules did not always correspond to traditional practices. But the territory's 5,700 people were thus ruled.[40] The navy only gradually relaxed its grip. After World War II, the Bureau of Insular Affairs of the Interior Department took over from the navy (as it did also in Guam), and in 1960 American Samoa finally had its own self-government, though it remained an "unincorporated, unorganized territory" of the United States.[41]

Why did the United States pursue and acquire Samoa? It had no guano. There was no thought of settling homesteaders there. Pago Pago harbor cried out to be a coaling station—if ships ever went by. But few did. It was south of the California–China routes, and Fiji was more attractive for Australian traffic. Samoa would hardly become a state of the union. It was not even part of a plan, of the omnivorous Seward or anyone else, to nail down another corner of the Pacific as an "American Lake." In short, it was, in historian David Pletcher's words, "a product of fuzzy geography, impulsive humanitarianism, and improvisations on the spot by ambitious but inexperienced consuls."[42] But it came essentially without conquest or cost—no $7.2 million or other sum payable to any European power. European "competition," the fear that Britain or Germany might get it all, played some role until 1899 and even to 1914. But in the last analysis, Samoa became, remained, and was administered as American, more than for any other reason, by force of acquisitory habit: a habit of empire.

Hawaii in Three Generations

The American procurement of the Hawaiian Islands may be thought of as a filibuster in very slow motion. It went on over three generations, from 1820 to 1898, but it ended much as the capture of West Florida did in 1810, and as Texas did in 1845: by an act of Congress rather than a bilateral negotiation. Unlike in those earlier episodes, however, almost no one was killed. The Hawaiians, relying on law, order, and peaceful petition, avoided bloodshed. Yet they lost their kingdom anyway.

The earliest Europeans to visit Hawaii were Captain James Cook and his crew in 1778. The first American was Captain Robert Gray in August 1789, on the same voyage that took him to the Columbia River and gave the United States a good claim to Oregon. By then, Kamehameha I, "the Great," was unifying the Hawaiian Islands under his personal rule, a process he completed in 1810. American missionaries from New England began arriving in 1820. Several kings and a queen later, in 1893, the Americans' sons and grandsons and other whites snuffed out the monarchy and replaced it with a republic they controlled, while seeking annexation by the United States, which took place five years later. In the intervening years, the whites—still known as haoles, the Hawaiian word for a white foreigner—first preached, then taught, inter-married (sometimes), planted, lawyered, and held public office, until they formed an elite minority holding the bulk of economic and, eventually, political power.

As that was happening, the number of native Hawaiians fell sharply (a decimation that began with Cook and the introduction of Western diseases) while contract laborers from China, Portugal, and Japan replaced them.[43] In demography, economics, and politics, Hawaii underwent a complete about-face in the eight decades after Kamehameha I died in 1819. The turnabout was imperceptible at first, picked up speed after a Western-style land reform became law in the late 1840s, and careened to its conclusion following a reciprocity (free trade) treaty with the United States in 1875. The road to American annexation was incremental, but in its final fifteen or twenty years, rapid and virtually irreversible.

The monarchs, particularly Kamehameha III (ruled 1825–1854), welcomed the missionaries and then other Americans (as well as British and Germans). Americans helped not only with religion but also with legal matters arising between Hawaiians and Europeans, and with education, finance, constitution writing, and counsel of many sorts. Americans held high public office, including judgeships. They persuaded the king that, while ancient laws, customs, and hereditary ranks should remain in place, he should rule within the bounds of a constitution, with the people electing officials (especially a house of representatives) democratically. To do this, it followed that people needed fee-simple rights to the land. Kamehameha graciously granted the "Great Mahele," a general land reform, to achieve that. But since it also allowed resident foreigners to own land, and since they had the wherewithal (and most natives did not) to pay for surveys, irrigation, and other costs of acquiring title, land gravitated to them and not to the natives. For Hawaiians the "reform" produced dispossession, not ownership. The result was great sugar plantations and imported contract laborers to work them.[44]

In 1863 the U.S. minister to Hawaii observed that Americans owned most of the plantations, the majority of merchant ships, nearly all the whalers that called at Honolulu, Lahaina, Hilo, or other ports, and "controlled perhaps four-fifths of Hawaiian trade."[45] A worried new king, Kamehameha V, reasserted some native rights in a revised constitution he promulgated in 1864. But the economic ligaments between the kingdom and the United States were already virtually unbreakable.

Seward in 1867 negotiated a treaty of reciprocity, which meant trade free of customs duties. The next secretary of state, Hamilton Fish, backed that treaty in 1870, as did his chief, President Grant. Although the Senate rejected it in June of that year—not from any meekness about becoming involved in Hawaii, but because protectionist senators carried the day—reciprocity returned in 1874, after the man who would become Hawaii's last king, David Kalakaua, ascended the throne.

In November 1874, a few months later, Kalakaua went to Washington. He signed a reciprocity treaty, which the U.S. Senate ratified on March 18, 1875. It radically changed Hawaii's economy, though the benefits did not fall evenly. From 1876 until 1890, sugar production rose from under 12,000 to 120,000 tons, the value of exports to the United States from $1.2 million to $12.3 million, and imports from the United States from under a million dollars to over five million. Ninety-eight percent of Hawaii's exports went to the United States. The kingdom became an economic satellite.[46] On the other hand, native farmers, who would supposedly have been able to sell their produce on the broad American market, pay less for imports, and enjoy higher profits and wages, gained very little. Instead, sugar production quickly concentrated in the hands of a few, led by the magnate Claus Spreckels. Contract workers arrived by the thousands. Prices and taxes rose, but not wages, and the native Hawaiians were squeezed.

Yet the haole elite complained. Their taxes, they said, were too high; Kalakaua spent recklessly (i.e., in ways they did not approve of); and they had no control over what he did with "their money." The Iolani Palace, begun in 1879, was costing too much, and a lavish coronation celebration in 1883—a grand reaffirmation of Hawaiian cultural traditions—was condemned by the elite as extravagant and even immoral (it included hula dancing).[47] Also considered profligate were the king's "welfare state measures"—expenditures to promote immigration, agriculture, railroad-building, public works, and schools. Several of the king's cabinet were haoles, and so was his prime minister, Walter Gibson, but they did not cater to the economic elite. Gibson, a Mormon, was "the prime example of a haole whose views and politics . . . were antithetical to the Hawaiianized white families" who constituted it.[48]

In January 1887 the elite decided to act. Some of its leaders conspired to create a "Hawaiian League," which by June had 405 members and an armed wing called the Honolulu Rifles. On June 30, they forced

Kalakaua to agree to a new constitution—aptly called the Bayonet Constitution—that made the cabinet responsible to the legislature and thus reduced the king to a figurehead. It also created a property qualification for voting and officeholding, thus disenfranchising the mass of native Hawaiians and Asians. The resemblance to franchise restrictions in the American South at that time was not accidental; at one point it was explained that Hawaii was now enjoying "Mississippi laws." With the electorate thus rearranged, an election on September 12, 1887, brought in a legislature controlled by the elite's "Reform" party.[49]

Other than the 1898 annexation itself, these actions were the decisive event in turning over Hawaii to American control. Several consequences flowed from it. First came renewal of the reciprocity treaty in November 1887, confirming Hawaii's economic satellite status. A new clause gave control of Pearl Harbor to the United States. Kalakaua agreed to that under duress. Then came the nationalization of crown lands, making them available to planters and other non-Hawaiians. Another act required that all schools, public and private, had to teach in English; Hawaiian was forbidden. The Bayonet Constitution and its sequels were a revolution by and for an elite. Claiming to be instituting good government and democracy, they certainly created it for themselves. The great majority were cast out of the political system, just as they had already become a lower tier in the islands' economic system.

A countercoup led by Robert Kalanihiapo Wilcox of Maui with several dozen armed men erupted in July 1889. It was suppressed after a hundred Marines from the U.S.S. *Adams* backed up the Honolulu Rifles with a loan of ten thousand rounds of ammunition. Congress was not so kind to the elite when it passed the McKinley tariff in 1890, giving preference to domestic sugar producers and reducing the Hawaiian planters' profits of 75 to 100 percent a year to a mere 10 percent.[50] The Wilson-Gorman tariff of 1894 and later acts restored their well-being, but in the early 1890s, "revolutionary sentiment"—support for annexation by the United States—increased.[51]

Kalakaua lived on for four years after the Bayonet coup, harassed and nearly powerless. At his death in January 1891, his sister Liliuokalani became queen. A talented composer and writer, she was also made of sterner stuff than her brother, and sought to reassert some powers of the monarchy and to restore a degree of native control. In response, the elite secretly formed an "Annexation Club" in early 1892. The American minister, John L. Stevens, regarded her as deeply anti-American and wrote to the secretary of state that "Hawaii . . . must now take the road which leads to Asia, or the other, which outlets her in America, gives her an American civilization and binds her to the care of American destiny."[52] Lorrin Thurston, the haole lawyer who was the principal drafter of the Bayonet Constitution, a grandson of early missionaries and leader of the Annexation Club, traveled to Washington that May. President Benjamin Harrison, speaking through his secretary of the navy, assured Thurston that if events led to a proposal that the United States annex Hawaii, it would "find an exceedingly sympathetic administration here."[53]

Such events did take place in January 1893. For the preceding year, Hawaiian politics had been unstable. Cabinets came and went. Finances were in poor shape because of the decline in the sugar market when the U.S. McKinley tariff of 1890 rescinded the duty-free status of Hawaiian sugar. Liliuokalani proposed a national lottery and a licensing of the opium traffic to raise public revenue. The legislature approved the lottery on December 31, 1892, and the opium tax on January 10, 1893, over the protests of haole moralists. The queen had received petitions in early 1892 from all around the islands, signed by more than two-thirds of the 9,500 registered voters, calling for a constitutional convention. She drew up a new constitution, similar to that of 1864, under which several kings had reigned prior to the Bayonet Constitution of 1887. Her document would have "removed the race and language requirements for the franchise, restored her executive powers, restored the inviolability of the sovereign's property, and either eliminated or lessened the property requirement for voters."[54] On Saturday, January 14, 1893, the queen prorogued the legislature and walked back to the Iolani Palace to receive and promulgate the new constitution.

The elite of the Annexation Club could not and did not let this happen. The queen had told her cabinet members what she intended to do, and they in turn leaked the news to Thurston and other annexationist leaders. Members of the cabinet persuaded her to postpone her announcement, and that afternoon she did so, "for a few days" or "until soon." Over the weekend the annexationists formed a "Committee of Safety" and took steps to stop the queen. They secured the support of Minister Stevens on the ground that as Americans their lives and property were in danger. Similarly, they contacted Captain Gilbert C. Wiltse of the U.S.S. *Boston*, docked in Honolulu harbor. Both sides held public meetings on Monday. With Stevens's approval and on Wiltse's orders,

154 Marines and 10 officers landed with Gatling guns and cannon. They posted themselves near Iolani Palace and the main government building. As an American admiral remarked, they "were well located if designed to promote the movement for the Provisional Government and very improperly located if only intended to protect American citizens in person and property." Cabinet members told Stevens that they were capable of preserving order themselves and did not want the troops on shore, but Stevens refused to call them back.

Monday night was tense, but no serious violence broke out. Early Tuesday afternoon, Thurston put out a proclamation deposing Liliuokalani and ending the monarchy. The resuscitated Honolulu Rifles of 1887 led the annexationist leader Sanford Dole in occupying the government building, and Stevens officially granted American recognition to the provisional government. The queen, wishing as always (as Kalakaua had done in 1887) to avoid armed confrontation and bloodshed, agreed not to resist, provided that a full account would be heard in Washington. She expected that a fair hearing by U.S. officials would repudiate Stevens and the revolutionaries and restore her authority.[55]

It was not to be. But neither, quite yet, was annexation. Thurston sped to Washington with some coconspirators to make their case to President Harrison, Secretary of State John W. Foster, and Congress. Foster and Harrison bought their version of events. By February 14 their annexation treaty was signed and approved by the Senate Foreign Relations Committee. An emissary from Liliuokalani arrived in Washington a few days later to present the queen's case. Possibly for that reason, possibly for others, the Senate did not vote to ratify before its session—and the Harrison administration—ended on March 3. The incoming Democratic president, Grover Cleveland, upset by the unseemly speed with which the queen and her case had been overridden, withdrew the treaty from Senate consideration. He furthermore sent a former congressman, James Blount, to Hawaii to conduct an impartial investigation.

Blount arrived in Honolulu on March 29. Stevens was replaced and soon repudiated by Cleveland, the troops were returned to the *Boston*, and Stevens's recognition of the provisional government was revoked. Following Blount's report on July 17 to the new secretary of state, Walter Q. Gresham, President Cleveland stated that the provisional government owed "its existence to an armed invasion by the United States." Thus, he concluded, "by an act of war, committed with the participation of a diplomatic representative of the United States [Stevens] and without authority of Congress, the Government of a feeble but friendly and confiding people has been overthrown."[56] In October the new American minister informed the queen that Cleveland regretted the "flagrant wrong" done to her and wished her reinstated, though with "full amnesty" to the insurgents. She wanted the insurgents prosecuted "as the law directs"—which could mean beheading. She later denied repeatedly that she had said any such thing. But the statement became part of a vile smear campaign against her, loaded with racist and sexually slanderous innuendo.[57]

Cleveland sent the Blount report to Congress on December 18, disavowed the annexation treaty, but left it to Congress to take further action. In February 1894, the House censured Stevens and disapproved of any power intervening, annexing, or asserting a protectorate over Hawaii. In the same month, the chair of the Senate Foreign Relations Committee, John T. Morgan (Democrat of Alabama), no Cleveland sympathizer, presented a report favoring annexation, but he was the only signer.[58] In May the Senate voted—55 to 0, with 30 not voting—to affirm the right of the Hawaiians to "establish and maintain their own form of government . . . which the United States ought in no wise to interfere with." But it did not restore the monarchy.

Why did the antiannexationist Cleveland leave the matter to the dubious mercies of Congress? Because he saw no choice; the only route to restoration of the queen and the unseating of the usurpers was to send an armed force. "Except by an American army," Cleveland's biographer Allan Nevins wrote, Liliuokalani "could no more be restored than Humpty-Dumpty. The wealthy and well-organized Americans who supported [President Sanford] Dole would never tolerate her return to power. As for using American bayonets to replace her, neither Congress nor public opinion would ever permit it."[59] The United States would not shrink from using force a few years later in the Philippines and the Caribbean. Then, however, it was "natives," not a white Anglo-American elite, who threatened law and order.

The annexationists in Hawaii then called for a new constitutional convention. To vote for a delegate, one first had to take an oath of loyalty to the provisional government. The new constitution openly followed Jim Crow "Mississippi laws" by disenfranchising native Hawaiians and Asians. On July 2, five thousand to seven thousand people protested at Palace Square against the new regime. But the American minister granted recognition, and on July 4, 1894, President Sanford Dole announced the existence of the Republic of Hawaii.

Supporters of Liliuokalani immediately began planning a counter-coup, importing arms for an uprising at Waikiki on January 6, 1895. Skirmishes went on for days, but the protest was squelched on January 14. Two days later the regime accused the queen of hiding weapons. She was arrested and detained for months at Iolani Palace. After her release she spent some time in Washington and elsewhere in the United States. She attracted much sympathy and financial support, but she never regained her crown. Instead, after Cleveland left office and the Republican William McKinley became president in March 1897, an annexation treaty resurfaced—the 1896 Republican platform had demanded that Hawaii should be "controlled" by the United States—and McKinley signed it on June 16. The treaty then went to the Senate.

Native Hawaiians mobilized two massive protest petitions. By September 11 they had obtained more than 21,000 signatures on one and more than 17,000 on the second from a native population of about 40,000. In other words, well over 90 percent of real Hawaiians objected to annexation. On September 14, Senator Morgan arrived in Hawaii with other members of Congress. At a mass meeting of thousands of Hawaiians—described as "well-informed . . . organized, articulate, and literate in two languages"—Morgan shamelessly announced that after annexation they would enjoy the right to vote, just as African-Americans did in the American South.[60] Representatives of the petition organizers carried the documents to Washington, where anti-imperialist senator George Frisbie Hoar (Republican of Massachusetts) placed them into the *Record*. The Hawaiians remained in Washington until February 27, by which time Senate votes for annexation dwindled from 58 to 46, well short of the necessary two-thirds. The annexation treaty seemed doomed.

But then war erupted between the United States and Spain. The government of the Hawaiian Republic offered all possible assistance to the United States, even before Commodore George Dewey's victory at Manila Bay. This impressed some members of Congress. Looking back at the Texas precedent of 1845, Congressman Francis Newlands (Democrat of Nevada) introduced a resolution of annexation. The Foreign Affairs Committee approved it on May 12. Speaker Thomas B. Reed (Republican of Maine) held it up in the House for three weeks. (Democrats usually opposed, and Republicans usually favored, annexation, but Newlands and Reed were exceptions.) Reed finally relented, and on June 15 the House passed it with 209 yeas, 91 nays, 6 present, and 49 not voting. The Senate took it up immediately and passed it on July 6 by a vote of 42 yeas, 21 nays, and 26 not voting.

The deed was done. Sovereignty was formally transferred on August 12, 1898. A historian—no Hawaiian nationalist—states that "there was scant enthusiasm. . . . Very few Hawaiians attended" the ceremony.[61] The acquisition was probably constitutional, since Hawaii might someday possibly become a state. But for the United States to support a coup, recognize the usurping regime as legitimate, and then annex the islands has been called "dirty pool."[62] In 1900 Hawaii was organized as a territory, and in 1959 it joined the union as the fiftieth state.

Hawaii was taken over, first economically and then politically, by a haole elite operating under the white supremacist conviction that it knew what was best for the native Hawaiians and the Asian immigrants. Taxes and public expenditure benefited them directly, and the rest by a trickle-down process, if at all. The majority were disenfranchised in 1887 and remained so until the 1950s, with law and order enforced by American authorities.[63] As in Samoa and in the West, native cultures and self-rule were suppressed. Liberty and freedom prevailed—for the elite and the new rulers. Expressions of nationalism and assertions of native rights have surfaced from time to time, including the bill introduced by Senator Daniel Akaka in 2004–2007. Opponents of the Akaka bill warned that giving recognition to native Hawaiians would make ethnic non-Hawaiians "subservient to a hereditary elite."[64] This is a startling irony, since it was a non-Hawaiian elite that thwarted and dispossessed the native monarchy in 1887, 1893, and 1898. Akaka's bill failed to pass the Senate in June 2006, needing 60 votes to stay on the floor but winning just 56 (with 41 nays); but he reintroduced it in January 2007 as "the Native Hawaiian Government Reorganization Act," noting that Americans had forced Liliuokalani to abdicate, leaving an unhealed wound festering "in the hearts of Hawaii's younger generation."[65]

Only once was Hawaii ever thought of as a "next frontier" extending the continental settlement process. In 1881 Secretary of State James G. Blaine proposed a "Hawaiian homestead act for the benefit of actual American settlers." But no action followed. If it had, would those settlers have replaced native Hawaiians, as they were replacing the Plains Indians at that moment? The haole elite was doing that job well enough in any case. And in the next and nearly final Pacific acquisitions, the Philippines and Guam, not only was there no homestead idea, but no haole elite either: only Filipinos and Chamorros, and the armed forces of the United States.

THE PHILIPPINES OVERNIGHT

The United States' post–Civil War forays into the Pacific began with the simplest and cleanest of acquisitions (Alaska) and concluded with the most complicated, lethal, protracted, and constitutionally dubious (the Philippines).

As 1898 opened, the American situation in the Pacific had developed over the preceding thirty years in the following ways. Alaska, somnolent and underpopulated, had proved that it would never be a homesteading frontier, but it was suddenly coming alive as hopeful thousands sailed to Skagway in 1897 to begin their climb to the Klondike gold fields. The navy and commercial surrogates had quietly planted the flag on guano-rich, uninhabited atolls and islands scattered across the vast sea. Samoa was settling down after the confrontations of the late 1880s with Germany and Britain. Within a year it ceased to be a diplomatic flash point, just an out-of-the-way naval base. Hawaiian annexation was on hold, awaiting a more eager president and a better opportunity than Cleveland had provided in 1893. Feelers toward east Asia, despite approaches such as the Burlingame Treaty of 1868 promoting trade and other relations with China, were virtually dormant.

Closer to home, however, a wide swath of public opinion became increasingly outraged at what it saw as Spain's repression of its Cuban colony. When the battleship U.S.S. *Maine* blew up in Havana harbor on February 15, 1898, the press and public blamed the Spanish. War pressure built irresistibly, and Congress declared war on Spain on April 22.[66] Cuba was the cause, and Cuban freedom from Spain the object. Spain also had a fleet and land forces on the other side of the world at Manila in the Philippines, claimed by her since Magellan visited the archipelago in 1521 and a colony since 1565. If war broke out over Cuba, other Spanish colonies, including the Philippines, became fair game.

Ten days after the *Maine* disaster, Assistant Secretary of the Navy Theodore Roosevelt (with President McKinley approving) cabled Commodore George Dewey, commanding the U.S. Pacific squadron at Nagasaki, to proceed to Hong Kong and be ready for further orders that events might make necessary. On April 24, two days after the declaration of war, Dewey was told to sail to Manila and capture or destroy the Spanish fleet there. He arrived in the early morning of May 1 and did so, wiping out nine Spanish warships with almost no casualties of his own. Spanish naval power was gone. Spain's land army remained, and so did 20 million Filipinos, some of whom had been rebelling against Spanish rule for years. Dewey requested ground troops to secure Manila. Already, however, the U.S. Army chief of staff, Nelson Miles, had recommended to McKinley that troops be sent to California and then embarked for Manila. The president agreed, and 1,200 troops left on May 25, arriving on June 30. By midsummer more than 10,000 were on the ground. At the same time, Representative Francis Newlands's Hawaiian annexation resolution was moving through Congress; Hawaii was now seen as a stepping-stone and supply base for the Philippines. Both would provide a pathway to China.

Just how strong, numerous, and well armed the Filipino *insurrectos* were, what classes in Filipino society supported them, and what districts they represented or controlled was not fully clear. Not every Filipino, everywhere in the islands, backed them. But that did not disqualify them as insurgents; after all, Americans had been divided in the 1770s. They were probably 20,000 strong outside and around Manila, and they were led by a charismatic young man from nearby Cavite, Emilio Aguinaldo. Aguinaldo hoped for U.S. support against Spain. He had had encouraging meetings with U.S. consuls in Singapore and Hong Kong, and now with Dewey. But Dewey and the navy played little role after U.S. Army troops under Major General Wesley Merritt began arriving. The actors became the Spanish, Aguinaldo's *insurrectos*, and the U.S. Army.

By early August the Spanish prepared to leave. To do so "with honor," they arranged a phony exchange of fire with the navy on August 13, and evacuated the walled inner city. (Six Americans and forty-nine Spaniards were killed in this "phony" encounter, which was unnecessary anyway because the United States and Spain had signed an armistice on the twelfth, but news of it had not arrived.) Now it was between the army and Aguinaldo. His forces had dug trenches all around Manila. General Merritt had been instructed not to confront the *insurrectos* directly, so he persuaded Aguinaldo to let the army into the city on the understanding that they would share the victory. But there was no sharing. Dewey and Merritt kept the Filipinos from the triumph and from the actual surrender ceremony.

Thus by mid-August 1898 the American army occupied Manila and Aguinaldo's forces surrounded it. Spain was gone, other powers such as Germany and Japan were unwelcome, and the Filipinos were deemed unable to rule themselves. The question boiled down to whether the Americans would create some sort of protectorate over Aguinaldo and his supporters, or just annex the islands and make them a colony. McKinley had probably already decided. Immediately after the Spanish evacuated Manila on August 13, with Aguinaldo shut out of the victory, the president ruled out "joint occupation with the insurgents" and ordered that they "must recognize the military occupation and authority of the United States."[67]

After Elwell S. Otis, a by-the-book desk general, replaced Merritt on August 30 as commander of U.S. ground forces, relations with Aguinaldo deteriorated rapidly. Otis warned Aguinaldo that if he did not remove his forces from Manila by September 15, the Americans would "be obliged to take forcible action." Aguinaldo pulled back, but also sent two emissaries to plead his case in Washington for recognition and a place at the peace conference, which was to start on October 1 in Paris. McKinley received them but granted the Filipino envoys no status except as private individuals and not as participants. The president had already stacked the American delegation with annexationists and then toured the Midwest prior to the fall elections gathering support.[68] At the end of October he instructed his peace commissioners to demand transfer of the entire Philippine Islands to the United States. The flag would not be "pulled down" in Manila as Cleveland had "pulled it down" in Honolulu after the 1893 coup there.

The consistent position of the president and others close to him was that the Filipinos were not capable of self-government. Aguinaldo, his colleagues, and other Filipinos were referred to by tribal names, and thus diminished in legitimacy. Their inferiority was assumed, not analyzed; it was conventional wisdom, resting on racial and religious biases prevalent among even educated Americans of that day. McKinley and missionaries talked of Christianizing the Filipinos, ignoring the fact that the Catholic Spanish had been doing so for over three hundred years. Imperialists and anti-imperialists alike regarded Filipinos as a non-Anglo-Saxon, nonwhite, and hence inferior race, like blacks or, more explicitly, Indians. During the debate in Congress in 1899 on the treaty and annexation, supporters openly drew parallels between Indians in the

West and Filipinos; both were unenlightened savages to whom civilization should be brought. Basically the same senators voted for Philippine annexation and for full federal control of Indians and their land. Virtually all of the thirty generals who served during the war against the *insurrectos* were from the West or had had Indian-fighting experience.[69] The racial and anti-Catholic prejudices of common soldiers and officers of the American army took blunt and aggressive forms. Despite Aguinaldo's proven success in organizing a prolonged rebellion against the Spanish, and despite Dewey's initial impression that he and his officers were well educated and intelligent, the McKinley administration simply refused to entertain the idea that the Filipinos could govern their islands, either by themselves or under American "protection."

The peace treaty was signed on December 10, 1898. Spain was to leave Cuba, turn over Puerto Rico and an island in the Marianas to the United States, and transfer the entire Philippines to the United States, for which Spain would receive $20 million. The Spanish objected but had no choice. McKinley interpreted the treaty to mean that Spain had ceded the Philippines to the United States alone. The *insurrectos* were not included. On December 21 the president wrote new instructions to General Otis, outlining what American sovereignty would mean. The orders were sent on December 29 and announced in Manila on January 4, 1899:

> It will be the duty of the commander of the forces of occupation to announce and proclaim in the most public manner that we come not as invaders or conquerors, but as friends. . . . It should be the earnest and paramount aim of the military administration to win the confidence, respect, and affection of the inhabitants of the Philippines by assuring them in every possible way that full measure of individual rights and liberties which is the heritage of a free people, and by proving to them that the mission of the United States is one of *benevolent assimilation*, substituting the mild sway of justice and right for arbitrary rule. In the fulfillment of this high mission, supporting the temperate administration of affairs for the greatest good of the governed, there must be *sedulously maintained the strong arm of authority*, to repress disturbance and to overcome all obstacles to the bestowal of the blessings of good and stable government upon the Philippine Islands under the flag of the United States.[70]

On the next day, January 5, Aguinaldo countered with his own proclamation. He would not acquiesce in a forcible American conquest. The *insurrectos* proceeded to hold a constitutional convention at Malolo, and on January 23 Aguinaldo became the first president of the Republic of the Philippines. The conflict was becoming joined: the *insurrecto* republic versus the American occupation.

Otis chose to emphasize "sedulously maintain[ing] the strong arm of authority" rather than "benevolent assimilation." In doing so he was behaving in a context very familiar to Americans at that moment. In 1887 Congress had passed the Dawes Severalty Act, which abolished tribal ownership and began forcing Indians into individual landholding, another manifestation of "benevolent assimilation." The Filipinos therefore had the bad luck of encountering American society and government at its most racist moment, when it was forcing conformity upon Indians, excluding Chinese immigrants, disenfranchising African-Americans in the South, affirming the "separate but equal" doctrine in schools and public accommodations, and lynching well over a hundred blacks (and some whites) every year.[71] The Filipinos were yet another people who would learn how benevolence and authoritarianism might be combined.

As conditions became more tense in Manila, the Treaty of Paris went to the Senate for ratification. While it removed Spain formally from the Philippines, the annexation-versus-protectorate question was technically still open. The Senate debated in executive session through January, with no certain victory by either side. Past and future Democratic presidential candidate William Jennings Bryan urged passage, arguing that final status of the islands could be dealt with afterward. The treaty passed by one vote more than the necessary two-thirds, 57 for and 27 opposed, on February 6. All but two Republicans (Hoar of Massachusetts and Eugene Hale of Maine) voted for; Democrats split, 10 for, 22 opposed; 5 Populists were opposed. Resolutions favoring Filipino independence then came close to passing. But they did not, and annexation proceeded.

Two days before the Senate vote, on the night of February 4, 1899, a Nebraska volunteer named William Grayson shot and killed two *insurrecto* soldiers. He shouted out to his comrades, "Line up, fellows; the niggers are in here all through these lines." Within a day, fifty-nine Americans and three thousand Filipinos were dead.[72] The war—minimized as an "insurrection" in American accounts and histories—had begun. From February 4, 1899, until July 4, 1902, the United States was at war with the Filipinos. By late October, Otis's troops had defeated their enemy in conventional settings after a campaign across northern Luzon. Aguinaldo, however, shifted to guerrilla warfare. His troops melted into the landscape, switched from being soldiers to farmers and back again, ambushed stray columns, and avoided pitched battles. An American officer reviled the Filipinos for refusing to stand up and be shot like men. Senior American officers who were veterans of the Indian wars easily equated the Filipinos with the "savages" of the Plains, deserving extermination. Common soldiers, many of them lightly trained volunteers, were unlimited in both their patriotism and their racism. One wrote, "I am in my glory when I can sight my gun on some dark skin and pull the trigger."[73] Other comments were much worse.

An American torture technique, the "water cure," became notorious for making prisoners talk. As an American soldier described it in a letter home, "The victim is laid flat on his back and held down by his tormenters. Then a bamboo tube is thrust into his mouth and some dirty water, the filthier the better, is poured down his unwilling throat."[74] One careful historian identified "fifty-seven verifiable instances when American soldiers committed atrocities," plus sixty cases of aggravated assault, including murder of prisoners, murder of civilians, rape, the water cure, and miscellaneous other acts. Incidents increased as the struggle wore on. From the other side, an American infantry company was surprised at Balangiga on Samar Island in September 1901 by disguised *insurrecto* infiltrators who killed forty-five and wounded eleven of them. General Jacob W. Smith then promised to make Samar "a howling wilderness" in retaliation, ordering that any Filipino capable of harming American troops should be killed on sight. Such persons were defined as anyone ten years old and up. Smith was later court-martialed and convicted for this, but he was let off with only his forced retirement.[75]

By then the insurrection on Luzon had wound down, leaving the fighting to outlying islands. In March, a colonel of Kansas volunteers, Frederick Funston, discovered Aguinaldo's hideout and on a ruse took him prisoner. Funston became an instant hero, and he was briefly talked of as a running mate for Theodore Roosevelt in 1904. But the public and Congress soon learned that Funston had bragged about executing prisoners and enforcing "bayonet rule," and—truly serious—had criticized the new civilian Philippines administration of William Howard Taft. Mark Twain loosed some of his bitterest satire against Funston in an essay in which he wrote that Funston was not truly to blame for his despicable actions, because his corrupt nature "took as naturally to moral slag as [George] Washington's took to moral gold." Funston was morally color-blind; he "had a native predilection for unsavory conduct." For Twain, the worst of it was that Funston was applauded and his conduct considered a model for others.[76]

In December 1901 the American commander at Batangas in southern Luzon began herding local people into protected zones around certain villages, warning that anyone who stayed outside was in mortal danger. This was, in effect, the same policy of "reconcentration" that the Spanish general Valeriano Weyler had effected in Cuba, and which Americans had condemned before the war. The American press in 1897–1898 denounced Weyler, but by 1901 the U.S. Army was doing just what Weyler had done. The tactic also prefigured the "strategic hamlets" policy that the Americans would use decades later in Vietnam.

At home a war of words between supporters and opponents of Philippine annexation heated up from late 1898 and continued to 1902. Anti-imperialists nearly defeated the treaty in the Senate in early 1899. The Anti-Imperialist League, founded by the Boston businessman-economist Edward Atkinson, included prominent people as diverse as Mark Twain and Andrew Carnegie. Atkinson called the annexation "criminal aggression," and proposed that the Philippines become a neutral commercial zone, run by experienced colonial administrators under whom "we can aid the inhabitants to bring order out of chaos [and] help them work out their own national salvation."[77] But no one adopted his suggestion. Instead, a War Department lawyer assured Secretary Elihu Root that the United States had full jurisdiction and a perfect right to annex the Philippines. Senator Albert Beveridge (Republican of Indiana), with Massachusetts's Henry Cabot Lodge the most vociferous of the Senate imperialists, proclaimed that Philippine annexation was no departure from America's past: "It is as old as our steady progress toward national power—yes, as old as the varying movements of civilization itself. . . . The mastery of that great ocean [the Pacific] in the future is to be ours." Lewis Cass had said so in the 1840s, and so had William Seward in the 1850s.[78]

President Theodore Roosevelt declared the war officially over on July 4, 1902. More than 126,000 American troops had gone to the Philippines; 4,234 were killed, more than 2,800 were wounded, and several thousand more died later of diseases or injuries. Upwards of 20,000 Filipinos were killed in combat, and probably 200,000 more died as a result of diseases, scorched-earth destruction of crops, burnt-down villages, and other disruptions. The war was as ugly as it was unnecessary.

In 1899 President McKinley appointed a civilian commission headed by Jacob Gould Schurman, president of Cornell University, to investigate conditions and advise him on policy. The Schurman commission reported in late 1899 and early 1900 that a degree of home rule would be good, but under U.S. sovereignty, and that no war had ever been "more humanely conducted." (Schurman later revised his views.) McKinley sent a second commission under a forty-three-year-old Ohio lawyer, William Howard Taft. Taft reported interviewing "many witnesses" who, whatever their "bias," agreed "that the masses of the people are ignorant, credulous, and childlike, and that under any government the electoral franchise must be much limited, because the large majority will not, for a long time, be capable of intelligently exercising it." Yet, Taft wrote, "the great majority of the people long for peace and are entirely willing to accept the establishment of a government under the supremacy of the United States"—though they did not always show their support for fear of reprisals from "the insurgents . . . [a] conspiracy . . . a Mafia on a very large scale."

McKinley was ready to establish a civil administration. General Otis had been getting bad press for his bluntness and insensitivity. General Arthur MacArthur replaced him in 1901 but fared little better. In March 1901 the president gave Taft full authority, and on July 1, 1901, civilians took over from the army. MacArthur was not pleased, and many military officers regarded such nation-building (as later generations would call it) as coddling a bunch of savages. Taft had Roosevelt's and Root's backing, however, and he prevailed. After McKinley appointed Taft as governor, MacArthur feuded with him. Whatever the virtues of Otis, MacArthur, and the other generals, diplomacy was not one of them. Taft took hold quickly despite the generals. He began establishing schools, improving public health, and putting in place the start of local governments from September 1900 onward. No one can defend contagious diseases or ignorance, and the American regime did much to reduce both. But it was not a democratic regime.[79]

In 1902 Congress passed an Organic Act for the Philippines. Construction of schools, sewerage, medical facilities, and agencies of local government proceeded. Another report of the ongoing Philippine Commission in 1904 informed Washington that Luzon was tranquil except for a few bands of "ladrones" (thieves) who needed to be "exterminated." In 1907 the first legislative elections among Filipino candidates and political parties were held.[80] The Philippines began to look very much like a species of American protectorate. But if that could happen in 1907 or even 1902, why did it not happen in 1898?

In 1916 the first bill promising future Philippine independence, the Jones Act, passed Congress. It created an all-Filipino legislature and Senate. The American governor-general remained the final authority, with power to override the legislature, but nevertheless, the administration of President Woodrow Wilson made a clear retreat from colonialism, becoming "the first country ever to declare its intention to free a colony."[81] In 1934 the Tydings-McDuffie Act actually promised independence in twelve years. Manuel Quezon became president in 1935 of the resulting Commonwealth of the Philippines, continuing in exile in the United States during the Japanese-American war and occupation until he died in 1944. Two years later, Manuel Roxas became president of the independent republic. In 1964 Emilio Aguinaldo died at age ninety-four. In 1992, after the Philippine government refused to renew a postwar treaty, the United States finally removed its remaining forces from Clark Air Force Base and the naval base at Subic Bay, north of Manila. After more than ninety years of occupation, the flag was finally lowered.

The United States turned a by-product of a campaign ostensibly to free Cuba into a half century of colonialism in the Philippines. Never was there the slightest intention of making the islands a frontier of settlement or a state. Quite the contrary. The "threat" was that Filipinos would migrate to the American mainland, and about 50,000 did so in the 1920s. The 1934 law promising independence put a stop to that, depriving Filipinos of any rights of citizenship and capping immigration at 50 people a year. A repatriation act in 1935 paid Filipinos their passage back home on the condition that they never return. The Great Depression was one context of those laws. Their immediate purpose was to reduce unemployment. But persistent racial prejudice was another motive. In the immediate aftermath of World War II, when Britain gave up its empire in India and the Dutch got out of Indonesia, the United States removed itself from its one true, thoroughgoing colony as well. A new immigration law in 1965 finally permitted Filipinos to migrate freely to the United States.

GUAM, BY-PRODUCT OF A BY-PRODUCT

Since 1668, Spanish government, friars, and soldiers had ruled the Chamorro people of Guam and the other islands now called the Northern Marianas. On the morning of June 20, 1898, in the 330th year of that presence, the Spanish governor, Colonel Juan Marina, awoke to explosions along the shore. They came from an American cruiser, the U.S.S. *Charleston*, commanded by Captain Henry Glass. He was accompanying three troop transports en route from San Francisco to provide ground forces for the takeover of Manila. Glass's orders, opened after he took on coal at Honolulu, were to proceed to Guam, capture and secure it, and then sail to Manila. Neither Glass nor the Navy Department knew much about Guam, except that its main harbor at Agana was protected by Fort Santa Cruz, which presumably would defend it.

No news about anything had come to Guam since April 9. Governor Marina sent a boat to greet the Americans. In it were Lieutenant Commander Don Francisco García Gutiérrez, the captain of the port; a surgeon; and an English-speaking Basque named Francisco Portusach, who was an American citizen (in fact the only one there). Gutiérrez apologized to Captain Glass for not returning what the Spanish had understood as a salute, on the ground that the fort had for some time been without operational guns. Glass explained that he had fired no salute but rather a bombardment, because Spain and the United States were at war. Glass took the three men prisoner, paroling them until the next day after they assured him that there would be, indeed could be, no resistance on shore.

The next morning brought a demand for surrender. Governor Marina replied that he was "under the sad necessity of being unable to resist such superior forces and regretfully accede to your demands, at the same time protesting against this act of violence." Glass imprisoned Marina and three of his staff on board the *Charleston* while his navigator, Lieutenant William Braunersreuther, supervised the disarming of the fifty-six Spanish soldiers on shore. On June 21, the American flag replaced the Spanish, and the United States owned another island. Glass sailed off to Manila, leaving no soldiers, Spanish or American, on Guam. Portusach, the only American, deemed himself in charge, as did the only remaining Spanish official, and the two quarreled with each other for control until December, when the Navy Department obligingly took over on an executive order from McKinley. A month later, another naval officer claimed the uninhabited atoll known as Wake Island. Guam remained a navy base, run by and for the navy. For many years it was off limits even to U.S. civilians, until the Truman administration transferred it to the Interior Department in 1950.[82]

The native Chamorros were not consulted at any point. Nor would they be, in a formal way, until the U.S. Congress sanctioned an elected legislature in the 1950s and a Chamorro became governor in 1960.

Empire II in the Pacific was nearly complete. After World War II, the Northern Marianas—Spanish in 1898, then German, then Japanese, and finally American—became "trust territories" or in "free association" with the United States, as did nearby Micronesia.[83] But they are really part of a later story. From Alaska to the Philippines, an offshore empire was in place. The United States had further interests in the western Pacific, such as preserving an "open door" in China and resisting Japanese expansion. American diplomacy and commerce had pointed to east Asia since before Seward's time, and there was a strong connection in many minds between the Philippine and Guam annexations and the desire for a firm American foothold in and near China. Secretary of State John Hay's "Open Door notes" of September 1899 and July 1900, along with McKinley's deployment of more than 3,400 American troops in June 1900 to join European powers in suppressing the antiforeign Boxer uprising in Beijing, revealed very strong American interest.[84]

The Caribbean became the other key theater of Empire II in the decades following the Civil War, though the major successes there did not begin until 1898. McKinley was certainly imperialist in his policies, but even more ardent expansionists would follow him. Theodore Roosevelt, Henry Cabot Lodge, Albert Beveridge, and Woodrow Wilson were yet to take power and assert American control, which they would do less in the western Pacific than in the Caribbean. Contrary to an older generation of historians who viewed 1898 as a "great aberration" from the nation's earlier history, the American search for empire continued from its continental base and sought new targets and emphases. At home, the last recalcitrant Indians were herded onto reservations and millions of homesteaders scrambled across the Great Plains. Seward took manifest destiny and put a commercial twist on it; the navy and the flag stuttered across the Pacific; Hawaii and the Philippines joined Empire II, the offshore empire, fairly peaceably in the first case and with much bloodshed in the second. Much of the Caribbean was about to follow, through a mixture of means but always with the continuing imperial motive.

Chapter Ten

AROUND THE CARIBBEAN

It would not be the part of wisdom for us to surrender the Government entirely into their hands, since they are of a different civilization, not looking upon matters of government in the same light as the Anglo-Saxon. They really have no conception of the true meaning of equality and liberty.

—William D. Boyce, 1914[1]

As far back as Thomas Jefferson's letter to Robert Livingston in April 1802, pointing out the new republic's dire need to control New Orleans, Americans with any sense of geopolitics and international trade had been casting covetous eyes on the Caribbean. Secretary of State William H. Seward wanted to buy the Dominican Republic, or at least Samaná Bay, on its coast. Seward sailed around the Caribbean in January 1866 and then negotiated a treaty with Denmark to purchase the Danish West Indies (now the U.S. Virgin Islands). The Danes agreed to it, but the U.S. Senate did not.[2] President Ulysses S. Grant also longed to acquire the Dominican Republic. Earlier, in the 1850s, American filibusters briefly took over Nicaragua. In 1850, Zachary Taylor's secretary of state, John Clayton, worked out a treaty with Britain to the effect that if a canal across Central America were ever built, the United States and Britain would do it jointly. (That was abrogated in 1901.) Tentative, sporadic, and without result before 1898, these initiatives into the Caribbean crystallized in the aftermath of the Spanish-American-Cuban war. As in the central and western Pacific, the American empire reached farther offshore than ever before, but more completely in the Caribbean. It became for the United States a "region of paramount interest," where its dominance was unthreatened by any other power.

Cuba Libre

No spot in the Caribbean had attracted voracious American eyes more often than Cuba. Ever since the United States captured the Floridas, Americans (especially in the South) hoped that Cuba would be next. In 1848 President James K. Polk offered Spain $100 million for its island colony, but he was turned down flat. Filibusters in 1850 and 1851 failed, but kept expansionist hopes alive. The Franklin Pierce administration, Democratic and expansionist, briefly considered a scheme in 1854 by three of its diplomats (one of whom was James Buchanan) to acquire Cuba, where slavery continued to exist. If Spain would not sell, "we should be justified in wresting it," they urged. But the contemporary furor over the possible extension of slavery into the Kansas and Nebraska Territories made the acquisition of Cuba or any other slave area politically untouchable.

In 1868, Cubans began a ten-year uprising, which they called *La Guerra Grande*, to end Spanish colonial rule. The Peace of Zanjón in 1878 gained them representation in the Spanish Cortes and freed any slaves who had fought on either side (slavery in Cuba conclusively ended in 1886).[3] But neither *La Guerra Grande* nor another uprising in 1879–1880, *La Guerra Chiquita*, brought independence. Americans watched, but during those largely depression-ridden years did not intervene. By the 1880s the United States had replaced mother-country Spain as Cuba's leading trading partner. Cuban expatriates living in New York and other American cities kept the vision of "liberty" and "freedom" alive as best they could—words to which Americans have always responded. When a third insurrection began in 1895, pressure began mounting toward an official, armed intervention by the United States.

The election of William McKinley and expansionist Republicans in 1896 made such an intervention possible, even likely. By then, the Democratic Party had largely pulled back from its spread-eagle expansionism of the 1840s. Grover Cleveland, elected in 1884 and again in 1892 as the first Democratic president since before the Civil War, was no shrinking violet in his foreign policy, but neither was he any enthusiast for annexations. While he stoutly defended American interests in Samoa in the late 1880s and in the Caribbean in 1895, he withdrew the treaty to absorb Hawaii from Senate consideration in early 1893, and he remained leery of entering Cuba, or even aiding the *insurrectos* there, in his second presidential term, which ended in March 1897.

McKinley and the Republican majorities in the Senate and the House that were elected with him in 1896 by no means lusted for war with Spain over Cuba. But they were ready to give an ear to popular outrage at reported Spanish brutalities and atrocities there, which were being publicized and magnified in the American press by the expatriate Cubans. They were also concerned about threats to American trade with Cuba and property there if the insurrection became more violent. It was an open question whether the *insurrectos* within Cuba would protect those American interests if they took over. The Spanish seemed less and less able to control the situation, but would it improve for American interests if the *insurrectos* came to power? Shrewd self-interest suggested that McKinley and his administration help send the Spanish home but also engineer substantial control of whoever succeeded them. The president did not personally favor annexation or even armed support of the rebels; instead he used diplomacy to pressure Spain to grant the Cubans autonomy, if not independence. With these strong efforts, Spain complied almost completely by late March and early April 1898. The Spanish ministry and the queen regent agreed to stop the tactics that Americans found most objectionable, and they consented to an armistice if the rebels asked for one. But the rebels continued to insist on full independence and Spain's complete withdrawal.

The Spanish monarchy had never truly recovered from the disasters of the reigns of Carlos IV and Fernando VII and the Napoleonic intrusion. It was too shaky to simply walk out of either Cuba or the Philippines without defending its colonies and its honor. Prime Minister Antonio Cánovas del Castillo, of the Conservative Party, backed the military high command in Madrid and General Valeriano Weyler, the commander in Cuba, in using tough measures against the Cuban insurgents. But Cánovas was assassinated by an Italian anarchist in early August 1897. Weyler's tactics were not winning anyway. Cánovas's successor, Práxedes Mateo Sagasta of the Liberal Party, did not have the military's confidence, and when he fired Weyler and took conciliatory steps toward the Cubans, he faced an officers' revolt. Sagasta saw his ultimate duty as saving the monarchy of the queen regent, Maria Christina, and her son the future king Alfonso XIII. He could risk a foreign war with the United States, but not another civil war at home. In March and April 1898, Sagasta and the queen went as far as they possibly could in offering concessions. They were almost too much for Madrid's Conservatives and military, and not enough for the Cubans. Therefore, they were also not enough for McKinley. What Spain would agree to, the *insurrectos* and McKinley could not. What the *insurrectos* demanded, the Spanish government could not give and still survive.[4]

After the American battleship U.S.S. *Maine* blew up in Havana harbor on February 15, 1898, killing 266 sailors, the road to war was almost irreversible. Although the real cause was much later proved to be an internal combustion of coal dust that exploded the ship's ammunition magazine, a navy investigation concluded that the cause was "external" to the ship.[5] The public blamed Spain—not very logically, as Spain would have had nothing to gain and a lot to lose. But pressure for intervention soared, both from the American public and the Cubans at home and in the United States. Despite Madrid's concessions, the *insurrectos* were adamant. On April 11, McKinley sent a message to Congress calling for "the forcible intervention of the United States as a neutral to stop the war."[6] (In no way did McKinley call for, or even refer to, annexation.) After debate, Congress responded on April 20 with a joint resolution that had four parts. First, it declared "that the people of the Island of Cuba are, and of right ought to be, free and independent." Second, it affirmed "the duty of the United States to demand . . . that . . . Spain at once relinquish its authority and government" in Cuba and "withdraw its land and naval forces." Third, it "directed and empowered" the president "to use the entire land and naval forces of the United States," and state militias, "to carry these resolutions into effect."

These were predictable, but the fourth part was not. Introduced by Senator Henry M. Teller (Republican of Colorado), and therefore known as the Teller Amendment, it stated that "the United States hereby disclaims any disposition or intention to exercise sovereignty, jurisdiction, or control over said Island except for the pacification thereof, and asserts its determination, when that is accomplished, to leave the government and control of the Island to its people."[7] Although personally in favor of annexations (he voted in July to annex Hawaii), Teller understood the public mood in April: that the United States should intervene to stop the fighting in Cuba and convert it from a Spanish colony to an independent republic, but that taking advantage of the situation for American territorial aggrandizement was unfair. Teller, and others agreed with him, believed that American motives should be seen to be pure. Many among the public (though not around the White House) wanted "Cuba Libre," a free Cuba, not territory. The Teller Amendment sailed through without a single nay vote. Teller explained the following December that his amendment "did not mean immediate absolute independence [for the Cubans], but rather American assistance in establishing self-government" and control of Cuba's foreign relations—in other words, "some kind of a protectorate."[8] Yet in April, his amendment expressed an undeniable altruism among much of the press and public, the popular belief that Spain was oppressing the Cubans, that the struggle paralleled Britain versus the Americans of 1776, that liberty, freedom, and "moral rights" (today, "human rights") demanded intervention.

The Teller Amendment appeared to stop annexation dead. So it did; but it did not kill the annexationist spirit, nor did it supplant the drive to control events in Cuba, and indeed to control Cuba itself. Instead it forced annexationists to invent a new way of exercising control: the device known as the "protectorate." In the Cuban case, the first of several begun during the next few years, the instrument would be the Platt Amendment, added in March 1901 by Congress to the military appropriations bill then before it. Mostly drafted by Secretary of War Elihu Root, but named after Senator Orville Platt (Republican of Connecticut), who introduced it, it provided legal cover for the United States to control Cuba's public finances, foreign affairs, and public order without actually annexing it. It remained in force in Cuba and several other republics around the Caribbean rim until 1934, serving as a new and major way to maintain Empire II. But this is getting ahead of our story.

Teller's amendment, on its face, expressed the idealism of the American people. Speeches in Congress and editorials in the press were studded with the traditional terminology of liberty and freedom. "The call to arms represented a crusade to deliver an oppressed New World people from the clutches of Old World tyranny," writes historian Louis A. Pérez, and thus it "served further to consecrate the American purpose in Cuba with lofty and selfless motives. . . . certain of the virtue of the Cuban cause, convinced of the nobility of the Cuban *insurrecto*, confident in their mission of liberation."[9] This idealism evaporated very quickly.

The original American plan was to land five thousand troops on the south shore of Oriente Province. There they would link up with the *insurrectos*, resupply them, and probably withdraw to Florida until more volunteer regiments could be trained. In the meantime, the navy would prevent Spain from resupplying its forces in Cuba. The American fleet

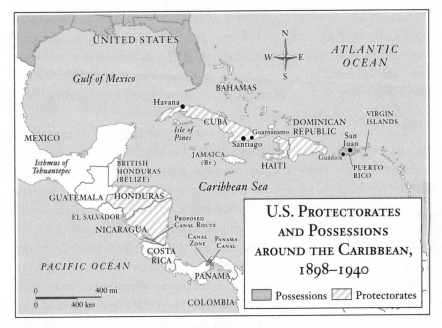

U.S. PROTECTORATES AND POSSESSIONS AROUND THE CARIBBEAN, 1898–1940

Possessions   Protectorates

The Caribbean theater of the Spanish-American War of 1898 was around Santiago, Cuba, and on Puerto Rico. In 1898 the United States took actual possession of Puerto Rico, and in 1903 of the Panama Canal Zone. In 1917 the United States bought the Virgin Islands (St. Thomas, St. John, and St. Croix) from Denmark.

U.S.-controlled "protectorates" existed all or most of the time in Honduras (1912–1919), Nicaragua (1911–1934), Panama (1903–1936), Haiti (1915–1934), the Dominican Republic (1905–1924), and Cuba (1898–1934).

Besides Panama, interocean canal routes were proposed from time to time across Nicaragua and the Isthmus of Tehuantepec in southern Mexico.

immediately steamed southward and discovered that the Spanish Caribbean squadron under Admiral Pascual Cervera had docked in port at Santiago on May 19. The location seems an odd choice; a better one would have been to put in at Havana harbor and reinforce the center of Spanish strength there. But Cervera's slow, overage ships were being chased by faster American ones, and had used too much coal crossing the Atlantic. Santiago harbor happens to be at the interior end of a narrow channel from the sea. Sailing in or out had to be done single file. Cervera and his fleet could be trapped there—and they were.

The Americans learned of Cervera's situation by the end of May and, shifting plans, quickly assembled a larger if poorly trained army. It sailed from Tampa on June 14, almost 17,000 strong. It landed on June 22–26 at Daiquirí and Siboney, two beach points ten or fifteen miles east of

Santiago. The two had been swept of Spaniards by the 3,000 *insurrectos* in the area. Facing them were about 9,000 Spanish at Santiago. Another Spanish force of 7,000 at Guantánamo, a few dozen miles to the east, was immobilized by guerrillas and blockaded by American warships. Slowly starving and out of contact, they could never be brought to bear in relief of Santiago.

Theoretically, the Americans were to reinforce 40,000 *insurrectos* on the island under the overall command of General Máximo Gómez and, in eastern Cuba, General Calixto García. The *insurrectos* had been living on the land, harassing and chipping away at the Spanish for three years. They had effectively forced the Spanish to retreat to the larger towns and cities, giving up the broad countryside. They successfully kept the Spanish away from the beaches, allowing the Americans to land without opposition. Of probably 70,000 effective troops in Cuba, Spanish commanders could deploy only the 9,000 at Santiago, because so many were needed in central and western Cuba to keep the insurrection at bay. Gómez's and García's effectives may have been ragtag, unkempt, and unmilitary-looking, but they weakened the Spanish at innumerable points.[10]

After landing, the American forces, commanded by Major General William Shafter, proceeded westward toward Santiago. The first skirmish, at Las Guásimas on June 24, resulted in more American casualties than Spanish, but since the Spanish then pulled back toward Santiago, the Americans called it a victory. Shafter spent the next week moving toward the city, focusing on taking two points on the way: the San Juan heights (preceded by a knob called Kettle Hill) and the village of El Caney. Shafter's units attacked both on July 1. The Spanish defenders, outnumbered twelve to one at El Caney and sixteen to one at San Juan heights, again fell back, but only after inflicting heavy damage. Using smokeless powder, they lost 593 killed and wounded, but the less well-equipped and minimally trained Americans lost 1,385.[11] The American advance had been a helter-skelter operation and it ground to a halt. The one outstanding result, in addition to the capture of the two positions, was the battlefield glory accorded to Lieutenant Colonel Theodore Roosevelt, leading his Rough Rider regiment up Kettle Hill (not San Juan Hill, as instant legend had it). Shafter had hoped and expected to take Santiago that day, but instead he felt forced to dig in. Early on July 3 he sent a surrender demand to the Spanish commander in the city, General José Toral. Toral declined.[12]

On that same day, however, sea power resolved the situation. Admiral Cervera had been ordered to leave Santiago harbor for the open sea, a predictably desperate maneuver. His fleet was slower and less than half the size in ship numbers and firepower than the Americans'. Threading single file down the narrow neck of the channel, his ships were either destroyed or driven ashore one by one as they emerged by the larger and faster American warships under Rear Admiral William T. Sampson. This time the casualty list greatly favored the Americans: one killed and one wounded, versus the Spaniards' 323 killed, 151 wounded, and 1,720 taken prisoner.[13] As with Dewey's demolition of Spain's eastern squadron at Manila two months earlier, sea power had decided the war against Spain in both theaters. A third Spanish fleet, which had been sailing eastward through the Suez Canal with the intent of relieving the garrison at Manila, was called back. The Spanish government had reflected on how vulnerable the country had become. No longer were the Caribbean colonies at issue; they could not be resupplied and were therefore lost. Now at risk were the Canary Islands and even the coast of Spain itself, if the Americans chose to bombard them. Spanish ground forces were on their own, without hope of reinforcement, facing the *insurrectos* as well as the Americans.

Shafter wisely chose to besiege Santiago rather than attack it. He resumed surrender negotiations with Toral, and after a four-hour naval bombardment on July 11—the last shots fired in the campaign—Toral capitulated on July 17, with Madrid's unhappy consent. Toral surrendered not only Santiago, but all of the 12,000 Spanish troops in eastern Cuba, seeing that further resistance, though it would damage the Americans severely, would ultimately be futile. Shafter later said that he was "thunderstruck" by this windfall. Washington, for its part, agreed to repatriate the Spanish armies.

In short, the Cuban campaign lasted three and a half weeks, from debarkation beginning on June 22 to Toral's surrender on July 17. The actual fighting was even briefer. Ground combat took place chiefly on July 1 just east of Santiago. Naval operations were confined to July 3. Casualties were close to equal on land, but very unequal at sea. The result was clear, however. Spain had lost Cuba and within weeks would evacuate it, not only from Santiago and the east, but from Havana and the west, where its armies were considerably larger but could not be brought to bear. The American strategy of attacking at a peripheral point, Santiago, rather than the most heavily guarded one, Havana, had paid off—better, however, for the United States than for the Cuban *insurrectos*. Years later, the Cuban historian Emilio Roig de Leuchsen-ring remarked that the Cubans had just about beaten the Spanish by themselves "when the United States intervened, not to ensure Cuban freedom but to prevent it."[14] It is difficult to see how the *insurrectos* would ever have defeated many thousands of Spanish regulars in the field without the Americans. But at the least, *insurrecto* harassments would likely have persuaded the Spanish eventually to withdraw.

The victory came none too quickly. Dysentery, malaria, and yellow fever began breaking out among the American troops. By late July the War Department was scurrying to evacuate its forces from Cuba, and by August 14, thousands (ultimately 20,000) began arriving at a makeshift hospital and camp at Montauk Point, Long Island. In the Cuban campaign, 243 American soldiers were killed in combat, while 771 died of disease there and at Montauk.[15]

The American action in Cuba in June–July 1898 paralleled the Philippine campaign in several ways. In both, Spanish navies were obliterated; Dewey's and Sampson's engagements were decisive. In both, the inexperience of the American officers and men was remedied in large part by technologically superior firepower and much better supply. And in both, amid the defeat of Spain, the Americans proved unable or unwilling to cooperate with or respect the *insurrectos* whom they had (in Cuba) ostensibly gone to war to help. In the Philippines, as we saw in the previous chapter, Americans negotiated the surrender, the ceremony of transfer, and the departure with honor of the Spanish, completely excluding Aguinaldo and his insurgents from these events. Much the same thing happened in Cuba.

From their first meetings with the Cuban *insurrectos*, Americans from foot soldiers to generals treated them with disdain and disgust. Ragged, ill-fed, and usually black or brown, they did not look like an army to the Americans. If they were to have any role in the fighting, it would be as trench diggers, messengers, or in other menial tasks—despite their combat experience. Shafter made no serious effort to coordinate with the Cuban commander, Calixto García. His units not only were not allowed to take part in the capture of Santiago, but Shafter would not let them participate in running the city (as he had earlier promised), administer liberated areas, or even come into the city after Americans took it. Shafter feared—and said so—that the *insurrectos* would loot and kill the citizenry.[16] The rebels regarded this as a profound insult. When García offered to send a division to join the Americans in the taking of Puerto Rico, he was simply ignored. No Cuban was invited to sign the document transferring power from Spain in December 1898. At the transfer ceremony on January 1, 1899, the American military governor in charge did allow nine Cuban generals to be present, but take no active role.[17]

The Americans did not give the *insurrectos* credit for softening up the Spanish during the previous three years. To the contrary, the Americans were under the impression that they had freed Cuba from Spain all by themselves, and they were displeased that the Cubans were not giving *them* the proper credit and gratitude. Undoubtedly the American action shortened the uprising and saved many Cuban lives. But the many put-downs of the Cubans during the conflict, and in the occupation that followed—indeed, the fact that it was an occupation rather than the beginning of self-government—soured relations and attitudes on both sides. As a rule, whenever the U.S. Army or Navy ran an occupation or civil government in this period, it behaved harshly and without consideration of the customs or sometimes even the humanity of those being occupied or "liberated." So it was in Samoa, Guam, and the Philippines; so it had been in the Indian wars throughout the nineteenth century; and so it was in Cuba. The American colonial administrators, it should be said in justice, were usually less harsh than its military, and often idealistic and selfless. But they too, like their superiors in Washington, reflected the racist hauteur so common among Americans of that time.

The rebels were poorly armed; they were "half-naked," that is, without proper uniforms or clean clothes; they did not "stand and fight" but employed hit-and-run tactics, like Indians in the West. In the Americans' racist eyes, they were, bluntly put, a bunch of savages. And, in a great many cases, they were black and Catholic. Shafter and other American commanders quickly decided that the rebel forces were worse than useless, unfit for combined operations, and a drag on battle plans. The journalists on the scene shaped American public opinion by painting the rebels in the same insulting terms.

When the time came, and it came quickly, when American policy makers had to decide on and devise a plan to deal with a Cuba no longer colonial, it could only conclude (as it did in the Philippines) that native self-government was out of the question. This assumption expressed the conventional wisdom in Washington. It was axiomatic that neither the Cubans nor the Filipinos, nor the Puerto Ricans nor the Chamorros of Guam, were in any way capable of running their own affairs without enlightened "civilized" guidance. The United States must control the situation. But there, alas, was that ticklish Teller Amendment. How could it be got around?

PUERTO RICO, THE GUAM OF THE EAST

An even easier conquest beckoned nearby, flowing as naturally in the wake of the Cuban conquest as Guam did after Manila. Although it was Spain's second and smaller colony in the Caribbean, Puerto Rico never-theless occupied a strategic location as the easternmost of the Greater Antilles (Cuba, Hispaniola, and Jamaica being the others). It was very much part of the Caribbean and Gulf region that the United States had thought it needed to control ever since Jefferson wrote Livingston about the geopolitical significance of New Orleans. Before the war, American strategists saw it as a possible base from which to reinforce Cuba, and it soon appeared to them anomalous to take Cuba but to leave Spain in possession of Puerto Rico. Capturing it would be relatively easy and would remove Spain completely from the Western Hemisphere. Spain had already given Puerto Ricans a large measure of home rule, and there was no *insurrecto* movement remotely like those in Cuba and the Philip-pines. Thus the capture of Puerto Rico seemed attractive, advisable, and feasible.

Consequently Nelson Miles, the army's commanding general, left Guantánamo on July 21 with 3,400 troops, to be joined soon by about 14,000 sailing directly from the States. Miles landed on the south side of the island near Ponce, skirmished on July 26 with a Spanish detachment, split his forces into four groups fanning out from northwest to north-east, to rendezvous at San Juan on the northeast shore. They were mak-ing their gradual way, about to meet significant Spanish resistance, when news came to Miles on August 12 that the American and Spanish gov-ernments had agreed in Washington to an overall armistice. No more fighting ensued. In fact, not much had occurred. The toughest engage-ment was at Coamo, a few miles east of Ponce, where the Americans and the Spanish each lost six men. The United States had taken Puerto Rico.

"Only a few would have imagined this outcome a few short months earlier," observes historian David Trask; it was "an unintended by-product of the war."[18] It was to Cuba as Guam was to the Philippine campaign—an island on the way, a satellite with measurable strategic value. Like Guam, it would tax the ingenuity of American empire builders to figure out a way to keep it and run it. An American military government was quickly put in place, to get rid of what the new chief, Brigadier General George Davis, called "the most absolute administrative corruption." Davis, immune to intercultural sensitivity, reported that it was "especially necessary to wipe out all those inherited vices and to prepare the country for a real democratic regime." An Organic Act, passed by Congress in 1900, installed "a Territorial government, which in due time could be raised to the highest dignity of membership as a State in the American commonwealth."[19] The Jones-Shafroth Act in 1917 granted citizenship to *Puertorriqueños* and let them elect their own legislature; in 1947 they could begin to elect their own governor; and in 1952 the colony became a commonwealth. But statehood never happened, nor did everyone want it. Fewer than half of the voters in a 1998 referendum supported it.[20]

COLONY-BUILDING IN THE CARIBBEAN

Once again, the United States had taken significant parts of Spain's empire—in fact, all that remained of it in the Caribbean and the western Pacific. As in 1795 after Pinckney's San Lorenzo treaty, as in 1803 with Louisiana (given Napoleon's defective title), and as in 1810, 1813, and 1819 in the Floridas, what was Spanish became American. Those earlier cases were on the North American continent and contiguous to the United States; their absorption was not problematical; they would all become states or parts of states. The offshore Spanish-become-American possessions, however, were not expected to do so. They were simply not thought of as future states, no matter what General Davis said about Puerto Rico. The very idea of an Asian Philippines or Guam, a black Cuba, or even a brown Puerto Rico joining the union was inconceivable to most Americans, southern or otherwise. With one fairly minor exception—the arrival of a few thousand hopeful citrus growers to Cuba before World War I, and the departure of most of them soon after—neither Cuba nor Puerto Rico were ever destinations for American settlement (though they certainly were sites for U.S. investment).[21] The Dakotas, Montana, west Texas, and other parts of the Great Plains were much easier to reach, and in those very years they were absorbing hundreds of thousands of settlers. What, then, should Spain's former colonies become?

The ultimate solution for Puerto Rico and the Philippines would be to invent a new colonial category, the commonwealth. Puerto Rico remains such an entity, with virtual home rule, not greatly different in its legal status from its final year or two as a Spanish possession. Cuba posed a greater difficulty, because the United States had foresworn annexation and promised an independent republic in the Teller Amendment. How that idealistic self-abnegation was circumvented, and American control (or hegemony, as some prefer to call it) was substituted, began immediately with the American conquest. The devices employed were, first, the military occupation after the Spanish went home; and second, the Platt Amendment of 1901.

The military government lasted from the end of 1898 until the Cuban republic was officially founded on May 20, 1902. The first military governor was Major General John R. Brooke, who got right to work and reported in late 1899 that the Spanish had withdrawn, the Cuban (*insurrecto*) army had dispersed, and civil government had been set up.[22] Brigadier General Leonard Wood, a physician turned field commander, took over from December 1899 until May 20, 1902. Under his rule the Americans conducted a "land reform" to clarify titles, a move destructive to peasant smallholders whose records had been destroyed during the insurrection, or who held land only by custom and tradition. The government decreed a moratorium on debt collection but then permitted claims to go through, bankrupting more small farmers. This policy was euphemistically called "creating a land market." Buyers often were Americans with cash or credit. The Foraker Amendment, an 1899 congressional measure, forbade granting concessions or licenses to Americans, but Wood finessed that by authorizing "revocable" concessions. Land was thereby confiscated and leased to companies to build railroads to ship sugar and tobacco grown on plantations in the interior, holdings that were increasingly attracting American investment.

In June 1900, Cubans voted in local elections and soon after for delegates to a constitutional convention. Or at least some Cubans voted. Secretary of War Root had instructed the military government that qualified voters must be male, twenty-one or older, Cuban citizens, and either be literate, hold property worth $250 in gold, or have served in the Cuban army before the armistice with Spain. This disenfranchised many peasants and, obviously, other poor or illiterate Cubans, and restricted the vote to the wealthier and better educated.[23] Despite the franchise rigging, and to Wood's disappointment, the annexationists among the Cubans were thoroughly defeated and Washington's efforts to control events proved flawed.

The constitutional convention of early 1901 was freely elected, if by a pinched electorate. It was not, however, entirely free to decide whatever it wanted to. The military government insisted that the Platt Amendment to the army appropriation bill of March 1901 be added to the new Cuban constitution. Root, an eminent corporate lawyer in private life, wrote all but one section, and that was authored by General (Dr.) Wood. It required that Cuban cities build sanitary systems to prevent "epidemics and infectious diseases" and thus to protect "the people and commerce of Cuba, as well as . . . the commerce of the southern ports of the United States and the people residing therein." Wood and many other Americans, particularly southerners, were well aware of the yellow fever epidemics and other contagions that had devastated American coastal cities such as Charleston and New Orleans and which, it was assumed, had been carried there by travelers from the Caribbean.

The Root-Wood-Platt provisions took away Cuba's power to make foreign treaties, or to incur any public debt that revenue would not cover. In the key Article III, Cuba had to recognize the United States' "right to intervene for the preservation of Cuban independence, the maintenance of a government adequate for the protection of life, property, and individual liberty" (not only of Cubans but of noncitizen persons and companies), and for "discharging the obligations with respect to Cuba imposed by the treaty of Paris [1899] on the United States." The military government's previous acts were "ratified and validated." Finally, Cuba promised to " sell or lease to the United States land necessary for coaling or naval stations at certain specific points to be agreed upon with the President of the United States." That became the open-ended authorization for the American naval base at Guantánamo Bay.[24] When the constitutional convention balked at these infringements on sovereignty, the Americans made clear that refusal would result in military action, that is, martial law. The convention acceded. In 1903 these provisions became part of the definitive treaty between Cuba and the United States, which also provided for trade reciprocity. Added to the railroad-building, the takeovers of land, and the Platt provisions, reciprocity became the final link in the chain tightly binding Cuba to the United States economically as well as politically.

On May 20, 1902, Tomás Estrada Palma took the oath of office as president of the Republic of Cuba. The Teller Amendment had been observed: Cuba was independent. The Spanish were gone. But the United States was very much present, watching and worrying whether annexation might still be possible or whether unsympathetic elements might begin winning elections. Another election in 1905 was condemned by the losers, the Liberal Party, as fraudulent. Uprisings threatened. To avoid them, Estrada asked the Americans to return and pacify the country, under the Platt provisions. President Theodore Roosevelt balked, but an armed uprising in August 1906 forced him to send William Howard Taft (by then secretary of war; Root had moved to State) and Assistant Secretary of State Robert Bacon to Havana to investigate and recommend. Their recommendation was to keep Estrada as president but elect a new congress, in return for the Liberals' behaving themselves. The Liberals agreed, but Estrada and his Moderates did not, and the American occupation forces had to return. They stayed until January 1909, when a newly elected government restored sufficient calm. Another uprising in Oriente (eastern Cuba) in the summer of 1917 put some railroad stations and American-owned houses and plantations to the torch. This brought back the Marines, who stayed until 1922.

By then—in fact well before then—any thoughts among American movers and shakers about annexing Cuba had evaporated. Annexation was not necessary. Cuba was already a safe place for Americans and their investments without the problems attendant on granting U.S. citizenship to Cubans, as had been done for Puerto Ricans. By 1934, not even the Platt Amendment was necessary (or worthwhile) any longer, and the United States abrogated it in May of that year. It consistently inflamed anti-American feeling, and "rather than forestalling disorder . . . [it] provided an incentive."[25] American forces occupied Cuba from 1898 to 1902, from 1906 to 1909, in 1912, and from 1917 to 1922, and the Platt protectorate lasted until 1934. Cooperative Cuban governments under the formal or informal control of Fulgencio Batista continued from 1933 until late 1958. The government of Fidel Castro that took over on January 1, 1959, was not cooperative at all, and quickly became an enormous, intolerable irritant to those Americans who personally or with historical hindsight regarded Cuba as virtually U.S. territory but without the obligations of ownership. For many Cubans, however, the Castro government realized their unfulfilled yearning for full independence, first from Spain, but then from the United States—the unfinished business, as they saw it, thwarted ever since 1898.

Were the colonial governments established by the United States in the Philippines, Puerto Rico, and other new possessions constitutional? Anti-imperialists insisted that the Constitution must follow the flag, and the rights guaranteed by it must be extended to the people of these new places. But the U.S. Supreme Court ruled otherwise, in a series of cases beginning with *Downes* v. *Bidwell*, handed down on May 27, 1901, and elaborated upon in more than thirty others over the next twenty years. A five-to-four decision, *Downes* made a distinction between "incorporated" and "unincorporated" territories. The former included the areas that had gone through, or would soon go through, the step-by-step process first outlined in the Northwest Ordinance of 1787, which took them from territorial status to statehood. Eventually these included the entire continental United States and even Alaska and Hawaii. But the "unincorporated" territories not only would not progress to statehood, but their residents would not enjoy the fullness of rights of American citizens. Secretary Root insisted that Puerto Rico, for instance, might "enjoy" its Organic Act, but that was an act created by, and solely under the discretion of, Congress, with no rights guaranteed or deemed inherent in the people of the island. The Constitution did not follow the flag.[26]

PANAMA

The United States was swiftly taking charge around the Caribbean. Puerto Rico's plain-and-simple transfer from Spain to the United States was explicitly stated in the Paris treaty of 1899. Cuba avoided annexation because the Teller Amendment was politically irreversible, but the Platt Amendment and its inclusion in the Cuban constitution rendered the country a protectorate. What remained? First, fulfillment of the long-standing dream of a canal across a narrow neck of Central America. Second, more protectorates—in the Dominican Republic, Nicaragua, and Haiti. And third, the purchase of the Virgin Islands from Denmark. The result would ensure U.S. control of the region, one way or another. European powers could keep their island possessions—Britain's Jamaica, Trinidad, Grenada, and the Bahamas; France's Guadaloupe and Martinique; the Netherlands' Curaçao and southern St. Maarten; and some smaller ones—but they must recognize the United States' "paramount interest" in the region. That they did. Jefferson, the pre-Louisiana imperialist who wrote to Robert Livingston in 1802 about how important New Orleans was to the United States, would have been astonished, proud, and fulfilled by the complete command his country had achieved over the Gulf and the Caribbean.

A centerpiece of that command was the Panama Canal. It opened for business in 1914. Theodore Roosevelt, not long after he left the White House, bragged to a congressional committee that "I took Panama." How did he manage it?

Ever since Balboa crossed Panama in 1513 to become the first European to look upon the Pacific, and since Magellan found out in 1519 how far it is to sail around South America, many dreamed of a canal across the nagging, narrow barrier of Central America. Three routes were possible: Tehuantepec, Nicaragua, or Panama. The northernmost, and therefore the closest to New Orleans and the Texas Gulf ports, was across the Isthmus of Tehuantepec in southern Mexico, a north–south stretch of about 135 miles between the Gulf of Mexico and the Pacific. It had none of Mexico's usual high mountains, at its highest point reaching only about 750 feet above sea level. Even that was beyond the engineering capabilities of the late 1840s. But the idea of a canal was mentioned during the annex-all-of-Mexico enthusiasm in early 1848, and the Gadsden Purchase treaty of late 1853 gave the United States the right to build a railroad (though not explicitly a canal) across Tehuantepec. The railroad was built some years later.

In the meantime, Secretary of State John Clayton signed a treaty in April 1850 with Britain agreeing that any isthmian canal would be built jointly by the United Kingdom and the United States. The site was not specified. By the mid-1850s, no canal was under way, but an American-built forty-seven-mile railroad opened across Panama in January 1855, meeting intense demand for a route to avoid sailing around South America to get from the eastern states to California and its newfound gold. The canal project, like other expansions, languished during the Civil War. That done, however, the indefatigable Seward negotiated a treaty with Colombia permitting a canal across Panama (then part of Colombia). It fell through; he approached Nicaragua in 1866, but he did not give up on Panama. Seward drummed up American funding in 1868 and 1869, and sent the veteran Massachusetts politician and diplomat Caleb Cushing as his agent to bring Colombia around. After two years' work, Cushing wheedled a treaty out of the Colombians in early 1869, delighting wealthy New York investors whom Seward and his friends had rounded up. Colombia was on board and the money was on the way.

But after Seward left office in March the Senate would not ratify the treaty, and the canal project slumbered again.

The opening of the Suez Canal in 1869 intensified interest. If the long sail around Africa could be avoided, couldn't the voyage around South America be shortened as well? The French company that built Suez thought so; and Ferdinand de Lesseps, the chief engineer of the Suez project, tried in the 1880s to build a canal across Panama. But Suez was a sea-level project. Panama required locks and a way to avoid the tropical diseases that could devastate and decimate whatever labor force anyone hired to do the digging. De Lesseps's Panama company could not overcome these problems, and it went bankrupt in 1889. The Nicaraguan option resurfaced. Although it would have to be more than three times the length of a Panama canal, at about 170 miles, much of it would cross natural rivers and lakes. It would require few locks, possibly none, and be basically a sea-level undertaking like Suez.

By 1900, both Panama and Nicaragua were live possibilities. With Cuba and Puerto Rico in hand, momentum for a canal surged. Two legal obstacles had to be cleared away. First, Britain agreed to cancel the Clayton-Bulwer Treaty of 1850, facing the reality of American "paramount interest" in the Caribbean. In February 1900, Secretary of State John Hay and British minister Julian Pauncefote signed a treaty freeing the United States to build a canal on its own. The Senate balked because the agreement failed to give full rights of defense to the Americans. But Hay and Pauncefote renegotiated in November 1901, correcting that "flaw," and the Senate ratified the new treaty.

The other legal obstacle was the rights of the bankrupt French company. If the United States chose the Nicaraguan route—and there was strong support for it in the government's Isthmian Canal Commission in 1899 and by early 1902 in the Senate—the French rights were worthless. But effective lobbying by the French company tilted the struggle toward Panama. On each senator's desk appeared a Nicaraguan postage stamp showing a volcano, Mount Momotombo, erupting along the proposed route. Senators also heard just then of a volcano that exploded in Martinique, killing 30,000 people. Within weeks, in June 1902, the Spooner Act authorized buying out the French company's rights for its asking price of $40 million. The United States had committed to the Panamanian route.[27]

All that remained was the matter of Colombia's sovereignty over Panama. Secretary Hay negotiated a treaty with the Colombian minister in Washington to lease to the United States a ten-kilometer-wide strip across the isthmus. The U.S. Senate ratified this in March 1903. But in August the Colombian Senate refused to do so. Yet Theodore Roosevelt, Secretary Hay, and Philippe Bunau-Varilla, the French company's agent, were not to be denied. Bunau-Varilla stirred up the ever-simmering independence movement in Panama. He met with Roosevelt, coming away with a wink-and-nod understanding that the United States would provide significant support. This included posting a U.S. Navy cruiser just off the Atlantic coast of the isthmus, to protect American persons and property—and also to prevent Colombian forces from quelling an uprising.

Long eager to become independent of Colombia and to run their own affairs, Panamanians declared themselves a republic on November 3, 1903. When Colombia tried to send troops from one coast to the other to put down the revolt, the railroad first carried the officers. It promised to bring their troops on the next train, but it never did. The Panamanian rebels arrested the officers; the troops went home; and the U.S. Navy blockaded the coast so that more Colombian forces could not land. The State Department recognized the new republic almost immediately, on November 5, and warned Colombia against further moves.

Secretary Hay drafted a "Convention for the Construction of a Ship Canal" giving the United States a lease "in perpetuity" to a zone five miles (not kilometers) on either side of a "ship canal across the Isthmus of Panama to connect the Atlantic and Pacific oceans." Bunau-Varilla, styling himself the diplomatic representative of the new republic, signed it with only one change. Hay's draft had given the United States full sovereignty within the zone, but Bunau-Varilla revised it to confer "all rights, power and authority within the zone . . . which the United States would possess and exercise *if it were* the sovereign" (italics added). Long arguments about what this meant kept surfacing for decades, but the language effectively granted control of the Canal Zone to the United States, which promised to pay the Republic of Panama $10 million upon ratification and $250,000 annually. The convention also made the new republic a protectorate of the United States, along the lines of the Cuban treaty earlier that year. Ratifications by each side were exchanged on February 26, 1904.[28] No real Panamanian ever signed that treaty, as the historian Walter LaFeber observed in his account of the gaining and giving up of the canal. When some Panamanian officials arrived in

Washington in late November, they were aghast, but the deed had been done.

THE POLICE POWER COROLLARY AND THE PROTECTORATES

The United States thus extracted protectorates on the east and west ends of the Caribbean in 1903—Cuba by adoption of the Platt Amendment, and Panama under the canal treaty. The next step in solidifying American control over the Caribbean was a unilateral declaration by President Roosevelt in December 1904 in his annual message to Congress. He claimed that it was "not true that the United States feels any land hunger or entertains any projects as regards the other nations of the Western Hemisphere save such as are for their welfare. All that this country desires is to see the neighboring countries stable, orderly, and prosperous." The word to small republics was clear and simple: keep order (no civil disturbances or threats to property) and pay your bills, and you "need fear no interference from the United States." But beware: "Chronic wrongdoing, or an impotence which results in a general loosening of the ties of civilized society, may . . . require intervention by some civilized nation, and in the Western Hemisphere . . . may lead the United States, however reluctantly, in flagrant cases of such wrongdoing or impotence, to the exercise of an international police power."

Roosevelt tied this self-bestowed license to Plattism. He continued, "If every country washed by the Caribbean Sea would show the progress in stable and just civilization, which with the aid of the Platt amendment, Cuba has shown since our troops left the island . . . all question of interference by this Nation . . . would be at an end." Definitions of "stable and just," "civilization," and other terms in the statement were of course not only American but aggressive imperialist American. They were spoken in the tradition of Jackson and Polk, and never with less embarrassment than by Theodore Roosevelt.

The chain of America's control around the Caribbean was now complete. The Cuban intervention, however well intentioned at first, produced the Platt Amendment; that in turn produced the Cuban republic as a protectorate; the Panama treaty affirmed a protectorate there; and Roosevelt's message took the process one further step, to a general policy, which came to be known as the Roosevelt or police power corollary to the Monroe Doctrine. Why was this being done? Most obviously, to defend American property and American strategic security when they were perceived to be threatened, if only potentially; and in the last analysis, because it could be done. The United States had the power. The popular president also was unshakably convinced of Anglo-Saxon racial superiority, and he aroused those atavistic and self-justifying feelings among millions of his fellow citizens. As the British historian Gordon Connell-Smith observed, "Roosevelt, with his belligerent policies and utterances (the 'Big Stick'), his unconcealed sense of Anglo-Saxon superiority and urge to play the policeman of the western hemisphere epitomized what Latin Americans would increasingly come to fear and hate."[29]

The policy was extended almost immediately to the Dominican Republic, and soon would be to Nicaragua and Haiti. In January 1905, on the heels of Roosevelt's proclamation of his police power corollary, the United States started talking with the Dominican Republic about its problems paying its debts to European powers. American planters began arriving in the 1890s, changing the small country's export crops and markets and infringing on European planter-investors. The Dominicans were indeed defaulting on their loans, and a combined European intervention was a real possibility; it was happening in Venezuela for the same reason. In February the two sides agreed to give the United States control over Dominican tax receipts and customhouses. Order and stability, civilized behavior, would reign. The U.S. Senate balked, but Roosevelt appointed a customs collector anyway, backed by warships offshore. In February 1907 a compliant Dominican government signed a treaty, creating another U.S. protectorate. More than half of the public revenue that the country—that is, its people—earned went to pay foreign debts. Nobody seems to have blamed the lenders for making bad loans or objected to foreigners' buying ownership of plantations. Default, whatever the hardship on the taxable public, had become no more an economic option than self-government was a political one. The Dominican people no longer owned or ran their own country.

Eleven years later, still not enough stability, order, and civilized behavior existed to satisfy President Woodrow Wilson and his secretary of state, William Jennings Bryan. In early 1914 they were unhappy with an interim president who would not leave office, and an empty Dominican treasury. So they maneuvered a new, legally elected government into office. Bryan's successor at State, Robert Lansing, took a harder line, appointing a financial controller in November 1915 and a new constabulary. Still more "order" was needed to prevent seething popular resentment, so hundreds of U.S. Marines (ultimately two thousand) began arriving in May 1916. The republic was wholly American-run. Wilson controlled its elections, then sent troops, and finally occupied it. The Marines stayed until 1924.[30]

Nicaragua was next. Since 1893 the country had been run by José Zelaya, who financed his quarrels with neighboring Honduras, El Salvador, and Guatemala with European loans. By 1909 his impatient creditors required him to turn over the customhouses to them. American property owners supported an indigenous uprising against Zelaya. In the process, two American citizens were killed. The Taft administration announced support of the rebels, Zelaya went into exile in Mexico, and a new government under Adolfo Díaz took over. Zelaya's was an early example of a series of U.S.-wrought regime changes.[31]

Díaz and the United States signed, in June 1911, an agreement called the Knox-Castrillo Convention, which made Nicaragua a protectorate. The United States underwrote a loan to pay off the country's creditors, with customs receipts as the collateral. The U.S. Senate balked at Knox-Castrillo, but after Zelaya's supporters attempted to return in 1912, the Taft administration sent a fleet of ships and 2,500 Marines to restore order. A new treaty (called the Bryan-Chamorro Treaty of 1914) gave the United States control over the public money. It also turned over the Corn Islands, off the country's east coast, as well as the rights to build a naval base on its Pacific coast and a canal across the country if the United States ever decided to.

The Díaz government had the support of the Wilson administration, but not of a majority of the Nicaraguan people.[32] A popular uprising in 1927 under Augusto Sandino brought back the Marines, and the Sandinistas, as their heirs were to be called, were put down. American forces departed in early 1933, entrusting the National Guard to Anastasio Somoza. Somoza killed Sandino a year later, and in 1937 claimed the presidency. He, and then two of his sons, ran Nicaragua as military dictators until the Sandinista National Liberation Front took over in 1979. Despite continued attacks by "contras" supplied by the Reagan administration, the Sandinistas remained in power until a free election in 1990 placed centrist Violeta Barrios de Chamorro in the presidency.

The protectorate system was already in trouble in 1934. It was expensive for the United States, then mired in the Great Depression, and both the Hoover and Franklin Roosevelt administrations backed away from it in the early 1930s. For the preceding two decades, however, Nicaragua's uneasy neighbors disliked the country's cozy acquiescence in American power. A Central American country had invited a U.S. protectorate. Objections would strengthen and multiply around the region through the 1920s.

Haiti with its checkered history came under the "protection" of the United States for similar reasons: inability to pay foreign debts and the threat, as perceived in Washington, of European intervention to collect them. The United States sought a Platt-type protectorate treaty in 1914 but the Haitians refused, despite the desperate shape of the country's finances. In July 1915 the president, Guillaume Sam, slaughtered more than 150 political opponents, and a revolt erupted. Washington sent a cruiser to Port-au-Prince, the capital. Rioters killed Sam. Two thousand Marines landed in August "to establish order," but in the process "nearly two thousand Haitians" died—perhaps more than ten thousand by the time the Marines departed in 1934. Meanwhile, the new U.S.-backed Haitian government agreed by treaty to turn over the public finances, which American operatives took charge of, thus running the country.[33]

To summarize: the protectorate system began with the Platt Amendment of 1901 and the insertion of it into the Cuban constitution in 1903. The Panama convention of late 1903 provided similar control there, as well as creating the Canal Zone, with its quasi-sovereignty clause. The Roosevelt police power corollary of late 1904 generalized the system to the Caribbean region. In early 1905, the Dominican Republic became a protectorate and remained so until 1924. Nicaragua's lasted from 1911 to 1924, with U.S. troops present except for a brief period until 1934. Haiti was a protectorate, with troops present, from 1915 to 1934. In none of these places did the United States annex any territory (except the Canal Zone until 1999).

Instead the United States exerted control in a new way, the protectorate device, which ironically was created as a way to get around the renunciation of power pledged by the Teller Amendment of 1898. The device was less direct but it was sufficient. It was expensive (all those Marines and ships cost money), but less so than annexation. As the 1910s and 1920s wore on, however, Washington gradually realized that the protectorate system continuously evoked popular uprisings, because it was experienced by the people as the intolerable suppression of sovereignty. That sense began with the Cuban *insurrectos* and was felt around the region, not least among those Latin Americans who were not themselves subjected to the system, but regarded it as a threat. By the mid-1920s, sometimes earlier, American policy makers knew that they did not need to send in the Marines and take over customhouses in order to achieve their goals of antirevolutionary stability and protection of American property and corporate interests. Supporting conservative or reactionary factions, politicians, and military cliques (frequently trained in the United States) did the job as well and more cheaply. This policy, in turn, "ironically helped cause revolutions in Central America" and in Cuba.[34]

The protectorates were not all alike. Nicaragua and Panama in different ways asked for American help and oversight, while the Dominican Republic and Haiti were essentially taken over as puppet states with few vestiges of sovereignty permitted.[35] But they all represented the United States' exertion of its own imperium in the region of its "paramount interest." The protectorates finally succumbed to Latin American outrage at such blatant Yankee interference. In 1930 the State Department issued a document by J. Reuben Clark, known as the Clark Memorandum, which renounced the Roosevelt corollary. Pinched financially by the Great Depression, the Hoover administration was pulling back. And in 1934, Franklin Roosevelt announced his "Good Neighbor" policy and the end of protectorates. Their successor governments, however, were often military-rightist authoritarian regimes, including Batista's in Cuba, Somoza's in Nicaragua, and Rafael Trujillo's in the Dominican Republic. Economies continued to be underdeveloped, and the announced ideals of democracy and freedom remained at best embryonic despite grand rhetoric from editors, politicians, and pundits.

FROM DENMARK, THE LAST PURCHASE

In a reversion to the typically nineteenth-century way of acquiring territory, the United States made the final acquisition to its fully sovereign areas in 1917, when it bought the Danish West Indies. They became the Virgin Islands of the United States. Forty miles east of Puerto Rico, the three principal (and several small) islands were, together, about two-thirds the size of Guam. They gave the nation no significant natural resources, but they were situated in a strategic location at the entrance to the most direct sea route into the Caribbean, and thus to the Panama Canal. Efforts to purchase them by Seward (1865–1868) and by McKinley and Theodore Roosevelt (1901–1902), as we have seen, had fallen through. Settlement, of course, was never the motive. Having a coaling station there, controlling access to the Caribbean, and preempting a strong power (possibly Germany) from taking over, were reasons enough.[36] The additions of Puerto Rico, the Cuban protectorate, and the Canal Zone only made the Danish islands more attractive, indeed seemingly essential.

The Theodore Roosevelt administration's interest stayed alive. The problem was to persuade the Danes that the Americans were not imperialists, materialists, or racists who would manhandle the largely black population of the islands. A genial American minister in Copenhagen, Maurice Francis Egan, managed to convince the Danes that Americans were in fact civilized. Nonetheless, enough reluctance remained among conservative Danes that the sale stalled, seemingly indefinitely.

The outbreak of World War I in August 1914 broke the impasse. Egan, still the American minister, feared that Germany might occupy Denmark, and its Caribbean islands as well. For their part, the Danes found themselves with an expensive budget item (the islands cost more than they earned) as well as an attractive nuisance that Germany might consider worth invading for. The United States was officially neutral early in the war, but the sinking of the British passenger liner *Lusitania* by a German submarine on May 7, 1915, tilted the Wilson administration away from professed neutrality toward the Allied side. Acquiring the Danish islands, protecting them from any possible German takeover, was increasingly urgent.

In October 1915, Secretary of State Lansing advised the Danish minister in Washington that the United States was again willing to talk about a purchase. From there the diplomatic ballet proceeded in both Copenhagen and Washington; the real questions were how much and when. Admiral George Dewey, by then the chief uniformed officer in the U.S. Navy, was asked what he thought. He replied that nearby bases in Puerto Rico were all that the navy really needed and that "the acquisition of the Danish Islands for the mere purpose of establishing a base upon which the United States fleet could rest would not be worthwhile. The Danish Islands, however, do afford harbors and anchorages . . . that would be very useful to a foreign nation conducting a campaign in the Caribbean. If that nation were an enemy of the United States the resulting situation would be exceedingly embarrassing. . . ."

In January 1916 the two countries agreed on $25 million as the price. A draft treaty went to Egan in March, and on August 4, 1916, Lansing and the Danish minister signed the sale document. The Senate, in a bipartisan vote, ratified it on September 17. The "German menace" was a powerful argument. In Denmark, approval was by no means certain, but a plebiscite in December ran almost two to one in favor. The Rigsdag approved overwhelmingly, and the king ratified the treaty on December 22. Woodrow Wilson did the same on January 16, 1917. As the treaty's historian, Charles C. Tansill, wrote, "a long and tedious chapter that had been started by Seward in January, 1865, was finally brought to a successful close."[37]

REFLECTIONS ON THE OFFSHORE EMPIRE, 1865–1934

The United States' creation of the offshore empire, its second, had almost nothing to do with the process of settlement, which characterized the first. That was still going on. Indeed, the larger part of it, both in terms of space occupied and the numbers of settlers, took place after 1865 rather than before. Historical periods do not always begin and end on a specific day or year, but often overlap, sometimes for decades. Sovereignty over the nation's continental empire was in place by the early 1850s, but settlement of it was not complete until around 1920. The offshore empire, meanwhile, began to take shape with the Alaska Purchase or even earlier. The westernmost reaches of the Louisiana Purchase, and of the Oregon country and Texas, were not settled by homesteaders until after 1900; nationally, homesteading did not peak until 1913. By then, the extensions of the second empire across the Pacific and around the Caribbean were practically complete. Annexations and protectorates were familiar by then, while settlement—the essence of the continental empire—remained confined to the continent, working out its completion.

Surprises had come in the eventful summer of 1898, so abruptly as to cause observers then, and many since, to regard that year as a critical turning-outward point in American history. It looked like a brand-new empire, in fact America's first forays into imperialism. On April 25, McKinley declared war on Spain. On May 1, Dewey destroyed the Spanish fleet in Manila Bay. On June 21, the U.S. Navy seized Guam. On July 1, Shafter's army captured the hills around Santiago de Cuba and began to lay siege to it. On July 3, Sampson destroyed the Spanish fleet at Santiago. On July 7, Congress annexed Hawaii. On August 12, Spain and the United States signed an armistice. On August 13, Ameri-

can forces captured the city of Manila. On August 14, Puerto Rico surrendered. On December 10, the Treaty of Paris was signed, giving the
Asian and Caribbean colonies of Spain to the United States and, nominally, to the Cubans. On February 4, 1899, Americans and Filipinos
went to war. Later in 1899, the United States and Germany divided up
Samoa, and the navy took over Wake Island. The Teller Amendment
deflected the annexation of Cuba, but in early 1901 the Platt Amendment provided the model for protectorates, and in that same year the
second Hay-Pauncefote treaty gave the United States a free diplomatic
hand to build its isthmian canal. All this happened within three years, all
within William McKinley's presidency.

But beneath these surprises lay continuities. Without an underlying
proclivity toward empire, an axiomatic belief in exceptionalism
(expressed as new manifest destiny, mission, racism-nativism-Anglo-
Saxonism, and the assumption that Filipinos and Cubans could not govern themselves), these extensions collectively called Empire II would not
have happened. The imperial urge was continuous, from Franklin and
Jefferson, Jackson and Polk, through Seward, McKinley, Theodore
Roosevelt, and Woodrow Wilson. The older model of outright annexation of territory was hardly discarded; Hawaii, Puerto Rico, Samoa, the
Canal Zone, and the Virgin Islands, not to mention Alaska earlier, and
the temporary anomaly of the Philippines, all speak to that. A new
model, the protectorate of the Platt Amendment kind, was now added
and employed where circumstances indicated.

Observers have wondered why English colonists who settled along
the Atlantic seaboard in the seventeenth century dealt so much more
harshly and antagonistically with the native peoples they encountered
than the French or Spanish did in their American empires. One answer
is that the English had just recently schooled themselves in imperial
methods by putting down the Irish. The incomplete subjugation of the
Irish in Elizabethan times was finished by Cromwell around 1650. The
Irish were defined as inferior, superstitious, unclean, unreformed, and in
all ways "uncivil." In short, they were savages.[38]

In contrast to Samuel de Champlain's efforts at Indian alliances in the
early years of French Canada, "early English settlers were too much in
the thrall of Ireland's example to conceive of accommodation" and
instead "followed a path that led more toward apartheid than cultural
engagement with native peoples."[39] Thus also the Pequots and Mahi-
cans of New England and the Powhatans of Virginia, the Creeks and

Seminoles confronting Jackson, the Comanches in Texas, the Lakota on the northern Plains, and all the other native peoples of North America. Thus also the Hawaiians, the Filipinos, the Cubans, and others who did not enthusiastically thank white Americans for freeing (and invading) them.

The frontier, as Frederick Jackson Turner frankly defined it in 1893, was the line between "civilization and savagery." It was the same to Americans of that historic moment whether in Luzon, Oriente Province, or the Great Plains. The frontier taught Anglo-Americans a way of dealing with other-looking people, defining them as inferior or just plain savages. This was done in the name of bringing civilization, liberty, and freedom—those very old, traditional terms and ideals—to benighted inferiors. The outward thrust continued from Empire I, the continental, through Empire II, the Pacific and Caribbean offshores. It would continue into Empire III, the virtual and global empire constructed after 1945, and it still continues—thankfully, with less of the overt and ardent racism, but with a conviction of superior righteousness still.

Historians in recent years have pointed to economic bases for all this imperialism. There can be no doubt that economics underlay a lot of it. The settlement process so important to completing the continental empire meant taking over millions of acres of land by millions of farmers and their families. It was justified in their eyes because the Native Americans so often hunted, gathered, grazed, and migrated, rather than making the "best use" of the land by farming it (though in fact many Indians did farm). The offshore empire, particularly in its early years, was commercial, and Seward said as much: the spread of civilization, liberty, freedom, across the Pacific (and anywhere else he could reach) was to be done by, for, and with the spread of American commerce. The protectorates around the Caribbean protected not just the small republics but also American interests, individual and corporate. Economics was without question part of imperialism.

But it was not the whole motivation or the deepest explanation. Sincere idealism did account for much of the urge to free Cuba, and to bring schools and sanitation to the Philippines, and, overprimly, to put coats and ties on Indian boys. Earlier, in certain parts of the United States, people believed sincerely that Indian removal and African slavery were morally justifiable and good. They had a mission, divinely or providentially sanctioned, which was manifest. Much of it, to be sure, was to acquire territory, ports, or markets, and in order to do so, the acquisitive thrust was clothed with missionary rhetoric that was expressed so vividly by Seward in his speeches and by Turner in his frontier essays. The frontier experience, ever since Plymouth and Jamestown, taught Americans a twisted ideology: that they should expand the area of civilization and shrink the area of savagery, first on the North American continent, then across the Pacific and around the Caribbean, and then around the world—the "free world." Americans recited their well-learned lesson on ever broader stages throughout the twentieth century and into the twenty-first.

The Global Empire

The GENERAL ASSEMBLY proclaims THIS UNIVERSAL DEC-
LARATION OF HUMAN RIGHTS as a common standard of achieve-
ment for all peoples and all nations, to the end that every individual and
every organ of society, keeping this Declaration constantly in mind, shall
strive by teaching and education to promote respect for these rights and
freedoms and by progressive measures, national and international, to
secure their universal and effective recognition and observance. . . .

—United Nations, "Universal Declaration
of Human Rights," December 1948[1]

Imperial Conjunctions: 1934

If world history in the twentieth century had to be confined to a single
line, it might read: two world wars, the Cold War, and population explo-
sion. Tens of millions died in wars, civil wars, and epidemics. The
empires that European governments built so laboriously and self-
righteously before 1914—British, French, Dutch, Belgian, Italian—all
collapsed within the two decades following the end of World War II in
1945. Others came and went—the German, the Ottoman, the Austro-
Hungarian, and the czarist Russian by 1918, and later, Japan's in east
Asia and the Soviet Union's in eastern Europe. The Soviet Union itself
ceased to exist in 1991, imploding from its own internal rot. Within this
global context, the United States of America was a huge success, exiting
the twentieth century much larger economically, demographically,
politically, and also imperially, than it had entered it. As of 2000, no
other country came close to it in military power; it ranked third in population behind only India and China; its economic reach was global. Its
victories in the two world wars and the Cold War did nothing to dampen
its people's convictions that they were singularly blessed; that theirs was
the optimal political and economic system; that the rest of the world
would do well to emulate it; that, in short, they were exceptional. Emu-

lation, of course, might happen by good example, or it might happen by forceful arm-twisting. Either way, the nation's underlying belief in its own exceptional virtues remained stronger than ever.

The outward thrust continued, the rhetoric of liberty and freedom needing little change. How it was to proceed took a new turn, however. From the continental empire-building of 1782 to 1853 and from the off-shore empire-building of the 1850s to 1917, the United States proceeded into a new phase. Empire III would not involve territorial acquisitions, but it would certainly involve the extension of American power—political (through treaties), military (through sowing military and naval bases around the planet), and economic (through multinational corporations and financial networks, and the supremacy of the dollar as the world's major reserve currency).

The shift from the continental and offshore forms of empire to the new, virtual-global empire took place in the context of the twentieth century's massive historical events. It was only embryonically evident during the interwar years of 1918–1939. In the 1920s and 1930s, the United States' imperial thrust languished, even ebbed. In the Caribbean, protectorates became more trouble than they were worth, and Washington stopped sending in the Marines. In the Pacific, doubts going back as far as Theodore Roosevelt about whether to keep the Philippines as a colony coalesced into relinquishing it. Within the continental United States, the true limits of agrarian settlement were finally reached, and Empire I concluded; the homestead era ended.

The year 1934 marked these shifts clearly. Amid the flurry of Franklin Roosevelt's New Deal and the disaster of the Great Depression, federal actions closed both Empire I and Empire II. Within three months, the president and Congress set the Philippines on the road to independence; abrogated the Platt Amendment for Cuba and the protectorates; and stopped virtually all further homesteading.

The blueprint for Philippine independence was laid out by Congress when it passed the Tydings-McDuffie Act on March 24, 1934. The Filipinos were to elect a convention that would write a constitution outlining a republican form of government with a bill of rights. After approval by the president of the United States, the Filipino people would vote on it. The act allowed two years for the constitution-making process, with full independence to come ten years later, in 1946. Despite World War II and the Japanese occupation of the islands, all this took place. Unpleasantly, Tydings-McDuffie also reduced Filipino immigration to the United States to only fifty people a year; and a Repatriation Act passed in 1935 authorized paying the fare for Filipinos in the United States to return home, on condition that they never come back. Prior to these acts, Filipinos could migrate freely to Hawaii or the U.S. mainland, and more than 50,000 were living and working in California and other states by the early 1930s. But after 1934, and for over thirty years until race-based immigration law changed in 1965, Filipinos were excluded. Independence was on the way, but liberty and freedom were hardly complete.[2]

The Platt Amendment was next to go. A new treaty with Cuba, dated May 29, 1934, abrogated the 1903 treaty that incorporated Platt. The base at Guantánamo Bay was specifically exempted; the permanent U.S. lease continued. Franklin Roosevelt's Good Neighbor policy was an imperfect pullback from the overbearing imperialism of 1898–1934 in Latin America. Although incomplete, however, the retreat was real.[3]

The carving of the United States' continental landmass into small farms, or "homesteads," as they were called in federal law and in common speech, had been going on since colonial times. It was Jefferson's agrarian ideal. On June 28, 1934, homesteading on U.S. public lands came to an end as the Taylor Grazing Act suppressed nearly all further homestead entries.[4] Entries had fallen off drastically during the 1920s, and a prolonged, dusty drought in the Great Plains discouraged the last hopefuls in the early 1930s. The Roosevelt administration fought the drought with several efforts at soil conservation, and the Taylor Act contained two: creating "grazing districts" to limit excessive livestock populations, and stopping any more small farms that would plow up the Plains even further. The surge of eager young farm families had finally reached the High Plains, the limits of the Louisiana Purchase. Young people, no matter how hard they worked, discovered that there was simply not enough water from the sky or under the earth to allow them to make a living on 320 or even 640 acres in that region. Henceforth the growth of America's population, and there was to be much more growth, would be almost entirely in cities and suburbs. The number of Americans multiplied six times over between 1900 and 2000, from just over 60 million to about 300 million. But the proportion living on farms or country villages dwindled from about half as recently as 1920 to 1 or 2 percent by the end of the century. Except for a few scattered exceptions, the most traditional kind of empire-building, the kind that Jefferson recognized, was finally over.

WORLD WAR II AND ITS AFTERMATH

A new sort of empire-building, unanticipated in 1939, was about to begin. In the next six to ten years, the years of World War II and its immediate aftermath, the world balance of power shifted drastically. By 1939 a militarist Japan had taken over Manchuria and much of coastal China. The Japanese then invaded the British colonies of Hong Kong, Singapore, and Burma; the Dutch in the East Indies; and soon U.S. possessions in the Philippines and the western Pacific. Nazi Germany invaded Poland; Britain and France responded by declaring war on Germany; and Europe collapsed into its second general cataclysm in twenty-five years. The Soviet Union, neutralized and bought off by the Molotov-Ribbentrop treaty of late August 1939, remained on the sidelines until Hitler, making an enormous strategic mistake, invaded it in June 1941. By then the Germans had overrun France, the Low Countries, Denmark, Norway, Poland, and Czechoslovakia, and were moving into the Balkans and across North Africa, aided by their Italian Fascist allies. Britain stood alone against Germany through 1940 and most of 1941, suffering countless bombing raids and the threat of actual invasion—Hitler's Operation Sea Lion—across the Channel in September 1940. For various reasons, Sea Lion was postponed and later abandoned. In 1940–1941, however, Britain's future appeared grim unless the United States joined the fight.

Bringing America into the war was no easy matter. Prime Minister Winston Churchill did everything he could to persuade and entice; President Franklin Roosevelt understood the Nazi threat not only to Britain but, if it succeeded there, to the Atlantic and the United States. Hobbled by neutrality laws passed during the 1930s, Roosevelt began maneuvering around them. He agreed in September 1940 to provide Britain with overage destroyers in return for American use of naval and air bases in Newfoundland, Bermuda, and the Caribbean. Selective service began in September 1940. By these and other moves, Roosevelt gradually committed the United States to material support of Britain.

Moral support came as well. Roosevelt invoked traditional rhetoric in ringing language. In his state of the union message to Congress in January 1941, the president spoke of "armed defense of democratic existence," "the democratic way of life," and added that "by an impressive expression of the public will and without regard to partisanship" (repeated three times) the United States would commit itself to "all-inclusive national defense" and "enduring peace." He concluded with one of his most famous statements, defining what was at stake: the "four essential freedoms"—of speech, of worship, from want, and from fear.[5] Eight months later, in August, Roosevelt met with Churchill at Argentia Bay, Newfoundland, and they announced "the Atlantic Charter." It was a succinct list of eight "common principles" to build "a better future for the world." Among them were "no aggrandizement, territorial or other," "no territorial changes that do not accord with the freely expressed wishes of the peoples concerned," and "abandonment of the use of force."[6] Apparently empires were passé.

Those principles were stated on the eve of what has later been called "the good war." "In no other war," historians Fred Anderson and Andrew Cayton have written, " has the American mission to extend the empire of liberty been less controversial; in no other has the rhetoric of liberation seemed more perfectly suited to circumstances."[7] The charter effectively helped rally public support. After the Japanese attack on Pearl Harbor on December 7, 1941, and Germany's declaration of war on the United States four days later, that support was virtually universal and remained so until victory in 1945.

The war ended with Germany and Japan crushed. Britain and France were nominally victorious but economically devastated and soon hard-put to maintain their prewar empires in Africa and Asia. The Soviet Union, which bore the brunt of the German Wehrmacht in northern Europe prior to the British, Canadian, and American landing in Normandy in June 1944, suffered terrible losses but found itself in May 1945 occupying eastern and central Europe as far west as the Elbe. The United States was the chief winner: sole owner of the atomic bomb; the leading force behind the creation of the United Nations; heir to Japan's northern Mariana Islands; co-occupier of Germany and Austria; and ruler of Japan. Furthermore, the United States had established land, air, and naval bases in Europe and elsewhere.

By the late 1940s, the nineteenth-century European empires started unraveling. Britain withdrew from India (and from what became Pakistan and Bangladesh) in 1947, the Dutch from Indonesia in 1949, the French from Vietnam in 1954 and Algeria in 1962, the Belgians from Congo in 1960. The United States, as promised, left the Philippines in 1946. As the traditional empires disappeared, however, a new one took shape. The Soviet Union retained control of eastern Europe as a bloc of political satellites with Marxist economies. It soon broke the Americans' nuclear monopoly and pursued what appeared to be an aggressive imperialism in south Asia, parts of Africa, and soon—to the great discomfort of American leadership—in Cuba. World politics by 1950 coalesced around two superpowers, the United States and the Soviet Union, confronting each other militarily, diplomatically, economically, ideologically, and culturally.

The blueprint for the American response to the Soviet challenge was the containment policy. Designed in late 1946 by the diplomat-historian George F. Kennan, it became public in his essay "The Sources of Soviet Conduct."[8] Its goal was to meet "an ideological-political threat emanating from Moscow," the *political* expansion of Stalinist Communism." "I did not believe," he later wrote, "that there was the slightest danger of a Soviet military attack."[9] But many in Washington did, which Kennan said he "never fully understood."[10] The invasion of South Korea by Communist North Korea in June 1950 confirmed the conviction that the Soviets would sponsor armed aggression anywhere on their perimeter. From that point on, up to the implosion of the Soviet Union in 1991, "containment" took on a military emphasis, which Kennan always opposed.

The United States had already, in 1944, led in creating international economic institutions for the postwar period, the World Bank and the International Monetary Fund. The expected replacement of Britain's pound sterling by the U.S. dollar as the world's chief reserve currency soon came to pass. Military containment arrived most vividly in 1949 with the creation of the North Atlantic Treaty Organization by the United States and eleven other governments, the United States' first broad mutual defense treaty. Other mutual defense treaties followed over the next two decades, forming a ring of alliances, "containing" and opposing the Soviet Union across the Pacific, the southern rim of Asia, and Latin America.[11] The U.S. president became "the leader of the free world." The traditional American rhetoric of "liberty" and "freedom" could be heard again and again as justifications for containing Communism in Korea and then in Vietnam, for ever larger Pentagon budgets, and for the overthrow of regimes in the Western Hemisphere or elsewhere that Washington regarded as leaning toward Communism or Soviet infiltration. The Korean War was at least initially understandable as a military extension of containment, waged out of the conviction that the invasion from the north was inspired from Moscow and Beijing, which were assumed (wrongly) to be acting in concert. While the results—including 53,000 dead Americans—hardly amounted to a total success for the United States, the engagement achieved no small outcome: the liberation of South Korea. A cease-fire in Korea came in late July 1953, early in the presidency of Dwight D. Eisenhower.

During his eight years in office, containment remained the United States' basic policy vis-à-vis the Soviet Union, but it became ever more militarized. Just before leaving office in 1961, Eisenhower—the most recent of the several generals who became presidents—repeated the rhetoric of peace, progress, and liberty. While recognizing that "a vital element in keeping the peace is our military establishment," Eisenhower warned that "the conjunction of an immense military establishment and a large arms industry is new in the American experience." Therefore "we must guard against the acquisition of unwarranted influence, whether sought or unsought, by the military-industrial complex. The potential for the disastrous rise of misplaced power exists and will persist."[12]

The Eisenhower administration had already begun supporting the government of South Vietnam with economic and counterinsurgency aid. The United States refused to proceed with free elections as it had agreed to, fearing (probably correctly) a Communist victory. As Eisenhower was leaving office, plans were well along to invade Cuba at the Bay of Pigs. That went disastrously awry in April 1961, four months after John F. Kennedy became president. In that instance, "regime change" failed.

Involvement in Vietnam increased under Kennedy and swelled under Lyndon Johnson to more than 550,000 troops. Following two almost certainly mythical attacks on American destroyers off North Vietnam on August 2 and 4, 1964, Johnson asked for, and Congress provided, authorization to "take all necessary steps" to "prevent further aggression" against American forces and to help a SEATO ally. The huge American investment did not result in even a Korea-like standoff. In its zeal for containment, its reliance on military power to carry it out, its fear that if Vietnam "fell" the rest of southeast Asia would fall "like dominoes," and its ignorance of the history and culture of Vietnam, Washington essentially took over from France as the colonial occupier. After more than a dozen years of fighting and the deaths of more than 58,000 Americans and over a million Vietnamese, the United States pulled out. As Kennan and many others said, the invasion was an enormous blunder. It was the country's first real loss in a war since the 1812–1814 conflict. "Vietnam fatigue" followed, a turning away from military adventures lasting for several years.

From the Korean War onward, the containment policy developed as a justification for American interventions and, often enough, "regime change." So it was in Iran in 1953, when the elected nationalist Mohammed Mossadegh was thrust aside and replaced with the Shah; in Guatemala in 1954, also replacing a democratically elected government; in South Vietnam in 1963, where Ngo Dinh Diem was deposed; in Chile in 1973, where the elected president Salvador Allende was assassinated and replaced by General Augusto Pinochet. The U.S. Central Intelligence Agency engineered or was involved in most if not all of these coups. Military invasions toppled the governments of Grenada in 1983 and Panama in 1989.[13] "Containment" of Communism, or anything remotely resembling it, became the perennial face of American policy during the Cold War. It meant armed intervention or, more often, establishing in power an authoritarian right-wing government, and building American military bases to ensure stability. From one angle, it looked like the post-1898 protectorate policy writ large, and it often was. Containment-as-imperialism took the United States into space and into the disastrous Vietnam intervention in the 1960s, clothed in "the classic idiom of the frontier"—Kennedy's "New Frontier," space as "the final frontier."[14]

Countering Vietnam fatigue, the political scientist Jeane J. Kirkpatrick published an influential essay in late 1979. She argued that the United States should distinguish between totalitarian and authoritarian regimes, always opposing the former but often embracing the latter, which "are less repressive . . . more susceptible of liberalization, and . . . more compatible with U.S. interests."[15] Ronald Reagan was much taken with this distinction, and his administration sold arms to Iran to raise money to support the anti-Sandinista "contras" in Nicaragua, money that Congress balked at providing. In Central America, any regimes or movements identified by Washington as leftist were presumed to be (or to become) Communist; those on the right therefore deserved support by almost any available means. In the region, such was the United States' approach. The urgency and reality of the Soviet nuclear threat added an almost unarguable justification for extending American military power, covert or open.

After the Cold War, a Peace Dividend?

The collapse of the Berlin Wall in 1989 and the implosion of the Soviet Union itself in 1991 brought the Cold War to its end. Containment had worked. When Soviet premier Mikhail Gorbachev denied support in 1989 to the East German government of Erich Honecker, the Wall fell. Within months so did the satellite governments of eastern Europe, and two years later, the USSR itself, from its internal economic, social, and political weaknesses.[16] Many people expected a "peace dividend," that NATO and the other regional defense alliances would wind down and disappear, that the American presence in so many military bases around the world would end, and that the tens of thousands of troops still in Korea, Okinawa, Germany, and elsewhere would come home, that Pentagon budgets would finally come down. None of that happened. The Cold War had ingrained a Manichaean mind-set, pitting the United States, the good force in the world, against the bad force, the Soviet Union.[17] When the Wall fell and the "velvet revolution" bloodlessly ended one Communist regime after another in eastern Europe, and then the Soviet Union itself, the longtime bad force was gone. Through the 1990s, no definite "bad force" lurked.

With the terrorist attacks of September 11, 2001, the symmetry was reestablished. Jihadism, international terrorism, radical Islam, "the clash of civilizations," overgeneralized and overreacted to, justified overseas interventions as easily as "international Communism" had done for over forty years. The Communist enemy was now replaced by the terrorist enemy.[18] After 9/11 came the invasion of Afghanistan and overthrow of its Taliban government, a legitimate response to the Al Qaida attackers insofar as they were state-based at all.

No purpose would be served here in drawing out all the permutations of American imperialism since 1989 or 1991, or in critiquing the Gulf and Iraq wars. Many others have discussed them in detail. We need only review some broad points. There was no significant peace dividend. The military form of internationalism strengthened, while "softer" kinds languished. U.S. Information Service libraries and cultural programs, for example, were reduced or closed; the U.S. Information Agency itself was abolished in 1999. Economic imperialism broadened during the 1990s into globalization, defined by one historian as "a process whereby American-style market economics engulfed nearly the entire world" in a manner similar to how white Americans put Indians' land "to better use" in the 1800s.[19]

No letup took place during the 1990s in establishing and staffing U.S. military, naval, and air bases domestically and around the world. The Cold War alliances continued in place. In fact, NATO was extended far beyond western Europe to within the borders of the former Soviet Union. NATO troops patrolled Afghanistan (or parts of it) after 9/11. Analysts described how decision makers around the world were bypassing American ambassadors and instead consulting the generals and colonels in charge of the nearby bases.[20] In 2002 the administration of George W. Bush announced a "National Security Strategy" asserting the American president's prerogative of starting preventive wars at his own discretion to promote and preserve "freedom, democracy, and free enterprise," using "unparalleled military strength and great economic and political influence."[21] Early in 2003 the Bush administration invaded Iraq, tying its regime to terrorism and weapons of mass destruction. These charges were in error and soon proved to be false, as were the stated reasons James K. Polk gave when he invaded Mexico, and when Lyndon B. Johnson claimed attacks on U.S. ships in the Gulf of Tonkin by North Vietnamese patrol boats in 1964. The powers of the president as commander in chief of the armed forces (and nationalized National Guard units) proved difficult to rein in, whether in 1846, 1964, or 2003. The Constitution gives Congress the purse strings and gives the president the military, but nothing prevents the president from deploying the troops before Congress can say no. Once they are deployed, Congress is politically snookered. So it was in 1846, and so it was again after 2003.[22]

Imperialism requires an emperor, in form if not name, and the American slouch into global imperialism has been accompanied by an augmentation of the power of the executive branch. Madison's behind-closed-doors support of the Florida filibusters was an early case. George W. Bush's many secrecies are contemporary ones. In between, there was Polk, who at least secured a declaration of war from Congress, which neither Truman in Korea, Johnson for Vietnam, nor the Bushes in Kuwait and Iraq did, acting instead on "authorizations."

Empire III, the global empire, extended by the early 2000s far beyond what earlier empire builders like Jefferson, John Quincy Adams, Polk, or even McKinley and Theodore Roosevelt could have hoped for. Exactly what kind of an empire it is, and how it compares with previous ones like Rome or Britain, is much argued. It is generally agreed that the United

States exercises, or could exercise, unparalleled power, at least of certain sorts, and without direct territorial absorption or even protectorate-like control. Perhaps the most sensible view is that, as the European Union is something new "for which we have not yet found a name," so too is the American empire. Some have drawn parallels to the history of Rome or Britain. Some exist, yet the American empire is unprecedented.[23]

Few observers doubt that a military-based empire existed by the time of the Iraq war. Books have proliferated, arguing that it does. They divide as to whether American empire is good or bad for the United States or the world. Both sides counted well more than seven hundred American military bases around the world and tens of thousands of troops stationed in Germany, Japan, and South Korea. There was no argument about the extent of the U.S. military reach.[24]

THE HABIT (AND RHETORIC) OF EMPIRE

The "why" of the American empire's existence can be explained both as the momentum of historical developments and more philosophically. Recent history records the sheer moment of inertia of Pentagon budgets, the political untouchableness of the military, the economic benefit of bases to hundreds of localities, and the repetition of traditional rhetorical ideals like "freedom" and "liberty." Philosophically, such world-historical power, and whether the United States was falling into "imperial overreach,"[25] were much argued. Was the republic losing its grip on first principles—no standing army, no entangling alliances, checks and balances between president and Congress, limits on power, the rule of law including humane treatment of prisoners, habeas corpus, and minimal government intrusion into citizens' lives? Were the imperatives of empire—same basic word—snuffing out the Bill of Rights and constitutional checks and balances?

The traditional consensus persisted that America has a unique set of values, way of life, and form of government to offer the world. But the consensus then divided, as it always had, between those who believed those goods were best spread benignly, by example, or assertively, by force. As the country and empire entered the new millennium, the forceful path clearly dominated the exemplary path. Lincoln's "last best hope of earth" would be made known, more than in any other way, by those hundreds of bases and hundreds of thousands of troops deployed all around the world.

Americans have been reluctant, as many have pointed out, to own up that theirs is an imperial nation. Jefferson talked of an "empire for liberty," but most have traditionally shunned the fact that the United States has been imperial and expansionist, and aggressively so. One reason may be that they have understood from the Roman example and more recently, the British, that empires decline and fall. But frontiers (including settlement frontiers), missions, and manifest destinies are not supposed to. Instead they expand. Indefinitely. The American experience and purpose, seen as the "expansion of the area of free land" and the replacement of "savagery" with "civilization," as Frederick Jackson Turner phrased it in 1893 and as a great many Americans before and since have almost instinctively believed, was all about beginnings, not endings. Americans still think about beginnings and deny endings. They are future-oriented.[26] Admitting to being an empire would be admitting that the United States some day, in some way, will decline and fall. But that would contradict the nation's historic sense of mission. How could the United States spread liberty, democracy, freedom, and free enterprise if it declined and fell? Those are perennial values, part of human rights and of human nature at its best, are they not?

As Turner wrote in 1896, "For nearly three centuries the dominant fact in American life has been expansion."[27] He by no means gave the expansion process a clean bill of health; he recognized how grimy and rough it was. But he regarded expansion as inevitable and good. With the benefit of early-twenty-first-century hindsight, one may think otherwise. The significance of the frontier in American history, to redirect Turner's famous thesis, may well be that it instilled in Americans bad habits of building empires.[28] Without the easy victories of the continental conquest, Americans might have paused and reflected before extending themselves across the western and southern oceans and, after 1945, around the world.

This history of national expansion reveals that it has not always been clean. America's preeminence, even its very territory, frequently resulted from force, subterfuge, or other reprehensible means, often varnished over by the language of liberty, freedom, and such terminology familiar since Jefferson, rephrased by Lincoln, and repeated in the American-inspired United Nations Universal Declaration of Human Rights. The beautiful rhetoric expresses the ideals of the republic. But the unspoken, unadmitted reality was and is that of an empire.

History cannot be rewound. What has happened cannot be repealed. But Americans can and should realize that they have behaved imperially, in the blameworthy sense that their hands have often been dirty. They should understand that their claim to exceptionalism is valid only in terms of their unparalleled growth and the remarkable natural resources their vast country has provided them. They are not exceptional, however, in any sense of moral innocence or purity. Since its beginning the United States has oscillated between republic and empire, the institutions and ideals of the first coexisting uneasily with the behavior of the second. The rhetoric of the republic continues, but the realities of statecraft, with wide popular support, have become increasingly imperial. The past is indeed irreversible, but the future demands a choice, and a historically informed one: republic or empire? The balance, never perfect, present since the country's first days, has been perilously tipping.

Notes

These notes cite works briefly, by author, title, and date.
For full citations, please consult the bibliography that follows.

FOREWORD

1. Few historians have connected America's continental and overseas empires. William Appleman Williams did so in several works, most extensively in *The Roots of the Modern American Empire* (1969). Williams understood that the acquisition and settlement of the West was empire-building, which he defined simply as "the use and abuse, and the ignoring, of other people for one's own welfare and convenience." He stressed Americans' search for overseas markets as a motivator of empire more than I do, but he correctly pointed out the most basic reason, and its frontier roots: "We are different only because we acquired the empire at a very low cost, because the rewards have been enormous and because until now we have masked our imperial truth with the rhetoric of freedom." "Empire as a Way of Life" (1980). Patricia Nelson Limerick also grasped the continuity of empire-building in *The Legacy of Conquest: The Unbroken Past of the American West* (1987); see also her "Dilemmas in Forgiveness: William Appleman Williams and Western American History" (2001), 293–300. These historians, however, did not treat each specific acquisition since 1782 as part of a connected narrative, as this book does.

2. For some comparisons see Walter Nugent, "Frontiers and Empires in the Late Nineteenth Century" (1989) and "Comparing Wests and Frontiers" (1994).

3. *Congressional Globe*, 29th Cong., 1st sess., 180 (January 10, 1846). Kennedy was a Democrat, representing the northeast corner of Indiana, from Fort Wayne to the Michigan and Ohio borders.

1. TRANSAPPALACHIA, 1782: FIRST LAND, FIRST GOOD FORTUNE

1. The Count of Aranda, Pedro Abarca de Bolea, was the Spanish ambassador in Paris during the peace talks. The full quotation is: "This federal Republic was born a pygmy, as such, it needed the aid and strength of two powerful states like Spain and France to accomplish its independence. The day will come when it will grow up, become a giant and be greatly feared in the Americas. Then it will forget the benefits that it had received from the two powers and only think [of] its own aggrandizement." From Thomas E. Chávez, *Spain and the Independence of the United States* (2002), 212. Chávez's source is a biography: Carmen de Reparaz, *Yo Solo: Bernardo de Gálvez y la Toma de Panzacola en 1781* (1986). Reparaz (p. 23) calls the quote "un famoso memorial atribuido a Aranda"—"a famous statement attributed to Aranda"—so it may be apocryphal. Nevertheless, it is well put.

2. William M. Van der Weyde, ed., *The Life and Works of Thomas Paine* (1925), 2:174–75.

3. Quoted in Don Gillmor and Pierre Turgeon, *Canada: A People's History* (2001), 1:142.

4. *Journals of the Continental Congress, 1774–1789* (1904), 1 (1774): 81, 83, 87, 88, 103, 112, 113; also, 2 (1775): 69 (May 29).

5. Walter Stahr, *John Jay: Founding Father* (2005), 6. Stahr discusses the "Address to the People of Great Britain" (47) but not the "Lettre" to the Quebecois.

6. "Conjectural": Russell Thornton's word, in "Population History of Native North Americans" (2000), 23. The numbers are an interpolation from the table in Douglas Ubelaker, "North American Indian Population Size: Changing Perspectives" (1992), 173.

7. The standard history is now Gregory Evans Dowd, *War under Heaven: Pontiac, the Indian Nations, & the British Empire* (2002).

8. Stahr, *John Jay: Founding Father*, 97.

9. For the war's military history see Christopher Ward, *The War of the Revolution* (1952); and Howard H. Peckham, *The War for Independence: A Military History* (1958). On the Montreal occupation (and quotation), see Gillmor and Turgeon, *Canada*, 1:152.

10. Dwight L. Smith, "The Old Northwest and the Peace Negotiations" (1977), 98. For the letter of Petre Sarget to Franklin, see Barbara B. Oberg, ed., *The Papers of Benjamin Franklin* (1993), 30:65–66; and Lewis J. Carey, "Franklin Is Informed of Clark's Activities in the Old Northwest" (1934–1935), 375–78. The French and Spanish took into account the influx of settlers, but not Clark's maneuvers.

11. Bradford Perkins, *The Creation of a Republican Empire, 1776–1865* (1993), 41.

12. Joseph J. Ellis, *His Excellency: George Washington* (2004), 127.

13. Jay's instructions, and the lengthy and blustery rationales with which Congress accompanied them, are in *Journals of the Continental Congress, 1774–1789* (1904), 18 (1780): 900–2, 935–47.

14. Jay and his wife, Sally, after more than two years of frustration at not being received at court and getting nowhere on boundary claims, left for Paris with alacrity. Congress also named Thomas Jefferson and Henry Laurens to the team, but Jefferson (whose wife was dying) declined to go and Laurens was captured on the trip over and spent until late November 1782 in the Tower of London.

15. Quoted in David R. Chesnutt and C. James Taylor, eds., *The Papers of Henry Laurens* (2000), 15: 461.

16. Livingston to Franklin, Philadelphia, January 7, 1782, in Ellen R. Cohn, ed., *The Papers of Benjamin Franklin* (2001), 36: 390–91.

17. María Pilar Ruigómez de Hernández, *El gobierno español del despotismo ilustrado ante la independencia de los Estados Unidos de America . . . (1773–1783)* (1978), 312–13: "inteligente prudencia de Franklin y la exaltación temeraria de John Jay." Spain's contributions came from its colonies too—from California, Sonora, Texas. Gálvez "executed the king's orders with *brillo*" and he won "stunning victories on the Mississippi and the Gulf," writes David J. Weber in his authoritative *The Spanish Frontier in North America* (1992), 266–70 (quotes, 267–68). For more detail see Francisco Morales Padron, *Spanish Help in American Independence* (1952); and Chávez, *Spain and the Independence of the United States.*

18. Lord Fitzmaurice (Edmond George Petty Fitzmaurice), *Life of William Earl of Shelburne, afterwards First Marquess of Landsdowne* (1912), 2:118.

19. C. R. Ritcheson, "The Earl of Shelburne and Peace with America, 1782–1783: Vision and Reality" (1983), 336; Vincent T. Harlow, *The Founding of the Second British Empire, 1763–1793* (1952), 249.

20. Oswald to Shelburne, Paris, July 10, 1782, reprinted in Mary E. Giunta, ed., *Documents of the Emerging Nation: U.S. Foreign Relations, 1775–1789* (1998), 88–89.

21. Vergennes' actions and objectives in the summer and fall of 1782 are detailed in Orville T. Murphy, *Charles Gravier, Comte de Vergennes* (1982), chap. 31, esp. 388–93.

22. The quoted words are Harlow's, *Founding of the Second British Empire*, 280.

23. Rayneval to Jay, Paris, September 6, 1782, in Richard B. Morris, ed., *John Jay: The Winning of the Peace: Unpublished Papers, 1780–1784* (1980), 2:331–32.

24. Harlow, *Founding of the Second British Empire*, 284.

25. Oswald to Townshend, Paris, October 2, 1781, in Morris, *John Jay*, 2:374.

26. Andrew Stockley, *Britain and France at the Birth of America: The European Powers and the Peace Negotiations of 1782–1783* (2001), 69. Stahr, Jay's biographer, agrees that "this was remarkable: he was urging Britain, with which America was still technically at war, to attack Spain, with which it was aligned if not allied." *John Jay: Founding Father*, 159.

27. Morris, *John Jay*, 2:451.

28. Ibid., 2:413 (Strachey to Townshend, Calais, November 8, 1782) and 2:415, the November 7 revised draft.

29. Harlow, *Founding of the Second British Empire*, 299, 303.

30. The position of the "patriot historians" appears in Morris's *John Jay* and *The Peacemakers* (1965) and Bemis, *The Diplomacy of the American Revolution* (1957). The more recent historians who suggest the Americans receded from the Nipissing Line too easily include Lawrence S. Kaplan, "The Treaty of Paris, 1783: A Historiographical Challenge" (1983), 436–37, citing an unpublished paper by Professor Bradford Perkins, who argued "Britain's readiness to relinquish the Nipissing country, present-day southern Ontario." Perkins elaborates on this in *The Creation of a Republican Empire*, 38–41, 44. Stockley, *Britain and France*, 64, agrees: "The Americans . . . backed down . . . and thereby failed to gain the 'Nipissing country.' "

31. Jonathan Dull, "Benjamin Franklin and the Nature of American Diplomacy" (1983), 351.

32. Morris, *John Jay*, 2:431.

33. Quoted in many places; in French it appears in Stockley, *Britain and France*, 65.

34. Harlow, *Founding of the Second British Empire*, 431, 433.

35. Ohio, Indiana, Illinois, Michigan, Wisconsin, and about a third of Minnesota in the Northwest; Kentucky, Tennessee, West Virginia, Alabama, and Mississippi to the south. This does not include Florida or Louisiana, which were not within the 1783 boundary.

2: LOUISIANA, 1803: SECOND GOOD LUCK

1. [François] Barbé-Marbois, *The History of Louisiana, particularly of the Cession of That Colony to the United States of America . . .* (1830), 310.

2. Robert R. Livingston to [Secretary of State] James Madison, Paris, May 20, 1803,

in David B. Mattern et al., eds., *The Papers of James Madison: Secretary of State Series*, vol. 5, *16 May–31 October 1803* (2000), 19.

3. Quoted in Reginald Horsman, *Expansion and American Indian Policy, 1783–1812* (1992 [1967]), 86.

4. Andrew R. L. Cayton, *Frontier Indiana* (1996), 138–39.

5. José A. Armillas Vicente, *El Mississippi, frontera de España: España y los Estados Unidos ante el tratado de San Lorenzo* (1977), 8–9, 93. Translations mine. For an overview of Spanish policy on the lower Mississippi and how European events affected it, see Paul E. Hoffman, "A History of Louisiana before 1813" (1996), 229–52.

6. Carondelet to Conde de Aranda, not dated but probably about September 1793, original in Archivo General Central in Alcala de Henares, Spain, in Louis Houck, *The Spanish Regime in Missouri* (1971 [1909]), 2:11–12.

7. Armillas Vicente, *El Mississippi*, 92, 173, 176.

8. John Mack Faragher, *Daniel Boone: The Life and Legend of an American Pioneer* (1992), esp. chap. 8.

9. Martin estimated the Caddos west of New Orleans at 500 warriors; the Transappalachian refugees (Delawares, Shawnees, Miamis, and others) around Cape Girardeau and New Madrid at 500 families (i.e., perhaps 2,500 people); Choctaws in the lower Mississippi Valley, 400–500 families; and unnumbered Osages west of St. Louis, whom he regarded as "cruel, treacherous, and insolent." A few years later Brackenridge also considered the Osage to be the dominant Missouri Valley nation and also thought them "warlike . . . treacherous and cowardly." He estimated the Osage at 5,500; the three bands of Pawnees, 5,100; Arikaras, 3,000; Mandans, 2,000; Blackfeet, 5,500; "Camanches," 8,000; "Algonquins," 5,000; "Chippoways," 4,000; and "Chactas" (Choctaws), 5,500. F.-X. Martin, *The History of Louisiana, from the Earliest Period* (1829), 2:205–8; H. M. Brackinridge, *Views of Louisiana* (1814), 72–88.

10. Brackinridge, *Views of Louisiana*, 69.

11. Alexander DeConde, *This Affair of Louisiana* (1976), 105, citing St.-Cyr to Cevallos, July 12, 1802, in *American State Papers, Foreign Relations*, 2:569.

12. Bernard Lugan, *La Louisiane Française, 1682–1804* (1994), 204.

13. Thierry Lentz, *Le Grand Consulat* (1999), 480, 495; DeConde, *This Affair of Louisiana*, 103. Different writers give different figures on the army's exact size, but all agree that more than 90 percent were killed in battle or by yellow fever.

14. Jefferson to Livingston, Washington, April 18, 1802, in Henry Steele Commager, *Documents of American History* (1963), 1:189.

15. *Annals of Congress* (1803), 7th Cong., 2d sess., 1059, 1062.

16. George Dangerfield, *Chancellor Robert R. Livingston of New York, 1746–1812* (1960), 358.

17. Ibid., 353.

18. DeConde, *This Affair of Louisiana*, 142–45; Elena Sánchez-Fabrés Mirat, *Situ-ación histórica de Las Floridas en la segunda mitad del siglo XVIII (1783–1819)* (1977), 247.

19. Madison to Livingston, January 18, 1803, in *Annals of Congress* (1803), 7th Cong., 2d sess., 1063–64.

20. Albert H. Bowman, "Pichon, the United States, and Louisiana" (1977), 266.

21. Livingston to Madison, Paris, and to Talleyrand and Joseph Bonaparte, February 18, 1803, and to Napoleon, February 27, 1803, in *Annals of Congress* (1803), 7th Cong., 2d sess., 1076–86, 1089–94.

22. Livingston to Madison, Paris, April 11, 1803, in *Annals of Congress* (1803), 7th Cong., 2d sess., 1126–27.

23. Barbé-Marbois, *History of Louisiana*, 263–64. Barbé-Marbois had served in the French ministry in Philadelphia during the 1782 peace negotiations. This book, which he published in French in 1829 and which was quickly translated, was written twenty-some years after the Purchase, as was the only other eyewitness participant's account, James Monroe's *Autobiography*. One must therefore allow for vagaries of memory in both. But Barbé-Marbois was intelligent and unbiased and his account corresponds with letters and documents from the time of the events.

24. Ibid., 263–64, 274–75, 277.

25. Livingston to Madison, Paris, April 13, 1803, in *Annals of Congress* (1803), 7th Cong., 2d sess., 1128–32.

26. The texts are in Peter J. Kastor, ed., *The Louisiana Purchase* (2002), 143–48.

27. U.S. Bureau of the Census, *Historical Statistics of the United States* (1975), 2:1104; DeConde, *This Affair of Louisiana*, 172–73; *Annals of Congress* (1851), 7th Cong., 2d sess., 1145–48. The actual signings of the documents and the English translations took place on May 2 and a few days later. Napoleon personally ratified them on May 22. Barbé-Marbois, *History of Louisiana*, 315.

28. *Annals of Congress* (1803–1804), 8th Cong., 1st sess., 11–14, 419–20, 432–88, 497–515, 546, 549, 781–82. After the 59–57 vote on October 24, subsequent favorable votes in the House were 60–15, 89–23, 85–7, and 88–13.

29. Gary Lawson and Guy Seidman, *The Constitution of Empire: Territorial Expansion and American Legal History* (2004), which analyzes the constitutionality of the territorial acquisitions, says that the Louisiana Purchase "easily passes" the constitutional test, though some later acquisitions are questionable or (in the case of the Philippine Islands) fail it; see their chap. 1, "Fundamentals: Lessons from Louisiana," 17–85 (quote, 5).

30. Henry Adams, *History of the United States of America during the First Administration of Thomas Jefferson* (1903), 2:56.

31. DeConde, *This Affair of Louisiana*, 194.

32. *Annals of Congress* (1803–1804), 8th Cong., 1st sess., 569. Also in Mattern et al., eds., *Papers of James Madison; Secretary of State Series*, 5:378, 464. Yrujo's notes were anything but a "caviling protest," as a modern-day historian claimed: Merrill D. Peterson, *Thomas Jefferson and the New Nation: A Biography* (1970), 775.

33. *Papers of James Madison*, 5:488–89.

34. DeConde's words, *This Affair of Louisiana*, 194.

35. *Annals of Congress* (1803–1804), 8th Cong., 1st sess., 2:570.

36. *Annals of Congress* (1803), 7th Cong., 2d sess., 1179.

37. E. Wilson Lyon, *Louisiana in French Diplomacy, 1759–1804* (1934), 231.

38. Barbé-Marbois, *History of Louisiana*, 297–98.

39. DeConde's incisive summation, *This Affair of Louisiana*, 202–3, 208.

40. Livingston to Madison, Paris, May 20, 1803, in *Papers of James Madison, Secretary of State Series*, 5:19.

41. F.-X. Martin, *History of Louisiana*, 2:193–200.

42. Martin, "Population Estimates for Louisiana, 1803," in Kastor, ed., *Louisiana Purchase*, 261–62.

43. Ibid., 273.

44. Gilbert Din, *Spaniards, Planters, and Slaves: The Spanish Regulation of Slavery in Louisiana, 1763–1803* (1999), 220–36.

45. Barbé-Marbois writes, "Six or seven thousand whites, who were received on board the English fleet [lying offshore], considered themselves fortunate in having thus got away from the fury of the rebels." *History of Louisiana*, 198.

46. L. Lagny, *La Cession de la Louisiane* (1968), 7–8, 87.

47. Lugan, *La Louisiane Française*, 217.

48. For the full story see Stephen Aron, *American Confluence: The Missouri Frontier from Borderland to Border State* (2005).

49. On Dehahuit and the Caddos, see Peter J. Kastor, "Dehahuit and the Question of Change in North America" (2002), 74–89. Also, F. Todd Smith, *The Caddo Indians, 1542–1854* (1995).

3. CANADA, 1812–1814: FAILED AGGRESSION NORTHWARD

1. In Thomas Jefferson Papers, Library of Congress.

2. The word "Canada" referred to what are now the provinces of Quebec and Ontario. In 1791 "Canada"—up to then, Quebec—was divided into "Lower Canada" (later Quebec) and "Upper Canada" (later Ontario).

3. Jefferson to William Duane [Monticello?], August 4, 1812. Jefferson Papers, LC, reel 46, series 1, no. 182. Jefferson wrote in the same vein to Kościuszko the next day (ibid., no. 183) and on June 28, 1812 (no. 176).

4. Patrick C. T. White, *A Nation on Trial: America and the War of 1812* (1965), 36.

5. American historians have argued for decades about the causes of the War of 1812. Was it primarily for westward expansion or the maritime issues? I find Reginald Horsman's position most persuasive:

> Even had there been no Indian problem, it seems likely that America would have gone to war in 1812. The increasing demand for war after 1809 arose naturally out of the failure of economic coercion as a means of resisting British maritime policy. The idea of conquering Canada had been present since at least 1807 as a means of forcing England to change her policy at sea. The conquest of Canada was primarily a means of waging war, not a reason for starting it. America in 1812 was acting essentially in reaction to British maritime policy. This British policy [laid out in "Orders in Council"], though influenced by jealousy of American commercial growth, stemmed primarily from the necessity of waging war against France. Had there been no war with France, there would have been no Orders in Council, no impressments, and, in all probability, no War of 1812. (Horsman, *The Causes of the War of 1812* [1962], 267)

A later and very illuminating essay by Horsman on the Canadian aspect is "On to Canada: Manifest Destiny and United States Strategy in the War of 1812" (1987), 1–24. To Canadian historians, of course, the invasion itself has been of primary concern, and the maritime issues only a "smokescreen for the conquest of

Canada." This is plausible. Congress's vote for war, and popular support for it, rested on both the maritime trade and impressment matters and on annexationism.

6. *Annals of Congress* (1811–1812), 12th Cong., 1st sess., 424, 427, 457–59, 466–67, 490, 515.

7. Ibid., 498, 533.

8. Reginald Horsman, "Who Were the War Hawks?" (1964), 121–36, the best analysis, congressman by congressman, vote by vote; William R. Barlow, "Ohio's Congressmen and the War of 1812" (1963), 175–94.

9. J. C. A. Stagg, "Between Black Rock and a Hard Place: Peter B. Porter's Plan for an American Invasion of Canada in 1812" (1999), 385–422, uses new evidence to analyze Porter's motives as of April 1812. His business interests favored building a canal from the Hudson to Lake Ontario (via Oswego) rather than to Lake Erie, and keeping commercial traffic away from Quebec via the St. Lawrence.

10. Leland R. Johnson, "The Suspense Was Hell: The Senate Vote for War in 1812" (1969), 247–67.

11. Carl Benn, *The Iroquois in the War of 1812* (1998), is a thoughtful monograph on Canada's Indian allies.

12. Reginald Horsman's "On to Canada," 15–21, laid out the annexationism of 1813 and documented it with the quotations from Jefferson (the emphasis on "cession" is mine), Matthew Clay, and Henry Clay. The annexation idea, pro and con, is also discussed in Reginald C. Stuart, *United States Expansionism and British North America, 1775–1871* (1988), 61–65, 76.

13. The American team insisted that the Paris treaties were "a permanent compact, not liable, like ordinary treaties, to be abrogated by a subsequent war between the parties." Donald R. Hickey, *Don't Give Up the Ship! Myths of the War of 1812* (2006), 293.

14. Henry Goulburn to Lord Bathurst (secretary for war and the colonies), September 16, 1814, as quoted in Charles M. Gates, "The West in American Diplomacy, 1812–1815" (1940), 506. Francis M. Carroll, *A Good and Wise Measure: The Search for the Canadian-American Boundary, 1783–1842* (2001), 23–31, describes the Ghent negotiations well.

15. Colin G. Calloway, "The End of an Era: British-Indian Relations in the Great Lakes Region after the War of 1812" (1986), 1–20.

16. Jane Errington, *The Lion, the Eagle, and Upper Canada* (1987), 86.

17. Donald W. Meinig, *The Shaping of America: A Geographical Perspective on 500 Years of History*, vol. 2, *Continental America, 1800–1867* (1993), 49–50.

18. *Ottawa Citizen*, November 12, 2003, as reproduced on History News Network, November 14, 2003.

19. George Woodcock, *The Century That Made Us: Canada, 1814–1914* (1989), 1–4 (quote, 1).

20. William F. Coffin, *1812: The War, and Its Moral: A Canadian Chronicle* (1864), 17.

21. G. Mercer Adam and W. J. Robertson, *Public School History of England and Canada* (1886), 167–68, 172–73.

22. Donald Harman Akenson, *The Irish in Ontario* (1984), 134. Woodcock writes, "There was no *Canadian* [Quebec] support for the American invaders in 1812; the *habitants* [felt] that they would have more chance to follow their own ways under the British than they would under the Americans, whose numbers would

have overwhelmed them and whose Protestantism was aggressive." *The Century That Made Us,* 5. The Quebecois attitude had apparently not changed since 1775–1776.

23. *Chicago Herald,* December 3, 1889, 7.

24. Floyd W. Rudmin, *Bordering on Aggression: Evidence of US Military Preparations against Canada* (1993), 77.

4: FLORIDA, 1810–1819: SOUTHWARD AGGRESSION I

1. Lord Acton (John Emerich Edward Dalberg-Acton), letter to Bishop Mandell Creighton, Cannes, April 5, 1887. Acton went on to write, "Great men are almost always bad men, even when they exercise influence and not authority; still more when you superadd the tendency or the certainty of corruption by authority. There is no worse heresy than that the office sanctifies the holder of it." From Add. Mss. 6871, Cambridge University. Reprinted in Lord Acton, *Selected Writings of Lord Acton,* ed. J. Rufus Fears (1986), 2:383. Acton's famous adage applies to absolute monarchs like the kings of Spain. It also applies to presidents who lack consistent and effective opposition, which was usually the case with Jefferson, Madison, and Monroe.

2. David J. Weber, *The Spanish Frontier in North America* (1992), 278–79.

3. Rodrigo Botero, *Ambivalent Embrace: America's Troubled Relations with Spain from the Revolutionary War to the Cold War* (2001), 29–30. Botero, a Colombian historian, called San Lorenzo "an enormous diplomatic success for the United States," a view shared by virtually all on whatever side.

4. Elena Sánchez-Fabrés Mirat, *Situación histórica de Las Floridas en la segunda mitad del siglo XVIII* (1977), 171.

5. Ibid., 228.

6. Stanley J. Stein and Barbara H. Stein, *Apogee of Empire: Spain and New Spain in the Age of Charles III, 1759–1789* (2003), 10.

7. Charles Carroll Griffin, *The United States and the Disruption of the Spanish Empire, 1820–1822* (1937), 22.

8. Jerónimo Becker, *Historia de los relaciones exteriores de España durante el siglo XIX* (1924), 1:120–22.

9. Wanjohi Waciuma, *Intervention in Spanish Floridas, 1801–1813: A Study in Jeffersonian Foreign Policy* (1976), 55–56, citing Talleyrand's letter to U.S. minister Armstrong, in *American State Papers,* 2:635.

10. Becker, *Historia de los relaciones exteriores,* 101–2n.

11. Mirat, *Situación histórica de Las Floridas,* 256: "un libelo atroz."

12. Nathan and Samuel Kemper, and a third brother, Reuben, have been described as "the most prominent troublemakers in West Florida . . . an uncouth, boozing, and violent trio." One reason why the 1804 coup failed was that "many residents recognized that the Kempers and their gang were not so much revolutionaries as opportunistic and unscrupulous marauders." Robert Higgs, " 'Not Merely Perfidious but Ungrateful': The U.S. Takeover of West Florida" (2005). The Kempers reappeared in the later, successful takeover of West Florida, and in a filibuster into Texas shortly after.

13. For details of these operations, and the involvement of President Madison and Secretary Smith, see Waciuma, *Intervention in Spanish Floridas,* 133–46; Joseph

Burkholder Smith, *The Plot to Steal Florida: James Madison's Phony War* (1983), 52–67; Isaac Joslin Cox, *The West Florida Controversy, 1798–1813* (1918), chap. 9.

14. Cox, *West Florida Controversy*, 331.

15. James A. Padgett, ed., "Official Records of the West Florida Revolution and Republic" (1938), 685.

16. Ibid., 693–98.

17. Stanley Clisby Arthur, *The Story of the West Florida Rebellion* (1935), 102.

18. Padgett, "Official Records," 728.

19. Holmes quote from J. B. Smith, *Plot to Steal Florida*, 66.

20. Arthur, *Story of the West Florida Rebellion*, 135.

21. J. B. Smith, *Plot to Steal Florida*, 108–12. Pickering was one of the last Federalists and has a reputation as one of the least pleasant public men of his time. Nevertheless he had the truth on his side on this occasion. Smith comments, "The Madison supporters reacted with the same ferocity that the Nixon administration displayed when the Pentagon Papers were published" (108). Also, Waciuma, *Intervention in Spanish Floridas*, 204.

22. Waciuma, *Intervention in Spanish Floridas*, 184.

23. Kemper quote from Arthur, *Story of the West Florida Rebellion*, 124; Padgett, "Official Records," 753.

24. Clarence Edwin Carter, *The Territorial Papers of the United States*, vol. 6, *The Territory of Mississippi, 1809–1817* (1938), "Judge Toulmin to the President," Fort Stoddert, October 31, 1810 (128–30), November 22 (135–39), November 28 (140–43), December 6 (149–51), December 12 (152–59). Regarding Harry Toulmin, see "I.J.C." (Isaac J. Cox), "Toulmin, Harry," in Dumas Malone, ed., *Dictionary of American Biography* (1936), vol. 9, part 2, 601–2.

25. Mirat, *Situación histórica de Las Floridas*, 270, 273–75.

26. "occupy and plunder": Thomas P. Abernethy, *The South in the New Nation, 1789–1819* (1961), 366.

27. Quoted in Rufus Kay Wyllys, "The East Florida Revolution of 1812–1814" (1929), 424, citing U.S. Senate, Miscellaneous Document 55, 36th Cong., 1st sess., 17–18.

28. Wyllys, "East Florida Revolution," 439–40.

29. James G. Cusick, *The Other War of 1812: The Patriot War and the American Invasion of Spanish East Florida* (2003), 240–43.

30. James W. Covington, *The Seminoles of Florida* (1993), 30.

31. First quote, J. B. Smith, *Plot to Steal Florida*, 264–65; second quote, Wyllys, "East Florida Revolution," 441.

32. Waciuma, *Intervention in Spanish Floridas*, 343–47, summarizes and documents this Monroe-Pinckney exchange.

33. Cusick, *The Other War of 1812*, 305–10.

34. Jackson to Claiborne, November 12, 1806, from John Spencer Bassett, ed., *Correspondence of Andrew Jackson*, 1:153, quoted in Griffin, *United States and the Disruption of the Spanish Empire*, 31.

35. Frank Lawrence Owsley Jr. and Gene A. Smith, *Filibusters and Expansionists: Jeffersonian Manifest Destiny, 1800–1821* (1997), 92.

36. Mirat, *Situación histórica de Las Floridas*, 284–86.

37. Cox, *West Florida Controversy*, 622.

38. Biographer: Robert V. Remini, *Andrew Jackson and the Course of American Empire, 1767–1821* (1977), 189–232 (quote, 231). I have also drawn on R. Douglas Hurt, *The Indian Frontier, 1763–1846* (2002), 124–33; Abernethy, *The South in the New Nation*, 367–72; J. Leitch Wright Jr., *Creeks & Seminoles: The Destruction and Regeneration of the Muscogulge People* (1986), 176–77; Owsley and Smith, *Filibusters and Expansionists*, 97; Owsley, *Struggle for the Gulf Borderlands: The Creek War and the Battle of New Orleans, 1812–1815* (1981), 187, 194.

39. Owsley, *Struggle for the Gulf Borderlands*, 104–7, 113–15, wrote that Juan Ruiz Apodaca, the captain-general at Havana, was decidedly unenthusiastic about the British presence; González Manrique "was acting on his own initiative" (107).

40. Covington, *Seminoles of Florida*, 34–37; Remini, *Jackson and the Course of American Empire*, 237–41.

41. For an excellent history of that action, see Robert V. Remini, *The Battle of New Orleans: Andrew Jackson and America's First Military Victory* (1999).

42. Rembert W. Patrick, *Florida Fiasco: Rampant Rebels on the Georgia-Florida Border, 1810–1815* (1954), 284–88; Covington, *Seminoles of Florida*, 37.

43. Remini, *Jackson and the Course of American Empire*, 325–30, 335–40; Francis Paul Prucha, *American Indian Treaties: The History of a Political Anomaly* (1994), 130–32, 145–55.

44. Hoffman, "History of Louisiana," 274; Wright, *Creeks & Seminoles*, 199 (Maroon quote); Owsley, *Struggle for the Gulf Borderlands*, 184.

45. Mirat, *Situación histórica de Las Floridas*, 290–95; William Earl Weeks, *John Quincy Adams and American Global Empire* (1992), 62–66.

46. Jackson to Monroe, January 6, 1818, quoted in Remini, *Jackson and the Course of American Empire*, 347.

47. William Earl Weeks, "John Quincy Adams' 'Great Gun' and the Rhetoric of American Empire" (1990), 28.

48. Mirat, *Situación histórica de Las Floridas*, 297–99.

49. Remini, *Jackson and the Course of American Empire*, 364.

50. Becker, *Historia de los relaciones exteriores*, 460–61.

51. José Fuentes Mares, *Génesis del expansionismo norteamericano* (1980), 88–89.

52. Philip C. Brooks, *Diplomacy and the Borderlands: The Adams-Onís Treaty of 1819* (1939), 84, explores this misunderstanding, which persisted into 1818.

53. Mirat, *Situación histórica de Las Floridas*, 293.

54. Ibid., 295.

55. Weeks, *John Quincy Adams and American Global Empire*, 76.

56. Brooks, *Diplomacy and the Borderlands*, 115, 136; Mirat, *Situación histórica de Las Floridas*, 306; Griffin, *United States and the Disruption of the Spanish Empire*, 94.

57. Weeks, "John Quincy Adams' 'Great Gun,' " 30.

58. Weeks, *John Quincy Adams and American Global Empire*, 139–49 (quote, 145).

59. Becker, *Historia de los relaciones exteriores*, 540.

5: Texas, 1811–1845: Overpopulating and Conquering

1. In Ephraim Douglass Adams, ed., "British Correspondence concerning Texas, XX" (1916), 186.

2. The figure of 30,000 Indians native to Texas living there in 1820, plus 10,000 migrating there during the 1820s, is in Gary Clayton Anderson, *The Conquest of Texas: Ethnic Cleansing in the Promised Land, 1820–1875* (2005), 4. Anderson writes

that perhaps 40,000 Comanches lived in Texas in the 1780s, but their numbers fell because of several smallpox and cholera epidemics (24) and continuing warfare from onrushing Anglos; by 1850 fewer than 10,000 Comanches survived (214).

3. Mexico's other patriotic holiday, Cinco de Mayo, May 5, celebrates the Mexican victory over a French army at the battle of Puebla in 1862.

4. Many histories of the Hidalgo revolt exist, short and long, English and Spanish. An accessible and good one is Hugh M. Hamill Jr., *The Hidalgo Revolt: Prelude to Mexican Independence* (1981 [1966]).

5. José Bernardo Gutiérrez de Lara and his older brother, the lawyer and priest José Antonio Gutiérrez de Lara, both held high office in the early years of Mexican independence. José Bernardo was a loyal follower of the later president Bustamante and "a friend and coreligionist" of Mier y Terán (see below). For biographical information on these two patriots see Lorenzo de la Garza, *Dos Hermanos Heroës* (1939); and Elizabeth H. West, "Diary of José Bernardo Gutiérrez de Lara" (1928–1929), 55–91, 281–94.

6. This took place contemporaneously with George Mathews's subvented "patriot war" in East Florida, and continuing moves by the West Florida insurrectionists to move on Mobile. As Harris Warren wrote,

> Gutiérrez was sent back to Texas with the understanding that he would execute an invasion of the Interior Provinces [Texas and likely Coahuila and more]. American officials provided him with funds and transportation from Washington to Natchitoches [Louisiana]. William Shaler was his adviser from the time he left New Orleans until the expedition crossed the Sabine. Recruiting was carried on at Natchitoches with little attempt at secrecy, and Shaler's warnings to Monroe were but poorly camouflaged reports on the progress being made. Claiborne and Shaler acted under the belief that they were carrying out the desires of Madison and Monroe. . . . Fully aware that a violation of Spanish territory was being planned at Natchitoches, American officials in Louisiana and Washington failed to take effective measures against the leaders of the project. (Harris G. Warren, *Their Sword Was Their Passport: A History of American Filibustering in the Mexican Revolution* [1943], 31–32)

Also on Madison's and Monroe's complicity, see Griffin, *The United States and the Disruption of the Spanish Empire, 1810–1822*, 54–55, 108–9; and Donald E. Chipman, *Spanish Texas, 1519–1821* (1992), 234–37. Richard W. Gronet, "The United States and the Invasion of Texas, 1810–1814" (1969), 281–306, the most detailed account, concludes that the Gutiérrez-Magee effort was "a United States sponsored scheme to aid the Mexican Revolution" (306).

7. Remini, *Jackson and the Course of American Empire*, 389–90, describes Jackson's positions. On Long, see Robert E. May, "Manifest Destiny's Filibusters" (1997), 150; Chipman, *Spanish Texas*, 240.

8. Figures are from Randolph B. Campbell, *An Empire for Slavery: The Peculiar Institution in Texas, 1821–1865* (1989), 11, citing work of Alice V. Tjarks and others. Before 1820, Campbell finds, there were never more than about three dozen enslaved Africans in Texas. Also, Gregg Cantrell, *Stephen F. Austin: Empresario of*

Texas (1992), 104, 107–8; Weber, *The Spanish Frontier in North America*, 299 (who notes that Arredondo purged *tejanos* suspected of disloyalty, after the Gutiérrez-Magee filibuster).

9. Austin's empresario grant is outlined in many places; see, e.g., Hubert Howe Bancroft, *History of the North Mexican States and Texas, 1801–1889* (1889), 2:60–61; Cantrell, *Stephen F. Austin*, 94, 123–24.

10. Eugene C. Barker, "Notes on the Colonization of Texas" (1923), 108–19, esp. 112, 116–17.

11. Jodella D. Kite, "A Social History of the Anglo-American Colonies in Mexican Texas, 1821–1835" (1990), esp. chaps. 2, 4, 8; quote, 196.

12. Jerónimo Becker, *La política española en Las Indias* (1920), 410–11, 414; Salvador de Madariaga, *The Fall of the Spanish American Empire* (1948), 76; Hugh Thomas, *Rivers of Gold: The Spanish Empire from Columbus to Magellan* (2003), 403, 410–11; Herbert S. Klein, *African Slavery in Latin America and the Caribbean* (1986), 25–27, 34–37, 83.

13. Rosalie Schwartz, *Across the Rio to Freedom: U.S. Negroes in Mexico* (1975), 6–7; Ernesto Lemoine, ed., *Insurgencia y república federal, 1808–1824: Documentos para la história del México independiente* (1987), 83 (quote), 145 (no. 24), 194.

14. R. B. Campbell, *An Empire for Slavery*, 15–16.

15. Schwartz, *Across the Rio*, 7–8.

16. Ibid., 11; R. B. Campbell, *An Empire for Slavery*, 19.

17. Bancroft, *History of the North Mexican States*, 2:73; Cantrell, *Stephen F. Austin*, 23, 115, 134, 160; David J. Weber, *The Mexican Frontier: The American Southwest under Mexico* (1982), 79–80; Gerald Ashford, "Jacksonian Liberalism and Spanish Law in Early Texas" (1953), 18.

18. Quoted in Joseph Carl McElhannon, "Imperial Mexico and Texas, 1821–1823" (1949), 139.

19. Nettie Lee Benson, "Texas as Viewed from Mexico, 1820–1834" (1987), 228; McElhannon, "Imperial Mexico," 122–31, 144–50 (quote, 144); F. Todd Smith, *The Wichita Indians*, 119; Edith Louise Kelly and Mattie Austin Hatcher, "Tadeo Ortíz de Ayala and the Colonization of Texas, 1822–1833" (1928–1929), 74–86, 152–64, 222–51, 311–43 (Austin quote, 343). A somewhat similar effort by an Irish priest, Eugene Macnamara, to settle ten thousand Irish peasants in northern California in 1845–1846 also failed. Had it happened a couple of years before the American takeover, rather than a few weeks, it might have changed California's history, as Ortíz's might have changed Texas's.

20. [Mexico], Ediciones de la Biblioteca de la Cámara de Diputados, *Documentos históricos inéditos del archivo* (1936), document 1, December 2, 1823, 6.

21. Mexico, Secretaría de Relaciones Exteriores, *La Diplomacia Mexicana* (1912), 2:74.

22. Bancroft, *History of the North Mexican States*, 2:70.

23. Eugene C. Barker, "Land Speculation as a Cause of the Texas Revolution" (1906), 76–77; Benson, "Texas as Viewed from Mexico," 244–45.

24. Weber, *Mexican Frontier*, 162–64.

25. The general is always referred to as "Terán," although the expected usage would be "Mier." The ten-month delay between the suppression of the Fredonian uprising and Terán's departure was all too typical of governmental responses, chronically impeded by distance and disputations.

26. Jack Jackson and John Wheat, *Texas by Terán: The Diary Kept by General Manuel de Mier y Terán on His 1828 Inspection of Texas* (2000), 29. This well-annotated translation includes his letters as well as diary entries.

27. Jackson and Wheat, *Texas by Terán*, quoting and translating Terán, 31–33.

28. An accessible version is Charles Wilson Hackett, ed., *Pichardo's Treatise on the Limits of Louisiana and Texas . . .* , vol. 1 (1931), which is a translation of the first part. A respected University of Texas historian, Hackett wrote, "On the whole Father Pichardo's conclusions are sane and correct" (xix).

29. Terán's letter of November 14 appears in Vito Alessio Robles, *Coahuila y Tejas: Desde la consumación de la independencia hasta el tratado de paz de Guadalupe Hidalgo* (1945), 1:349, 352–57; Alleine Howren, "Causes and Origin of the Decree of April 6, 1830" (1913), 400–4, 406–13; Jackson and Wheat, *Texas by Terán*, 178–79 (they date it November 24 but the contents are the same as quoted in Robles and Howren).

30. Jackson's biographer described Butler as not only sleazy but two-faced; he "proceeded to execute every cheap trick his febrile mind could devise to offend the Mexicans and hoodwink the Jackson administration." Robert V. Remini, *Andrew Jackson and the Course of American Freedom*, 218–19.

31. Robles, *Coahuila y Tejas*, 1:239–44; Schwartz, *Across the Rio*, 16.

32. The text of the April 6, 1830, law (translated into English) appears in Howren, 415–17.

33. Petition of April 13, 1833, by Wily Martin and others, San Felipe de Austin, in Mexico, *Documentos históricos inéditos del archivo*, 15–28.

34. Ibid., 19, 25–27.

35. Juan Nepomuceno Almonte, *Noticia estadística sobre Tejas* (1835), 25, 50, 67. The leading settlements were, in the Department of Bejar, "Bejar" (San Antonio) with 2,400 (down from 5,000 in 1806), Goliad 700, Victoria 300, and San Patricio, an Irish colony, 600. In the Departamento de los Brazos, San Felipe had 2,500, Columbia 2,100, Matagorda 900, and Mina 1,100. In the Departamento de Nacogdoches, Nacogdoches had 3,500, San Agustin 2,500, and Johnsburg 2,000. Weber, *Mexican Frontier*, 177n, points out that Almonte did not tally his figures quite correctly; his total is 21,000 but should be 24,700.

36. Weber, *Mexican Frontier*, 177.

37. Austin's calamitously indiscreet remarks in San Antonio and Mexico City, his incarceration, and the process of his release are detailed comprehensively in Cantrell, *Stephen F. Austin*, 263, 274, 275, 281–82, 305–9.

38. Barker, "Land Speculation as a Cause of the Texas Revolution," 78–88.

39. C. A. Hutchinson, "Mexican Federalists in New Orleans and the Texas Revolution" (1956), 40, 46–47.

40. Schwartz, *Across the Rio*, 27.

41. Eugene C. Barker, "The Annexation of Texas" (1946), 52; Remini, *Jackson and the Course of American Freedom*, 368; Michael A. Morrison, "Westward the Curse of Empire: Texas Annexation and the American Whig Party" (1990), 224–25.

42. Carlos Bosch Garcia, *Historia de las relaciones entre México y los Estados Unidos 1819–1848* (1961), 85.

43. A recent discussion by legal scholars argues that the joint resolution method of annexation, rather than a treaty that would have required a two-thirds Senate approval, was entirely constitutional. Lawson and Seidman, *Constitution of Empire*,

93. However, it was unprecedented and was resorted to because garnering a two-thirds vote was out of the question.

44. *Memoirs of John Quincy Adams*, 12:173–74, reprinted in Walter LaFeber, ed., *John Quincy Adams and American Continental Empire: Letters, Papers and Speeches* (1965), 148.

45. F. Todd Smith, *The Wichita Indians*, 48–51, 57–61, 145 (quote), 150; Smith (62) likens the Comanche-Apache activity against the Mexican frontier to the Viking invasions in the *Anglo-Saxon Chronicle*. Also see T. R. Fehrenbach, *Comanches: The Destruction of a People* (1944), 315, 333, 348–51; Anderson, *Conquest of Texas*, chaps. 12–22.

6: Oregon, 1818–1846: Fixing the Canadian Border

1. E. W. Tucker, *A History of Oregon, from Its Discovery to the Present Time, Showing the Grounds of the Claim of the United States to That Territory* (1844), v.

2. Adam Thom, *The Claims to the Oregon Territory Considered* (1844), 15–16, 24. Thom was one of the highest British officials in western Canada.

3. Quoted in London *Times*, October 1, 1845, and March 5, 1846.

4. P[ierre] J[ean] DeSmet, S.J., *Oregon Missions and Travels over the Rocky Mountains in 1845–46* (1847), 24.

5. Ibid., 26.

6. Tucker, *History of Oregon*, 71, 73.

7. Figures and quotations are from Robert Boyd, *The Coming of the Spirit of Pestilence: Introduced Infectious Diseases and Population Decline among Northwest Coast Indians, 1774–1874* (1999), 107, 110, 117, 129–30, 135–36, 138, 232, 262, 278.

8. DeSmet, *Oregon Missions*, 54.

9. Ibid., 54, 22–23.

10. In a curious backlash, the famous "Whitman massacre" east of Walla Walla on November 29, 1847, resulted from a measles epidemic that killed a third to a half of the Cayuse tribe that fall. The baffled and enraged Cayuse rose up and killed the missionaries Narcissa and Marcus Whitman and their companions, who had been "doctoring" them. The measles continued, killing hundreds more Indians after that.

11. Walter N. Sage, "The Oregon Treaty of 1846" (1946), 351.

12. Rezanov's trip back to St. Petersburg was, in part, to seek imperial permission to marry the daughter, Maria de la Concepcion Argüello. But he died on the way at Krasnoyarsk, and she waited vainly in a convent in Benecia until she died fifty years later.

13. For specifics see C. P. Stacey, "The Myth of the Unguarded Frontier, 1815–1871" (1950), 1–18; Stanley L. Falk, "Disarmament on the Great Lakes: Myth or Reality?" (1961), 69–73.

14. For the text of the Convention of October 20, 1818, see Frederick E. Hosen, *Unfolding Westward in Treaty and Law* (1988), 106–9. Also, C. O. Paullin, "The Early Choice of the 49th Parallel as a Boundary Line" (1923), 127–31, on the Utrecht "precedent"; William E. Lass, *Minnesota's Boundary with Canada: Its Evolution since 1783* (1980), 33–34; Samuel Flagg Bemis, "Jay's Treaty and the Northwest Boundary Gap" (1922), 480, 484; and (no author given) "Correspondence of 1817–18 among British diplomats, President Monroe, Secretary Adams, Secre-

tary Rush, and others concerning the *Ontario* and the return of Astoria," in "Message from the President of the United States . . . in relation to Claims set up by Foreign Governments to Territory of the United States upon the Pacific Ocean, north of the forty-second degree of latitude . . . , April 17, 1822" (1822), 7–18.

15. Helpful treatments are Anatole G. Mazour, "The Russian-American and Anglo-Russian Conventions, 1824–1825: An Interpretation" (1945), 303–10; and Mykhaylo Huculak, *When Russia Was in America: The Alaska Boundary Treaty Negotiations, 1824–25, and the Role of Pierre de Poletica* (1971), esp. chaps. 2–4.

16. John S. Galbraith, *The Hudson's Bay Company as an Imperial Factor, 1821–1869* (1957), 21. Much of my information on the HBC relies on this history.

17. Ibid., 19–20.

18. Hall J. Kelley, *A Geographical Sketch of That Part of North America Called Oregon . . .* (1830), 7, 9, 17. Jefferson, Monroe, Senators Thomas Hart Benton and John Calhoun, and others also made the Louisiana Purchase assertion, based on the false Treaty of Utrecht claim; see, for example, Lawson and Seidman, *Constitution of Empire*, 95.

19. G.-T. Poussin, *Question de l'Oregon* (1846), 99. "Incontestablement," he wrote, the rights to Oregon "sont du côté des Americains" (91).

20. DeSmet, *Oregon Missions*. It first appeared in 1846 in French.

21. Ibid., 23, 54.

22. Sage, the Canadian historian, put it gently: "As a class . . . the frontiersmen were distinctly different from New England missionaries; neither were they interested in them. A vital connection between the two groups does not appear to have existed." "Oregon Treaty of 1846," 356.

23. Galbraith, *Hudson's Bay Company*, chap. 10, esp. 205, 211–12. For the Red River colony see R. Louis Gentilcore, ed., *Historical Atlas of Canada*, vol. 2, *The Land Transformed, 1800–1891* (1993), plate 18 and text. DeSmet counted "about 5,500 souls, of whom 3,175 are Catholics," in 730 houses in the Red River settlement (*Oregon Missions*, 162).

24. Galbraith, *Hudson's Bay Company*, 242, quoting a letter of Aberdeen's to Prime Minister Robert Peel, October 17, 1845.

25. W. Kaye Lamb, introduction to E. E. Rich, ed., *The Letters of John McLoughlin from Fort Vancouver to the Governor and Committee; Second Series, 1839–44* (1943), xviii. Galbraith's discussion (*Hudson's Bay Company*, 222–24) of Simpson's decision concluded that for the London management the "economic purpose" was foremost. Lord Aberdeen, about to send Lord Ashburton to Washington to settle boundary problems (preeminently the Maine–New Brunswick line), was more mindful of British-American relations. Thus, McLoughlin opposed de-emphasizing Fort Vancouver, which he had built up over the previous seventeen years; Simpson, among other considerations, feared the settlers; London saw better profits farther north; the Foreign Office still considered good relations with the United States less important than Oregon's "few miles of pine swamp."

26. W. Kaye Lamb, "The Founding of Fort Victoria" (1943), 83–86.

27. Simpson to "Governor and Committee," quoted in W. Kaye Lamb, introduction to E. E. Rich, ed., *The Letters of John McLoughlin . . . ; Third Series, 1844–46* (1944), xxxiv.

28. Lamb, introduction to *Letters . . . Third Series*, xxxvii–xxxviii, xlv.

29. Ibid., li–liii, lx–lxii; William G. Robbins, *Landscapes of Promise: The Oregon Story, 1800–1940* (1997), 70–73.

30. Robert E. Ficken and Charles P. LeWarne, *Washington: A Centennial History* (1988), 21; Ruth Kirk and Carmela Alexander, *Exploring Washington's Past: A Road Guide to History* (1990), 367.

31. Will Ferguson, *Canadian History for Dummies* (2000), 206 (first quote). Detailed accounts are in Carroll, *Good and Wise Measure*, part 3; and Carroll, "The Passionate Canadians: The Historical Debate about the Eastern Canadian-American Boundary" (1997), 83–101 (second quote, 101). Also, Howard Jones and Donald A. Rakestraw, *Prologue to Manifest Destiny* (1997), chaps. 5 and 6.

32. "Mr. Falconer's Reply to Mr. Greenhow's Answer, with Mr. Greenhow's Rejoinder," June 24, 1845; Thom, *The Claims to the Oregon Territory Considered*.

33. Pakenham to Aberdeen, late August 1844, in James J. Barnes and Patience P. Barnes, *Private and Confidential: Letters from British Ministers in Washington to Foreign Secretaries in London, 1844–67* (1993), 25.

34. Polk, Inaugural Address of March 4, 1845, in 28th Cong., 2d sess., House Document 540, 89. Settlement, not simply acquisition, was in his mind.

35. James K. Polk, *The Diary of James K. Polk During His Presidency, 1845 to 1849*, ed. Milo Milton Quaife (1910), 1:135.

36. David M. Pletcher, *The Diplomacy of Annexation: Texas, Oregon, and the Mexican War* (1973), 330–31.

37. Polk, *Diary*, 1:209.

38. Quoted in Wilbur Devereux Jones, *Lord Aberdeen and the Americas* (1958), 80, and in Charles Sellers, *James K. Polk: Continentalist, 1843–1846* (1966), 380, citing a letter from McLane to Buchanan, London, February 3, 1846.

39. Julius W. Pratt, "James K. Polk and John Bull" (1943), 346. Stuart Anderson, "British Threats and the Settlement of the Oregon Boundary Dispute" (1975), 153–60, disagreed with Pratt on the ground that Polk never really wanted or expected to get all of Oregon up to 54°40'. This is not certain. Anderson believed (160) that the "thirty sail of the line" note did succeed in inducing Polk to say what he really wanted: the forty-ninth parallel. Webster quote: from *Writings and Speeches of Daniel Webster*, 4:20–21, quoted in Sage, "The Oregon Treaty of 1846," 367.

40. *Senate Journal*, 29th Cong., 1st sess., 555; *Congressional Globe*, August 10, 1846, 1224.

41. The treaty provided that the border extended along the forty-ninth parallel "to the middle of the channel which separates the continent from Vancouver's Island; and thence southerly through the middle of the said channel, and of Fuca's Straits to the Pacific Ocean." However, there were two such channels, on either side of the San Juan Islands, and the choice had to be settled years later. The treaty did not say anything about the HBC's rights expiring in 1859. It did guarantee "the possessory rights" of the company, such as Fort Vancouver and lands belonging to the Puget Sound Agricultural Company; these also caused some future disputes. For the treaty, see Hosen, *Unfolding West in Treaty and Law*, 169–71.

42. Galbraith, *Hudson's Bay Company*, 249.

43. Frederick Merk, "The Oregon Pioneers and the Boundary," (1914), reprinted in Merk, *The Oregon Question: Essays in Anglo-American Diplomacy and Politics* (1967), 245.

44. Charles Elliot to Aberdeen, June 15, 1845, quoted in E. D. Adams, ed., "British Correspondence Concerning Texas," 186.

45. Sellers, *James K. Polk*, 384, citing a letter from Frank Blair to Martin Van Buren, January 18, 1846, stating that the Castlereagh remark had been quoted by John C. Calhoun.

46. Norman A. Graebner, *Empire on the Pacific: A Study in American Continental Expansion* (1955), emphasized Polk's and other presidents' "goal . . . to control the great harbors of San Francisco, San Diego, and Juan de Fuca Strait" both for national glory and imperial expansion and for a share of the China trade (quote, xiv, and conclusion, passim). One cannot suppress a doubt that these motives were foremost in the minds of the thousands of settlers on the Overland Trail.

47. J. D. B. DeBow, *Statistical View of the United States . . . being a Compendium of the Seventh Census* (1854), 40, 43, 45, 48, 51, 63, 116–17, 141–44, 169, 332, 373.

48. John D. Unruh, Jr., *The Plains Across: The Overland Emigrants and the Trans-Mississippi West, 1840–60* (1979), 119–20.

49. Robbins, *Landscapes of Promise*, 77.

50. A meticulous treatment is John W. Long Jr., "The Origin and Development of the San Juan Island Water Boundary Controversy" (1952), 187–213.

51. Francis Paul Prucha, *American Indian Treaties*, 246–50 (quote, 249).

7: CALIFORNIA AND MEXICO, 1846–1848: SOUTHWARD AGGRESSION II

1. Ulysses S. Grant, *Memoirs and Selected Letters*, ed. Mary Drake McFeely and William S. McFeely (1990), 41.

2. José Fernando Ramírez, *México durante su Guerra con los Estados Unidos*, translated as *Mexico during the War with the United States* (1970 [1905]), 139.

3. Isaiah Berlin, *The Hedgehog and the Fox: An Essay on Tolstoy's View of History* (1986 [1953]).

4. Unruh, *The Plains Across*, 119. California in 1846 had at least 6,000 Spanish-Mexicans and 1,500 Anglos—and perhaps 70,000 Indians. Walter Nugent, *Into the West: The Story of Its People* (1999), 51. David Weber's figure is slightly higher but close: Weber, *The Mexican Frontier, 1821–1846* (1982), 206.

5. Hubert Howe Bancroft discussed the Macnamara plan, but the best modern treatment is John Fox, *Macnamara's Irish Colony and the United States Taking of California in 1846* (2000).

6. Castro to Larkin, Monterey, March 8, 1846, Larkin Papers, Bancroft Library, University of California at Berkeley, C-B 102:4.

7. Frémont's most recent and best biographer saw the meeting with Gillespie as "a turning point—away from exploration, toward operations fraught with more dangerous and complex military and political consequences." Tom Chaffin, *Pathfinder: John Charles Frémont and the Course of American Empire* (2002), 303.

8. On the deep-seated character of ideological divisions in Mexico, see, e.g., Pedro Santoni, *Mexicans at Arms: Puro Federalists and the Politics of War, 1845–1848* (1996), chap. 1 and passim.

9. Pletcher, *Diplomacy of Annexation*, 230–31, notes that Bancroft did not make this claim until forty years later, but did so to both the historian James Schouler and to the then-elderly Frémont. Pletcher also notes (94) that Jackson in 1835 and again in 1836 had offered to buy Alta California, and that in mid-1846 "Polk kept very quiet about California until the United States and Mexico were actually at war,

although he never took his eyes off his goal for long" (422). Pletcher concludes, "There was never any question that Polk regarded permanent possession of California as the first goal of the Mexican War" (422).

10. Polk, *Diary*, 1:71, entry of October 24, 1845.

11. Richard Griswold del Castillo, *The Treaty of Guadalupe Hidalgo: A Legacy of Conflict* (1990), 10–12. This is as explicit and succinct a statement of the matter as I have seen, and it is supported consistently by Spanish, Mexican, and American scholarship. Disagreeing with it are nineteenth- and some twentieth-century defenses of the Texan claim as far as the Rio Grande.

12. Pletcher, *Diplomacy of Annexation*, 260.

13. Bustamante, in Cecil Robinson, trans. and ed., *The View from Chapultepec: Mexican Writers on the Mexican-American War* (1989), 67.

14. See, e.g., "Problema por la posible ocupación estadounidense de la franja entre los rios Bravo y Nueces" (1846), in Mercedes de Vega and María Cecilia Zuleta, eds., *Testimonios de una guerra: México 1846–1848*, vol. 2 (2001), 329.

15. Sellers, *James K. Polk*, 400.

16. The war message may be found in the *Congressional Globe* for Monday, May 11, 1846 (29th Cong., 1st sess., 782–83). The House debate follows, 791–95; the Senate discussion, 783–88, 795–804.

17. Breakdowns of the votes are in John R. Collins, "The Mexican War: A Study in Fragmentation" (1972), 228–29.

18. For a detailed chronology and narrative, stressing the military aspects, consult Edward H. Moseley and Paul C. Clark Jr., *Historical Dictionary of the United States–Mexican War* (1997). For a vivid military-naval history, see Robert Leckie, *From Sea to Shining Sea: From the War of 1812 to the Mexican War, the Saga of America's Expansion* (1993). An excellent, brief modern account from the Mexican side is Orlando Martinez, *The Great Landgrab: The Mexican-American War, 1846–1848* (1975).

19. Buchanan to Larkin, State Department, January 13, 1847, in Mariano G. Vallejo Papers, box 3, Huntington Library, San Marino, Calif.

20. Figures are from Paul Foos, *A Short, Offhand, Killing Affair: Soldiers and Social Conflict during the Mexican-American War* (2002), 84–85.

21. Thomas R. Irey, "Soldiering, Suffering, and Dying in the Mexican War" (1972), 285–98.

22. On the San Patricios, a unit that included not only Irish but German, Polish, and British immigrants as well as native-born Americans, see Michael Hogan, *The Irish Soldiers of Mexico* (1998). Hogan stated some of the main points in his essay "The Irish Soldiers of Mexico" (1997), 38–43. The hanging contributed to the Mexican War having the highest rate of executions for desertion of any American war; see Robert Ryal Miller, *Shamrock and Sword: The Saint Patrick's Battalion in the U.S.-Mexican War* (1989), 176.

23. See Foos, *A Short Affair*, chap. 6, "Atrocity: The Wage of Manifest Destiny"; also John C. Pinheiro, " 'Religion without Restriction': Anti-Catholicism, All Mexico, and the Treaty of Guadalupe Hidalgo" (2003), 69–96, which reproduces dozens of contemporary expressions, many of them insults.

24. *Exposición de una persona residente en la República Mexicana sobre la guerra que actualmente sostiene con los Estados Unidos del Norte* (1847).

25. Polk, *Diary*, 2:75.

26. *The Conquest of Mexico! An Appeal to the Citizens of the United States, on the Justice and Expediency of the Conquest of Mexico . . .* (1846), 26, 32.

27. Roy P. Basler, *Collected Works of Abraham Lincoln*, 1:441, quoted in Norman Graebner, "Lessons of the Mexican War" (1978), 342.

28. William H. Herndon and Jesse W. Weik, *Herndon's Life of Lincoln: The History and Personal Recollections of Abraham Lincoln* (1936), 221–23. Herndon, Lincoln's law partner and biographer, states that Lincoln badly damaged his chances of reelection by introducing the "spot resolutions," "as his constituents began to manifest symptoms of grave disapproval of his course on the Mexican war question" (221).

29. Polk, *Diary*, 2:283–84 (December 19, 1846).

30. From *Niles' National Register*, January 22, 1848, quoted in Graebner, "Lessons," 332; Whitman quote, 333.

31. Dean B. Mahin, *Olive Branch and Sword: The United States and Mexico, 1845–1848* (1997), 140.

32. *Congressional Globe*, 30th Cong., 1st sess., Senate: Calhoun and Cass, December 15, 1847, 26, 53, 55, 114; Cass and Butler, January 17, 1848, 184, 186–88.

33. See Pittsfield, Mass., and other papers for late 1847 and early 1848 opinion on "all Mexico," in *Early American Newspapers* database.

34. The most complete discussion of the all-Mexico movement is John D. P. Fuller, *The Movement for the Acquisition of All Mexico* (1936). A handy brief treatment is Paul F. Lambert, "The Movement for the Acquisition of All Mexico" (1972), 317–27. Its connection with manifest destiny and slavery is explored in Sam W. Haynes, *James K. Polk and the Expansionist Impulse* (1997), 177–84; and Horsman, *Race and Manifest Destiny* (1991), 236–43. See also Pletcher, *Diplomacy of Annexation*, 551–57.

35. Polk, *Diary*, 2:467 (April 10, 1847).

36. Ibid., 2:467, 472, 478.

37. Scott's biographer calls Pillow

> Mr. Polk's faithful personal watchdog with the army. . . . General Pillow, whose gratuitous advice had been disregarded by Scott at the time of the armistice [of Tucubaya, August 24 to September 6, 1847, after which Scott invaded Mexico City], had written to his former partner [Polk] privately, criticizing the gross blunders of the commanding general and probably hinting that Trist had now become the mere tool of Scott, their combined purposes representing something that boded no good to either Polk, the Democratic party, or such able military Democrats as Gideon J. Pillow himself. (Charles Winslow Elliott, *Winfield Scott: The Soldier and the Man* [1937], 558)

38. Polk, *Diary*, 3:185–86 (October 4–5, 1847).

39. Ibid., 3:199 (October 23, 1847).

40. Trist to General Scott, January 28, 1848, in Nicholas P. Trist Papers, Library of Congress, Special File, container 11, folder 2.

41. Trist to Buchanan, February 2, 1848, in Trist Papers, Special File, container 11, folder 3. The original of the treaty, with the red-wax seals of Trist and the three Mexican negotiators, is in this folder. A detailed account of the January negotiations is in Dean B. Mahin, *Olive Branch and Sword*, 141–63.

42. Trist-Butler letters, March 1848, in Trist Papers, Special File, container 11, folder 4.
43. Mahin, *Olive Branch and Sword*, 171.
44. Polk, *Diary*, 3:345 (February 19, 1848), and 3:348 (February 21, 1848).
45. On Trist's final negotiations and the ratification process, Wallace Ohrt's *Defiant Peacemaker: Nicholas Trist in the Mexican War* (1997), 140–49, is helpful. Also see Collins, "The Mexican War: A Study in Fragmentation," for analysis of this and related votes in Congress. The Senate debate was initially secret, but was released by resolutions of May 31 and June 2, 1848; the minutes appear in 30th Cong., 1st sess., Senate Executive Document 52, and are analyzed in Hunter Miller, ed., *Treaties and Other International Acts of the United States of America*, vol. 5 (1937), 246–53, 378–80. The Senate vote is broken down by party and section in George Lockhart Rives, *The United States and Mexico, 1821–1848* (1913), 636–37.
46. The text is in Hosen, *Unfolding Westward*, 175–87.
47. John L. O'Sullivan, "Annexation" (July–August 1845), 9.
48. Translation in Cecil Robinson, *View from Chapultepec*, 93.
49. Letter of Manuel González Cosío, governor of Zacatecas, to former president Valentín Gómez Farías, Zacatecas, February 11, 1848 (quote); and letter of General Ignacio de Mora y Villamil to Mariano Riva Palacio, Mexico City, April 18, 1848, in Vega and Zuleta, eds., *Testimonios de una guerra: México 1846–1848*, 1:22–24.
50. The "Address" is reprinted in translation in Robinson, *View from Chapultepec*, 103–12. In it, says Robinson, "the dignity, honor, and sincerity of the man shine clearly through" (102). I agree.
51. Thornton to Trist, Mexico City, May 26, 1848, in Trist Papers, Special File, container 11, folder 5. The Trist Papers are full of correspondence between Trist and the three Mexican commissioners, but not between Trist and President Peña y Peña himself, which would not have been proper protocol.
52. Polk, *Diary*, 3:431, 444–45. For context see Mary Wilhelmine Williams, "Secessionist Diplomacy of Yucatan" (1929), 132–43.
53. Quoted in Haynes, *James K. Polk and the Expansionist Impulse*, 184; and in Pletcher, *Diplomacy of Annexation*, 574. For the cabinet discussion, see Polk, *Diary*, 3:446, 469, 475–82.
54. For details see J. Fred Rippy, "The Negotiation of the Gadsden Treaty" (1923), 1–26.
55. *Apuntes para la história de la guerra entre México y los Estados-Unidos* (1848), 3, 28, 402.
56. Martinez, *The Great Landgrab*, 5–6.
57. Graebner, *Empire on the Pacific*.

8: Populating the Empire

1. Thomas Robert Malthus, *An Essay on the Principle of Population, as it affects The Future Improvement of Society* . . . (1798), 20–21, 342–43.
2. "Message of President Monroe on Indian Removal, January 27, 1825," in Prucha, ed., *Documents of United States Indian Policy*, 39–40.
3. Boudinot, editor of the *Cherokee Phoenix*, March 13, 1828, as quoted in Stuart Banner, *How the Indians Lost Their Land: Law and Order on the Frontier* (2005), 211.

4. "Jeffersonian philanthropy" is best described in Bernard W. Sheehan, *Seeds of Extinction: Jeffersonian Philanthropy and the American Indian* (1973).

5. Banner, *How the Indians Lost Their Land*, 221–22.

6. Ellis, *His Excellency: George Washington*, 237–38: "But despite his sincerity and personal commitment, this was one promise that even Washington could not keep."

7. The Senate debate ran from April 9 to 26, 1830, and may be found in *Gales & Seaton's Register of Debates in Congress* (1830), 29th Cong., 1st sess., 305–83 (intermittently). Theodore Frelinghuysen, a lawyer, served one term (1829–1835) in the Senate and was chancellor of New York University (1839–1850) and president of Rutgers College (1850–1862); he was Henry Clay's running mate on the Whig ticket in 1844. John Forsyth was minister to Spain from 1819 to 1823 and as such promoted the ratification of the Adams-Onís treaty; he was secretary of state from 1834 to 1841.

8. The House proceedings are in *Gales & Seaton's Register of Debates in Congress*, 988, 993–1133 (May 13–24, 1830). The Storrs quotation is on 1015; Lumpkin's, 1025; Foster's, 1036; Everett's, 1064 and 1070. Storrs was a Whig from central New York. Everett, a Boston Whig, was later governor of Massachusetts, secretary of state under Millard Fillmore, and U.S. senator. Of the 102 in favor, 99 were Democrats (Jacksonians), 3 National Republicans. Of the 98 opposed, 67 were National Republicans, 26 Democrats, 5 Anti-Masons. The South (Alabama, Georgia, Louisiana, Mississippi, North Carolina, South Carolina, Virginia) voted in favor, 44–11, with 5 negatives from North Carolina and 5 from Virginia. New England voted 9 in favor (6 of those were New Hampshire's six Democrats) and 28 opposed. The Middle Atlantic states (Delaware, Maryland, New Jersey, New York, Pennsylvania) voted 28 for, 41 against, with New York split 16–16 and Pennsylvania 7–16; of the 26 Democratic negatives, 14 were Pennsylvanian. The West (Illinois, Indiana, Kentucky, Missouri, Ohio, Tennessee) voted 21 for, 18 against. Roughly speaking, supporters were Jacksonian Democrats from the South and the border; opponents were National Republicans from north of the Mason-Dixon line and the Ohio River. Slave states voted 66–20 in favor; nonslave states voted 36–78 against.

9. Banner, *How the Indians Lost Their Land*, 196, 226. The numbers are estimates and almost certainly are undercounts.

10. The major law providing this was the Dawes Severalty Act of 1887.

11. The white birthrate in 1800 is estimated at 55 live births per thousand people per year. In 1920 it was 28, and recently has stayed around 14. Total U.S. population counted in the 1790 census was 3,929,214; in the 1890 census, 62,947,714; and in the 2006 estimate, 300,000,000.

12. Meinig, *Shaping of America*, vol. 2, 193.

13. Robert W. Johannsen, "The Meaning of Manifest Destiny," in Johannsen et al., *Manifest Destiny and Empire: American Antebellum Expansionism* (1997), 10.

9: To Alaska and across the Pacific

1. Report on Alaska of General Thomas, commander in the Pacific, to the secretary of war, included in President Grant's first annual message to Congress, 41st Cong., 2d sess., House Executive Document 1, 2:119–20.

2. U. S. Adjutant General's Office, *Correspondence Relating to the War with Spain and Conditions Growing Out of the Same* (1902), 2:858–59.

3. St. Barthélemy, Swedish until 1877, when it reverted to France.

4. Fred C. Hadden, "Midway Islands" (1941), 179; 40th Cong., 2d sess. (1867), Senate Executive Document 79, 1713; 40th Cong., 3d sess. (1868), Senate Report 194, 1362.

5. It was more complicated than that, however. See Amy S. Greenberg, *Manifest Manhood and the Antebellum American Empire* (2005), 14 and passim; for the turn of the century, Kristin L. Hoganson, *Fighting for American Manhood: How Gender Politics Provoked the Spanish-American and Philippine-American Wars* (1998).

6. Michael Adas, *Dominance by Design: Technological Imperatives and America's Civilizing Mission* (2006), explains at length the American sense of mission and how technology has helped drive it, from interaction with Indians in the seventeenth and eighteenth centuries to the "industrialization and conquest of the western frontiers" and on to the Philippines, the Caribbean, and the expansions of the twentieth century.

7. W. H. Seward, pamphlet, "The Elements of Empire" (1844), quotes from 6, 7, 10, 21. Capitals and italics are Seward's.

8. W. H. Seward, "Commerce in the Pacific Ocean," speech in the U.S. Senate, July 29, 1852 (1852), 11–13.

9. W. H. Seward, "The Continental Rights and Relations of Our Country," speech in the U.S. Senate, January 26, 1853 (1853), 2, 4, 8.

10. W. H. Seward, "The Destiny of America," speech at the dedication of Capitol University, Columbus, Ohio, September 14, 1853 (1853), 8.

11. Glyndon G. Van Deusen, *William Henry Seward* (1967), 209, 549.

12. Stephen Haycox, *Alaska: An American Colony* (2002), 175. The figures are Russian estimates made in the 1860s.

13. For details see Nikolay N. Bolkhovitinov, "The Crimean War and the Emergence of Proposals for the Sale of Russian America, 1853–1861" (1990), 15–49; Norman E. Saul, *Distant Friends: The United States and Russia, 1763–1867* (1991), 388–96.

14. Several good accounts of the March negotiations exist. A lively and succinct one is in Ronald J. Jensen, *The Alaska Purchase and Russian-American Relations* (1975), 67–79; on the czar's pro-Union position and the negotiations, see Van Deusen, *William Henry Seward*, 537–41.

15. On Seward's campaign of persuasion, see Howard I. Kushner, *Conflict on the Northwest Coast: American-Russian Rivalry in the Pacific Northwest, 1790–1867* (1975), 148–51. On press support, see Virginia Hancock Reid, *The Purchase of Alaska: Contemporary Opinion* (1939), 14, 22–31.

16. Reid's words, *Purchase of Alaska*, 15.

17. "Speech of Hon. Charles Sumner, of Massachusetts, on the Cession of Russian America to the United States . . ." (1867); quotes from 11. Sumner's initial misgivings, his discussions with his Foreign Relations Committee, and his final support are discussed in Van Deusen, *William Henry Seward*, 543, and in David Herbert Donald, *Charles Sumner and the Rights of Man* (1970), 304–10. Donald also reports that Sumner "succeeded in blocking plans to annex lands in the Caribbean," including the Danish West Indies treaty and the Dominican Republic project (354–58). Sumner's speech, and indeed the entire debate, took place during executive session of the Senate and does not appear in the *Congressional*

Globe, but this printed version probably reproduces it well, though perhaps not precisely as he delivered it.

18. "Letter of Hon. R. J. Walker, on the Purchase of Alaska, St. Thomas and St. John," Library of Congress "Meeting of Frontiers" Web site.

19. Brainerd Dyer, "Robert J. Walker on Acquiring Greenland and Iceland" (1940), 263–66.

20. Haycox, *Alaska: An American Colony*, 173. Paul S. Holbo maintains that "there is no doubt that [Stoeckl] disbursed some of the moneys at his disposal" to Walker and others, but Walker claimed they were for legal fees as Stoeckl's lawyer. Congressman Nathaniel P. Banks, chair of the Foreign Affairs Committee, was also a suspect, but Holbo concludes that "the verdict should be not guilty, or at least not proven." Holbo, *Tarnished Expansion: The Alaska Scandal, the Press, and Congress, 1867–1871* (1983), 49, 109.

21. Handwritten document, "Transfer of Alaska to the United States," in Seward Papers, Library of Congress, reel 184.

22. Lawson and Seidman, *Constitution of Empire*, 105–8.

23. Ted C. Hinckley, *The Americanization of Alaska, 1867–1897* (1972), 23, 52.

24. 41st Cong., 2d sess., House Executive Document 1, "Report of Major General George H. Thomas," San Francisco, September 27, 1869, 115, 117, 119. Thomas was in command of the military division of the Pacific, which included Alaska.

25. Frank Norris, *North to Alaska: An Overview of Immigrants to Alaska, 1867–1945* (1984), xi, 3–5.

26. Hinckley, *Americanization of Alaska*, 59–60.

27. Ted C. Hinckley, "Alaska as an American Botany Bay" (1973), 1–19.

28. Jeannette Paddock Nichols, *Alaska: A History of Its Administration, Exploitation, and Industrial Development during Its First Half Century under the Rule of the United States* (1924), 49.

29. On Alaska as a post-Klondike frontier to 1929, see James R. Shortridge, "The Alaska Agricultural Empire: An American Agrarian Vision, 1898–1929" (1978), 145–58.

30. W. H. Seward, "The Darien Canal," in George E. Baker, ed., *Works of William H. Seward* (1884), 5:589–92.

31. Guano, "from Quechua *huanu* dung. 1. a substance that is found on some coasts or islands frequented by sea fowl, is composed chiefly of their partially decomposed excrement, is rich in phosphates, nitrogenous matter, and other material for plant growth. . . ." *Webster's Third New International Dictionary* (1971), 1007. On some islands the guano deposits were initially 150 feet deep. More recently, bat excrement has also been called "guano" and also serves as fertilizer.

32. The guano island annexations are detailed in Dan O'Donnell, "The Pacific Guano Islands: The Stirring of American Empire in the Pacific Ocean" (1993), 43–66; and more extensively in Jimmy M. Skaggs, *The Great Guano Rush: Entrepreneurs and American Overseas Expansion* (1994). They show that the annexations belie the traditional view that American imperialism suddenly began in 1898.

33. It is still U.S. law: 48 *U.S. Code*, chap. 8, sections 1411–1419. The first section (1411) reads: "Whenever any citizen of the United States discovers a deposit of guano on any island, rock, or key, not within the lawful jurisdiction of any other government, and not occupied by the citizens of any other government, and takes peaceable possession thereof, and occupies the same, such island, rock, or key

may, at the discretion of the President, be considered as appertaining to the
United States."

34. Seward was then a senator from New York, his Alaskan "icebox" years in the
future. Skaggs writes, "surely the Guano Islands Act, which resulted in America's
first overseas territorial acquisitions, was Seward's Outhouse." *The Great Guano
Rush,* 56.

35. Ibid., 208–9.

36. Ibid., 230–36, includes a list of all "Places Claimed and/or Acquired under the
U.S. Guano Islands Act," with their "alleged location," "discoverer or claimant,
and filing date," and ultimate "disposition." Of the dozen still in U.S. hands,
nearly all are in the Pacific.

37. 40th Cong., 3d sess., Senate Report 194, January 28, 1869; quotes from 2, 6.

38. Samoan society and leadership are discussed in Francis J. Vest, *Political Advance-
ment in the South Pacific: A Comparative Study of Colonial Practices in Fiji, Tahiti, and
American Samoa* (1961), 126–29; Paul M. Kennedy, *The Samoan Tangle: A Study in
Anglo-German-American Relations, 1878–1900* (1974), 2–5.

39. John Bassett Moore, in his 1933 introduction to George Herbert Ryden, *The Foreign Policy of the United States in Relation to Samoa* (1975 [1933]), xv.

40. Population rose rapidly, reaching about 57,000 by the late twentieth century. See
Chai Bin Park, "Population of American Samoa" (1979); and Jerry W. Combs Jr.,
"Population Growth in American Samoa" (1974).

41. Helpful for history and description are William Albert Setchell, *American Samoa*
(1924), 3–5; Kennedy, *Samoan Tangle,* 2–21, 52–53, 65, 87–88, 95–97, 251–54,
279–80.

42. David M. Pletcher, *The Diplomacy of Involvement: American Economic Expansion
across the Pacific, 1784–1900* (2001), 90.

43. The native Hawaiian population has been estimated to have been as high as
800,000 when Cook came in 1778. Surely it was at least 400,000. Dysentery,
measles, smallpox, syphilis, gonorrhea, mumps, chicken pox, leprosy, and
influenza led the list of infections against which the natives had no immunity.
Missionaries reported in 1830 that the population was 130,000. A census in 1850
reported 84,000; three years later, after a smallpox epidemic, it was 73,000. The
native population was counted as 38,000 in 1898. By then the islands also held
around 18,000 Chinese, 12,000 Japanese, and 10,000 Portuguese—mostly contract workers on sugar plantations—and smaller numbers of others. There were
about 2,000 Americans there in 1884. Merze Tate, *The United States and the
Hawaiian Kingdom: A Political History* (1965), 44; David E. Stannard, "Disease and
Infertility: A New Look at the Demographic Collapse of Native Populations in
the Wake of Western Contact" (1990), 325–50; Robert C. Schmitt, "Catastrophic
Mortality in Hawai'i: An Update" (1989), 217–27; Nugent, *Into the West,* 128–29.
Infertility helped cause the Kamehameha family line to die out by the 1870s, con-
tributing to the instability of the monarchy.

44. Good discussions of the Great Mahele of 1845–1850 and its results are in Tate,
United States and the Hawaiian Kingdom, 18, and Jonathan Kay Kamakawiwo'ole
Osorio, *Dismembering Lāhui: A History of the Hawaiian Nation to 1887* (2002),
44–53. Osorio writes that the division was "disastrous" (44) for the ordinary
native people but a boon to haoles.

45. Pletcher, *Diplomacy of Involvement,* 47.

46. Ibid., 57.

47. Noenoe Silva, *Aloha Betrayed: Native Hawaiian Resistance to American Colonialism* (2004), 225.

48. Osorio, *Dismembering Lāhui,* 199.

49. Nationalist historians such as Osorio and Silva see the Bayonet Constitution—correctly—as the crucial event in the Hawaiians' loss of control. See Osorio, *Dismembering Lāhui,* 193–203; and Silva, *Aloha Betrayed,* 126–27. So do non-nationalist historians; Gavin Daws, *Shoal of Time: A History of the Hawaiian Islands* (1968), 248–53, writes that the Reformers believed in white racial supremacy, and in the supremacy of property owners, and that they did one thing after another "to knock Kalakaua over and bind him hand and foot. [They] seemed to enjoy kicking the king while he was down."

50. Merze Tate, *Hawaii: Reciprocity or Annexation* (1968), 245.

51. Words of historian Charles S. Campbell, *The Transformation of American Foreign Relations, 1865–1900* (1976), 179; his stance is nationalist, but American, not Hawaiian.

52. Quoted in ibid., 180.

53. Tate, *United States and the Hawaiian Kingdom,* 117.

54. Silva, *Aloha Betrayed,* 167 (quote); Tate, *United States and the Hawaiian Kingdom,* 156; Daws, *Shoal of Time,* 270–71.

55. For close accounts of the events of January 14–17, see Daws, *Shoal of Time,* 270–77; Silva, *Aloha Betrayed,* 123–30; Tate, *United States and the Hawaiian Kingdom,* chap. 5. Tate points out that the annexationist-insurrectionists were very solid citizens—"lawyers, legislators, merchants," etc., not a wild-eyed radical among them, but they had one aim in common: "the extirpation of the Hawaiian monarchy" (165). They are reminiscent of the "patriots" of West and East Florida in 1810–1813. The Hawaiian insurrectionists, however, had the direct and immediate support of U.S. armed forces.

56. Silva, *Aloha Betrayed,* 134.

57. Ibid., 167.

58. Joseph A. Fry, *John Tyler Morgan and the Search for Southern Autonomy* (1992), 84–88.

59. Allan Nevins, *Grover Cleveland: A Study in Courage* (1932), 559–60: "The provisional government had prepared to defend itself by placing sandbags about its buildings, and by a general issuance of arms to its supporters. Plainly it could not be ejected by force without much bloodshed." Two more recent biographies offer no further explanations: Richard E. Welch Jr., *The Presidencies of Grover Cleveland* (1988), 174; and Henry F. Graff, *Grover Cleveland* (2002), 123.

60. Silva, *Aloha Betrayed,* 148; Fry, *John Tyler Morgan,* 167. Morgan had been a Confederate brigadier general and after Reconstruction served six terms in the U.S. Senate. As one of the leading Democrats on foreign policy, he might have become secretary of state had William Jennings Bryan been elected president in 1896. Morgan was "the New South's foremost expansionist," and he was also a leading segregationist, with "an unbending devotion to white supremacy." Fry, *John Tyler Morgan,* xii. An academy in Selma, Alabama, his hometown, is named after him. For a time Morgan's Senate colleague was Edmund Pettus, another former Confederate general from Selma. A bridge is named after him—the one that the Selma civil rights marchers crossed in 1965 on their way to Montgomery.

61. For this account I rely on Tate, *United States and the Hawaiian Kingdom*, 298–307 (quote, 307); and Silva, *Aloha Betrayed*, 148–61.

62. Lawson and Seidman, *Constitution of Empire*, 109–10.

63. The "Massie Affair" of 1931–1932, over the alleged rape of the wife of a young American naval officer by several Hawaiian men and the kidnapping and murder of one of them by the officer and his wife's mother, demonstrated the white-supremacy attitudes of the white civilian elite and also of the navy. A jury con-victed the officer and mother-in-law of manslaughter, but the U.S. territorial governor commuted their ten-year sentences to one hour. For detail see David E. Stannard, *Honor Killing: How the Infamous "Massie Affair" Transformed Hawai'i* (2005). About American racism in Hawaii in general, see John Gregory Dunne, "The American Raj" (2001), 46–54.

64. *Chicago Tribune*, May 29, 2006, story on the Akaka bill.

65. *Chicago Tribune*, June 9, 2006. All 41 nays were from Republicans; the yeas included 42 Democrats, one Independent, and 13 Republicans. In January 2007, Senator Lamar Alexander (Republican of Tennessee) objected to Akaka's bill, contending that Hawaiians "do not meet the requirements under current law of being sovereign for the last 100 years, living as a separate and distinct community, and having a preexisting political organization," like recognized tribes of Indians. He did not refer to the Hawaiian monarchy, which was surely a "preexisting polit-ical organization," whose absence for 114 years resulted from the haole coup. For the Akaka and Alexander quotations see http://www.hawaiireporter.com/story for January 20, 2007.

66. To be described in Chapter 10.

67. Lewis L. Gould, *The Spanish-American War and President McKinley* (1980), 99–100.

68. Gould writes, "The president made the difference. From Dewey's victory onward, he guided events so that American acquisition of the Philippines became logical and, to politicians and the people, inevitable" (ibid., 118).

69. Walter L. Williams, "United States Indian Policy and the Debate over Philippine Annexation: Implications for the Origins of American Imperialism" (1980), 810, 815, 820, 824, 827–28. This essay documents how nineteenth-century treat-ment of Indians provided precedent for treatment of Filipinos in 1899–1902. In both cases, U.S. actions were based on a "dichotomy between savagism and civilization" (831).

70. *U.S. Statutes at Large*, March 1897 to March 1899, XXX (1899). Italics added.

71. U.S. Bureau of the Census, *Historical Statistics of the United States, Colonial Times to 1970*, 1:422 (series H 1168–70, "Persons Lynched, by Race, 1882 to 1970").

72. Fred Anderson and Andrew Cayton, *The Dominion of War: Empire and Liberty in North America, 1500–2000* (2005), 333; David Haward Bain, *Sitting in Darkness: Americans in the Philippines* (1984), 185; Brian McAllister Linn, *The Philippine War, 1899–1902* (2000), 46–52. Linn gives lower figures: on February 4–5, he writes, "American casualties totaled 238, of whom 44 were killed in action or died of wounds. . . . Filipino losses can only be estimated. . . . The army's official report listed total Army of Liberation [Filipino] casualties as 4,000, of whom 700 were killed, but this is guesswork" (52).

73. Quoted in Mark D. Van Ellis, "Assuming the White Man's Burden: The Seizure of the Philippines, 1898–1902" (1995), 618. This is one of many sources docu-

menting prevalent racism and parallels with Indian fighting. Others include Stuart Creighton Miller, *"Benevolent Assimilation": The American Conquest of the Philippines, 1899–1903* (1982), esp. chaps. 10–12; Stanley Karnow, *In Our Image: America's Empire in the Philippines* (1989), esp. chaps. 5–7; Linn, *Philippine War*, esp. index listings under "Misconduct, American," and "Misconduct, insurgent"; Richard E. Welch Jr., "American Atrocities in the Philippines: The Indictment and the Response" (1974), 233–53.

74. Glenn A. May, "Private Presher and Sergeant Vergara: The Underside of the Philippine-American War" (1984), 43.

75. Welch, "American Atrocities," 238–39; Karnow, *In Our Image*, 191–94.

76. Twain's satire, "A Defence of General Funston," in three segments, appears online at http://www.boondocksnet.com/ai/twain/deffunst.html; quotations here are from part 3, page 1. The piece was published in *North American Review*, May 1902. For a brief biography of Funston and his wartime activities, see Stuart Creighton Miller, "Funston, Frederick," in *American National Biography*, at www.anb.org/articles/06/06-00206.html.

77. Edward Atkinson, "Criminal Aggression: By Whom Committed?," 55th Cong., 3d sess., Senate Document 163, March 1, 1899, 12. Presented by Senator Jefferson Caffery (Democrat of Louisiana), one of the anti-imperialists.

78. "The Philippine Situation," 57th Cong., 1st sess., Senate Document 422, including "Speech of Hon. Albert J. Beveridge, of Indiana, in the Senate of the United States, Tuesday, June 3, 1902," 77–78. Also, Charles E. Magoon, "Report on the Legal Status of the Territory and Inhabitants of the Islands Acquired by the United States during the War with Spain . . . ," 56th Cong., 1st sess., Senate Document 234, February 12, 1900.

79. For details consult Paul T. McCartney, *Power and Progress: American National Identity, the War of 1898, and the Rise of American Imperialism* (2006), 230–65. McCartney points out the good and the bad: "Unquestionably, American rule in its new colonies was far superior in every respect to Spain's. . . . But it was not benign, and it was not consistent with American ideals" (276).

80. Gould, *Spanish-American War*, 124–26; Miller, *Benevolent Assimilation*, 250. All but two Republicans voted for the Organic Act, and all but one Democrat voted against. The Schurman Commission's report is 56th Cong., 1st sess., Senate Document 138, in four volumes; the Taft Commission's report is 56th Cong., 2d sess., Senate Document 112, January 25, 1901 (quotes, 15, 17); the Fifth Annual Report (for 1904), under Luke E. Wright, is 58th Cong., 3d sess., House Document 232, (quote, 14).

81. Anna Leah Fidelis T. Castaneda, "The Board of Control: Cases in the Philippine Islands: Containing Colonial Conflict in Constitutional Categories" (2007); Kenton Clymer, review of Paul Kramer's *The Blood of Government: Race, Empire, the United States, and the Philippines* (2007), 473. The Democratic Congress passed the Jones Act over vigorous Republican opposition.

82. The takeover story may be found in several sources, without substantial variance. See, e.g., Paul Carno and Pedro C. Sanchez, *A Complete History of Guam* (1964), 170–77; Robert F. Rogers, *Destiny's Landfall: A History of Guam* (1995), 109–15; Timothy P. Maga, *Defending Paradise: The United States and Guam, 1898–1950* (1988), 5–17; Leslie W. Walker, "Guam's Seizure by the United States in 1898" (1945), 1–12.

83. The formerly Japanese islands came under U.N. trusteeship after 1945, with the U.S. as trustee. Eventually the Northern Mariana Islands became a U.S. Commonwealth, and the Republic of the Marshall Islands, the Federated States of Micronesia, and Palau each signed a Compact of Free Association with the United States.

84. The "myth of the China market" developed at least as early as Seward's time and gathered strength after the Panic of 1893 and the ensuing depression, which lasted through most of the 1890s. See Thomas J. McCormick, *China Market: America's Quest for Informal Empire, 1893–1901* (1967), esp. 17–19, 54ff. Like William Appleman Williams, McCormick connects empire-building across North America to empire-building across the Pacific: "continentalism was not (and never had been) the sole avenue of expansion" (18).

10: Around the Caribbean

1. William D. Boyce, *United States Colonies and Dependencies Illustrated: The Travels and Investigations of a Chicago Publisher in the Colonial Possessions and Dependencies of the United States* . . . (1914), 414–15. Boyce is speaking here of Puerto Ricans, but his racial attitudes applied equally to Filipinos, Cubans, and others. Boyce was a philanthropic man, the founder of the Boy Scouts of America. He was an invincibly Republican progressive, fearing that the (Democratic) Wilson administration was about to undo all the civilizing efforts of the (Republican) Theodore Roosevelt and Taft administrations. (See, e.g., 403.) My thanks to Burt Chudacoff for his copy of Boyce's book.

2. Seward's Caribbean voyage is described in journals by his son Fred and daughter-in-law Anna Wharton Seward in box 2, Seward Papers "Additions," Special Collections, University of Rochester Library.

3. U.S. Congress, 45th Cong., 2d sess., Senate Executive Document 79 (May 14, 1878), " . . . information respecting the terms and conditions under which the surrender of the Cuban insurgents has been made . . . ," 1, 19.

4. For a good analysis of the Spanish situation, see John L. Offner, *An Unwanted War: The Diplomacy of the United States and Spain over Cuba, 1895–1898* (1992), 225–27.

5. (Admiral) Hyman G. Rickover, *How the Battleship Maine Was Destroyed* (1976).

6. McKinley, in more detail, asked Congress "to authorize and empower the President to take measures to secure a full and final termination of hostilities between the Government of Spain and the people of Cuba, and to secure in the island the establishment of a stable government, capable of maintaining order and observing its international obligations, insuring peace and tranquillity and the security of its citizens as well as our own, and to use the military and naval forces of the United States as may be necessary for these purposes." In Commager, *Documents of American History*, 2:3,4, taken from James Richardson, ed., *Messages and Papers of the Presidents*, 1:139ff.

7. Commager, *Documents of American History*, 2:5, reprinting *U.S. Statutes at Large*, 30:738. Teller was a "Silver Republican," one of the western Republicans who split with the McKinley administration and mainline Republicans on the currency question, the overriding issue in the 1896 election.

8. Elmer Ellis, *Henry Moore Teller: Defender of the West* (1941), 316. Ellis opined that

Teller, "like most of them [his fellow Americans], was trying to eat his cake as imperial glory and to keep it as the American dream of freedom and liberty" (314). Historian Louis Pérez and Teller biographer Duane Smith have suggested that Teller may have been motivated in part by the potential competition from Cuba's cane sugar to the beet sugar production of Teller's Colorado, but if so that did not explain the Senate's unanimous vote for Teller's resolution. Louis A. Pérez Jr., *Cuba between Empires, 1878–1902* (1983), 186; Duane A. Smith, *Henry M. Teller: Colorado's Grand Old Man* (2002), 217. Another motive for avoiding annexation, present though hard to measure, was the likelihood of having to assume Cuban debts incurred in the insurrection. Teller also shared commonly held racial views, believing that as "Asiatics," Filipinos were less capable of self-government than Anglo-Saxons; tropical climates inhibit intelligence and morality, etc. See McCartney, *Power and Progress*, 248–49, 254–55.

9. Pérez, *Cuba between Empires, 1878–1902*, 197.
10. John Lawrence Tone, *War and Genocide in Cuba, 1895–1898* (2006), 273–80.
11. David F. Trask, *The War with Spain in 1898* (1981), 245. I have followed Trask's clear and detailed account of the military operations in Cuba and Puerto Rico.
12. Ibid., 255.
13. Described in ibid., chap. 11, 259–85.
14. As cited in David Healy, *Drive to Hegemony: The United States in the Caribbean, 1898–1917* (1988), 47.
15. Trask, *War with Spain*, 324–35, relates the threat and reality of the epidemics and the creation of the Montauk camp. He sums up the Cuban campaign praising McKinley:

> The campaign at Santiago de Cuba had been hastily decided upon, after Cervera [and the Spanish navy] had been penned up, as a means of applying immediate pressure on the enemy in a location as propitious for the Americans as it was unfavorable for the Spanish. Unable to mount an early campaign against Havana, the center of Spanish strength in Cuba, President McKinley wisely chose to conduct an operation in this peripheral location where a modest military accomplishment still might well yield important political results. (335)

16. Pérez, *Cuba between Empires*, 208–10. Tone adds that American officers and men "experienced a change of heart about the insurgents. In part, it was simply a matter of the racism of white officers and soldiers reasserting itself." Americans could not stomach "the destitution of the Cuban guerrilla forces." Contrariwise, as in the Philippines, the American attitude toward the Spanish warmed; they became "brave and honorable and . . . bulwarks of civilization against the insurgents. Above all, they turned out to be white." Tone, *War and Genocide in Cuba*, 283–85.
17. Herminio Portell Vilá, *Historia de Cuba en sus relaciones con Los Estados Unidos y España* (1939), 3:472, 540–41.
18. Trask, *War with Spain*, 367.
19. Quoted from 56th Cong., 1st sess., House Document 2, "Annual Reports of the War Department for the Fiscal Year Ended June 30, 1899: Report of Brig. Gen. Geo. W. Davis on Civil Affairs in Puerto Rico," 484, 486–87.

20. Warren Zimmermann, *First Great Triumph: How Five Americans Made Their Country a World Power* (2002), 489.

21. Carmen Diana Deere, "Here Come the Yankees! The Rise and Decline of United States Colonies in Cuba, 1898–1930" (1998), 729–65.

22. 56th Cong., 1st sess., House Document 2, "Annual Reports of the War Department for the Fiscal Year ended June 30, 1899: Report of Maj. Gen. J. R. Brooke on Civil Affairs in Cuba," 6.

23. In 1902 the War Department reported to Congress that nearly 32,000 acres of land in Cuba had come into American ownership. 57th Cong., 2d sess., House Document 51, "Purchase of Land by Nonresidents in Cuba since Date of American Occupation, Etc.," December 3, 1902, 9.

24. Commager, *Documents of American History*, 2:29. Article VI provided that the Isle of Pines, off the southwest coast of Cuba, which had attracted some thousands of American would-be citrus farmers, "shall be omitted from the boundaries of Cuba," but this article was annulled a few years later.

25. Louis A. Pérez Jr., *Cuba under the Platt Amendment, 1902–1934* (1986), 338. Also helpful is Jules R. Benjamin, *The United States and the Origins of the Cuban Revolution: An Empire of Liberty in an Age of National Liberation* (1990), 76–91; and Deere, "Here Come the Yankees!," 754–55, 764–65.

26. The most recent and complete history of the "Insular Cases" is Bartholomew H. Sparrow, *The Insular Cases and the Emergence of American Empire* (2006). Sparrow writes, "The immediate impact of the Supreme Court's decisions in 1901 was to ratify the expansionism of . . . McKinley . . . Theodore Roosevelt . . . Taft . . . Root . . . Lodge, and other prominent Republicans" (6).

27. The Nicaraguan route still remains a possibility, especially as both naval and merchant vessels have outgrown the Panama Canal. See "Nicaragua Hopes Ship Comes In: Backers Say Building a Canal to Rival Panama's Would Fulfill the Nation's 'Destiny' . . . ," *Chicago Tribune*, December 23, 2006.

28. The story of the U.S. acquisition of the Canal Zone is well known and requires no elaborate documentation. For fair and detailed treatments, see Walter LaFeber, *The Panama Canal: The Crisis in Historical Perspective* (1978); and John Major, *Prize Possession: The United States and the Panama Canal* (1993).

29. Gordon Connell-Smith, *The United States and Latin America: An Historical Analysis of Inter-American Relations* (1974), 121. On Wilson carrying an even bigger stick into Central America than Theodore Roosevelt did, see Walter LaFeber, "Wilson's Corollary to the Monroe Doctrine," in *Inevitable Revolutions: The United States and Central America* (1993), 51–55.

30. G. Pope Atkins and Larman C. Wilson, *The Dominican Republic and the United States: From Imperialism to Transnationalism* (1998), 45; Healy, *Drive to Hegemony*, 193–97.

31. Stephen Kinzer, *Overthrow: America's Century of Regime Change from Hawaii to Iraq* (2006), 70. Kinzer describes other coups: Iran, 1953; Guatemala, 1954; South Vietnam, 1963; Chile, 1973; Grenada and Panama in the 1980s; Afghanistan, 2001; Iraq, 2003.

32. Connell-Smith, *United States and Latin America*, 129–32; Healy, *Drive to Hegemony*, 184–87.

33. Connell-Smith, *United States and Latin America*, 142; Robert D. Schulzinger, *U.S. Diplomacy since 1900* (1998), 50; Healy, *Drive to Hegemony*, 187–92.

34. LaFeber, in *Inevitable Revolutions*, 13. This book details "how North Americans turned away from revolution toward defense of oligarchs" (13).

35. For a full description of the Dominican case, consult Bruce J. Calder, *The Impact of Intervention: The Dominican Republic during the U.S. Occupation of 1916–1924* (1984).

36. 55th Cong., 2d sess., Senate Report 816 (March 31, 1898), "Naval Station in the West Indies," 6.

37. Charles Callan Tansill, *The Purchase of the Danish West Indies* (1932), 455, 467, 468, 476, 481–82 (Dewey quote), 484, 505, 515 (Tansill quote).

38. One well-put expression of the Irish precedent for English imperial methods and attitudes (though not the only one) is in Anderson and Cayton, *Dominion of War*, 43–44.

39. Ibid., 44. Similarly, Edmund S. Morgan and Marie Morgan, "Our Shaky Beginnings" (2007), reviewing Karen Ordahl Kupperman, *The Jamestown Project:* "The Irish shared with American Indians a profound deficiency that required correction if they were to make proper subjects: they were not *civil*."

POSTSCRIPT: THE GLOBAL EMPIRE

1. United Nations, "Adopted and proclaimed by General Assembly resolution 217 A (III) of 10 December 1948," Preamble.

2. Nugent, *Into the West*, 238.

3. Historian Fredrick B. Pike points out that people on the left and the right will never agree about Roosevelt's New Deal, and therefore about the Good Neighbor policy either; they "will lie in wait, ready to pounce on anyone who attempts this assessment either from the pole opposite to the one they defend or from the perspective of the center: the perspective that—properly, it seems to me—always most appealed to FDR himself." Pike, *FDR's Good Neighbor Policy: Sixty Years of Generally Gentle Chaos* (1995), xiv.

4. Nugent, *Into the West*, 251–52.

5. Franklin D. Roosevelt, *The Public Papers and Addresses of Franklin D. Roosevelt*, "1940 Volume," 672.

6. Ibid., "1941 Volume," 314–15.

7. Anderson and Cayton, *Dominion of War*, 392.

8. "X" [George F. Kennan], "The Sources of Soviet Conduct" (1947), 566–82.

9. George F. Kennan, *At a Century's Ending: Reflections, 1982–1995* (1996), 94 (italics Kennan's), and 111, reprinting addresses that Kennan gave in 1983 and 1985. Also, Kennan, "Reflections on Containment" (1987), 15.

10. Kennan, *At a Century's Ending*, 94.

11. As of 1959, the United States was party to NATO, ranging from Canada and Iceland to Greece and Turkey; to CENTO (Central Asia), including Pakistan and Iran; to the ANZUS treaty with Australia and New Zealand; to SEATO, the Southeast Asian Treaty Organization, including Thailand and the Philippines; the Organization of American States, including twenty Latin American republics; plus treaties with Japan, Korea, and Taiwan.

12. Dwight D. Eisenhower, *Public Papers of the Presidents: Dwight D. Eisenhower*, 1960–61 (1961), 1038; paper 421, given January 17, 1961.

13. For a useful survey of these coups, see Kinzer, *Overthrow*.

14. William Appleman Williams, "Empire as a Way of Life," 116.

15. Jeane J. Kirkpatrick, *Dictatorships and Double Standards: Rationalism and Reason in Politics* (1982), 49; these pages "originally appeared in the November 1979 issue of *Commentary*."

16. For a thorough, country-by-country explanation of the fall of the Soviet and East European Communist regimes, see Tony Judt, *Postwar: A History of Europe since 1945* (2005).

17. Manichaeanism was a third-century A.D. Persian religion that influenced Christianity from then into the Middle Ages. It "rests on a dualistic concept of the world's structure. A radical duality between Light and Darkness, Good and Evil, existed from the beginning." Richard P. McBrien, *Encyclopedia of Catholicism* (1995), 810.

18. Brian Urquhart, "World Order & Mr. Bush" (2003), reviewing Clyde Prestowitz, *Rogue Nation: American Unilateralism and the Failure of Good Intentions*, 10. According to Urquhart, Prestowitz "deplores Washington's tendency to view world events through a single prism—formerly fear of communism, and now fear of terrorism."

19. Robert Kagan, *Dangerous Nation: America's Place in the World from Its Earliest Days to the Dawn of the Twentieth Century* (2006), 85.

20. The Republican staff of the Senate Foreign Relations Committee reported in late 2006 that "some embassies have effectively become command posts, with military personnel in those countries all but supplanting the role of ambassadors in conducting American foreign policy." *New York Times*, December 20, 2006.

21. Office of the President, "The National Security Strategy of the United States of America, September 2002," 1, 2, 29. From the White House Web site, www .whitehouse.gov/nsc/nss/2002.

22. For cases of how two presidents led the United States into wars for reasons that were (or shortly proved to be) false, and their exertions of executive power, see Walter Nugent, "The American Habit of Empire, and the Cases of Polk and Bush" (2007), 5–24.

23. See Robert Skidelsky, "Hot, Cold & Imperial" (2006), 55, reviewing Charles S. Maier's *Among Empires: American Ascendancy and Its Predecessors*. In the reviewed book, Maier

> decided to avoid claiming that the United States is or is not an empire. I have found such assertions so polarizing that readers never get past the definition. . . . The United States reveals many, but not all—at least not yet—of the traits that have distinguished empires. . . . For many observers, the United States has become an empire of a new type [as Skidelsky suggests], its ascendancy based not only on military superiority, but on economic and technological prowess and the appeal of its popular culture. . . . [It may] emerge as the most problematic empire of all—controlling not so much a stable territory as global finances and naval, air, and electronic spectrum space. (3, 8, 32)

Maier discounts—unfortunately, to my mind—the acquisition of the transcontinental empire, chiefly by regarding Native Americans as "nomads" (26) or "partly settled, partly nomadic" (89), and "sparse and already depleted" in numbers by 1800 or so. Except for the Plains Indians, however, very few were nomads; Acoma

Pueblo, New Mexico, for example, has been continuously settled for over a thousand years. Aided by pathogens, the white conquest was easier than for other empire builders on the Eurasian landmass. But it was a conquest nonetheless, and Jefferson and his followers called it "empire."

Joseph A. Fry provides a sensible "working definition" of imperialism. "The key considerations are power, control, and intent. Imperialism and hence empire exist when a stronger nation or society imposes or attempts to impose control over a weaker nation or group of people. This control may be formal (via annexations, protectorates, or military occupations) or informal (via economic control, cultural domination, or threat of intervention). The informal species of empire might involve businessmen, missionaries, and other non-state actors." Joseph A. Fry, "Imperialism, American Style, 1890–1916" (1994), 53.

24. The favorable side includes Niall Ferguson, *Colossus: The Price of America's Empire* (2004), esp. 7, 23; Robert D. Kaplan, *Imperial Grunts: The American Military on the Ground* (2005), esp. 3, 7, 8. Kaplan remarks on the continuity between nineteenth-century continental empire-building and today's: "By the turn of the twenty-first century the United States military had already appropriated the entire earth, and was ready to flood the most obscure areas of it. . . . 'Welcome to Injun Country' was the refrain I heard from troops from Colombia to the Philippines, including Afghanistan and Iraq." Critical of empire-building is Chalmers Johnson (*The Sorrows of Empire: Militarism, Secrecy, and the End of the Republic* [2004]; see, e.g., 4); and the colonel-turned-professor Andrew Bacevich (*American Empire: The Realities and Consequences of U.S. Diplomacy* [2002]; see, e.g., viii, 215–20, 244). The Pentagon's installations are listed in Department of Defense, *Base Structure Report: A Summary of DoD's Real Property Inventory*, issued annually since 1999. The 2006 edition is available online at www.acq.osd.mil/ie/irm/irm_library/BSR2006Baseline.pdf.

25. As suggested by Paul M. Kennedy, *The Rise and Fall of the Great Powers: Economic Change and Military Conflict from 1500 to 2000* (1987).

26. Yehoshua Arieli, *The Future-Directed Character of the American Experience* (1966).

27. Frederick Jackson Turner, "The Problem of the West" (1986 [1896]), 219. Turner was right about the three centuries, now more than four, though his next sentence was wrong: "With the settlement of the Pacific coast and the occupation of the free lands, this movement has come to a check." He did not see that the Alaskan expansion was part of the story, and he did not know that the so-called free lands would not fill up until around 1920.

28. Turner's classic essay stating the "Turner thesis" appeared slightly earlier: "The Significance of the Frontier in American History," originally a paper delivered at the 1893 meeting of the American Historical Association in Chicago. It is reprinted in Turner, *The Frontier in American History* (1986 [1920]), and in many other works.

Bibliography

This bibliography lists only the items cited in the Notes. I consulted many more, very usefully, and specialists may wonder at their absence. But including them would have greatly extended this list to no good purpose. Works are listed alphabetically, regardless of the provenance or form of publication.

Abernethy, Thomas P. *The South in the New Nation, 1789–1819.* Baton Rouge: Louisiana State University Press, 1961.

Acton, Lord (John Emerich Edward Dalberg-Acton). *Selected Writings of Lord Acton.* J. Rufus Fears, ed. Indianapolis: Liberty Classics, 1986.

Adam, G. Mercer, and W. J. Robertson. *Public School History of England and Canada.* Toronto: Copp, Clark, 1886.

Adams, Ephraim Douglass, ed. "British Correspondence concerning Texas, XX." *Southwestern Historical Quarterly* 20 (October 1916), 154–93.

Adams, Henry. *History of the United States of America during the First Administration of Thomas Jefferson.* Vol. 2. New York: Scribner, 1903.

Adams, John Quincy. *Memoirs of John Quincy Adams.* Vol. 12, 173–74. Reprinted in Walter LaFeber, ed., *John Quincy Adams and American Continental Empire: Letters, Papers and Speeches,* 148. Chicago: Quadrangle Books, 1965.

Adas, Michael. *Dominance by Design: Technological Imperatives and America's Civilizing Mission.* Cambridge, Mass.: Belknap Press of Harvard University Press, 2006.

Akenson, Donald Harman. *The Irish in Ontario: A Study of Rural History.* Kingston, Ont.: McGill-Queen's University Press, 1984.

Almonte, Juan Nepomuceno. *Noticia estadística sobre Tejas.* Mexico: Impreso por Ignacio Complido, 1835.

Anderson, Fred, and Andrew Cayton. *The Dominion of War: Empire and Liberty in North America, 1500–2000.* New York: Viking, 2005.

Anderson, Gary Clayton. *The Conquest of Texas: Ethnic Cleansing in the Promised Land, 1820–1875.* Norman: University of Oklahoma Press, 2005.

Anderson, Stuart. "British Threats and the Settlement of the Oregon Boundary Dispute." *Pacific Northwest Quarterly* 66 (October 1975), 153–60.

Annals of Congress. 7th Cong., 2d sess.; 8th Cong., 1st sess.; 12th Cong., 1st sess. Washington: Gales and Seaton, 1851–1853.

Apuntes para la história de la guerra entre México y los Estados-Unidos. Mexico City: Tipografía de Manuel Payne, 1848.

Arieli, Yehoshua. *The Future-Directed Character of the American Experience.* Jerusalem: Magnes Press, 1966.

Aron, Stephen. *American Confluence: The Missouri Frontier from Borderland to Border State*. Bloomington: Indiana University Press, 2005.

Arthur, Stanley Clisby. *The Story of the West Florida Rebellion*. St. Francisville, La.: St. Francisville Democrat, 1935.

Ashford, Gerald. "Jacksonian Liberalism and Spanish Law in Early Texas." *Southwestern Historical Quarterly* 57 (July 1953), 1–37.

Atkins, G. Pope, and Larman C. Wilson. *The Dominican Republic and the United States: From Imperialism to Transnationalism*. Athens: University of Georgia Press, 1998.

Atkinson, Edward. "Criminal Aggression: By Whom Committed?" In U.S. Senate Document 163, 55th Cong., 3d sess., March 1, 1899.

Bacevich, Andrew. *American Empire: The Realities and Consequences of U.S. Diplomacy*. Cambridge, Mass.: Harvard University Press, 2002.

Bain, David Haward. *Sitting in Darkness: Americans in the Philippines*. Boston: Houghton Mifflin, 1984.

Bancroft, Hubert Howe. *History of the North Mexican States and Texas, 1801–1889*. Vol. 2. San Francisco: History Company, 1889.

Banner, Stuart. *How the Indians Lost Their Land: Law and Order on the Frontier*. Cambridge, Mass.: Belknap Press of Harvard University Press, 2005.

Barbé-Marbois, [François]. *The History of Louisiana, particularly of the Cession of That Colony to the United States of America. . . .* Philadelphia: Carey & Lea, 1830.

Barker, Eugene C. "The Annexation of Texas." *Southwestern Historical Quarterly* 50 (July 1946), 49–74.

———. "Land Speculation as a Cause of the Texas Revolution." *Quarterly of the Texas State Historical Association* 10 (1906), 76–95.

———. "Notes on the Colonization of Texas." *Southwestern Historical Quarterly* 27 (October 1923), 108–19.

Barlow, William R. "Ohio's Congressmen and the War of 1812." *Ohio History* 72 (July 1963), 175–94.

Barnes, James J., and Patience P. Barnes. *Private and Confidential: Letters from British Ministers in Washington to the Foreign Secretaries in London, 1844–67*. Selinsgrove, Pa.: Susquehanna University Press, 1993.

Becker, Jerónimo. *Historia de los relaciones exteriores de España durante el siglo XIX*. Vol. 1. Madrid: Establecimiento Tipográfico de Jaime Ratés, 1924.

———. *La politica española en Las Indias*. Madrid: Imprenta de Jaime Ratés Martin, 1920.

Beisner, Robert L., ed. *American Foreign Relations since 1600: A Guide to the Literature*. 2 vols. Santa Barbara, Calif.: ABC Clio, 2003.

Bemis, Samuel Flagg. *The Diplomacy of the American Revolution*. Bloomington: Indiana University Press, 1957.

———. "Jay's Treaty and the Northwest Boundary Gap." *American Historical Review* 27 (April 1922), 465–84.

Benjamin, Jules R. *The United States and the Origins of the Cuban Revolution: An Empire of Liberty in an Age of National Liberation*. Princeton: Princeton University Press, 1990.

Benn, Carl. *The Iroquois in the War of 1812*. Toronto: University of Toronto Press, 1998.

———. *The War of 1812*. Oxford, U.K.: Osprey, 2002.

Benson, Nettie Lee. "Texas as Viewed from Mexico, 1820–1834." *Southwestern Historical Quarterly* 90 (January 1987), 219–91.

Berlin, Isaiah. *The Hedgehog and the Fox: An Essay on Tolstoy's View of History*. New York: Touchstone, 1986 (1953).

Beveridge, Albert J. "The Philippine Situation." In U.S. Senate Document 422, 57th Cong., 1st sess., June 3, 1902, 77–78.

Bolkhovitinov, Nikolay N. "The Crimean War and the Emergence of Proposals for the Sale of Russian America, 1853–1861." *Pacific Historical Review* 59 (February 1990), 15–49.

Bosch Garcia, Carlos. *Historia de las relaciones entre México y los Estados Unidos 1819–1848*. Mexico City: Escuela Nacional de Ciencias Politicas y Sociales, Universidad Nacional Autónoma de México, 1961.

Botero, Rodrigo. *Ambivalent Embrace: America's Troubled Relations with Spain from the Revolutionary War to the Cold War*. Westport, Conn.: Greenwood, 2001.

Bowman, Albert H. "Pichon, the United States, and Louisiana." *Diplomatic History* 1 (summer 1977), 257–70.

Boyce, William D. *United States Colonies and Dependencies Illustrated: The Travels and Investigations of a Chicago Publisher in the Colonial Possessions and Dependencies of the United States. . . .* Chicago: Rand McNally, 1914.

Boyd, Robert. *The Coming of the Spirit of Pestilence: Introduced Infectious Diseases and Population Decline among Northwest Coast Indians, 1774–1874*. Vancouver, B.C.: UBC Press, and Seattle: University of Washington Press, 1999.

Brackinridge, H. M. *Views of Louisiana*. Pittsburgh: Cramer, Spear and Eichbaum, 1814.

Brooks, Philip C. *Diplomacy and the Borderlands: The Adams-Onís Treaty of 1819*. Berkeley: University of California Press, 1939.

Calder, Bruce J. *The Impact of Intervention: The Dominican Republic during the U.S. Occupation of 1916–1924*. Austin: University of Texas Press, 1984.

Calloway, Colin G. "The End of an Era: British-Indian Relations in the Great Lakes Region after the War of 1812." *Michigan Historical Review* 12 (fall 1986), 1–20.

Campbell, Charles S. *The Transformation of American Foreign Relations, 1865–1900*. New York: Harper & Row, 1976.

Campbell, Randolph B. *An Empire for Slavery: The Peculiar Institution in Texas, 1821–1865*. Baton Rouge: Louisiana State University Press, 1989.

Cantrell, Gregg. *Stephen F. Austin: Empresario of Texas*. New Haven: Yale University Press, 1992.

Carey, Lewis J. "Franklin Is Informed of Clark's Activities in the Old Northwest." *Mississippi Valley Historical Review* 21 (1934–1935), 375–78.

Carno, Paul, and Pedro C. Sanchez. *A Complete History of Guam*. Rutland, Vt.: Charles E. Tuttle, 1964.

Carroll, Francis M. *A Good and Wise Measure: The Search for the Canadian-American Boundary, 1783–1842*. Toronto: University of Toronto Press, 2001.

———. "The Passionate Canadians: The Historical Debate about the Eastern Canadian-American Boundary." *New England Quarterly* 70 (March 1997), 83–101.

Carter, Clarence Edwin, ed. and comp. *The Territorial Papers of the United States*. Vol. 6, *The Territory of Mississippi, 1809–1817*. Washington, D.C.: Government Printing Office, 1938.

Castaneda, Anna Leah Fidelis T. "The Board of Control: Cases in the Philippine Islands: Containing Colonial Conflict in Constitutional Categories." Paper read at the annual meeting of the Organization of American Historians, Minneapolis, March 31, 2007.

Cayton, Andrew R. L. *Frontier Indiana*. Bloomington: Indiana University Press, 1996.

Chaffin, Tom. *Pathfinder: John Charles Frémont and the Course of American Empire*. New York: Hill & Wang, 2002.

Chávez, Thomas E. *Spain and the Independence of the United States: An Intrinsic Gift*. Albuquerque: University of New Mexico Press, 2002.

Chesnutt, David R., and C. James Taylor, eds. *The Papers of Henry Laurens*. Vol. 15, December 11, 1778–August 31, 1782. Columbia: University of South Carolina Press, 2000.

Chicago Herald, December 3, 1889.

Chicago Tribune, May 29, June 9, December 23, 2006.

Chipman, Donald E. *Spanish Texas, 1519–1821*. Austin: University of Texas Press, 1992.

Clemens, Samuel L. [Mark Twain]. "A Defence of General Funston." Three segments, at www.boondocksnet.com/ai/twain/deffunst.html. Originally published in *North American Review*, May 1902.

Clymer, Kenton. Review of Paul Kramer, *The Blood of Government: Race, Empire, the United States, and the Philippines*. In *American Historical Review* 112 (April 2007), 473.

Coffin, William F. *1812: The War, and Its Moral: A Canadian Chronicle*. Montreal: John Lovell, 1864.

Cohn, Ellen R., ed. *The Papers of Benjamin Franklin*. Vol. 36. New Haven: Yale University Press, 2001.

Collins, John R. "The Mexican War: A Study in Fragmentation." *Journal of the West* 11 (April 1972), 228–29.

Combs, Jerry W., Jr. "Population Growth in American Samoa." Washington, D.C.: National Institute of Child Health and Human Development, 1974.

Commager, Henry Steele, ed. *Documents of American History*. 7th ed. New York: Appleton-Century-Crofts, 1963.

Congressional Globe. 29th Cong., 1st sess. (1846); 30th Cong., 1st sess. (1847–1848).

Connell-Smith, Gordon. *The United States and Latin America: An Historical Analysis of Inter-American Relations*. London: Heinemann Educational Books, 1974.

The Conquest of Mexico! An Appeal to the Citizens of the United States, on the Justice and Expediency of the Conquest of Mexico. . . . Boston: Jordon & Willey, 1846.

"Correspondence of 1817–18 among British diplomats, President Monroe, Secretary Adams, Secretary Rush, and others concerning the *Ontario* and the return of Astoria. . . ." In "Message from the President . . . in relation to Claims set up by Foreign Governments to Territory of the United States upon the Pacific Ocean, north of the forty-second degree of latitude . . . April 17, 1822," 7–18. Washington: Gales & Seaton, 1822.

Covington, James W. *The Seminoles of Florida*. Gainesville: University Press of Florida, 1993.

Cox, Isaac Joslin. ["I.J.C."] "Toulmin, Harry." In Dumas Malone, ed., *Dictionary of American Biography*, 9, part 2. New York: Scribner, 1936.

———. *The West Florida Controversy, 1798–1813*. Baltimore: Johns Hopkins University Press, 1918.

Cusick, James G. *The Other War of 1812: The Patriot War and the American Invasion of Spanish East Florida*. Gainesville: University Press of Florida, 2003.

Dangerfield, George. *Chancellor Robert R. Livingston of New York, 1746–1812*. New York: Harcourt Brace, 1960.

Daws, Gavin. *Shoal of Time: A History of the Hawaiian Islands*. New York: Macmillan, 1968.

DeBow, J. D. B. *Statistical View of the United States . . . being a Compendium of the Seventh Census*. Washington: Beverley Tucker, 1854.

DeConde, Alexander. *This Affair of Louisiana*. New York: Scribner, 1976.

Deere, Carmen Diana. "Here Come the Yankees! The Rise and Decline of United States Colonies in Cuba, 1898–1930." *Hispanic American Historical Review* 78 (November 1998), 729–65.

DeSmet, Pierre-Jean. *Oregon Missions and Travels over the Rocky Mountains in 1845–46*. New York: Edward Dunigan, 1847.

Din, Gilbert. *Spaniards, Planters, and Slaves: The Spanish Regulation of Slavery in Louisiana, 1763–1803*. College Station: Texas A&M Press, 1999.

Donald, David Herbert. *Charles Sumner and the Rights of Man*. New York: Knopf, 1970.

Dowd, Gregory Evans. *War under Heaven: Pontiac, the Indian Nations, & the British Empire*. Baltimore: Johns Hopkins University Press, 2002.

Dull, Jonathan. "Benjamin Franklin and the Nature of American Diplomacy." *International History Review* 5 (August 1983), 346–63.

Dunne, John Gregory. "The American Raj." *New Yorker*, May 7, 2001, 46–54.

Dyer, Brainerd. "Robert J. Walker on Acquiring Greenland and Iceland." *Mississippi Valley Historical Review* 27 (1940), 263–66.

Early American Newspapers. Online database, for "all Mexico" items, 1848.

Eisenhower, Dwight D. *Public Papers of the Presidents: Dwight D. Eisenhower, 1960–1961*. Washington, D.C.: Government Printing Office, 1961.

Elliott, Charles Winslow. *Winfield Scott: The Soldier and the Man*. New York: Macmillan, 1937.

Ellis, Elmer. *Henry Moore Teller: Defender of the West*. Caldwell, Idaho: Caxton Printers, 1941.

Ellis, Joseph J. *His Excellency: George Washington*. New York: Knopf, 2004.

Errington, Jane. *The Lion, the Eagle, and Upper Canada*. Kingston, Ont.: McGill-Queen's University Press, 1987.

Exposición de una persona residente en la República Méxicana sobre la guerra que actualmente sostiene con los Estados Unidos del Norte. Mexico City: R. Rafael, 1847.

Falconer. "Mr. Falconer's Reply to Mr. Greenhow's Answer, with Mr. Greenhow's Rejoinder." June 24, 1845. Pamphlet in the Huntington Library, San Marino, Calif.

Falk, Stanley L. "Disarmament on the Great Lakes: Myth or Reality?" *U.S. Naval Institute Proceedings* 87 (December 1961), 69–73.

Faragher, John Mack. *Daniel Boone: The Life and Legend of an American Pioneer*. New York: Henry Holt, 1992.

Fehrenbach, T. R. *Comanches: The Destruction of a People*. New York: DaCapo Press, 1944.

Ferguson, Niall. *Colossus: The Price of America's Empire*. New York: Penguin, 2004.

Ferguson, Will. *Canadian History for Dummies*. Toronto: Wiley, 2000.

Ficken, Robert E., and Charles P. LeWarne. *Washington: A Centennial History*. Seattle: University of Washington Press, 1988.

Fitzmaurice, Lord (Edmond George Petty Fitzmaurice). *Life of William Earl of Shelburne, afterwards First Marquess of Landsdowne*. London: Macmillan, 1912.

Foos, Paul. *A Short, Offhand, Killing Affair: Soldiers and Social Conflict during the Mexican-American War*. Chapel Hill: University of North Carolina Press, 2002.

Fox, John. *Macnamara's Irish Colony and the United States Taking of California in 1846*. Jefferson, N.C.: McFarland, 2000.

Fry, Joseph A. "Imperialism, American Style." In Gordon Martel, ed., *American Foreign Relations Reconsidered, 1890–1993*, 52–70. New York: Routledge, 1994.

———. *John Tyler Morgan and the Search for Southern Autonomy*. Knoxville: University of Tennessee Press, 1992.

Fuller, John D. P. *The Movement for the Acquisition of All Mexico*. Baltimore: Johns Hopkins University Press, 1936.

Galbraith, John S. *The Hudson's Bay Company as an Imperial Factor, 1821–1869*. Berkeley: University of California Press, 1957.

Gales & Seaton's Register of Debates in Congress. 29th Cong., 1st sess. Washington: Gales & Seaton, 1830.

Garza, Lorenzo de la. *Dos Hermanos Heroës*. Mexico City: Editorial Cultura, 1939.

Gates, Charles M. "The West in American Diplomacy, 1812–1815." *Mississippi Valley Historical Review* 26 (March 1940), 499–510.

Gentilcore, R. Louis, ed. *Historical Atlas of Canada*. Vol. 2. Toronto: University of Toronto Press, 1993.

Gillmor, Don, and Pierre Turgeon. *Canada: A People's History*. Toronto: McClelland & Stewart, 2001.

Giunta, Mary E., ed. *Documents of the Emerging Nation: U.S. Foreign Relations, 1775–1789*. Wilmington, Del.: Scholarly Resources, 1998.

Gould, Lewis L. *The Spanish-American War and President McKinley*. Lawrence: University Press of Kansas, 1980.

Graebner, Norman A. *Empire on the Pacific: A Study in American Continental Expansion*. New York: Ronald Press, 1955.

———. "Lessons of the Mexican War." *Pacific Historical Review* 47 (August 1978), 325–42.

Graff, Henry F. *Grover Cleveland*. New York: Times Books, 2002.

Grant, Ulysses S. *Memoirs and Selected Letters*. Mary Drake McFeely and William S. McFeely, eds. New York: Library of America, 1990.

Greenberg, Amy S. *Manifest Manhood and the Antebellum American Empire*. Cambridge, U.K.: Cambridge University Press, 2005.

Greene, Jack P. *The Intellectual Construction of America: Exceptionalism and Identity from 1492 to 1800*. Chapel Hill: University of North Carolina Press, 1993.

Griffin, Charles Carroll. *The United States and the Disruption of the Spanish Empire, 1820–1822: A Study of the Relations of the United States with Spain and with the Rebel Spanish Colonies*. New York: Columbia University Press, 1937.

Griswold del Castillo, Richard. *The Treaty of Guadalupe Hidalgo: A Legacy of Conflict*. Norman: University of Oklahoma Press, 1990.

Gronet, Richard W. "The United States and the Invasion of Texas, 1810–1814." *The Americas* 25 (January 1969), 281–306.

Hackett, Charles Wilson, ed. *Pichardo's Treatise on the Limits of Louisiana and Texas.* . . . Vol. 1. Austin: University of Texas Press, 1931.

Hadden, Fred C. "Midway Islands." *The Hawaiian Planters' Record* 45 (1941).

Hamill, Hugh M., Jr. *The Hidalgo Revolt: Prelude to Mexican Independence.* Westport, Conn.: Greenwood, 1981 (1966).

Harlow, Vincent T. *The Founding of the Second British Empire, 1763–1793.* London: Longmans, Green, 1952.

Haycox, Stephen. *Alaska: An American Colony.* Seattle: University of Washington Press, 2002.

Haynes, Sam W. *James K. Polk and the Expansionist Impulse.* New York: Longman, 1997.

Haynes, Sam W., and Christopher Morris, eds. *Manifest Destiny and Empire: American Antebellum Expansionism.* College Station: Texas A&M Press, 1997.

Healy, David. *Drive to Hegemony: The United States in the Caribbean, 1898–1917.* Madison: University of Wisconsin Press, 1988.

Herndon, William H., and Jesse W. Weik. *Herndon's Life of Lincoln: The History and Personal Recollections of Abraham Lincoln.* "With an introduction and notes by Paul M. Angle." New York: Albert & Charles Boni, 1936.

Hickey, Donald R. *Don't Give Up the Ship! Myths of the War of 1812.* Urbana: University of Illinois Press, 2006.

Higgs, Robert. " 'Not Merely Perfidious but Ungrateful': The U.S. Takeover of West Florida." *Independent Institute Working Paper no. 55,* vol. 10, no. 2 (fall 2005). Accessible at www.independent.org/publications/working_papers/article.asp?id= 1478.

Hinckley, Ted C. "Alaska as an American Botany Bay." *Pacific Historical Review* 42 (Feburary 1973), 1–19.

————. *The Americanization of Alaska, 1867–1897.* Palo Alto, Calif.: Pacific Books, 1972.

Hoffman, Paul E. *A History of Louisiana before 1813.* Baton Rouge: privately published, 1996.

Hogan, Michael. *The Irish Soldiers of Mexico.* Guadalajara: Fondo Editorial Universitario, 1998.

————. "The Irish Soldiers of Mexico." *History Ireland* 5 (winter 1997), 38–43.

Hoganson, Kristin L. *Fighting for American Manhood: How Gender Politics Provoked the Spanish-American and Philippine-American Wars.* New Haven: Yale University Press, 1998.

Holbo, Paul S. *Tarnished Expansion: The Alaska Scandal, the Press, and Congress, 1867–1871.* Knoxville: University of Tennessee Press, 1983.

Horsman, Reginald. *The Causes of the War of 1812.* Philadelphia: University of Pennsylvania Press, 1962.

————. *Expansion and American Indian Policy, 1783–1812.* Norman: University of Oklahoma Press, 1992 (1967).

————. "On to Canada: Manifest Destiny and United States Strategy in the War of 1812." *Michigan Historical Review* 13 (fall 1987), 1–24.

————. *Race and Manifest Destiny: The Origins of American Racial Anglo-Saxonism.* Cambridge, Mass.: Harvard University Press, 1991.

————. "Who Were the War Hawks?" *Indiana Magazine of History* 60 (June 1964), 121–36.

Hosen, Frederick E. *Unfolding Westward in Treaty and Law.* Jefferson, N.C.: McFarland, 1988.

Houck, Louis. *The Spanish Regime in Missouri.* Vol. 2. New York: Arno Press, 1971 (1909).

Howren, Alleine. "Causes and Origin of the Decree of April 6, 1830." *Southwestern Historical Quarterly* 16 (1912–1913), 378–422.

Huculak, Mykhaylo. *When Russia Was in America: The Alaska Boundary Treaty Negotiations, 1824–25, and the Role of Pierre de Poletica.* Vancouver, B.C.: Mitchell, 1971.

Hurt, R. Douglas. *The Indian Frontier, 1763–1846.* Albuquerque: University of New Mexico Press, 2002.

Hutchinson, C. A. "Mexican Federalists in New Orleans and the Texas Revolution." *Louisiana Historical Quarterly* 39 (January 1956), 1–47.

Irey, Thomas R. "Soldiering, Suffering, and Dying in the Mexican War." *Journal of the West* 11 (April 1972), 285–98.

Jackson, Jack, and John Wheat. *Texas by Terán: The Diary Kept by General Manuel de Mier y Terán on His 1828 Inspection of Texas.* Austin: University of Texas Press, 2000.

Jefferson, Thomas. Papers. Reel 46. Library of Congress Manuscripts Division.

Jensen, Ronald J. *The Alaska Purchase and Russian-American Relations.* Seattle: University of Washington Press, 1975.

Johannsen, Robert, et al., eds. *Manifest Destiny and Empire: American Antebellum Expansionism.* College Station: Texas A&M Press, 1997.

Johnson, Chalmers. *The Sorrows of Empire: Militarism, Secrecy, and the End of the Republic.* New York: Metropolitan Books/Henry Holt, 2004.

Johnson, Leland R. "The Suspense Was Hell: The Senate Vote for War in 1812." *Indiana Magazine of History* 65 (December 1969), 247–67.

Jones, Howard, and Donald A. Rakestraw. *Prologue to Manifest Destiny.* Wilmington, Del.: SR Books, 1997.

Jones, Wilbur Devereux. *Lord Aberdeen and the Americas.* Athens: University of Georgia Press, 1958.

Journals of the Continental Congress, 1774–1789. Vols. 1, 2, 18. Washington, D.C.: Government Printing Office, 1904.

Judt, Tony. *Postwar: A History of Europe since 1945.* New York: Penguin, 2005.

Kagan, Robert. *Dangerous Nation: America's Place in the World from Its Earliest Days to the Dawn of the Twentieth Century.* New York: Knopf, 2006.

Kaplan, Lawrence S. "The Treaty of Paris, 1783: A Historiographical Challenge." *International History Review* 5 (August 1983), 431–74.

Kaplan, Robert D. *Imperial Grunts: The American Military on the Ground.* New York: Random House, 2005.

Karnow, Stanley. *In Our Image: America's Empire in the Philippines.* New York: Ballantine Books, 1989.

Kastor, Peter J. "Dehahuit and the Question of Change in North America." In Kastor, *Louisiana Purchase,* 74–89.

———, ed. *The Louisiana Purchase: Emergence of an American Nation.* Washington: CQ Press, 2002.

Kelley, Hall J. *A Geographical Sketch of That Part of North America Called Oregon.* . . . Boston: J. Howe, 1830.

Kelly, Edith Louise, and Mattie Austin Hatcher. "Tadeo Ortíz de Ayala and the Colonization of Texas, 1822–1833." *Southwestern Historical Quarterly* 32 (1928–1929), I, 74–86; II, 152–64; III, 222–51; IV, 311–43.

Kennan, George F. *At a Century's Ending: Reflections, 1982–1995.* New York: Norton, 1996.

———. "Reflections on Containment." In Terry L. Deibel and John Lewis Gaddis, eds., *Containing the Soviet Union: A Critique of U.S. Policy,* 15–19. Washington: Pergamon-Brassey's International Defense Publishers, 1987.

———. ["X."] "The Sources of Soviet Conduct." *Foreign Affairs* 25 (July 1947), 566–82.

Kennedy, Paul. *The Rise and Fall of the Great Powers: Economic Change and Military Conflict from 1500 to 2000.* New York: Random House, 1987.

Kennedy, Paul M. *The Samoan Tangle: A Study in Anglo-German-American Relations, 1878–1900.* St. Lucia, Australia: University of Queensland Press, 1974.

Kinzer, Stephen. *Overthrow: America's Century of Regime Change from Hawaii to Iraq.* New York: Times Books/Henry Holt, 2006.

Kirk, Ruth, and Carmela Alexander. *Exploring Washington's Past: A Road Guide to History.* Seattle: University of Washington Press, 1990.

Kirkpatrick, Jeane J. *Dictatorships and Double Standards: Rationalism and Reason in Politics.* New York: American Enterprise Institute/Simon and Schuster, 1982.

Kite, Jodella D. "A Social History of the Anglo-American Colonies in Mexican Texas, 1821–1835." Ph.D. dissertation, Texas Tech University, 1990.

Klein, Herbert S. *African Slavery in Latin America and the Caribbean.* New York: Oxford University Press, 1986.

Kushner, Howard I. *Conflict on the Northwest Coast: American-Russian Rivalry in the Pacific Northwest, 1790–1867.* Westport, Conn.: Greenwood, 1975.

LaFeber, Walter. *The American Search for Opportunity, 1865–1913.* Vol. 2 of *The Cambridge History of American Foreign Relations.* New York: Cambridge University Press, 1993.

———. *The Panama Canal: The Crisis in Historical Perspective.* New York: Oxford University Press, 1978.

———. "Wilson's Corollary to the Monroe Doctrine." In LaFeber, *Inevitable Revolutions: The United States and Central America,* 51–55. 2d ed. New York: Norton, 1993.

Lagny, L. *La Cession de la Louisiane.* Paris: Editions Cabiro, 1968.

Lamb, W. Kaye. "The Founding of Fort Victoria." *British Columbia Historical Quarterly* 7 (April 1943), 71–92.

———. Introduction to E. E. Rich, ed., *The Letters of John McLoughlin from Fort Vancouver to the Governor and Committee; Second Series, 1839–1844.* London: Champlain Society for the Hudson's Bay Record Society, 1943.

———. Introduction to E. E. Rich, ed., *The Letters of John McLoughlin from Fort Vancouver to the Governor and Committee; Third Series, 1844–46.* London: Hudson's Bay Record Society, 1944.

Lambert, Paul F. "The Movement for the Acquisition of All Mexico." *Journal of the West* 11 (April 1972), 317–27.

Larkin, Thomas O. Papers. Bancroft Library, University of California at Berkeley.

Lass, William E. *Minnesota's Boundary with Canada: Its Evolution since 1783.* St. Paul: Minnesota Historical Society Press, 1980.

Lawson, Gary, and Guy Seidman. *The Constitution of Empire: Territorial Expansion and American Legal History.* New Haven: Yale University Press, 2004.

Leckie, Robert. *From Sea to Shining Sea: From the War of 1812 to the Mexican War, the Saga of America's Expansion.* New York: HarperCollins, 1993.

Lemoine, Ernesto, ed. *Insurgencia y república federal, 1808–1824: Documentos para la historia del México independiente.* Mexico City: Miguel Angel Porrúa, 1987.

Lentz, Thierry. *Le Grand Consulat.* Paris: Fayard, 1999.

Limerick, Patricia Nelson. "Dilemmas in Forgiveness: William Appleman Williams and Western American History." *Diplomatic History* 25 (spring 2001), 293–300.

———. *The Legacy of Conquest: The Unbroken Past of the American West.* New York: Norton, 1987.

Linn, Brian McAllister. *The Philippine War, 1899–1902.* Lawrence: University Press of Kansas, 2000.

Long, John W., Jr. "The Origin and Development of the San Juan Island Water Boundary Controversy." *Pacific Northwest Quarterly* 43 (July 1952), 187–213.

Lugan, Bernard. *La Louisiane Française, 1682–1804.* Paris: Perrin, 1994.

Lyon, E. Wilson. *Louisiana in French Diplomacy, 1759–1804.* Norman: University of Oklahoma Press, 1934.

Madariaga, Salvador de. *The Fall of the Spanish American Empire.* New York: Macmillan, 1948.

Maga, Timothy P. *Defending Paradise: The United States and Guam, 1898–1950.* New York: Garland, 1988.

Magoon, Charles E. "Report on the Legal Status of the Territory and Inhabitants of the Islands Acquired by the United States during the War with Spain. . . ." In U.S. Senate Document 234, 56th Cong., 1st sess., February 12, 1900.

Mahin, Dean B. *Olive Branch and Sword: The United States and Mexico, 1845–1848.* Jefferson, N.C.: McFarland, 1997.

Major, John. *Prize Possession: The United States and the Panama Canal.* Cambridge, U.K.: Cambridge University Press, 1993.

Malthus, Thomas Robert. *An Essay on the Principle of Population, as it affects The Future Improvement of Society . . .* London: J. Johnson, 1798.

Mares, José Fuentes. *Génesis del expansionismo norteamericano.* Mexico City: El Colegio de México, 1980.

Martin, F.-X. *The History of Louisiana, from the Earliest Period.* Vol. 2. New Orleans: Lymann and Beardslee, 1829.

Martinez, Orlando. *The Great Landgrab: The Mexican-American War, 1846–1848.* London: Quartet Books, 1975.

Mattern, David B., et al., eds. *The Papers of James Madison: Secretary of State Series.* Vol. 5, May 16–October 31, 1803. Charlottesville: University Press of Virginia, 2000.

May, Glenn A. "Private Presher and Sergeant Vergara: The Underside of the Philippine-American War." In Peter W. Stanley, ed., *Reappraising an Empire: New Perspectives on Philippine-American History,* 35–57. Cambridge, Mass.: Harvard University Press, 1984.

May, Robert E. "Manifest Destiny's Filibusters." In Sam W. Haynes and Christopher Morris, eds., *Manifest Destiny and Empire: American Antebellum Expansionism,* 146–79. College Station: Texas A&M Press, 1997.

Mazour, Anatole G. "The Russian-American and Anglo-Russian Conventions, 1824–1825: An Interpretation." *Pacific Historical Review* 14 (1945), 303–10.

McBrien, Richard P. *Encyclopedia of Catholicism*. New York: HarperSan Francisco, 1995.

McCartney, Paul T. *Power and Progress: American National Identity, the War of 1898, and the Rise of American Imperialism*. Baton Rouge: Louisiana State University Press, 2006.

McCormick, Thomas J. *China Market: America's Quest for Informal Empire, 1893–1901*. Chicago: Quadrangle Books, 1967.

McElhannon, Joseph Carl. "Imperial Mexico and Texas, 1821–1823." *Southwestern Historical Quarterly* 53 (October 1949), 117–50.

Meinig, Donald W. *The Shaping of America: A Geographical Perspective on 500 Years of History*. Vol. 2, *Continental America, 1800–1867*. New Haven: Yale University Press, 1993.

Merk, Frederick. "The Oregon Pioneers and the Boundary." *American Historical Review* 29 (July 1914), reprinted in Merk, *The Oregon Question: Essays in Anglo-American Diplomacy and Politics*, 234–54. Cambridge, Mass.: Belknap Press, 1967.

Mexico. Ediciones de la Biblioteca de la Cámara de Diputados. *Documentos históricos inéditos del archivo*. Mexico City, 1936.

Miller, Hunter, ed. *Treaties and Other International Acts of the United States of America*. Vol. 5. Washington, D.C.: Government Printing Office, 1937.

Miller, Robert Ryal. *Shamrock and Sword: The Saint Patrick's Battalion in the U.S.-Mexican War*. Norman: University of Oklahoma Press, 1989.

Miller, Stuart Creighton. *"Benevolent Assimilation": The American Conquest of the Philippines, 1899–1903*. New Haven: Yale University Press, 1982.

———. "Funston, Frederick." In John Garraty et al., eds., *American National Biography*. New York: Oxford University Press, at www.anb.org/articles/06/06–00206.html.

Mirat, Elena Sánchez-Fabrés. *Situación histórica de Las Floridas en la segunda mitad del siglo XVIII (1783–1819): Los problemas de una región de frontera*. Madrid: Ministerio de Asuntos Exteriores, Dirección de Relaciones Culturales, 1977.

Monroe, James. *Autobiography*. Stuart Gerry Brown, ed. Syracuse: Syracuse University Press, 1959.

Moore, John Bassett. Introduction to George Herbert Ryden, *The Foreign Policy of the United States in Relation to Samoa*. New York: Octagon Books, 1975 (1933).

Morgan, Edmund S., and Marie Morgan. "Our Shaky Beginnings." *New York Review of Books* 54 (April 26, 2007).

Morris, Richard B., ed. *John Jay: The Winning of the Peace: Unpublished Papers, 1780–1784*. New York: Harper & Row, 1980.

———. *The Peacemakers: The Great Powers and American Independence*. New York: Harper & Row, 1965.

Morrison, Michael A. "Westward the Curse of Empire: Texas Annexation and the American Whig Party." *Journal of the Early Republic* 10 (summer 1990), 221–49.

Mosely, Edward H., and Paul C. Clark Jr. *Historical Dictionary of the United States-Mexican War*. Lanham, Md.: Scarecrow Press, 1997.

Murphy, Orville T. *Charles Gravier, Comte de Vergennes: French Diplomacy in the Age of Revolution, 1719–1787*. Albany: State University of New York Press, 1982.

Nevins, Allan. *Grover Cleveland: A Study in Courage*. New York: Dodd, Mead, 1932.

Nichols, Jeanette Paddock. *Alaska: A History of Its Administration, Exploitation, and Industrial Development during Its First Half Century under the Rule of the United States*. Cleveland: Arthur H. Clark, 1924.

Norris, Frank. *North to Alaska: An Overview of Immigrants to Alaska, 1867–1945.* [Juneau]: Alaska Historical Commission Studies in History, 1984.

Nugent, Walter. "The American Habit of Empire, and the Cases of Polk and Bush." *Western Historical Quarterly* 38 (spring 2007), 5–24.

———. "Comparing Wests and Frontiers." In Clyde A. Milner II, Carol A. O'Connor, and Martha A. Sandweiss, eds., *The Oxford History of the American West,* 803–33. New York: Oxford University Press, 1994.

———. "Frontiers and Empires in the Late Nineteenth Century." *Western Historical Quarterly* 20 (November 1989), 393–408.

———. *Into the West: The Story of Its People.* New York: Knopf, 1999.

Oberg, Barbara B., ed. *The Papers of Benjamin Franklin.* Vol. 30. New Haven: Yale University Press, 1993.

O'Donnell, Dan. "The Pacific Guano Islands: The Stirring of American Empire in the Pacific Ocean." *Pacific Studies* 16 (March 1993), 43–66.

Offner, John L. *An Unwanted War: The Diplomacy of the United States and Spain over Cuba, 1895–1898.* Chapel Hill: University of North Carolina Press, 1992.

Ohrt, Wallace. *Defiant Peacemaker: Nicholas Trist in the Mexican War.* College Station: Texas A&M University Press, 1997.

Onuf, Peter S. *Jefferson's Empire: The Language of American Nationhood.* Charlottesville: University of Virginia Press, 2000.

Osorio, Jonathan Kay Kamakawiwo'ole. *Dismembering Lāhui: A History of the Hawaiian Nation to 1887.* Honolulu: University of Hawaii Press, 2002.

O'Sullivan, John L. "Annexation." *United States Magazine and Democratic Review* 17 (July–August 1845).

Ottawa (Ont.) *Citizen,* November 12, 2003.

Owsley, Frank L., Jr. *Struggle for the Gulf Borderlands: The Creek War and the Battle of New Orleans, 1812–1815.* Gainesville: University Press of Florida, 1981.

Owsley, Frank Lawrence, Jr., and Gene A. Smith. *Filibusters and Expansionists: Jeffersonian Manifest Destiny, 1800–1821.* Tuscaloosa: University of Alabama Press, 1997.

Padgett, James A., ed. "Official Records of the West Florida Revolution and Republic." *Louisiana Historical Quarterly* 21 (January–October 1938), 685–765.

Padron, Francisco Morales. *Spanish Help in American Independence.* Madrid: Publicaciones Españoles, 1952.

Park, Chai Bin. "Population of American Samoa." Bangkok: United Nations Economic and Social Commission for Asia and the Pacific, 1979.

Patrick, Rembert W. *Florida Fiasco: Rampant Rebels on the Georgia-Florida Border, 1810–1815.* Athens: University of Georgia Press, 1944.

Paullin, C. O. "The Early Choice of the 49th Parallel as a Boundary Line." *Canadian Historical Review* 4 (1923), 127–31.

Peckham, Howard H. *The War for Independence: A Military History.* Chicago: University of Chicago Press, 1958.

Pérez, Louis A., Jr. *Cuba between Empires, 1878–1902.* Pittsburgh: University of Pittsburgh Press, 1983.

———. *Cuba under the Platt Amendment, 1902–1934.* Pittsburgh: University of Pittsburgh Press, 1986.

Perkins, Bradford. *The Creation of a Republican Empire, 1776–1865.* New York: Cambridge University Press, 1993.

Peterson, Merrill D. *Thomas Jefferson and the New Nation: A Biography.* New York: Oxford University Press, 1970.

Pike, Fredrick B. *FDR's Good Neighbor Policy: Sixty Years of Generally Gentle Chaos.* Austin: University of Texas Press, 1995.

Pinheiro, John C. " 'Religion without Restriction': Anti-Catholicism, All Mexico, and the Treaty of Guadalupe Hidalgo." *Journal of the Early Republic* 23 (spring 2003), 69–96.

Pletcher, David M. *The Diplomacy of Annexation: Texas, Oregon, and the Mexican War.* Columbia: University of Missouri Press, 1973.

————. *The Diplomacy of Involvement: American Economic Expansion across the Pacific, 1784–1900.* Columbia: University of Missouri Press, 2001.

Polk, James K. *The Diary of James K. Polk during His Presidency, 1845 to 1849.* Milo Milton Quaife, ed. 4 vols. Chicago: McClurg, 1910.

————. "Inaugural Address." In U.S. House Document 540, 82d Cong., 2d sess.

Portell Vilá, Herminio. *Historia de Cuba en sus relaciones con Los Estados Unidos y España.* Havana: Jesus Montero, 1939.

Poussin, G.-T. *Question de l'Oregon.* Paris: W. Coquebert, 1846.

Pratt, Julius W. "James K. Polk and John Bull." *Canadian Historical Review* 24 (December 1943), 341–49.

Prucha, Francis Paul. *American Indian Treaties: The History of a Political Anomaly.* Berkeley: University of California Press, 1994.

————, ed. *Documents of United States Indian Policy.* 2d ed. Lincoln: University of Nebraska Press, 1990.

Ramírez, José Fernando. *México durante su Guerra con los Estados Unidos.* Translated as *Mexico during the War with the United States.* Columbia: University of Missouri Press, 1970 (1905).

Reid, Virginia Hancock. *The Purchase of Alaska: Contemporary Opinion.* Long Beach, Calif.: Press-Telegram, 1939.

Remini, Robert V. *Andrew Jackson and the Course of American Empire, 1767–1821.* New York: Harper & Row, 1977.

————. *Andrew Jackson and the Course of American Freedom, 1822–1832.* New York: Harper & Row, 1981.

————. *The Battle of New Orleans: Andrew Jackson and America's First Military Victory.* New York: Viking, 1999.

Reparaz, Carmen de. *Yo Solo: Bernardo de Gálvez y la Toma de Panzacola en 1781: Una contribución española a la independencia de los Estados Unidos.* Barcelona: Ediciones del Serbal, 1986.

Rickover, Hyman G. *How the Battleship* Maine *Was Destroyed.* Washington, D.C.: Government Printing Office, 1976.

Rippy, J. Fred. "The Negotiation of the Gadsden Treaty." *Southwestern Historical Quarterly* 27 (July 1923), 1–26.

Ritcheson, C. R. "The Earl of Shelburne and Peace with America, 1782–1783: Vision and Reality." *International History Review* 5 (August 1983), 322–45.

Rives, George Lockhart. *The United States and Mexico, 1821–1848.* New York: Scribner, 1913.

Robbins, William G. *Landscapes of Promise: The Oregon Story, 1800–1940.* Seattle: University of Washington Press, 1997.

Robinson, Cecil, trans. and ed. *The View from Chapultepec: Mexican Writers on the Mexican-American War.* Tucson: University of Arizona Press, 1989.

Robles, Vito Alessio. *Coahuila y Tejas: Desde la consumación de la independencia hasta el tratado de paz de Guadalupe Hidalgo.* Mexico City: Tallers Gráficos de la Nación, 1945.

Rogers, Robert F. *Destiny's Landfall: A History of Guam.* Honolulu: University of Hawai'i Press, 1995.

Roosevelt, Franklin D. *The Public Papers of Franklin D. Roosevelt.* "1940 Volume." New York: Macmillan, 1941. "1941 Volume," Samuel I. Rosenman, comp. New York: Harper, 1950.

Rudmin, Floyd W. *Bordering on Aggression: Evidence of US Military Preparations against Canada.* Hull, Que.: Voyageur, 1993.

Ruigómez de Hernández, María Pilar. *El gobierno español del despotismo ilustrado ante la independencia de los Estados Unidos de America: Una nueva estructura de la politica internacional (1773–1783).* Madrid: Ministerio de Asuntos Exteriores, 1978.

Sage, Walter N. "The Oregon Treaty of 1846." *Canadian Historical Review* 27 (December 1946), 349–67.

Santoni, Pedro. *Mexicans at Arms: Puro Federalists and the Politics of War, 1845–1848.* Fort Worth: Texas Christian University Press, 1996.

Saul, Norman E. *Distant Friends: The United States and Russia, 1763–1867.* Lawrence: University Press of Kansas, 1991.

Schmitt, Robert C. "Catastrophic Mortality in Hawai'i: An Update." *Hawaiian Journal of History* 23 (1989), 217–27.

Schulzinger, Robert D. *U.S. Diplomacy since 1900.* New York: Oxford University Press, 1998.

Schwartz, Rosalie. *Across the Rio to Freedom: U.S. Negroes in Mexico.* El Paso: Texas Western Press, 1975.

Sellers, Charles G. *James K. Polk: Continentalist, 1843–1846.* Princeton: Princeton University Press, 1966.

Setchell, William Albert. *American Samoa.* Washington: Carnegie Institution, 1924.

Seward, William H. "Commerce in the Pacific Ocean." Speech in the U.S. Senate, July 29, 1852. Washington, D.C.: Buell & Blanchard, 1852.

———. "The Continental Rights and Relations of Our Country." Speech in the U.S. Senate, January 26, 1853. Washington: Buell & Blanchard, 1853.

———. "The Darien Canal." In George E. Baker, ed., *Works of William H. Seward,* Vol. 5, 589–92. Boston: Houghton Mifflin, 1884.

———. "The Destiny of America." Speech at the dedication of Capitol University, Columbus, Ohio, September 14, 1853. Albany: Weed, Parsons, 1853.

———. "The Elements of Empire." New York: C. Shepard, 1844.

———. Papers. Library of Congress Manuscripts Division. Also, University of Rochester Special Collections.

Sheehan, Bernard W. *Seeds of Extinction: Jeffersonian Philanthropy and the American Indian.* Chapel Hill: University of North Carolina Press, 1973.

Shortridge, James R. "The Alaska Agricultural Empire: An American Agrarian Vision, 1898–1929." *Pacific Northwest Quarterly* 69 (October 1978), 145–58.

Silva, Noenoe. *Aloha Betrayed: Native Hawaiian Resistance to American Colonialism.* Durham, N.C.: Duke University Press, 2004.

Skaggs, Jimmy M. *The Great Guano Rush: Entrepreneurs and American Overseas Expansion*. New York: St. Martin's, 1994.

Skidelsky, Robert. "Hot, Cold & Imperial." *New York Review of Books*, July 13, 2006.

Smith, Duane A. *Henry M. Teller: Colorado's Grand Old Man*. Boulder: University Press of Colorado, 2002.

Smith, Dwight L. "The Old Northwest and the Peace Negotiations." In *The French, the Indians, and George Rogers Clark in the Illinois Country*, 92–105. Indianapolis: Indiana Historical Society, 1977.

Smith, F. Todd. *The Caddo Indians: Tribes at the Convergence of Empires, 1542–1854*. College Station: Texas A&M Press, 1995.

———. *The Wichita Indians: Traders of Texas and the Southern Plains, 1540–1845*. College Station: Texas A&M University Press, 2000.

Smith, Joseph Burkholder. *The Plot to Steal Florida: James Madison's Phony War*. New York: Arbor House, 1983.

Sparrow, Bartholomew H. *The Insular Cases and the Emergence of American Empire*. Lawrence: University Press of Kansas, 2006.

Stacey, C. P. "The Myth of the Unguarded Frontier, 1815–1871." *American Historical Review* 56 (October 1950), 1–18.

Stagg, J. C. A. "Between Black Rock and a Hard Place: Peter B. Porter's Plan for an American Invasion of Canada in 1812." *Journal of the Early Republic* 19 (fall 1999), 385–422.

Stahr, Walter. *John Jay: Founding Father*. New York: Hambledon and London, 2005.

Stannard, David E. "Disease and Infertility: A New Look at the Demographic Collapse of Native Populations in the Wake of Western Contact." *Journal of American Studies* 24 (1990), 325–50.

———. *Honor Killing: How the Infamous "Massie Affair" Transformed Hawai'i*. New York: Viking, 2005.

Stein, Stanley J., and Barbara H. Stein. *Apogee of Empire: Spain and New Spain in the Age of Charles III, 1759–1789*. Baltimore: Johns Hopkins University Press, 2003.

Stockley, Andrew. *Britain and France at the Birth of America: The European Powers and the Peace Negotiations of 1782–1783*. Exeter: University of Exeter Press, 2001.

Stuart, Reginald C. *United States Expansionism and British North America, 1775–1871*. Chapel Hill: University of North Carolina Press, 1988.

Sumner, Charles. "Speech of Hon. Charles Sumner, of Massachusetts, on the Cession of Russian America to the United States. . . ." Washington, D.C.: Congressional Globe Office, 1867.

Tansill, Charles Callan. *The Purchase of the Danish West Indies*. Baltimore: Johns Hopkins University Press, 1932.

Tate, Merze. *Hawaii: Reciprocity or Annexation*. East Lansing: Michigan State University Press, 1968.

———. *The United States and the Hawaiian Kingdom: A Political History*. New Haven: Yale University Press, 1965.

Thom, Adam. *The Claims to the Oregon Territory Considered*. London: Smith, Elder, 1844.

Thomas, Hugh. *Rivers of Gold: The Spanish Empire from Columbus to Magellan*. New York: Random House, 2003.

Thornton, Russell. "Population History of Native North Americans." In Michael R.

Haines and Richard H. Steckel, eds., *A Population History of North America*, 9–50. New York: Cambridge University Press, 2000.

Tone, John Lawrence. *War and Genocide in Cuba, 1895–1898*. Chapel Hill: University of North Carolina Press, 2006.

Trask, David F. *The War with Spain in 1898*. New York: Macmillan, 1981.

Trist, Nicholas P. Papers. Library of Congress Manuscripts Division, Washington, D.C.

Tucker, E. W. *A History of Oregon, from Its Discovery to the Present Time, Showing the Grounds of the Claims of the United States to That Territory*. Buffalo, N.Y.: Wilgus, 1844.

Turner, Frederick Jackson. *The Frontier in American History*. Wilbur R. Jacobs, ed. Tucson: University of Arizona Press, 1986 (1920).

———. "The Problem of the West." *Atlantic Monthly*, September 1896. Reprinted in Turner, *The Frontier in American History*, 205–21.

———. "The Significance of the Frontier in American History." Originally in American Historical Association, *Proceedings 1894*. Reprinted in Turner, *The Frontier in American History*, 1–38.

Ubelaker, Douglas H. "North American Indian Population Size: Changing Perspectives." In John W. Verano and Douglas H. Ubelaker, eds., *Disease and Demography in the Americas*, 169–76. Washington, D.C.: Smithsonian Institution Press, 1992.

United States. Adjutant General's Office. *Correspondence Relating to the War with Spain and Conditions Growing Out of the Same*. Vol. 2. Washington, D.C.: Government Printing Office, 1902.

United States. Bureau of the Census. *Historical Statistics of the United States, from Colonial Times to 1970*. Washington, D.C.: Government Printing Office, 1975.

United States. Department of Defense. *Base Structure Report: A Summary of DoD's Real Property Inventory*. Annual since 1999. The 2006 edition is accessible at www.acq .osd.mil/ie/irm/irm_library/BSR2006Baseline.pdf.

United States. House of Representatives. 41st Cong., 2d sess. House Executive Document 1. "Report of Major General George H. Thomas." September 27, 1869.

———. 56th Cong., 1st sess. House Document 2. "Annual Reports of the War Department for the Fiscal Year ended June 30, 1899: Report of Brig. Gen. Geo. W. Davis on Civil Affairs in Puerto Rico," and "Report of Maj. Gen. J. R. Brooke on Civil Affairs in Cuba."

———. 57th Cong., 2d sess. House Document 51. "Purchase of Land by Nonresidents in Cuba since Date of American Occupation, Etc." December 3, 1902.

———. 58th Cong., 3d sess. House Document 232. "Fifth Annual Report of the Philippines Commission."

United States. Office of the President. "The National Security Strategy of the United States of America, September 2002." At www.whitehouse.gov/nsc/nss/2002.

United States. Senate. 29th Cong., 1st sess. (1846). *Journal*.

———. 30th Cong., 1st sess. (1848). Senate Executive Document 52. Off-the-record debate on the Treaty of Guadalupe Hidalgo.

———. 40th Cong., 2d sess. (1867). Senate Executive Document 79. On Midway Islands.

———. 40th Cong., 3d sess. (1868). Senate Report 194. On Midway Islands.

———. 45th Cong., 2d sess. (1878). Senate Executive Document 79. On Cuban insurgents.

———. 55th Cong., 2d sess. (1898). Senate Report 816. "Naval Station in the West Indies."

———. 56th Cong., 1st sess. (1900). Senate Document 138. "Report of the Schurman Commission on the Philippines" (4 vols.).

———. 56th Cong., 2d sess. (1901). Senate Document 112. "Reports of the Taft Philippine Commission."

United States. Statutes at Large, March 1897 to March 1899. Vol. 30. Washington, D.C.: Government Printing Office, 1899.

Unruh, John D., Jr. *The Plains Across: The Overland Emigrants and the Trans-Mississippi West, 1840–60.* Urbana: University of Illinois Press, 1979.

Urquhart, Brian. "World Order & Mr. Bush." *New York Review of Books,* October 9, 2003.

Vallejo, Mariano G. Papers. Huntington Library, San Marino, Calif.

Van der Weyde, William M., ed. *The Life and Works of Thomas Paine.* Vol. 2. New Rochelle, N.Y.: Thomas Paine National Historical Association, 1925.

Van Deusen, Glyndon G. *William Henry Seward.* New York: Oxford University Press, 1967.

Van Ellis, Mark D. "Assuming the White Man's Burden: The Seizure of the Philippines, 1898–1902." *Philippine Studies* 43 (fourth quarter 1995), 607–22.

Vega, Mercedes de, and Maria Cecilia Zuleta, eds. *Testimonios de una guerra: México 1846–1848.* Vol. 2. Mexico City: Secretaria de Relaciones Exteriores, 2001.

Vest, Francis J. *Political Advancement in the South Pacific: A Comparative Study of Colonial Practices in Fiji, Tahiti, and American Samoa.* Westport, Conn.: Greenwood, 1961.

Vicente, José A. Armillas. *El Mississipi, frontera de España: España y los Estados Unidos ante el tratado de San Lorenzo.* Zaragoza: Institución Fernando el Católico, 1977.

Waciuma, Wanjohi. *Intervention in Spanish Florida, 1801–1813: A Study in Jeffersonian Foreign Policy.* Boston: Branden, 1976.

Walker, Leslie W. "Guam's Seizure by the United States in 1898." *Pacific Historical Review* 14 (March 1945), 1–12.

Walker, Robert J. "Letter of Hon. R. J. Walker, on the Purchase of Alaska, St. Thomas and St. John." Library of Congress "Meeting of Frontiers" Web site.

Ward, Christopher. *The War of the Revolution.* John R. Alden, ed. Vols. 1, 2. New York: Macmillan, 1952.

Warren, Harris G. *Their Sword Was Their Passport: A History of American Filibustering in the Mexican Revolution.* Baton Rouge: Louisiana State University Press, 1943.

Weber, David J. *The Mexican Frontier, 1821–1846: The American Southwest under Mexico.* Albuquerque: University of New Mexico Press, 1982.

———. *The Spanish Frontier in North America.* New Haven: Yale University Press, 1992.

Weeks, William Earl. *John Quincy Adams and American Global Empire.* Lexington: University of Kentucky Press, 1992.

———. "John Quincy Adams' 'Great Gun' and the Rhetoric of American Empire." *Diplomatic History* 14 (winter 1990), 25–42.

Welch, Richard E., Jr. "American Atrocities in the Philippines: The Indictment and the Response." *Pacific Historical Review* 43 (May 1974), 233–53.

———. *The Presidencies of Grover Cleveland.* Lawrence: University Press of Kansas, 1988.

West, Elizabeth H. "Diary of José Bernardo Gutiérrez de Lara." *American Historical Review* 34 (October 1928 and January 1929), 55–91, 281–94.

White, Patrick C. T. *A Nation on Trial: America and the War of 1812.* New York: Wiley, 1965.

Williams, Mary Wilhelmine. "Secessionist Diplomacy of Yucatan." *Hispanic American Historical Review* 9 (May 1929), 132–43.

Williams, Walter L. "United States Indian Policy and the Debate over Philippine Annexation: Implications for the Origins of American Imperialism." *Journal of American History* 66 (March 1980), 810–31.

Williams, William Appleman. "Empire as a Way of Life." *The Nation,* August 2–9, 1980.

———. *The Roots of the Modern American Empire: A Study of the Growth and Shaping of Social Consciousness in a Marketplace Society.* New York: Random House, 1969.

Woodcock, George. *The Century That Made Us: Canada, 1814–1914.* Toronto: Oxford University Press, 1989.

Wright, J. Leitch, Jr. *Creeks & Seminoles: The Destruction and Regeneration of the Muscogulge People.* Lincoln: University of Nebraska Press, 1986.

Wyllys, Rufus Kay. "The East Florida Revolution of 1812–1814." *Hispanic American Historical Review* 9 (November 1929), 415–45.

Zimmermann, Warren. *First Great Triumph: How Five Americans Made Their Country a World Power.* New York: Farrar, Straus and Giroux, 2002.

Acknowledgments

My first thank-yous go to the patient students in my undergraduate seminars on "The Territorial Acquisitions of the United States," the first of which I conducted during the academic year at University College Dublin in 1991–1992, followed by three at the University of Notre Dame later in the 1990s.

I am greatly indebted to John T. McGreevy, department chair and historian, and to deans Mark Roche and Greg Sterling, at Notre Dame, who provided me with research support after I retired from teaching. I am also grateful, in the researching of this book as in earlier ones, for grants from the Henry E. Huntington Library in San Marino, California, and its gracious and genial director of research, Robert C. Ritchie.

I have relied on the resources of several libraries: the University of Notre Dame's Hesburgh Library most of all; but also the general, special, and documents collections of Northwestern University, Lake Forest College, the Newberry Library in Chicago, the Regenstein Library of the University of Chicago, the University of Rochester's Special Collections (with particular thanks to Jean Lombard and Melissa Mead), the Bancroft Library at the University of California at Berkeley, the Library of Congress, and (as mentioned) the Huntington. My thanks to the staffs of all of them. Without librarians and archivists, we historians would be virtually mute.

For photographs and other images, I was helped courteously and promptly by Theresa Langford at the Fort Vancouver (Wash.) National Historic Site; Gina S. Vergara-Bautista at the Hawaii State Archives; Kim Curtis at the Monticello/Thomas Jefferson Foundation; Susan Sutton at the Indiana Historical Society; Claudia Martínez in Mexico City; Jim Akerman, Pat Morris, John Powell, and Diane Dillon at the Newberry Library, Chicago; and the anonymous but efficient staff at the Library of Congress Prints and Photographs Division and Photoduplication Service.

For all sorts of tips, leads, courtesies, conversations, and other forms of support: Robert C. Carriker of Gonzaga University for information on Pierre-Jean DeSmet; Charles Bittner, academic liaison at *The Nation*, for a Bill Williams essay I had not known of; former fellow grad student Robert L. Beisner, for his monumental editing of *American Foreign Relations since 1600: Guide to the Literature*, which saved me an enormous amount of searching; Alan H. Lessoff, editor of *Journal of the Gilded Age and Progressive Era*, for intensely satisfying conversations about imperialism; Michael Ebner for arranging access to the Lake Forest College Library (and many other collegial favors); Richard White and Samuel Truett for leads into the latest ongoing research on the Southwest; Thomas LeBien of Hill & Wang for books; Ellen Skerrett for various leads; and my daughter Rachel Nugent and her husband, Brian Baird, and their "boyos," Walter and William, for many stays at their home near the Library of Congress.

I am deeply grateful to the historians whose time I imposed upon with requests to read chapters on subjects that they know better than I. They unfailingly provided detailed critiques and saved me from many errors of fact and from problematic interpretations. I have taken most of their advice, but I have been stubborn on some points. Thus I am entirely responsible for the content of *Habits of Empire*, not they. Most of them I have known for some time: Steven Aron, Andrew Cayton, Brian W. Dippie, Gregory Dowd, Joseph A. Fry, Paul E. Hoffman, Ann Durkin Keating, Walter LaFeber, Alan H. Lessoff, Anna K. Nelson, William G. Robbins, Malcolm J. Rohrbough, Bernard W. Sheehan, Thomas Slaughter, Robert M. Utley, David J. Weber, and Bernard A. Weisberger. Two others I look forward to meeting and to thanking for so readily assisting a stranger: Carl Benn and Robert Wooster.

Suellen Hoy, as always, read every word in every chapter. I could not get along without her exceptional editorial skills, her historical sense, her candor, and above all her good heart and her companionship.

My editor, Ashbel Green, has been the soul of cooperativeness and encouragement, on this book as in the past. My deep thanks to him, to his assistant, Sara Sherbill, to Andrew Miller, who took over when Ash retired, and to their colleagues at Knopf.

I dedicate the book to the memory of three friends and historians, who helped and inspired me in innumerable ways over many years. Yehoshua Arieli (1916–2002) migrated from the Sudetenland to Mandate Palestine in 1931; in the 1960s founded the American studies program at the Hebrew University of Jerusalem; was generally recognized as the doyen of American studies in Israel; and was a winner of the Israel Prize. Robert F. Byrnes (1917–1997) was one of the founders of Soviet studies in the United States and chaired the Department of History at Indiana University for nine years; first he hired me, then inspired me. Martin Ridge (1923–2003) was my colleague at Indiana when he edited the *Journal of American History*, and we maintained close contact after he became director of research at the Huntington Library. These credentials indicate only the external achievements of these men. Within, they were at once generous, brilliant, and inspiring. I hope this book is worthy to bear their names in dedication.

Index

Illustration Credits

The author gratefully acknowledges and credits the following for permission to reprint illustrations or quotations:

Fort Vancouver National Historic Site, National Park Service

Joseph A. Fry

Hawaii State Archives

Indiana Historical Society

Library of Congress "American Memory"

Library of Congress Prints and Photographs Division

Gordon Martel

Monticello/Thomas Jefferson Foundation

The Nation and Charles Bittner, Academic Liaison

National Archives and Records Administration, Pacific Region

The Newberry Library (Chicago)

Ross County (Ohio) Historical Society